That Paris Year

That Paris Year

JOANNA BIGGAR

à Michelle Vigne,
Grande artiste, grand esprit -
Joanna Biggar, March 2011

Alan Squire Publishing
Bethesda, Maryland

That Paris Year is published by Alan Squire Publishing in association with Left Coast Writers and The Santa Fe Writers Project.

ISBN: 978-0-9826251-0-1

Cover painting by Gregory Robison
Jacket design by Randy Stanard, DeWitt Designs,
www.dewittdesigns.com
Back cover photo by Douglas Hale
Copyediting and interior design by Nita Congress
Editorial assistance by Bernadette Geyer
Printed by ProForma Mactec Solutions, Oakland, CA

First Edition
Ordo Vagorum

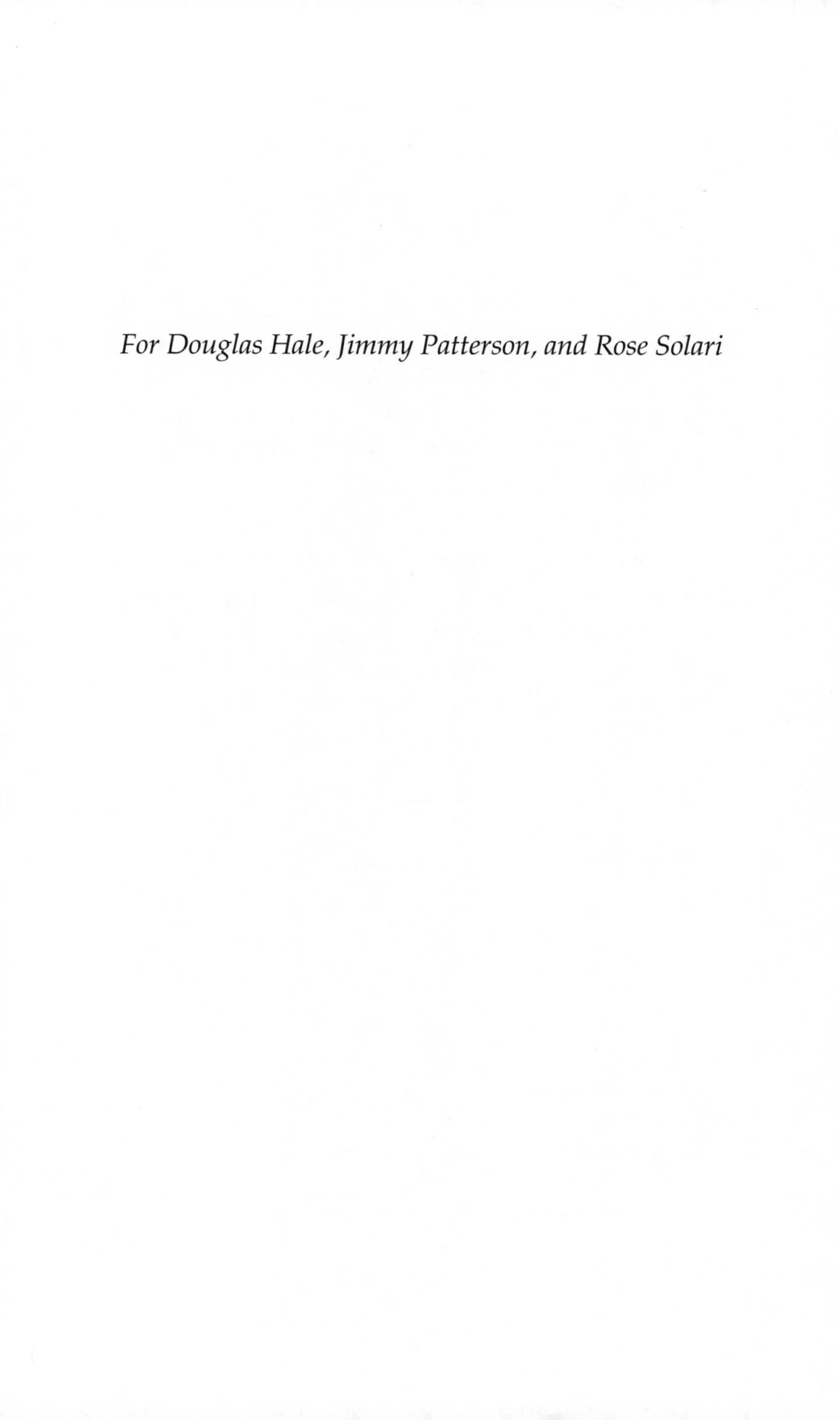

For Douglas Hale, Jimmy Patterson, and Rose Solari

"I will write here. I will live quietly and alone. And each day I will see a little more of Paris, study it, learn it as I would a book. It is worth the effort… The streets sing, the stones talk. The houses drip history, glory, romance." —Henry Miller, letter, 1930

"We do not say anything special to each other, only that Paris is beautiful. But in that word beautiful are centuries of lives, of wars, of work, of faith, of deaths… Paris is beautiful. It aches to say so, one's arms are never big enough to hug such an immensity." —Etel Adnan, *Paris, When It's Naked*, 1993

Contents

If I desire the water of Europe, it is
Only the black, cold pool in a scented twilight
Where a squatting child full of sorrow sets the sails of
A boat, fragile as a butterfly in May.

—Arthur Rimbaud, "The Drunken Boat,"
translation by Joanna Biggar

Prologue

How can I convey to you what this is like?

How it is to pass down this quiet Claremont street, through the iron college gate again ("Eager, Thoughtful, and Reverent" it still announces) and feel that old hint of breeze from the desert, hot, yet virginal, against my cheek.

Now it's 1972, and they probably don't have virgins anymore. Surely these girls I'm about to address will find what I have to say about our struggles, our desires, quaint. (God, how Jocelyn would laugh!)

It's been only ten years, but it seems a hundred since I walked this shaded street, passing the open grassy quad, the somnolent ivied walls, the buildings and bell tower beyond, where California Spanish makes an impressionist's blur of whitewash splashed with red tile, orange cannas, deep pink geraniums. The palm trees still scrape the eastern horizon before the rise of Old Baldy and fan the memory of heat—its breeze still scented with orange blossoms. But today it is the sycamores lining this street, the sycamores with their puzzling bark and their offer of shade, that I seek. Perhaps because I now know their cousins, the plane trees of Paris.

The sun gathers itself imperially, dictating heat from that high desert throne already hidden in ghastly haze. If I glance behind myself, perhaps the smog has settled so low I can't really see the outline of Old Baldy, the palm fronds against the horizon, the tangle of rooftops and flowers. Perhaps even the scent of orange groves is only a figment of memory. No matter. Memory, I see now, is the vital organ of reality; our best, if fragile, link to the immortal. Otherwise, how could I be here?

I would not now be turning down the little street with the old, cracked pavement to follow it to the end where it wanders into the wash. Would not be walking toward la Maison, its unkempt shingles and chipping porch paint, dingy living room with the puckered, dusty rose chairs, the persistent, if neglected, ivy on the mantle hung with a cheap and too fleshy Renoir. The room, the overstuffed furniture, and dark floors where I danced once dressed like a French whore and Gracie grasped love as a principle of physics. It is, all of it, you see, etched on the lids of my inner eyes.

How can I tell you what it is like then, to open them and find it has all disappeared?

But unfortunately I am not alone. Dean Lutowsky, the rather hip replacement for that dragon of my youth (Spinster Krauss, we called her), walks beside me, her fashionable boots crunching the gravel as we veer up a new path. She actually seems pleased. "About time, don't you think?" she says, assuming my approval of the "improvement" and gesturing broadly to the pseudo-Spanish monstrosity, rising like a bad joke on the buried bones of la Maison. *Ma maison. Mal maison.*

Streaks of gray hair glance off her shoulders like swords. She is talking feverishly, but I can't seem to get what she says, as if she is speaking Esperanto. I brush my hand once, quickly, across my eyes. She assumes assent in this, my only visible flicker of grief.

So I follow her through the thick, thoroughly modern, glass doors declaring *Soyez la Bienvenue* and enter the dusky, rose-scented, slanting oak-floored room of memory. It is effaced of course by the shine of overhead fluorescent lights. In the cavernous all-purpose room, the plastic chairs have been pushed aside, and my audience, *les demoiselles de la Maison Française*, awaits me, sprawled on new linoleum.

I gaze at them. Eager, thoughtful, and reverent perhaps, but something else. Something urgent. I take in the tattered jeans, the bandanas, the fatigues and realize they do not look like girls, but like women. What can I tell them, then, standing here, a throwback from some other world in heels and silk, daubs of Ma Griffe on the soft undersides of my ears? Should I start by saying we were in fact girls, and that is the difference?

Or should I simply do as the college asked and speak about the virtues of going abroad, sticking with the prepared script and the messages I bring from the others?

Or perhaps I should just confess that for want of sufficient poetry and lack of revolutionary will I have become a journalist. That my single talent is as a collector. That I am a hunter and gatherer, an archeologist of the present who picks through others' lives trying to assemble some unforeseen design, some exquisite tapestry, some denouement, some clue. That as acquisition is my true and single gift (a trait I now believe hereditary; I am, after all, the only child of my parents' import business), it fell quite naturally to me to become the chronicler of our group of five, of Jocelyn and Melanie, of Grace, Evelyn, and myself.

"…and how her travels—right from this very spot—led to the work we all admire today, and to her breaking ground, that soil of the patriarchy if I may say so, where other women have often feared to tread…" It goes on, Dean Lutowsky's introduction, until I've been transformed into a post-modern Jeanne d'Arc, fearless revolutionary of the Women's Section.

Perhaps, then, I should tell them about my newspaper assignment. How Bud Purvis, travel and features editor, fat cigar hanging out of his thick grin, called me in. "Say, sweetheart, how about some nice foreign travel stuff for a change. Jesus Ke-rist, the public's tired of all this bad news all the time. War, drugs, hippies, disaster. Something light, you know? Didn't you rich college broads go abroad once to gay Paree? Yeah, how about that? A little follow-up nostalgia piece. Innocents 'n' broads." He sucked on the cigar, laughing so hard he choked. "That's it, J.J. The good old days, for Ke-rist sakes, and something far away from Asia."

Maybe we could, all of us together, have a laugh at Bud Purvis, and I could share the good news: that Bud's almost ready to laugh at himself. Even if he was enraged at what I gave him.

"Jesus H. Christ, what the fuck (pardon my French) is this? I wanted a little levity here. You know what I'm saying? Maybe even a little *romance*. So what is this, *Psychology Today*? Feminism 101, for God's sake? *C'mon*, sweetheart."

I did keep on. And Purvis switched me out of Travel—into Women. It was a demotion. But by then, I didn't care.

What I've discovered is this: after the first voyage, like the first love, nothing exists apart. I wrote one piece for Travel, and that was the beginning. Now I want to rediscover all that I left behind. I want what I hope the *demoiselles* will forebear from asking me just yet, because I'm still researching them: the lives of Jocelyn and Evelyn, of Gracie and Melanie. Of myself.

With increasing apprehension, I keep glancing at my prepared remarks and the witty, sanitized, grammatical—oh, the flawlessly untruthful—responses from my *vielles copines*, my friends. Worse, now the eyes of the wary young women are riveted on me, waiting for me to persuade them of the *virtues of going abroad*.

Damp, wet-palmed, I try to find the old door to the porch, the way out, the way back. Could I impart Paris to them, where all primary roads (*la rue* being of the feminine gender) would take them still, first, before all the world's imperial Romes and sweltering Meccas? Because before the Revolution, there was Paris, and Paris is a woman.

What would they think if I said that only now, ten (or is it a hundred?) years later, can I articulate a little of why I went? That it had something to do with absence, something to do with history, something to do with sex? And that only when I reentered this thirsty land, this Los Angeles, this native city without particular gender did the questions come like waves? Were we daughters of the sea, the mountains, the desert—the forgotten elements—or transplants from some other, distant, half-buried place? Or, like flickers on a silver screen, were we no more than flashes in the hot lights of the city, destined to burn out quickly without name or definition? In France, you see, everyone begins with a past; we Californians seem mere creatures of an overwrought and anonymous imagination.

I suspect this is not the sort of thing the *demoiselles* want to hear. Nor this piece of hard news: that youth is the province of answers, even if quickly discarded, while age, I'm beginning to see, brings with it the season of questions.

Well. I could reach into that file box of stuffed manila folders my mind has become and retrieve my tangle of notes, clips, scraps, letters (you see I have not invented my friends). That is, I could tell the truth.

But I glance down at them, jean-clad, sprawled, determined on the unrelenting floor. I clear my throat. "First, greetings from Jocelyn," I say. They would know her, of course, the immaculate profile an image as imbedded in the American psyche as flag-burning, and I watch the *demoiselles* stir. They know her latest film, *A Walk on the Woman Side,* in which she'd made a stunning leap from *femme fatale* to *femme de guerre,* an immortal silhouette in jackboots and chains.

"She was my roommate, here in la Maison Française and in Paris," I say, trying shamelessly for a sliver of refracted glory. But what can I tell them, anyway? That there were three things about Jocelyn, not counting her skin?

I stick instead to the prepared banalities and to Jocelyn's message itself.

> Claremont Women of l'Ancienne Maison Française:
>
> *Salut!*
>
> As you know, I've been asked to share some reflections and thoughts with you about the virtues of the French experience. And advice. In these times—"and the times they are a'changin," and thank God for that—should

> you go? And why did I? Well, the times are dangerous, but so were they back then—my mother was always terrified, still is by what I do (can you relate?). But we women have come a long way, so the first thing I'd say is, if you want to do this, go for it. As for me, it was J.J.'s craziness first of all that got me into it (I still bless her for it) and without such a roommate, I would never have dreamed to travel so far so young. Too trapped in my little life, I guess.
>
> But beyond J.J.'s determination—her passion, you could say—should I tell you I just went for the banks of the Seine in springtime, and an insane craving to improve my verbs? Or should I say, lacking a better way to put it, that I went looking for freedom, longing for possibility, and of course desire—all the things I'd best not go into here?

I hesitate before going on, looking down at my audience, now supine and a little dazed, just imagining Jocelyn. Deceit becomes her, I have to admit. But then it always did. And I'll not reveal that the only truth here has to do with French verbs.

Shifting weight, I look down again, searching out the faces beneath the varied hair, check for signs of fatigue. No, what I really fear is skepticism. Can they see the lie in Jocelyn's message, or the edges of my storytelling where it has glazed the truth?

To my surprise, they seem genuinely interested. The heavy round-faced girl stares intently beneath a jagged fringe of bangs. Next to her the light-skinned black child (she seems more child to me than woman, though I'd never dare express such an observation) watches me carefully, her gorgeous green eyes open questions.

Only Dean Lutowsky taps her boot impatiently, her face a mask of swirling cigarette smoke. When it clears, I suddenly see the stairs again, the stairs of the old Maison rising behind her, and the spot where I stood.

How clear it had been that Parents' Day when Evelyn came down those stairs and met herself—her mother coming up. How she saw the future in that remorseless light, the face shattered by lines and rimmed with circles, the rose-tinged cheeks webbed with fifty years of fatigue, the fire-licked hair put out with strands of gray. It was only a passing moment, but there she stood, witness to a forgotten beauty beneath the quiet ruins of her mother's face. The pastor's wife. Despite resolve, was she, Evelyn, also to be so condemned by some angry God or genetic flaw? Did it lurk in the bloodline, this turning from hot into lukewarm? As she reached forward in greeting, I could almost hear the passionate vow of obedience to a newly discovered Eleventh Commandment: "And this above all, thou shalt not become thy mother."

It is hard to bring myself to the present, to the *demoiselles*, the puffing dean, the amazing image of Evelyn now, wearing some kind of cowl. And I wonder, briefly, how many of her calamities they know of, for scandal does linger on long after fact. Or, given the shallow memory of youth, perhaps the headlines are too far in the ancient past.

I smooth out her letter.

Chères soeurs:

I imagine you all in la Maison, or whatever stands in for it now, and I know there are bloodlines between us. Should you go to France? you have asked. Well, if you have to ask, then the answer is given, in my humble opinion.

And why did I go? I think I'll let J.J., who knows more about that than maybe even I do, field that one.

But the Virtues of Going Abroad? Who comes up with these things? Okay, I confess I know less about virtue than ever. Maybe some folks are preaching to you that to go is to commit an act of Old-Worldism, a sin of backwardness, self-indulgence, or counter-revolution. Maybe they're saying you should become *involved* instead, or *engagé* as Sartre would have it. That the place to be is where the action is—so stick around because we've got plenty of our own devils right here in our own backyards—and the real action is very far away from the *ancien régime* and miserable halls of the Sorbonne. Personally, I didn't hang around there nearly as much as I should have, but I do know something about devils, foreign and domestic!

But I also know that there are many things ticking in this world. True, some of them are bombs. But some of them are hearts. And sometimes you need to travel very far to tell the difference. So if the blood is rushing to your chest and what you think you feel is lust for this adventure, then for damn sure you better not deny it.

No. Listen to yourself. Pay attention to your own pulse and all the little things so small that you may not yet be used to seeing them. For preparation? I guess I'd recommend brushing up on your Proust and keeping in mind what can come from something so simple as a cup of tea. I swear it's true. A whole world spilled out for me once from a can of beans. Perhaps J.J. can explain. But then she may have become prudent and restrained in her "old age."

So, *mes soeurs, amitié. Bon voyage. Et cherchez toujours et partout l'amour.*

Sister Eve

Unconsciously almost, my eyes seek out and come to rest upon the most unnoticeable *jeune femme* in the room. The girl who would be Gracie. Plain, you could say politely. Impolitely, stubby, frumpy, frizzly, or—here's to the point—acned. The worst of it is, even if she hasn't been called such names, she has tormented herself with them.

I struggle to resist calling out to her. And she resists my gaze. Perhaps it's only my imagination that this Grace, too, carries the great burden of mind.

And I wonder if her dean, the hard-bodied Lutowsky who wears large tortoiseshell glasses and serious leather, infuses her with inspiration. Or derision. Or fear. I can only imagine the general disbelief if I told them about the old days, and the reign of Spinster Krauss with her strict imposition of The Rules, which came in the form of sign-ins and sign-outs, blaring lights, permission slips, and cocked eyebrows to make sure there were no infractions of their larger purpose: the thwarting of wandering hands, furtive caresses, fervent kisses.

The reaction to The Rules, of course, was hilarious mockery followed by compulsive sabotage. Except for Gracie. For Gracie, the reign of Spinster Krauss was a particular reign of terror because in Gracie Krauss had one triumphant case of clear compliance, if only because Gracie had no reason not to comply.

I begin the letter beneath the letterhead from Caltech, Department of Physics.

Chères mademoiselles:

They say time dims the view, but I have found that true only if I lose my contact lenses. The mere thought of where you are, what you are on the verge of, fills me with that surprising (there it is again) surge of caprice, joy, desire, freedom. I can honestly say nothing was ever more wonderful than the French connection.

I could tell you dozens of reasoned, thoughtful things about whether to go or not to go, but you've heard them all before. And do you believe them? In a way, it's ridiculous to think we *vielles filles* could advise you anyhow. But, that's the college for you, *plus ça change…*

So, what advice can I possibly give? Only three little words come to mind, and they surprise me as much as they may you. But for better or for worse, reflect on these: *Liberté, Égalité, Maternité.*

Grace Battaglia, Ph.D.

I finish Gracie's note and notice the other, second Grace looking back at me unsparingly. I am gratified to see her hand go up.

"So, how did she do that, um, go to Paris on this French deal when she was supposed to be a science major?"

"Ah, well," I answer, avoiding any brush with Grace's most loathed epithet—*sell-out.* "Matter of fact, she did become a French major." Better, she once explained, for one with matrimonial ambitions.

Then the hands sprout up quickly. Questions about what it was like *back then*. When Civil Rights were young. And Vietnam. When JFK lived. When JFK died. When women were forced into marriages. And bras.

Unconsciously, I step out of my shoes. Not because my feet hurt, but because I want to get a bit closer to their level. Behind the purposeful headbands and fringes, I glimpse the face of innocence. I see the moment has come to speak of Melanie. But I don't know where she is.

In my mind, I try to call her up—the compact, delicate body, the feathered crown of yellow-white hair, the darting, transparent eyes—try to imagine what she'd say. There would be a letter, addressed to me.

> Dear J.J.,
>
> I know you've been trying to reach me, and I'm sorry I haven't reached you. You know how it is with me. Don't you? (Even if I never exactly said.)
>
> It's hard to imagine who I was during those long-ago days, and the idea of giving advice to the young frightens me. (But I can just hear that little wry tone of yours, tossing off a line of Rimbaud, then saying "Well, someone's got to do it.") So what can I say, given what messes I've made, except maybe "Don't do as I have done?"
>
> There is only one bit that has stuck with me all the years, which I know to be true. Pascal, may he rot forever, got it right. *"Le coeur a les raisons que la raison ne connaît point."*
>
> All these years, and that's still as much as I know.
>
> Love always,

I got stuck trying to sign her letter. Who was she now?

"There was one among us whose remarks unfortunately did not arrive on time. Her name was Melanie, and like many of us, she fled because she didn't want to be like her mother—and because she was desperately in love…"

As I begin this excursion, making it up as I go, I can almost hear Bud Purvis purring in my ear, pleased to finally get it.

For Dean Lutowsky, this tale, so far from her evolved world where girlish romance no longer exists, is the final catastrophe. She can only try to put the best spin on the damage I have done. "...shared power..." I hear her say. I nod politely.

Afterwards, she offers perfunctory thanks and an apology. "Terribly sorry about the lunch mix-up." There is a brisk handshake and the sound of her boots, striding rapid fire across the all-purpose linoleum.

I am back outside on familiar ground, following the cracked pavement, blinking in the light. Then a shadow in my path, foreshortened by the midday sun. It is "Grace."

"Excuse me, Ms...., but we were wondering, well, that is, we'd like to know if you'd have time for lunch with us? I know you're busy, but—"

I interrupt the breathless invitation, the nicest I've had in a long time. "I'd be honored. Except I've about exhausted all the useless advice I've got."

"Oh, no. You were great." Her round face shines like a breakaway moon. "It's just like there's so much stuff you didn't get a chance to say."

I surrender myself, happily, to the center of their small circle, turning back toward the dining hall. "What else are you interested in? I was afraid you were dying of boredom."

"No, you were cool," a willowy blonde assures, "and I loved how you sidestepped old Lutowsky." There is a small ripple of laughter, shrugs, rolling eyes. "But you didn't say much about yourself, you know?"

"Yeah," Gracie adds. "What about you?"

I have not addressed the large questions of my fevered leaving. No reason then, to confess the small, personal ones: that I went in search of Rimbaud, the gaudy, rowdy nineteen-year-old captain of the drunken boat, whose poetry careened through my veins. That I went, like everyone goes, to escape. And worse, most prosaic of all, that I went in the wake of a lover's quarrel, though at this moment I could not say what Guy and I had quarreled about. Nor do I say what it took so many years to understand, that I went mostly in search of a woman, one who was definitely not my mother, one I only began to discover in my grandmother's territory.

"What was it like? Was it worth it?" Gracie was saying. "And what happened to everybody afterwards?"

Afterwards?

There was a wedding. It was fall, one of those perfect days of sun where the palms seem to brush the sky clean and the mountains behind Pasadena rise clear and violet-tinged to the west, as if cradling the valley, or offering a buffer to the endlessness of the sea. As if promising definition.

The immense old hotel seemed to swagger a little on that hillside not far from Gran's, its dark Victorian shingles fussy beneath a filigree of flowering vines. I watched Ivan arrive, feeling lost as he adjusted his wire-rim glasses and tried to tame his unruly black hair before entering the vast reception hall beneath chandeliers mounted in gold. He blinked, hesitated a moment before stepping onto the huge roses in the carpet, and made his way slowly down through the ballroom, where the band in white tie was already playing waltzes. The tables were piled in dizzying display. He noticed the heaps of caviar, but the rest was a blur. Behind him, the limousines kept entering the curving drive, disgorging guests in gloves and capes, satin, silk, dark suits, and tuxedos. He smoothed his sports coat with his hands, hoping the stains from eggs thrown at the last demonstration were no longer visible. I watched him struggle with the extravagance in front of him, which would have unsettled him in the best of times, but now, right out of jail…

Soon the wedding party would arrive, Pastor and Mrs. Richter a little pale perhaps, a little overcome, arriving straight from the First Lutheran Church. And Gracie, the only one of *les demoiselles de la Maison Française* to be in the wedding, would come, nestled like a weed in the bouquet of Eve's tall, languorous sisters. And the bride herself, of course, in a dress of ivory satin and beadwork across the bodice, her red hair in a *bouffant à la* Jackie as if to hold a crown—Eve, the color of roses but scented of gardenia. Ivan took a breath. I imagined he was trying to place himself in such a world. Like one described by Tolstoy or scorned by Zola, or worse, hawked by the pretentious classes in…what publications? *Elle*? *Vogue*? He wouldn't even know the names.

He stepped outside the vast ballroom, airy and light-filled as Versailles's Hall of Mirrors, and stood for a minute in the sun to compose himself. Then, noticing the terrace steps cascading to a pool festooned with floating camellias, he came down looking in every direction. I watched him, reading his mind, and took a goblet of champagne from a passing waiter.

"Hey you," I finally called out. He rushed over to embrace me. "There you are! Thank God. I love them all, but this is a bit hard to take, you know, without a friend."

"Indeed." I grabbed his hand. "Anyway, you are supposed to be my date." I was feeling a little unsettled myself. All my *copines* would be there, regrouped for the first time since Paris. So much had happened in so short a time that time itself seemed to elongate. "I feel like I'm in a looking glass myself," I said. "Want to walk around a little before we go in to face the music? This is my old neighborhood. Well, Gran's actually."

Ivan slipped his arm through mine in that awkward yet delicate way of his, and we strolled, just as we had on the grounds of Versailles, down the gentle hill with its Japanese gardens and dainty bridge, its cactuses and rock formations, its flowering lily ponds. As exotic as the Chinese book of love poems he had unexpectedly delivered from Guy that rainy night in Paris. Then, just as we had in France, we spun our thoughts into each other's sentences.

"Well," he said at last, "guess it's time to face reality again."

Reality being the wedding dance. I crossed the threshold into the ballroom, the filtered sunlight behind lost to the glitter inside. In the center I watched Eve, the crown of her hair threaded with pearls and gardenias, her neck encircled with diamonds, as she twirled and smiled, sparkling in that rose light between window and chandelier and candelabra. I saw Jocelyn, too, now made up by Hollywood. Her long blonde perfection dazzled in a slim gold gown. She, too, was waltzing with a tall, deeply handsome dark man, a man who appeared to be Samuel.

"Jo!" I called out, waving. But she did not hear me, and her face turned to the light, a plaster cast.

Despite the late afternoon glow, I felt a bit of a chill. As if absence were again my best companion. I pulled my wrap around my shoulders. It was French lace. Ivan had gone limp on my arm. I looked over at him, but the lights so filled his glasses, I could not see his eyes.

"Want to dance?" I asked.

"You know I don't know how," he whispered loudly.

"Piece of cake," I answered, glancing down at what might well have been three actual left feet. "I'll teach you—think of it as taking radical steps."

"What the fuck," he finally said, giving his goofy, half-twisted grin and offering his arm. "Shall we?"

So we turned, stumbling and spinning, giving in to the gods of laughter. Then, coming down the long hall from the reception, as if down the corridor of my recurring dream—the one where I drop a finished jigsaw and can't find a missing piece—Guy walked in.

Part 1

Children of the Fire

Chapter 1

Why? Why did we go, you ask? Perhaps if not for one strange and haunting night, we would not have. We might have stayed in the warm cocoon of Los Angeles, its eternal present, and let doubts, questions, hungers dissipate, like all things do in time. Or perhaps we would have simply dissipated ourselves in the caress of breezes blowing from the beach. Or perhaps my own emptiness was so acute, my desire for that one wild ride on Rimbaud's boat so strong, I would have gone alone—and then have had to face the consequences of making a woman out of one insubstantial person instead of from many. I don't know. But as I have promised as best I can to tell the truth of the matter, I will lay out the facts as I know them and leave it to others to judge.

I'll begin with Jocelyn, the one closest to me, the one I thought I knew best. I took my readings of her as if from a thermometer, watching the way light tipped in her eyelashes and flickered green then golden, her eyes changing color to match some mysterious hidden cell. Not that

I believed the light in her eyes, any more than I believed the weather report, nor the innuendo in her long confusion of limbs. But I did believe her skin.

I saw it first that afternoon when Jocelyn and I had floated on rafts in the kidney-shaped pool that extended like a shimmering organ from her family's Hollywood hillside home. I watched, fascinated and a little horrified, as Jocelyn's naked perfection (an unkind mirror to my own blotched color) quickly toasted to the shade of golden grass.

Although I'd been her roommate for many months, I'd never seen her in such a light, and as she stretched and turned, the full splendor of her six feet trailed the edge of the raft. (Ah, Jocelyn, *mon enfant, ma soeur*, such a familiar view to so many now, I know—the snapshot look in glossy copy, the trailers, the vision splashed across the billboards of suburban dreams.) How pale and fragile her face appeared, how creamlike the flesh drawn taut across her breastbone and ribs, as if presenting this side of herself to the sun for the first time. It startled me to see this vestal underside of her in such contrast to the back, shoulders, and limbs so quickly bronzed. It seemed she was two-toned.

I was already used to the shifting color of her eyes, at that moment a blue as aseptic as the chlorinated water. I took them to be a reflection of her rare, complex intelligence, their changes an act of will. But as we slipped from the pool and toweled ourselves, shivering a bit as the sun, in setting, took the heat from our city (reminding us it was, at heart, a desert), I noticed she was no longer the two-toned creature I had only just remarked in the pool. She had, in so short a time, synthesized all over a rosy sameness like the last rays of the sun.

Of all her singular qualities, this was the most original. And it sprang from some place so profound, so primeval, it seemed the only part of her beyond artifice. Because she changed color so quickly, as if a function of nature rather than the intent of her own will, perhaps it is uniquely Jocelyn of whom I could say her deepest character could be seen only on the surface.

It was that day, too, I came to grasp the first thing about Jocelyn—meaning Madge, her mother. That I was startled is an understatement. Though as an Angelino myself, used to my city's inherent peculiarities of parentage, perhaps I should not have been.

Still, no vision of her ever erased the first of Madge flinging open the red door of the house clinging to the hill, lashed down by nothing more than tendrils of bougainvillea. Madge, her smooth white body covered by strips of a skimpy two-piece bathing suit.

"Oh, lovely dears," she beamed with a kind of maternal pride. Behind her Burt, a white-haired gnome in undershorts, rummaged through the living room, a blur of curved glass and stainless steel with magenta accents and orange carpet. He groped like a blind detective. "Confound it, anybody seen my glasses?"

Later, floating, Jocelyn explained.

"I adore Madge, of course, but I don't want to end up like her. I mean, an eccentric ex-artist married to a dear old madman, an inventor with a wind tunnel in the basement. She had talent too. You should see, well you can see, her paintings are all over the house. And once she was ready to defy everything—Grandfather, the family, all that Mormon debris—to come to California and paint.

"The family begged her to come back to Utah, to the fold, and she used to laugh about it, how they preached love and marriage to her. The purpose of marriage, if there was one, she said, was to raise a passel of free spirits and live by the sea."

She paused there, and we floated in silence. I could think of nothing to say.

"We've never been sure who my father is," Jocelyn went on. "She narrowed it down to three. An English professor at UCLA, another artist from down toward Laguna, or maybe a flier from back East who was stationed here before going to war. Madge always rather favored the flier, because he was tall and blond, but you never know.

"The professor went back to his wife, the flier got killed, and the artist fell in love with the paperboy. But then I came along, and that changed everything."

Her arrival, Jocelyn explained with a tinge of guilt, was the event that drove Madge back to Utah and the family. But in time Madge, suspicious of all that wholesomeness and clean living, afraid it would have a bad effect on her child, packed Jocelyn up. Answering a postwar call for engineers, she moved back to California. Madge, who by training was an engineer, and a brilliant one, got less and less work because she was a woman. Then she met Burt.

"When he offered marriage, she figured, why not? He could be a father for me. Or at least grandfather. Anyway, she quit her awful job and we were suddenly rich."

"What happened to the painting?" I asked.

"She never went back to it," Jocelyn answered, looking at me directly with one startling blue eye, the other closed against the sun. "I think parts of a person can die as surely as a whole person, don't you? I mean Madge as an artist—I hate to say this—seems as dead to me as Father."

That evening, Burt, in a thirty-year-old suit with wide lapels and a tie that should have been condemned, led us beneath a young and twinkling sky down the stone steps of the hillside to the teasing lights of the Strip below. When we reached the Châlet, the maître d' already had Burt's stinger waiting, and we were escorted to the family's regular table, where I got another glimpse of Jocelyn's uncommon parentage.

"Confound it!" Burt began, glasses now in place as if he could see. "I don't see how any intelligent, good-looking woman could get herself into such a pickle as to get pregnant. Imagine turning yourself into a big, broad cow." He slammed his glass on the white table linen for emphasis.

I was mildly surprised at this, and thought maybe we were being challenged to formulate a response. But Madge and Jocelyn went right on discussing Marilyn Monroe and Sammy Davis Jr. and the Rat Pack and paid no attention. "No siree," the harangue continued, "can't understand it. Divorced three of my wives on just such an account."

I was about to object—after all, one result of this sort of catastrophe was Jocelyn herself. But I hardly got a chance.

"Now you take this Miss Jo here." He began waving his fork at me, a clear case of mis-identity. "Why, when I first took her in, she was a skinny thing with flapdoodle ears. Just look at her now. A beauty for sure, but a beauty with brains. Too smart to do such a damn-fool thing. Yesiree."

I sputtered a little and tried lamely to engage in this nonsense, but without success.

Soon enough we reversed course, and he talked all the way back up the hill, a wild-haired dwarf leading three tall women completely indifferent to his ranting. He seemed not the slightest bit offended.

The path now wound beneath a dark sky smudged with overripe moon, and the stars twinkled not above, but below, in millions of lights that spun across the hills and across the vast bowl of the city. This was the view from Jocelyn's house, acres of lights dancing like angels fallen from a soiled heaven.

We entered the cool recesses of her room on the bottom floor, and there I encountered for the first time the huge, red, round inviting bed. It was there just waiting for Jocelyn and whomever she might invite to share it.

"For heaven's sake," Madge had admonished for years, laying out her unique maternal guide for healthy living. "Bring your little friends inside. You don't want to stay out in the night air and catch cold, do you?"

With such an invitation—with such a mother—Jocelyn had done the only thing she could. She had refused.

Not that anyone would believe it. Least of all Burt, whose wind tunnel drowned out all but what he wanted to hear. "Take all precautions," he had warned.

As if there were any.

It was I who shared the round red bed that night, just as I would later a lumpy one in Paris, and our exchanges were the dark whispers of sisters ludicrously wrapped in flannel, another of Madge's remedies against the hazards of the night.

I was not, of course, the "little friend" Madge had in mind. Samuel was. But Jocelyn was devout in her refusal.

Samuel. That was the second thing about Jocelyn.

Samuel Rosen. Whenever I think of him, a roaring sound comes over me. Perhaps because it always accompanied his arrival. The motorcycle, the leather jacket, the gloves, the tall, muscled frame swinging from the bucking seat as if from a stallion. A helmet hid his vulnerabilities, the black rings of curls, the weak, pointed chin beneath the chin strap. But those added to the air of theater he created. No wonder she loved him.

Or perhaps the roaring was the sound of his mind, its frightening rush of uncontrolled energy. Samuel, who by sixteen was a philosopher at Berkeley, by eighteen a musician, and by twenty a medical student. Samuel the poet, stand-up comedian, commentator, politician. Samuel the lover, most ardent, most determined, most thwarted, and most afraid. Jocelyn matched him mind and length. If they had not found each other, each would have had to invent the other. What kept them together was what kept them apart—the thin bikini strip Jocelyn would never surrender.

"Why, in God's name?" I asked her that night lying in the dark.

"To keep from unraveling," she answered.

I eventually came to see Madge's fears—that Jocelyn would make some dull, safe, bourgeois alliance—were unfounded. Had Samuel been solid, prosperous, responsible, "going somewhere," and talking of marriage, then (perhaps because of the pernicious lingering effect of those early years) he might have found his way to the round bed, because he would have been harmless.

But because Samuel was who he was—and because Jocelyn loved him—it was proof in a way that Madge, whatever she thought, had not failed completely.

There was one more thing about Jocelyn. It could be summed up, I suppose, in two words: Miss Calbrew. Miss Calbrew, goddess of beer.

It was that same year, on the fateful night of the *bal masqué*, that I first glimpsed the glossy publicity prints she stuffed under her bed as we vainly tried to tidy our little room in la Maison Française.

Jocelyn stretching, writhing, smiling like a cat. Jocelyn, pouty, lank-haired, leggy in a bikini. Jocelyn a milkmaid in gingham. Jocelyn the sequined empress.

And it was on the basis of these shots circulated by her agent that, improbable as it seemed at the time, she was selected Miss Calbrew, beer queen. Accepting the title would mean dropping out of school for a year to tour. But it would also mean the launching of her Hollywood career.

"Jeez, to beer or not to beer," Eve had quipped as Jo pushed the shots out of sight.

She was closer to the truth than she knew. For Jocelyn, who could be anything, suffered the tyranny of her possibilities. And as possible approached probable, she experienced a melancholy uncertainty.

"What if I become some one thing and it's the wrong one thing?" she once lamented. Acting was a natural outgrowth of this condition, giving her the chance to try on the many faces and personalities that sprang forth from her in a kind of desperate fertility. But when the stardom she craved was as close at hand as her publicity shots, she panicked, ready to flee.

This is not what she said though later, as we looked at the pictures again, then affixed to her wall near the round bed and interspersed with watercolors of a small blond cherub clutching wildflowers, painted by Madge in the Utah years.

What she said was, "So, of course I can't do it."

"Why not?" I asked.

"Well, it's a moral thing, don't you see. I mean, I can't sell beer...Mormons don't drink."

Chapter 2

NIGHT ON FIRE
Bal Masqué
Les Demoiselles de la Maison Française
Vous invitent à Danser

Yellowed and slightly curled at the corners, this piece of paper recently fell from the cardboard file stuffed with evidence and labeled simply "*Maison*." As to why we hosted such a seemingly medieval event I could not begin to explain.

Even now, after so much time has passed, it is difficult to revisit the night of the masked ball without seeming to fall into fiction. But ever since, I have known one thing to be true: the devil does live and can be found in the Santa Ana.

The story to be told here is not strictly my own. But if you are to understand it, you should know how I came to be there that night atop Old Baldy with Guy, and where my descent from that place carried me.

Guy had been in my line of vision long before I knew him, because he was so visible. Tall, sandy-haired, fine-featured, and already two years out of college, he came back to campus as a recruiter, a speechmaker, a man of the world. Voting rights, Peace Corps, House Un-American Activities Committee—he evoked these as if distinct countries, drawing their contours with passion. Everyone listened. I, too, but what he said seemed to have so little to do with me, I who had chosen to study French by way of choosing nothing. Or as a means of deferring the future.

Perhaps that's why he noticed me, the one on the edge of the crowd always ready to turn away. He had called out, inviting me to a little brain-storming session in a dorm. And I began coming to these events, in campus basements and pizza parlors, and to noon rallies, fascinated by the charge of energy that surged through the gatherings of fellow students even as I felt apart. I was in no way inclined or ready to charge forward to fix an imperfect world. And the more Guy made his pitch to join students going to the South—especially during that pivotal Parent's Day speech—the more I resisted. With every mention of Mississippi, it became clearer to me that my ticket was punched for Paris.

Then, that night before the masked ball, we'd called a sort of truce. "Look," I said, "I'm just a bad candidate. Hopeless, in fact. You've done your best to convert me, so don't blame yourself. How about a well-deserved evening off? I'm going to a movie."

There was a festival of old Bogart films at the Claremont Cinema. Of course the film showing that night was *Casablanca*. Afterwards we had dinner in the modest Old Europe a little ways out of town. I ordered snails as a kind of defiance, and Guy, who was old enough, ordered wine. By the end of the evening, he had become at least a sympathizer if not a recruit to my libertine (*louche*, the French would say) view of political theory and action. Then outside la Maison, he kissed me, holding on way past the time for letting go. Or was it that I held onto him?

That night was the first time I felt the danger of falling in love with him, and the next day could have gone in any direction. The prospect of a picnic on Old Baldy and the masked ball at la Maison loomed like doors that could either shut behind us, closing on a pleasant but ill-matched flirtation, or through which we could pass on our way to somewhere new.

About halfway up the mountain, we found a flat, smooth rock beside a brook, a gnarled California oak, a stand of pines. Guy spread a checked cloth on the rock and began extracting things from his basket: smoked oysters, sourdough bread, cheese, mustard, a bottle of burgundy. "Here's looking at you, kid," he smiled, touching his glass to mine and looking at me, his searching eyes seeming to see me for the first time.

I watched his hands, nimble, long, elegant at their work, and I knew.

We could have lain then on the ground, soft by the stream bed and spread with the tablecloth. But the wind came up. The paper plates began to overturn; the checkered cloth curled at the edges, like a sail to carry us away. We scurried to pack up before the next gust, and Guy cursed the fickle gods of rain.

There would be no rain, of course, only the Santa Ana, the fire in the wind, but we didn't know it then. What we knew was that we had salvaged the wine and a bit of cheese to reassemble on the dashboard in the safe cocoon of the car. And that the rattling wind sent us laughing and soon half-naked into each other's arms.

"I want…you are so…lovely." He spoke several times, whispering as if the wind would hear. And I said only "Yes," not knowing if he imagined some romantic deflowering, or desire and sweet, deep connection.

But, and here is the thing I blush even now to recount, it was not Guy's passion that rose in conquest that night—it was the gearshift. It stood maddeningly, implacably, between us. He shoved and moaned, I groped and wriggled. With less uncertainty, we might have gotten round it. As it was, Guy buried his head in my hair, crying out, "Damn it, J.J., there isn't enough room." So we just held on, remaining ludicrously entwined and quiet for a few minutes, then pulled on shirts and looked each other in the eye. It was too ridiculous for words or even remorse.

Besides, we had the night and all the world ahead of us. We would dance at the masked ball, a French whore rocking with Robespierre, and let the rest unfold. For the moment, there was only one place to go, and as Guy turned the little bug around, we dissolved in laughter, believing we would find our time again. We climbed up to the lodge and lingered enough at the fraternity party to know there was nothing for us there, then we headed down the mountain.

Perhaps if I believed that things could be written in the wind, I would have paid more attention to all the signs and foreseen disaster. It was everywhere.

Just take Gracie, for one example. Reviewing all the odd things I would witness that night, nothing seemed more peculiar than Gracie in her harlequin suit. She had dressed early, hours early actually, but even then the rose-tinged sliver of the moon, like its own telltale, had beaten her and was rising in daylight from the desert sandstone to the east. And there she was, a ridiculous oversized elf in a pointed hat. I wanted to shout. *Quick, Gracie, change. You don't have to do this. It's not too late…* But even if I had figured out what to say, Gracie was already lost in her own reverie. That is, Jay Greene's arrival and the unfolding drama of Eve's life. Jay Greene with his tall stride and blue-eyed smiling had come to fetch Eve. Or, in Gracie's view, to claim her.

"Am I okay?" Eve asked, straightening her skirt over her rounded hips in that room across from Jocelyn's and mine. "God, and J.J. thinks she's too fat," she went on, oblivious to my presence, not waiting for Gracie to reply. "Remind me to go on that disappearing diet soon, eh?" Then she adjusted a pair of dangling gold earrings. "How about these? Good? I borrowed—hey thanks J.J.," and she waved toward my open door. She did not have to mention that borrowing was the curse of being the minister's daughter, that she raided my better-grade stuff all the time. For Gracie, whose poverty wasn't even genteel, no explanations at all were necessary.

"Yeah, you look great." Gracie swung her short legs and slippered feet off Eve's bed, standing straight in her costume of patchwork and pompon buttons. "Actually, you look too good for that creep."

Eve laughed. "Oh come *on*, Gracie. He's fun. And exciting. And smart. He knows stuff—like about politics. And he is drop-dead handsome, you've got to admit. You know, like your secret heartthrob, JFK." Gracie didn't so much as blink, and Eve tried again. "Besides, he's even been known to wear a cravat."

"A cravat? That proves he's a jerk—and no JFK, either. If you like cravats, why not go to Paris where you can get the real thing?"

"I'm working on it, *chérie*, but you know…" Gracie, who was poorer than any of us, did know.

At last satisfied with the mirror, Eve turned her voluptuous silhouette to face Gracie. "Look, Battaglia, I know you're in Tomacello's pay. Old country ties and all that. Tom's a really good guy, and I know it, okay? It's just that, you know, gather ye rosebuds while ye may, meaning while you're young…" She stopped there, considering. The one thing Gracie was not nor ever would be was young. "And Tom's so possessive. If you went out with him, you'd know what I mean."

She turned then, her slim pink legs made longer in the heels that tapped hard on the stairs as she went down, leaving behind an empty echo. And I watched Gracie watching, looking down in her clown suit and slippers. For a moment, her broad face opened like a book. I read its messages of hurt and surprise. As ever, I suppose, she wondered if Evelyn knew how desperately she was attracted to Tom. Of course, Evelyn did not.

Everyone heard Eve leaving la Maison, the sounds of Jay Greene's arrogant little Triumph, which was soon probably speeding fast enough along the sinuous Baldy Road to cheat several of the curves below the lodge. Guy and I followed that road not too long after, but by reason of the wind and a gearshift, it wasn't until much later that we arrived at the fraternity party. By then it had become the definition of a fraternity party, couples heaped in a fumy haze on the edges of an ill-defined room, or in an imitation of dance, swaying together like sea plants on the bottom of the ocean, or gyrating in silent screams to the percussion bleating convulsively through the loud speakers. And so we soon left.

It was later I found out from Ivan what had happened. How Jay Greene, swaggering and proud, Evelyn draped on his arm like a coat, had entered the party and instantly owned it. How his fraternity had hung around him, brought him beer, and how the more he drank, the more he talked. How eventually, Eve, ignored, had slipped from his side to sit in the anonymous shadows at the edges of the room, away from his heat and light. That's where Ivan was, at once fascinated and disgusted by the unfolding scene.

Then, out of nowhere, Tom came in and stood in front of her, blocking what little light had filtered her way. Eve asked what he was doing there, and who his date was. When Tom answered "you," Eve laughed, then started to argue. "'Well, you can't be here with me,'" is what she said. "'I'm here with Jay.'"

"That's when he had her," Ivan reported. "Because that's when he answered, 'Is that a fact? Looks to me like old Jay's over there by himself spouting off and getting pissed. Looks to me like his date is the crowd. Looks to me like you're over here with me.'"

Tom, despite his size and strength, had the knack of gentleness. Quiet and persistent, he began to make his case that she should leave *right then* with him, and that he would deliver her to the party at la Maison safely. How she protested that she couldn't just leave, like that, without saying good-bye. But Tom stood firm. His parting shot was, "Like hell, Evelyn. If there are apologies, he can deliver them to you. Tomorrow. And sober. Now you come with me. If he makes it to the party at la Maison tonight, you'll just wish he hadn't." Then Ivan saw them leave in Tom's car.

I know what they saw as Tom's battered old Ford with the leopard seat covers made the descent down the Baldy Road, for Guy and I had gone down just before them. They, too, must have witnessed how the city unfolded in coils like a diamondback from the desert, while the sky above rippled with peculiar, gusty winds. And once down, in the parking lot next to the woods, they, too, must have seen la Maison transformed with partygoers. Its lights poured like musical notes from its opened windows, and its small frame bulged like a pumpkin. By the time they came inside, the word "Santa Ana" was already on everybody's lips. Soon the eerie calm cracked open, and the full force of the wind broke loose. The devil's breath, Guy called it, as it carried off leaves, twigs, branches, boxes, pieces of roof, and debris that danced like dervishes twirling fire.

They, too, must have seen that odd vision of Jocelyn, the improbable saint in medieval garb, standing transfixed and utterly still, stiff in her bodice and long, pointed headdress like an ornament affixed to a ship's rail. Or a statue cast in a waiting pose. Waiting for Samuel.

"Hey, Jo," I had said, punching a hole in her reverie. "What is this? I thought you were going as a Modigliani."

"Saint Geneviève," she'd answered. "Savior of Paris. Defender against Attila the Hun. Nun from the age of seven."

I pushed on through the crowd of costumed dancers, not bothering to point out she looked more like Rapunzel waiting for her lover than a nun of any age, not bothering to ask why she was in such a state. It was then Eve bumped into me.

"Oh my God, J.J," she blurted, "you do look like a French streetwalker. Check out those plumes and black stockings." Then she turned to Tom. "Holy shit. I forgot about my costume. Marie Antoinette's milkmaid. Can you wait a sec while I change?"

"Well," he said, squeezing her hand, "you could just come as you are. Frighten everybody with that lovely, unmasked face. That French schoolgirl innocence."

"You mocking me, Tomacello?" she shot him a sidewise glance, then slipped upstairs.

La Maison was hot and crowded and strangely charged. I pushed through the costumed dancers crushed beneath flickering lights to make my way upstairs, first passing into the little anteroom that held the telephone. *La chambre des secrets*, we called it. There I was startled to see Gracie in her clown suit sitting on the window seat. Tom was standing in front of her. "You know me in a manner of speaking," I heard her say, "but in French my name is Arlequin."

"Arlie-gan," he answered smiling. "Well, French isn't my forte, as they say. So come a bit closer so I can guess."

I could almost feel Gracie's heart beating like a rabbit's beneath her costume as he came closer and she awkwardly brushed against him. "Let's see," he was saying, "pretty eyes behind that mask. Gray? I know I should know you. So, you clowns wise? What can you tell me about love?"

She backed up a step, groping for the window seat. "Love?" I heard her say. "Mostly it seems not to work out. To occur between the unmatched and the unwilling. Or the unnoticing. Mostly it's a felt phenomenon, unobserved." By then I had stepped out of the room.

Back in my own room, trying to smooth my crooked seams and brace myself for the night ahead with Guy, I found the letter tossed open on Jocelyn's bed. Samuel's letter. I skimmed over the treatise on Kafka and went straight to the page that began

> ...empress of all my desire. I LOVE YOU. There it is. Despicable, decadent, and the truth. So, here I am in Berkeley, wandering around the eucalyptus groves like a madman, in my mind fucking every girl in sight. In my mind trying to purge you from me.
>
> Why? Why? Why do you keep doing this, wrapping up your precious virginity like an offering to some impotent god? And worse, why do I want you more for it?
>
> So tighten up your chastity belt if that's the way you really want it, my creamy white princess of perversion, because I'm coming to that damn party of yours. To paraphrase another madman who came before me, "Tonight, Jocelyn. Tonight."

I know only the ending, but can imagine the rest. She was, no doubt, half-surprised that he actually came, the roar of his arrival lost in the tossing of the wind, and in her unlikely dress, so far outside herself as to be beyond pretending. Perhaps she believed that in the guise of Saint Geneviève she could at last act with honesty as Jocelyn.

"Les Feuilles Mortes" played on the phonograph. While I danced with Guy, my private Robespierre, in the crowded living room, black fishnet stockings crooked and head-plume askew, Jocelyn invited Samuel up to our little room, not giving a thought to Spinster Krauss or the inconvenience of The Rules.

Then deliberately, too slowly for his impatient hands, she let everything fall, the medieval bodice, the pointed headdress, her long golden hair. And she watched his fingers worship her, the slender neck, small mounds of breasts, tender abdomen with its taut golden skin beating like a drum.

Perhaps it was then, believing the words to be her own, that she cried out like Molly Bloom, "Yes, Sam, I will yes I will yes," and then that she uttered, "run off together…babies…live by the sea."

She was certainly astonished, as she had been so many times, by the beauty of Samuel, his sculpted torso, his eyes a burning dark blue as they uncovered her layer by layer, his hustler's lips and little boy chin. Perhaps it was just as she moved her hands slowly down his hips, wanting to find the swollen, forbidden sex inside his jeans, that he pulled away.

The smile turned quickly too, into an almost-sneer, as he bowed in mocking jest. "Ratfink that I am, I cannot do this to you. Things are as they are. I leave you inviolate." He stood at the door for a moment, gazing at her nakedness. Then he headed into the pitching wind. She believed he was crying. It wasn't until much later she thought to ask herself just what it was he meant.

Piaf sang a *cri d'amour* on the phonograph as the lights blew out for the last time.

A strange mélange of spiced wine, perfume, and scented wax rose from the living room to the stairs where Jocelyn sagged against me as I helped her down. "Help me get out of here," was all she said, and then went limp.

Through the flickering candlelight downstairs, I searched for Guy. The evening had not gone as we imagined, but then neither had the afternoon. There was always tomorrow. He held me very close, saying "I want you. Come back very soon." Then he walked me outside to Jocelyn's red convertible.

The wind now blew without the definition of gusts, but in hot waves from the desert beyond the mountains. Tall things—the thicket of oak, sage, and pine in the woods—bent over to the breaking point. The cap on Robespierre's head blew off, leaving Guy as himself, a shock of sandy hair whiplashing his forehead. "I..." he shouted, words lost in the wind.

"Tomorrow night latest," I called back.

Jocelyn seemed semicomatose beside me. Swallowing panic, I tried to decide where to go. Gran's was the only refuge I could think of. At the very moment I struggled out of the car to go back inside and call Gran, I saw the blinking red lights careen through the chaotic dark. Two police officers reached the front steps just as I did.

"Miss Evelyn Richter here?" one of them bellowed over the roar.

Eve came to the door as I slipped past toward the phone. "That's me," she said.

All I could hear of what followed was "...nothin' but trouble tonight, as you can see. There's been an accident, miss, on the Baldy Road. One Jay Greene. Some said you were with him. Since we didn't find any body...evidence of you bein' along for the ride, we wanted to verify your safety.

"Body!" Eve screamed. "Oh, God, is he dead?"

"No, miss. But just about as close as you can come without bein' so."

Eve let out a muffled cry, then seemed to fall. Tom caught her in his arms.

Jocelyn said nothing all the way to Pasadena. It was the longest trip there I had ever taken. We found Gran in her darkened sitting room, creamy white hair pulled back, blue cameo at her throat, waiting for us.

Gran shut the heavy glass-paned door with a definitive bang against the now ferocious night. Then she took a long look at the pair of us and said, "Oh dear. *Mon dieu.* Sit right here."

The dark-shingled house with deep front porch, the front room with its polished oak and old-fashioned damask and antimacassars, its antiques and scents of tea and rosewater, this was the only place I could count on. As a child I had lain on the thick red Chinese carpet, fingering the unknown code of its design while feigning naps.

In a few minutes she handed us jasmine-scented tea in porcelain cups, then turned to Jocelyn, pronouncing her name in the French fashion, as though she were the empress. "*Ma petite,* what sorrow could lie so heavily on you as to streak that lovely face?" She passed a sugar bowl without looking up. "I could guess a young man…"

Jocelyn looked out for the first time from behind her fallen hair and gave a kind of nod.

Gran continued: "They say time heals, but that's not quite it, is it dear? No. Time buries, but the offender is still there, always waiting to be visited again—or liberated—if you wish. Sometimes that may be the very best course. But then sometimes not. *Voilà.* The difficulty is to know which is which, no?"

The large oil portrait of Grandfather, with the blue-eyed bewilderment I always saw in his godlike good looks, stared down quizzically, as if the conversation of women were incomprehensible to a man of great posture wearing an aviator's leather jacket and goggled helmet. I wondered, once again, about Gran's American hero and the stories I'd never been told. But Gran was focusing on me, seeming to see inside, just as she always did.

She laid her hand, always so warm, against my icy knuckles. "Listen to it, dear. So many people fear the fire in its coming. But like you, they must look fire in the face."

She smiled then, that dreamy eyes-closed serene smile that drove Mother mad.

"I hear this, *et voilà*, I'm a child again in Provence hearing the mistral. Some say they smell the fire in the wind, but me, I smell the lavender."

It was Gran who awoke us the morning after the Santa Ana started. She came up the polished oak stairs carrying a tray with fresh-squeezed orange juice, toast and jam and café au lait. That was how she brought the news. Fire had broken out over many western parts of the city. The seafront by the Palisades, Malibu, the canyons along Mulholland and Sunset, the Hollywood Hills.

Jocelyn and I leaned against goose-down pillows propped on the four-poster bed and waited for Gran to finish. Both our homes were in the fire zone. "Your mother and father are evacuated but safe, *ma petite*," she said to me, calling me the pet name, so improbable now, of my childhood, "and for now it is forbidden to go anywhere near. But for you, my poor Jocelyn, I do not know. I have taken the liberty of calling your number, but there is nothing, and from the reports I cannot tell exactly where the fire is stopped."

That was all Jocelyn needed to hear. She inflated with energy as surely as she had gone limp the night before. "Come with me, J.J.," she nearly commanded, then added, "please."

Gran gave slight signals of alarm. "It is very dangerous," she stated calmly. "The winds still shift fast, making the fire unpredictable. They ask on the radio that everyone stay away so they can get the trucks through." But even as she was saying "it's dangerous," she seemed also to be saying *Be careful*, not *Don't go.*

We assured her that we would be very careful, and dashed toward Jocelyn's car carrying our small bags.

The sky bucked and tossed with ashes and smoke, and the palm trees bent like reeds in a fast current. At times it felt as if the little red car would be picked up and blown away like a broken leaf as we followed Jocelyn's back route to Sunset Boulevard.

A police blockade stopped us a good two miles from where the road wound up the hill to her house. Forced to leave the car at a gas station, we walked on and on until we got to the forbidden intersection, just in time to see the fire curve down the ravaged hill, then in a gust blow back up and take the stone path to the top.

Shouts of firefighters charging with trucks and hoses, screaming sirens, explosions, then the thud of a misplaced water bomb. We watched it devour Jocelyn's house level by level, from Burt's wind tunnel to the roof, only four minutes and then only burning embers, as if the fire had been determined to pick even our memories clean.

Jocelyn said nothing, and seemed not even to blink, as we backed slowly away.

Finally she said "Samuel's. It's the only place we can get to that I know will be safe."

I did not ask how she knew this, and followed miles on the long, twisted walk through Hollywood's streets and dirty sky to reach the safe haven of the Rosens' Spanish-style mansion behind sturdy wrought-iron gates. Though no one was home, she knew the secret code and where the door key was hidden.

I wandered, more than a bit dazed, inside the Rosens' empty, opulent house. It makes a strange collage in my memory, red tile floors and Persian carpets, low leather furniture and brass antiques, highly polished inlay, marbled-topped tables, crystal chandeliers—and in every room, it seemed, a menorah. A lanai with straw mat flooring led to a terrace and a recessed swimming pool, dark with ashes and appearing to heave with waves of protest. Overhead the sky sank low under a burden of smoke.

Jocelyn said little. I recall only her sobbing from a distant room, a sound which faded as I searched for her. At last I found a messy bedroom. Samuel's, of course. There she lay, asleep in a bed beneath two self-portraits of van Gogh. Perhaps just then I couldn't see how like willful, passionate children she and Samuel were. But I did know that because he had run from her she could at last sleep in his bed.

When the telephone rang at Samuel's house, Jocelyn was still asleep. Madge had been looking for us everywhere. It fell to me to give her the news that it was all gone, even the wind tunnel. I hung up, woke Jocelyn, and together we waited for the oversized black Cadillac—now her family's only tangible possession—to pull up outside the Rosens' gate. As we waited, it became increasingly clear to me that all I wanted was to go home and verify for myself what the radio said: that the entire canyon was burned, perhaps burning still, sparing nothing.

Had Madge known what I was thinking, she would have been aghast. So I guessed would Mother, though she might have dropped any objection if she thought I could save her inventory of imported treasures. And Gran? Well, Gran did not fear fire but respected ashes. Perhaps if Guy had been with me, he would have become my accomplice; perhaps from that moment, we would have gone on together.

But only one person was there who knew what I wanted and why, and was prepared to go back into the flames with me. "Jo," I said waiting for the Cadillac, "I need to go now to my house. To see."

"Of course." She gave a crooked nod and put her long arm around my shoulder. And soon we were in the backseat of the Cadillac on our way to find where we had parked her car, giving some excuse to her parents, and promising to join them later at the grand old hotel in Pasadena where they had taken refuge.

Jocelyn then chauffeured us again through a labyrinth of streets until we approached the charred mouth of my canyon, that narrow indentation into the coastal hills where I lived. What had been a thicket of live oaks and sycamores was now only a residue of ash. The Santa Ana had stopped, replaced by winds off the coast nearby. But the ground held the heat.

A barricade and forbidding signs warned all comers to Keep Out, but no one manned the entrance, and there was no question of obedience. For me, the drive up that curving road where my family had lived for more than a dozen years was like feeling my way blind. The landmarks—the trees, the houses, fences, and gardens—were gone, anchors of my physical world suddenly turned into blackened silhouettes, burnt stumps, collapsed walls, or simply nothing. What remained was the road, its every bend and bump committed to deep memory by the child who had walked it, watching closely how it led out into the world.

When we reached that bend around which my house should have been, Jocelyn slowed, as if to cushion my shock—for which neither of us, in truth, were prepared. Because when she turned, there, naked against the evening where the trees had once been, stood the house set deep back into the land. The sidewall facing the road, the chimney, two stories high sprouting from the roof, the cement steps which stretched far across the front, all were intact.

I gasped, while Jocelyn said, "My God, my God. The only house left in the whole canyon. It's a miracle." I got out and ran through the smoldering earth and rubble to see the rest. But the Santa Ana's tricks were not over. When I reached the steps, I saw that there was no front door, no front wall, no house. All that remained was that western face closest to the road, the charred wall, the unbroken chimney. A shell. A trick.

I crumpled on the blackened steps and cried. Jocelyn ran to comfort me. But while I wept against her shoulder, I realized what I had never known before—that my true home remained. It was Gran's house where I had first loved what was beyond my own time and place; it was from her that I had learned to cherish the meaning of old things, a concept alien to Mother, who only bought and sold them.

"Do you know why we call her Gran, my grandma? It's short for *grand-mère*. She grew up somewhere in

Provence, you know, where they make perfume and the hills are wild with lavender."

I know this was such a bizarre comment that anyone would have thought I'd momentarily lost my mind. Anyone but Jocelyn.

What she said was, "Come on, J.J. We've got to get you to Pasadena for now. Then to Paris."

The night the houses burned was the night, one way or another, everyone decided to go to Paris. Not that anyone realized it at the time. For me, the desire was already strongly beating in my brain. But with the fire came a kind of clarity, an urgency. Jocelyn, with the Hollywood house gone, and with it Madge's paintings, the round red bed, and all the contortions of color, had lost her foundation. "Now we're both orphans," she had said with just the right amount of melodrama before the remains of my house, as she put her arm around my shoulder and led me back to her car.

I liked to think she felt our twinship acutely just then, after our parallel loss, and so decided to come with me. But that was wishful thinking on my part. Jocelyn had many reasons to go to Paris—to escape the Miss Calbrew dilemma, to run from the tortures she and Samuel inflicted on each other, to experience the freedom of flight itself. Still, I preferred to believe that her bond with me lay beyond the reach of will.

Chapter 3

For the others, whose homes lay outside the zone of fire, the impact of that night revealed itself more slowly. Evelyn, for example. I think it's fair to say that the night of the *bal masqué* and the wind and the fire, her life really began, but it was not until the next year, in Paris, that she knew it.

But that night, for the first time, she walked to the edge youth never believes is there—that the *demoiselles* certainly don't believe is there—and peered over. The first time she saw Jay with his white, immobile face, hard to distinguish from the white bandages that encased it, she thought she was looking at death. And that night the dreams began.

"There's the Triumph flying around the curve," she recounted, sitting on my bed in la Maison, "the city dazzling below, and then it's off the curve flying in the air and the sensation of flying, flying, then nothing. In the distance I see the heap of the car and know Jay's still there in the driver's seat. But I myself am dead. I watch as the police come and find me, just a lump, sometimes by the side of the road, sometimes in a tree branch, here or there. But dead and *never coming back*."

That was the terrifying part, *never coming back*. "How can that be, J.J.?" she wailed, and started in with me about resurrection. I understood the dream's threat. If the minister's daughter lost faith in resurrection, as her own dream's logic would suggest, it represented her greatest break yet with her childhood faith and family.

I expected that, after a few perfunctory calls, she would stop visiting Jay. No one would have blamed her. But a strange thing happened: instead of shunning him, she became his ministering angel, as if the whole burden of his rising again were hers. To my knowledge, guilt and the uplifting nature of expiation were never mentioned. Not even by her mother, the mother superior of ministering angels, who hovered in those days, worrying the way any mother would after a close call. Worn and gentle like the clothes she wore, those rayon prints and seersucker dresses, those low-heeled sensible pumps, she came often in those months after the accident, bringing homemade food and magazines as if she were making a parish call.

But Eve's own vigil, her watch over Jay, had begun. Almost daily she would go, taking the bus or borrowing Jocelyn's car to visit the Foothill Hospital at Baldy's base, where Jay still clung to that edge she dreamed of every night. After the first couple of encounters, she looked like a ghost. "I hate this, J.J.," she said, trembling on the porch of la Maison. "He looks like death and I feel like it every time I'm in his presence. And he doesn't even know I'm there."

"You don't have to do this, you know," I said, not stating the obvious, that it wasn't her fault.

"But I do. That's the strange part."

And so she did. She complained: "He smells bad, and drools from the mouth, and then he *moans*." But still she went and sat with him by the hour, read to him, or sometimes played music on a little transistor radio. On the day he opened his eyes to greet her, her heart gave a little. "It seemed so encouraging to me, like maybe he's going to make it," she said. "I felt kind of faint with gratitude."

It wasn't gratitude, that much I knew—and knew enough not to say. Maybe she knew it, too, as the weeks progressed and one by one Jay's wraps fell away. He began to banter with her, ask for books, and then for her to read passages to him. She told me how the conversations had shifted from politics and news—his things—to hers. I heard this with no little envy. "A captive audience." Her grin had its old wickedness back. "We're doing all the theologians and thinkers, Adler to Wittgenstein, and the novelists and poets. I think it's important for a man to go through an entire volume of Emily Dickinson, don't you?"

I could picture him, lying there defenseless, and believed briefly in divine retribution myself. But by the time they got to Baudelaire, Eve didn't discuss it anymore. By then, Jay was in traction and mostly immobile, but, in a sense, a more seductive force than he had ever been. She would open the window wide, even when a chill was in the air, and let the night into his room, and with it the wavering scent of oranges and the looming shadow of the old mountain, which now seemed more guardian than killer. She would also stay late, until the moon dipped down into the desert, or the last bus left, convincing herself more than Jay that it didn't matter if her grades slipped a bit or she slacked a little at her job waiting tables in the women's dining hall. "All that matters, kiddo, is that you rise again and walk." Perhaps she did convince him of that.

But it is also important to understand what Eve did not say. Leaning heavily on the facility of mind that allowed her to compartmentalize, she simply neglected to mention Tom to Jay. "What's the point, J.J.?" she asked, more of herself than me, as she pinched a bracelet from my bureau. "I mean, knowing that Tom is a darling friend is really not going to advance Jay's health, now, is it?" So, to my knowledge, she never said a thing about Tom. How he came afternoons, evenings, and nights, whenever football practice released him, and waited for her. How he brought food swiped from meals she'd missed or notes cadged from classes she'd skipped, or a wrap to keep the chill off when she walked home from the late bus.

"Can't have you walking alone in the dark and cold, *bella*," I can hear him say, as he noted again that she was getting kind of skinny.

"You're very sweet, but you don't have to do this, you know," she'd reply. To which he'd raise his palm, saying only, "Please!"

Of course, nobody in the world knew better than Eve about doing what one is driven to do. So her protests must have been at best half-hearted. And it didn't hurt that, as she put it, "you know, with those shiny curls and humongous shoulders, he ain't bad. It kills me how these freshmen girls always just kind of stumble into his path." It was hard not to notice the swath they cut crossing the quad, his arm around her shoulders drawing her tight, while other, ordinary girls looked at her with undisguised envy.

In the end, she never did mention Tom to Jay. Likewise, she explained, it was best not to mention Tom to her mother. "God, all I have to do is *hint* that I'm going out with someone, and she begins wringing her hands and starts with the 'is this serious?' routine. Meaning 'are you behaving?' So if she thinks there's a Papist lurking in the woodpile, when I've got enough troubles already, she'll have a heart attack. Besides, it's not like we're dating. Not in the ways that really count."

Given how well the walls of denial were working, I guess it was not surprising that she neglected to say anything about what was, at least to my mind, the most surprising thing she did that fall. I was left to figure out for myself what it meant when she put a picture of Jackie, wearing that dreamy half-smile, a pale green suit, and three strands of pearls, over her bed. It was in the spot where, if she'd still been a believer, maybe a Catholic like Tom, a Madonna might have hung.

I believe it was around the time Jackie's picture went up that Eve began to speak of France.

All I know is that one day after her mother had gone, leaving behind a plate of oatmeal cookies, Eve burst through my door, her skin that high pink tone she turned after a close call, a hot bath, or a sensation of pleasure.

"J.J., you aren't going to believe this! Where's Jocelyn? Oh, God," she hugged herself, "Mother has just told me the church is starting a scholarship fund for advanced study. The Sorbonne is definitely advanced, no? And what better way to launch it than one of the Richter offspring let loose in the world to set a fine, *Christian* example. Oh, I'm so excited. Can you believe this? *I'm coming with you. To France."*

Chapter 4

I feel here that, despite myself, I hear Dean Lutowsky's mocking laugh, as if to say, "*That's* the best case you can make?" Well, perhaps not. Perhaps Eve was just another rich bitch in disguise without a trace of proletarian pedigree. But what would she—would anyone—make of Grace?

By Parents' Day, Mama, who stared out with bewildered resignation from that photo on Gracie's bureau, was already a year dead. And Papa, who had arrived from the shadowy purple hills of Napa to this alien college world, perhaps tried to bestow benediction—or extract the sense of that big brain beneath—by patting her thick dark curls with his knobby, winemaker's fingers. "Datsa real gude," he said to her, as if in parody, then repeated to Dr. Hart, who took him for the gardener, and to Pastor Richter, who smiled ingratiatingly and then said slowly, "Sorry, but I don't speak Spanish."

Papa just then was concentrating on Gracie, feeling a rising pride mingling with confusion. After that visit from the nuns Gracie had told me about, both Papa and

Mama began to grasp the fact of her uncommon intelligence, and then the bewildered resignation started to set in. Especially for Mama, who tried to greet it with the force of faith. "Sort of like Mary, Mother of God, learning the extraterrestrial facts of her son's conception. What could Mama do but God's will? She threw up her hands and prayed a lot," Gracie said. "And when I came here, sequestering myself in a place dedicated to the life of the mind, she said she could understand if only I'd gone to a convent."

It probably didn't help that her brothers—dreamy-eyed Marcello and the dark-haired, muscular Favio in particular—were such screw-ups. Marcello (Mark, he insisted) could think of nothing but cars, while Favio dreamed endlessly of going south to the beach "to find some blonde Anglo broads with long legs." I didn't say what I was thinking: That Mama had probably wished she could shift things, to give Favio some brains and Gracie a little beauty; that it seemed a waste to have a girl with such a head; that perhaps she'd made a mistake giving her daughter that beautiful American name, the name that became attached to a movie star.

I know that, like all of us, Gracie felt she must not turn into her mother, that she desperately needed to find some other kind of woman to be. And that when Gracie left home as a Governor's Scholar, declaring her intention to become a physicist, Papa stormed out of the house, into the vineyards, while Mama, ever defined by family and her Tuscan kitchen, wept into Gracie's collar. "I'm gonna lose you," she repeated, and Gracie said her own silent prayer of thanksgiving.

This is what I'm guessing: in those days when Tom Tomacello hung around la Maison waiting for Evelyn, and Gracie shivered a little every time she passed near him, she trembled from the excitement of the forbidden and the familiar. Tom, the godlike football hero, who sat on the couch struggling with his work in the half-lit living room, was somebody who, in the ordinary way of the world, would never know she existed. Yet with his dark curls, muscular body, and Roman profile, he might be a cousin. She felt that frisson of familiarity. And in those early evenings passing by him, before they spoke, it was Papa's words that came back to her, the ones he was always repeating about how the sun hits the vine. "Two branches on same stock, one makes da sour grape, one da sweet. Some grapes for *vino*, some for *vinagre*."

Like Tom, who had two sources of angst. One she knew from the beginning—his uphill battle for Eve's affection. It came to her slowly that she and Tom had another thing in common: they were both scholarship students. Tom, whose real purpose was football, found his studies a major pain in the gluteus maximus. This came to Gracie with time, as every night she peered over his shoulder while he sat in the slanting living room, head in hands. One night, after discovering him bowed over a formula for mass and weight, she bounded up the stairs to my room, filled with purpose.

"Say, J.J.," she said, pushing open my door, "I see poor old Tom down there every night beating himself up over his courses. Then tonight I, um, noticed, he's kind of struggling with physics. Think I should offer to help?"

Of course I said yes. So a new watch was set in *la chambre de secrets*. Sometimes when the phone rang it was Tom, who sometimes asked for Gracie. And it went that way for months, the two mops of Italian curls, one large round head, the other shapely on a massive neck, bending together over books in the corner of the living room.

There was one night whose memory she pressed and kept the way some girls press corsages from their first dance. "Let's go to Mama Maria's for pizza," he said. "My treat," and he winked, making her blush. She told me how he laughed. What she didn't tell, I already knew: the gestures that came so easily to him, the way he lightly touched her hair and eased her with his strong hand into the booth at Mama's. Then Tom and Mama broke into rapid Italian, and for once Gracie could see being Italian might be an asset. "I wish to God I'd paid more attention at home and learned to speak."

I could almost hear her rabbity heart beating, see her eyes furtively skimming the room to see who was there to witness this pivotal moment in her life, when she, Gracie Battaglia, was the one in a booth at Mama's drinking a tankard of beer and sharing a pizza with Tom Tomacello.

So I knew what she meant when, on another night, she burst into my room to declare, "J.J., I just lost my virginity." There had been another stroll back from Mama's, when Tom, his mind swirling with equations, beer, and a sense of gratitude, reached out, grabbed her in his massive arms, and picked her up. In one brief, lighthearted embrace, he had caught her by surprise and awakened what even the nuns and a lifetime of homeliness could not extinguish. She felt the power of his rough cheek before he brushed her lips. For the first time, Gracie had been kissed.

I don't know if she ever saw the irony of it, the fact that the one thing Mama wished the most, she had done. She had fallen in love with a nice Italian boy, a strong boy, none too smart, who kept the faith and loved his mother.

By the end of the year, though, changes were evident. Physics had been put down like an inconvenient dog, and Gracie made the switch to becoming a French history major as if it were a conversion. She began to openly study the dress and movements of the rest of us, long-legged, long-haired, easy in our own skin. And by year's end, it also became clear: if Evelyn was going to spend her junior year studying French at the Sorbonne, Gracie would be there too.

Chapter 5

That leaves only Melanie. I don't know how she got through the night of the Santa Ana. Her parental manse, a stately, shingled home with gables, remained safe in Pasadena (as did the aspirations of her parents, her socially prominent surgeon father and her ambitious if unpedigreed mother). Despite my best efforts, I don't remember her at the *bal masqué*. Was she there? Wherever she was, she was with Hans in a world already at risk for burning in rarefied air.

For Melanie, starlight was most becoming. She might have lived forever if she'd found some warmth in it. At least that's what I came to believe. Her stars were not those of Jocelyn, the ones that hung in bright, false clusters off a Hollywood hill; hers were the stars of Pascal—frigid, distant, hard, but irresistible in their beauty. That was her discovery, and something always pulled her toward their brilliance and the fields of darkness so vast between.

In part this was because she was so unsuited to the naked heat of the California sun. She lacked the pigment for it. Her small, white blondeness kept her to the shadows; her see-through blue eyes jittered in too much light. In the end, it was the need for darkness that led her below the earth. That is what linked her to Hans. I saw how they shunned daylight together.

Ordinary days, as she scurried on her rounds, Melanie passed the music building. Along its path, she walked the brick edge of the flower bed to find shade, a stingy commodity in the feathered shadows of palm and mimosa. Ivy on the old adobe walls gave an illusion of cool between the fiery blooms of hibiscus and birds-of-paradise.

Still, sunlight caught her and set her ablaze.

From the basement practice window, Hans looked up and saw her aglow, a wondrous candle, pale as himself. After the first day he spotted her, be began stopping all sound, hushing his violin as she passed, so he could look. But one Wednesday, when the light was especially strong, he could not restrain the impulse to play. Mozart. Liszt. Chopin. Thursday and Friday he fairly sawed his violin. Melanie hurried past. Saturday and Sunday she didn't come. Hans kept vigil. Monday he opened the window, and she heard.

The next day and the week to follow, she slowed a little as she rounded the corner, and she listened. Bach. He played beautifully. Her pause in sunlight—Hans thought of it perhaps as an arrest—he no doubt took to be his own invention. But then she'd glance at her watch, ever eager to be on time, and slip away.

Then, the Tuesday following, the bells in the Spanish tower struck hard at noon. Melanie didn't come. At ten past twelve, I can see him throwing down his bow in disgust, thinking how for these few days he had stopped her with his playing, touched her with his notes. But now she hadn't come.

He would have gone then to the courtyard and sought the shade of the farthest avocado tree, to plant himself and stand watch, thinking maybe she was late.

But Melanie was never late. That day she had spent her lunch hour in French lab, doing extra work to improve her grammar. I know, because I was her partner. I was also the cause of the buzz that had started around la Maison, the talking that had been only about my intentions but had come to embrace all the *demoiselles*, about the possibility, no, the fact, that we were all going to France. She could hardly believe it. And was she going? It hadn't crossed her mind.

But then there was that one day, and the shadow that she couldn't see of Hans beneath the avocado tree, and the wind of the rumor. I believe that right there, the small subtle net of the idea caught her too. And on that day, she thought to herself in French lab, *"Et moi aussi? Et pourquoi pas?"* And then, being Melanie, she leapt immediately to the steps to be taken, and the first thought was to improve her French. Yes, if she could get up to speed and go too, it was definitely worth a few French labs.

So beginning that Tuesday, she skipped taking time to walk through the shaded garden of the music building. For four days, Hans waited at noon. I can see him each morning, the music drying up in him a little earlier. The sound of the bells approaching, and his fingers trembling. By Friday, he had to know she wouldn't come. He must have tried, however briefly, to think why this mattered, tried to play it on his violin. And that is how he finally understood: this girl, this vision of a girl, affected his music.

The next week, I know, he stood in the middle of the grassy quad, in the open, without even the protection of the mottled sycamores to shield him, and he watched. Within two days he spotted her, only a blur of hair, a streak of melting butter in the sun.

By Wednesday, he was prepared. I can see him pacing the garden, circling the music building. Without thinking precisely how he got there, he finally found himself in front of the dean's large Victorian house with the full rose garden. As many times as he had noticed the roses in passing, now he really saw them for the first time. He would have looked carefully, making his selection, before sailing high over the iron fence, making no sound as he landed to pick the rose, and none as he jumped back. And yes, he would have whistled—perhaps a little aria from *Madame Butterfly*—while running, a white rose tucked safely in his breast pocket.

When Melanie briskly crossed the path along the quad, Hans, neat in a crisp white shirt and black shoes, stepped out in front of her.

"Miss," she heard him say. "Please. Accept this. I am sorry for troubling you, but you seemed to like my music. Perhaps you like roses also, yes?"

This is what she saw as she stopped sharply and looked up from the soft petals on the prickly stem: ice-blue eyes that held her fast, as if she were looking into herself. Then she heard the voice that was speaking so intently, so oddly, in front of her. "...but as you see, I have been missing you," she heard him say.

"Oh, but I..." and she noticed right then how fair he was, how likely to burn. She might have blushed when his hand slipped under her elbow as naturally as if they had been born together. Then he would have said, "Forgive me, but it is so warm here. Might we take lunch together and find something to drink?"

The outline of this story she recounted to me herself. But I was a witness when they first walked into the dining hall, already locked in step together. "Would you get a load of that?" Eve sputtered over French fries.

"So, Mel, who's the blond?" Eve called out to her later that evening. But Melanie had a way with silence that could not be broken. She gave what could only be called noncommittal shrugs.

Still, the young Swiss musician from the borderland of Germany (or was it the borderland of France; who could tell given the promiscuousness of history?) began appearing often at la Maison. Most young men who showed up, casual and self-assured in loafers, jeans, and jerseys, could accurately be called boyfriends. But Hans dressed with an alien correctness, a demeanor that could only be called that of a suitor. What he did was conduct a courtship.

Roses arrived regularly in the house, perhaps more fragrant for having been stolen. To keep the offense from the prying eyes of Spinster Krauss, all winter the thick teacups of house crockery were stained with forbidden red wine, so if she caught them sipping together, she'd have no hint of a beverage stronger than tea.

Once, as first Sunday light came through the east window over the hush of the wash, I found Mel at the sink. She had not, I think, been to bed and was twisting thick ropes of her hair to keep them out of dishwater as she tried to scrub the incriminating stains. "To tell you the truth, it's only Hans who really drinks the stuff," she said, as if I cared that she drank. "I don't actually like the taste of it, though the idea is romantic. Do you suppose that would win me any points with old Krauts if she finds out?"

The courtship continued into spring. Daffodils filled Melanie's room, and she came into la Maison with the faint perfume of orange blossoms clinging to her, acquired on afternoons spent deep in orange groves. The rest was easy to imagine. Books of poetry exchanged on soft beds of newly mown grass. And always music. Under the magic of Hans's fingers, even the old piano out of tune in the sunroom swelled in serenade of Melanie.

Her silence became more telling—"the golden swoon," Eve called it—though she never said exactly where she'd been or what she'd been doing. She never told, for instance, how many hours she spent in that basement room, listening to Hans practice the violin. And she certainly never told the thing everyone wanted to know most—and Evelyn asked once outright—how and when they had become lovers.

It was only later, on the *Jeanne d'Arc*, wrung out like a couple of limp socks and trying to gather some fresh air on the deck, when we lay on lounge chairs in the feeble sun that she spoke of it. Melanie was the first of our group to reach the awesome age of twenty-one, but only Hans had known it. Though the number had no great meaning in Europe, he understood that in America it marked a passage.

So on that special day in April, champagne replaced the jug of red wine in the kitchen pantry. Then, pushing aside the thick teacups, he poured the silver bubbles into hollow-stem glasses, asking playfully, "Surely you drink this, *ma petite*?"

"Of course," she said. And, given all the events in her past—the receptions, cocktail parties, weddings, and galas that were part of her life on the socialite circuit—of course she'd had her share. But the question as to whether she liked it or not still had not been broached. It was, she admitted, better than red wine, and she complimented Hans for the special surprise. Meaning not the champagne itself, but the hollow-stemmed glasses.

"But how else to drink champagne? For some things, important things, it is necessary to do them right, no?" She blushed as she recounted this. Then she confessed slowly, having played these words verbatim over and over to herself. "And after that, J.J., he said the dearest thing: 'I love the way the light catches your hair. You could be an angel, Mel-an-ee'—you know the way he says my name like that, Mel-an-ee—'An angel from a painting. Or a song. I pray you never change.' Then he toasted me. 'To you…to us.'"

I could only imagine how she held up her own glass, toasting him back through its transparency, and swallowed hard courageously, blood drumming in her ears.

It wasn't until all these years later, with her papers now in my possession, a gift from Ivan who stumbled on them by chance, that I know what really happened. The journal entry from that day in April 1962 is as explicit as anything she ever wrote.

> We went to Hans's new place. It is a small room behind a professor's house with high ceilings and a large stone fireplace. He moved from the dorm because he needed privacy and quiet for music—"to pluck it out and hear it bounce from the corners," he said. Still, I guess that wasn't the only reason. I think he was thinking of me. Of course he was thinking of me! Dear Hans, he even said, "Mel-an-ee" (I adore how he says my name) "I cannot take you in the leaves."
>
> We went inside and he lit a match to the fireplace and everything was flickering shadows. Then he gave me

> a rose from the mantle and I understood. But first he gave me my present—a paper wrapped in blue ribbon. I opened it, but it was just a blur of notes. (How shameful I don't even read music.) Across the top was written "Song for Melanie."
>
> I couldn't believe it. I still can't. He played it on a guitar, just the melody he said, just a thin skeleton, the basis for his first serious composition. But me! He played *me*! At least the tune, and I can't imagine how it will sound when he's finished the whole piece.
>
> And then... I've never been so delirious. How could I ever forget the first time? And now I don't even know the words for my feelings. It must be happiness. But so strange too, I don't know, like bitter chocolate, with a taste of sadness.

With that testimony in hand, it is easy now to fill in what I only guessed at that gray afternoon at sea. How he had let himself down on her, as if on a rope of flaxen silk, and how they both cried out, trying to fill in the thin tune with the whole symphony, his sounds of pleasure swallowing her cries. Without the anesthetic wine, she might have known how much she bled. Without the aphrodisiac wine, she might have known that only imagination carried her away, leaving the hollow of herself, her body unfulfilled.

I believe, too, that on her birthday, when she died to herself as much as she lived in Hans, Melanie made the decision to come to Paris. Of course she'd thought of it that day in French lab, and it was certainly in her mind as long ago as Parents' Day, when she tentatively introduced Hans to her impeccable mother, so cool and minty looking in green beneath the blonde helmet of her perfect hair. "Mother, I'd like you to meet my friend, Hans Boucher.

He's, he's a musician. From, Basel, or Bâle in French, near France, but in the German part of Switzerland..."

"Madame 'art," he said, dropping the H in her name as he bent slightly over her hand, stopping short of kissing it.

I can see now as clearly as yesterday how Mrs. Hart turned, noiselessly, on that steep high heel in the color they called bone and faced him, a lethal smile on her face. "A musician? How charming! I don't believe we've ever had one of those in our family." She extended the fingers of her right hand, nails frosted with a slight green tint. "And Belgium did you say? Such a quaint little country..."

Of course Melanie couldn't say exactly when she decided to go, still being a stranger to her own mind. But her growing passion for Hans, who, like herself, had been consigned to the deep freeze by her mother, had by necessity become a secret. She imagined only running toward him and their future together. What she couldn't see was the twin impulse to run away from him and toward the dark she carried within. The dark she so deliberately avoided entering, although her name was over the door. But there, in the recesses of her conscience, like a light in the hold, the decision to go flickered and ignited.

Escape doesn't begin to describe it. If there is a word for what she embarked on, it is salvation.

Part 2

The Passage

Chapter 6

Perhaps it was seasickness, or merely a dream. How did we cross from one world to the other? I look back and wonder, the files in my head tossing like that pathetic rust bucket, the *Jeanne d'Arc*, as she lurched through the waves.

This much I can report as fact: Wooden deck chairs, chipped blue paint. In repose under a slab of sun, eyes closed to keep from seeing that woozy gray line, sometimes vertical, sometimes horizontal, that separates sky from sea. It, too, a fiction. Mel beside me, hidden beneath a light blanket and hat, trying vainly to escape the sun. Trying vainly, like me, to breath the wet salt spray, pretend it is air, pretend the *mal de mer* has been vanquished.

For myself, perhaps never before did a wretched (yes, that is the word!) hollowness so perfectly match my mind to my physical state. As I lay, eyes shut against the painful light, I tried deliberately to transport myself somewhere else, to find in the tossing ship the gentle rocking of the swing on Gran's porch. To find again in the slanted shade light filtering through the awning and the spreading avocado tree of my childhood, to contemplate the treasure of those early, compulsively sorted collections: spools, balls of yarn, buttons. Did this impulse come from Gran, whose urge to collect sprang, I think, from a longing of the spirit, as if the artful gathering of plain things could beautify a spare, inner cathedral? Or did my passion come from Mother, who collected out of appetite, with all those mismatched beads, primitive African masks, and evil-eyed totems displayed without regard to the nature of their provenance, things flung together in sheer acquisitive delight?

I couldn't resolve just then which one I followed. I only know that from an early age, my pockets were always full. And that as I reached to pat them for reassurance at that rocky moment, found with alarm that they were singularly empty.

There was only that one slight letter from Guy, reminding me how quickly the wind can shift. He had left for Mississippi before Christmas, and we had begun our intense, intimate, long-distance love affair, each reporting in letters like foreign correspondents from a different front, punctuated by occasional phone calls and too short, passionate, unfulfilled rendezvous. Each ended as the one before had: unresolved, filled with desire and reproach. Then there was the quarrel, and the *demoiselles'* cost-cutting decision to sail on the *Jeanne d'Arc*—sooner than originally planned—before he could return to say good-bye. Leaving felt like an amputation.

On that miserable deck, I shifted onto my left hip, fingering the letter, Guy's last. It was no use pulling it out to read; I had already, despite myself, memorized it. Why not get rid of the damn thing, I asked myself again, even as Guy's maddening, tantalizing truths and half-truths worked me over.

> The problem is that we are so profoundly different, that we're attracted to the opposite of each other at the same time we want each other to see things the same way. But sometimes, when I have to face how small-minded men can be (even ones I admire) or when I think this is pretty hopeless and that racism will defeat us all or when I'm just plain scared, like I was last week when they brought out attack dogs to face little kids, then I dream of the boat you are taking. Rimbaud's of course—I've been reading that "Drunken Boat"—and I keep coming to these lines: "I drifted on a river I could not control/No longer guided by the bargeman's ropes" and I just want to jump on it with you. But I can't, you see, I can't give up just yet, even as I long to lie beside you...as always you fill my dreams.

Disgusted by my inability to move, to make so small a gesture as ridding myself of Guy's lingering presence, of turning my pockets at last into an authentic void, I rolled over again and squinted at Mel, and wondered if she experienced the kind of emptiness tinged by nausea that I was feeling. Then, startled, I realized she had been speaking all along from beneath her wraps, telling me her life's story as though it had begun only last year, when Hans had taken possession, as though there had been no struggle with her family before they hated him, no desire to find out who she was before he composed her. No dark and empty place inside, a hollow she could call her own.

I could almost say that was the whole of it, adrift without meaning or memory on a scruffy little boat suitable only to foreign students, that passage was no more or less than survival in a deck chair and the vague awareness of a swirl of languages passing through the heavy salt air. But

Gracie, who in Paris would insist on telling everything, would not let me get away with so little.

It was she who plopped down in the deck chair beyond Mel. Out of it as I was, even I had to notice and to speculate. In her coy deck dress, ridiculously out of place, a pair of outsized, white-rimmed sunglasses propped just so on her head, her shapeless legs crossed awkwardly at the knee, what exactly was she trying to prove? Or more to the point, who was she trying to be? Through half-shut eyes, I watched her watching Jo, alone on the prow and aloof as an ornamental goddess, impervious to the rush of cold spray splashing over her, a sleek, unapproachable tangle of limbs, and thought I knew. But that didn't take into account whatever poses Eve struck out of view of my limited vision.

She was, Gracie informed me, giving great performances in the smoky lounge of the A-deck. Gracie followed Eve doggedly, not just in her usual worshipful way, but because she now felt bound by her secret love of Tom. Gracie could hardly keep the pain out of her voice as she described the Eve she saw. "Surrounded as usual, J.J., by men, inviting them to her really, you know, winking the way she does, tossing her head, and promising who knows what with that smile." But it was not the multitudes that really bothered Gracie, it was one in particular and the fact that Eve had discovered first what we all longed to know: the true secret of voyaging abroad. The ability to float free, to exist in the present, to act suspended from consequences.

The scene of Gracie's dismay: Eve at the bar, drinking Scotch, the Frenchman approaching. The laugh, the wink, the nod, another drink, and the Frenchman, a dark, slim, curly-headed cliché of a Frenchman, and Eve maneuvering to the crowded dance floor. The Frenchman—"Call him Pierre," Gracie said with disgust, "say he was the med student from Bordeaux"—kissing her neck, holding her hips close against him, his hands caressing her buttocks. "And the way he looked at her—you know the way they do. In other countries that kind of look could get you arrested for indecent exposure."

Indeed. I did know the look that asks the question, *"Tu veux, chérie?"* to which evidently Eve had responded, *"Je veux,"* or maybe even, "Yes, I will yes, I will, yes," forgetting to cite the source. And so she left the bar, his arm across her shoulder, guiding her into the night. A few minutes later, Gracie, pulled together enough to go below to her bunk, left too. She ran down the dimly lit stairs to reach the cabin she shared with Eve, where she stopped outside the slightly opened porthole. There everything was revealed. The sounds of love, the moans, the cries small and large, the final shuddering gasps of joy—his and hers—and the telltale voices. "Pierre" saying, astonished, *"Mais, Evelyn, tu étais vierge?"* Evelyn answering, as if to the waning moon beyond her invisible, listening roommate, *"Non, chéri. Demi. Je suis née demi-vierge."*

Born a half-virgin. Maybe that revelation more than any other propelled Gracie, ever imprisoned in her physiognomy, or her formation by the nuns, or the unfortunate misnomer of her name. For whatever reasons, Gracie moved. Kissed once by Tom, yes, but in spite of her delighted brag to me, a virgin still.

But what course could she take? She did the logical thing. Taking a page from Eve's book, or Jocelyn's, or even possibly mine, she studied what she considered successful techniques and set about to emulate them. Hence the dress and shades, the studied nonchalance of Gracie's pose as she perched—awkwardly, it has to be said—upon the lounge chair. And hence, she explained, the determination to hang out in the lounge where the action seemed to be. "Something," she said, "was bound to happen."

Something did. He arrived in the form of a slight, nineteen-year-old, wispy-haired pig farmer with acne. Not only that, but he was Canadian, which hardly even counted as foreign. But Gracie said, when he first bumped into her in the lounge, it was pretty dark and she couldn't see clearly what she was getting into. She was sitting in a corner, nose in a German book, when George McKay approached her, clearing his throat. *"Fräulein,"* he said, which, Gracie reported, "I figured was a promising start. Didn't realize he was also taking German and wanted a study buddy. He asked if he could sit down. I said, 'Sure,' and I should have seen where this was going right then, when he ordered a Cherry Coke. Too young to drink, he said! But then, when he told me he was going to study in Germany, I figured, you know, Heidelberg or something. When I found out it was a mechanical and agricultural school, I figured, well, okay, something technical. It wasn't until several conversations later and…you know…that I discovered he was really going on some kind of 4-H scholarship to look at German tractors!"

The elusive "you know" covered the heart of the story, which partially came out in awkward drabs, forcing me to fill in the rest. It seemed that even George (whom by then she derisively called Georgie) was not blind to what Gracie, a perfect match for his unsurfaced desire, advertised in her contorted deck pose. "After we got out of those lounge conversations about German grammar, he began to see me in a different light," she explained matter-of-factly. "Then he started inviting me back inside, safety in the dark I guess, and despite the Cherry Cokes, we began dancing, and then, well, you know..."

He turned up everywhere, his raw complexion now further reddened from salt wind and sun to say nothing of perennial blushing brought about, Gracie guessed, by "hardening in public view." Still, it pleased her, made her even a little feverish to be for once the object of such open, if vulgar, worship. I can almost picture him as she climbed the winding metal stairs to the A-deck, staring with rapture as if he were glimpsing the underside of a love goddess, maybe Brigitte Bardot. But despite his adoration, things, according to Gracie, didn't seem to be going anywhere. And perhaps determined to follow Eve's example and float in the present, she decided she needed to push for a change in direction.

"That was my fatal mistake," she recounted, "telling him pretty directly it was dumb to just sit there and drink Cherry Cokes. I mean it was the middle of the ocean and who cared about being under age and why not at least drink a beer, for heaven's sake? So he ordered this whiskey." There were a couple more, I gathered, before they both left the lounge and its warped recordings of boozy jazz to lurch out on the open deck. I'm not sure how, exactly, they ended up in a lifeboat hidden under a tarp, but I do know enough to say that one horrific kiss—"French," she informed me—was enough to shake Gracie's faith in the romantic course she'd cut out for herself. And every gesture, every rough caress and awkward grope carried her farther and farther from herself—and farther still from the erotic paradise she imagined Eve reached so easily. She fled the lifeboat half-dressed, a *demi-vierge* at last.

Of course, I knew nothing of this at the time and noticed only that the deck chair Gracie had so conspicuously adorned was suddenly abandoned. So, meeting her on the ship's stairs one evening, I asked what happened. "Seasickness," she replied, to which I nodded sympathetically, not realizing that Gracie's nausea was born of deep revulsion.

Unhappily, the lifeboat affair did not end with the night. Georgie, it seemed, was a bit fuzzy about what had really transpired, but assumed it all meant an engagement. Gracie, an overnight refugee taken to hiding in her bunk or the women's head, never wanted to see him again and sent word through Eve that she was terminally indisposed.

But lovestruck and determined, Georgie barraged her with notes. "There were references," she winced recounting this, "to *Mother*. And the assumption of our life together because I had let him go so far." The letters, telling of progress with the new German tractors and encouraging numbers of piglets interwoven with a craven pining, even followed her to Paris. "How did they get to me here, you may well ask? Well wouldn't you know, he found the address of la Maison on something and copied it. So he writes me there, where sweet Tom, who regularly goes to collect stuff for Eve, finds them and forwards them to me."

Only once do I remember entering the A-deck lounge myself. I cannot say if I saw Eve there in a steamy embrace on the dance floor with Pierre, or if my eye caught Gracie in a darkened corner, her inflamed inamorato downing Cherry Cokes by her side. I was probably as invisible to myself and my purposes as Mel beneath her wraps, who at least had her object of adoration upon which to focus. But all my conscious attention was riveted on Jocelyn, whom otherwise I recall speaking to during our voyage only in late-night muffled half-thoughts in our stifling cabin. I had accepted that she had chosen the spot on the prow as her private throne, her unique seat of passage. Such militant solitary confinement, although in a setting to make the most of her beauty, did not quite square with the fact that she seemed to always have crowds around her wherever she went. I couldn't figure out exactly what she was up to and was mostly too seasick to care.

Then that one night I made my foray into the lounge only to discover that after a dayshift on deck, Jocelyn, my roommate, my soulmate, my *soeur*, nightly moved inside to live the other half of her life as celebrated performer. It was startling to see her there in the yellow spotlight on the small, makeshift stage, like a pale Ophelia suddenly come to life, golden hair falling wonderfully over a perfect face, strumming a plaintive guitar. Her clear voice rang out with the ballad recently made new again by Joan Baez:

> All men are false, says my mother.
> They tell you wicked, cheating lies,
> And the very next evening, go court another
> Leave you alone to pine and sigh.
> Go court another tender maiden
> And hope that she will be your wife,
> For I've been warned and I've decided
> To sleep alone all of my life.

I reached in my nearly empty pocket for my touchstone, but couldn't find the letter. Either to answer Guy or as a silent rebuttal to Jocelyn, or a hymn to the Paris I was about to enter, I began reciting more Rimbaud lines under my breath:

> Deliriums that streak the glowing sky
> Stronger than drink and the songs we sing,
> It is boiling, bitter, red; it is love!

Chapter 7

When, in a dark dawn, the *Jeanne d'Arc* groaned mightily and pitched against the massive lines that tied her to the dock in Le Havre, I knew that at last the sea voyage had ended. But much as that had been a kind of suspension between time and realities, so, too, would be the next phase of our journey. As I peered down into the oily black water while a bleak sun struggled to pierce the fog-filled sky, I realized that although the ship had stopped sailing, we hadn't landed either. And when, hours later, we gave up a collective little cheer as we actually stepped on French soil, it hardly felt like land.

Eve, a scarf pulled around her ears against the lingering damp, rocked unsteadily as she stepped off the gangplank onto cement. "Holy moly," she shouted out, "this feels like walking on water, again."

"Really? I'm surprised you noticed," Gracie shot back, uncharacteristically sharp, "I thought you spent most of the time aboard on your back."

"Well, I did," I jumped in. "Aboard I could hardly walk, and now I feel like a drunken sailor."

In a way, that feeling of always seeming to keel a little, of perpetually stepping on ground that gives way, became more a metaphor for landing in a strange land than a problem of sea legs never attained. And rolling toward Paris on the lurching train, the French countryside a blur outside the windows, only fueled our unsteadiness. Then, too, the giddy *joie de vivre* we gave into as we boarded a train actually bound for Paris loosened and slowly—oddly—grew into something closer to melancholy by the time we reached the outer suburbs of the City of Light. Not that any of us would have admitted it.

Only now, in hindsight, can I venture to say what that was all about. It was that we were at last arriving in that place we longed, but secretly feared, to go. And we were venturing there without the protection and bravura of our little group, because *les demoiselles de la Maison Française* were splintering off from each other to find their own ways in Paris. Even those of us who went with a roommate, like Jocelyn and I, would soon lead separate lives. No sooner did the wheels of the train screech to a halt in the station than I saw how we were to scatter like seeds carried on the wind to disparate worlds within the city.

How disparate and how different our lives were to be one from the other was clear from the moment we set foot in the Gare Saint-Lazare. The beautiful webs of Paris, full of irony, contradiction, glorious seductions, and unforeseen despair, would soon enmesh us all, and were already being spun.

We were foreign, American, out of place, and none more obviously so than Gracie. There, standing on the platform as soon as Gracie stepped down was a stout, severe French woman in a plain brown suit, her head adorned by a brown felt hat with a lonely brown feather stuck into its band. This was without question Madame Gautier, a renowned former professor of French cuisine. What might have been a sliver of a smile—like a slice of lemon, Eve remarked—passed quickly on and off her lips. Then casting a disapproving glance at the lot of us, she barked, *"Et qui est Mademoiselle Battaglia?"* severely mispronouncing Gracie's last name. As Gracie stepped forward, rumpled in a shirtwaist dress and unfashionable flat shoes, her unruly hair flying in all directions, Madame Gautier visibly flinched. Then she stuck out her gloved hand, and it took a thoroughly startled Gracie several awkward seconds to realize she was meant to shake it. "It is I, Madame. I am Mademoiselle Battaglia," Gracie sputtered at last.

"Oh God, Madame *Gout*-ier, wouldn't you know? Well, at least she didn't have to go through the kissing routine," Eve whispered as Madame thrust her arm through Gracie's and began to yank her away. "That would be like kissing an old sow—not the sort of kiss for arriving in Paris." And we stood, startled, watching, while Gracie and her former professor of cuisine began to disappear into the crowd. Before she was out of sight, Gracie turned and gave a wan wave. We all waved back, worried. What had we let her get into?

We, of course, had nothing to do with it. The truth and the irony was that Gracie, vying with Evelyn to be the poorest of our band, had landed in the best, most comfortable, living arrangements of us all. That was because she was also the smartest and the best endowed with scholarships. A special travel abroad fund was attached to her main stipend and provided living arrangements "suitable to a young woman scholar" as well as any tuition and book fees for the Sorbonne. It was through agents administering the money that Gracie had been placed in "an airy and gracious apartment for up to three young women students in a desirable, close-in, Left Bank district with a respectable, upstanding patron." We had long giggled at the language and imagined what the upstanding patron might prove to be. A sort of Maurice Chevalier with a cane, a bandy-legged fop with a monocle who loved opera, or, Jocelyn's contribution, a gigolo? Gracie went along with a good-natured sort of mock horror. But nobody had come up with the idea that patron might really be *patronne*, a woman. Nobody had come close to imagining Madame Antoinette Gautier and Gracie's Old-World lifestyle on the tree-lined Boulevard Raspail that came with a maid and daily dining exercises from hell.

By the time Gracie was out of sight, the rest of us headed for the huge baggage carts that carried out luggage from the train and wondered again at Gracie's luck. Madame Gautier, not one to be bothered by unpleasant details like bags, had arranged to have Gracie's delivered. When at last we had claimed our own, we ventured to the huge doors that opened to the streets of Paris and an inviting September sun.

There, as we blinked into the prospect of another parting, I could glimpse how it was going to be, with Melanie about to disappear too, taking Eve with her. "Well, I guess this is where we try to catch a cab," Melanie said, her searching eyes trying to make contact with mine. "I've got this wad of francs, and the address, so how hard can it be?" she swallowed.

"Right," Eve said. "It's 10 *bis* Rue Boileau, *16ième arrondisement*. All in my head." She smiled uncertainly. "A piece of cake, *n'est-ce pas*?"

With that, she turned toward a stand of taxis, and Mel followed. Jocelyn soon turned too, dragging her bags the few meters down the sidewalk, and I came in her wake. We stood back a little, watching our two friends, one tall, voluptuous, and red-haired, the other blonde and slender as a small flame, lean into a taxi to negotiate in untested French. When the matter was resolved, a short mustached man jumped out of the driver's side and began opening doors and a trunk. In a moment, they were all inside, ready to head for that distant, chic side of the city near the Bois de Boulogne to share an apartment with another young woman, English as it turned out. The neighborhood, the apartment, even the roommate had all been arranged by Melanie's eternally striving mother, who wanted to make sure her daughter was going to the "right" place in the strictest social sense. Only after a lot of pleading from Melanie did her parents consent to allow Evelyn as the third roommate, and that only because Eve was a pastor's daughter and likely, they concluded, to be a good influence. Just as the cab started to pull away, Mel leaned from the window to call out, "So where are you going? Where to find you?"

"No idea," Jocelyn called back. "We'll find you."

Suddenly Jocelyn and I were left on the curb in that honeyed afternoon, alone and without a notion about what was to come next. I glanced up at her and can still see that profile, the classical perfection of it, her lashes shuttered and sweeping her cheeks, the way her hair melted into the yellow of the day. I watched myself watching her, as I had when she molded herself to the prow of the ship like its icon and understood how alluring her unpredictability was, why she naturally collected fans who would follow her anywhere. I myself was among them, quietly thrilled by her ability to change roles, to become anyone. It gave me the sense of living not with just a single person, but a whole cast of characters, within a demimonde of unspoken desires and secrets.

So when I asked, "What next?" and she replied, "I've got some addresses here to check out," I was ready to go. I already knew the fantasy she had in mind: She was determined to spend this year as a poor student living in splendid bohemian poverty. It seemed a romantic enough illusion to me, and I agreed to bypass the comforts we both could have afforded to find suitably shabby student quarters near the Sorbonne. In a small way, too, it was a gesture to Guy, who would have respected my choice of living poor and close to the people, however silly in actuality that notion was, there in the Latin Quarter in the heart of Paris.

Jocelyn began circling addresses in her battered copy of *Student Living in Paris*, and I suggested that I could stand in line for a cab.

"Oh no," she countered, with a look of horror crossing her face like a late summer storm. "We'll just take the Métro." And so, her suitcases and battered guitar case in hand, and my shoulders sinking under the weight of a bag with too many books, together we stepped off the curb and into that Parisian light for the first time. And when Jocelyn gestured for me to follow her down into the street and the black hole of the Métro, I did so without a backwards glance.

Above ground again, Jocelyn's book creased open at the map of the Quartier Latin, our intended home, we were soon making our way down Boulevard Saint-Michel—Boul'Mich as we would learn to call it. Jo stopped suddenly at a small, narrow street. "This is it, then," she said. I looked up to see the street sign declaring Rue de l'École-de-Médecine and tagged after her until we reached, for the first time, the badly painted sign indicating *Hôtel*. She pushed open the door, and we found ourselves in a dimly lit foyer where, behind a cheap wood reception area, a florid-faced man with a mustache read a newspaper.

"Bonsoir," Jocelyn said boldly as we approached the desk.

"Bonsoir," the man replied wearily without looking up.

"Do you have a room?" she went on.

"That depends," he answered, still buried in his paper.

"That depends?"

"Yes. For how many nights?"

"Oh forever, I guess, if we like it." Jocelyn moved flush against the desk, towering over it.

"For eternity, eh?" This was a concept that obviously grabbed his attention, because he looked up, and for the first time we stared face to face with the small, boring eyes and whimsical fleshy cheeks of Monsieur Lepic. "Well, in that case..." and he stood, reaching for a key.

Soon we were following him up the darkened staircase with threadbare carpet. But not before Jo turned to me with a catlike grin on her face to say, *"Eh bien, voilà."*

I figured I was now at home in Paris.

Part 3

LESSONS AND YELLOWING TREES

Chapter 8

"Les Feuilles Mortes." An old song, the wind, the present. The plane trees shake, bow to winds out of the west. A collection of yellowing leaves, curling with the last light of summer sun, swirls, then falls in a neat pile on the pavement near the curved art nouveau sign above the Métro. Exit Boulevard Saint-Michel. A rush of footsteps, high heels, and scuffed shoes, students' feet—it's easy to imagine Jocelyn among them as they hurry up the stairs, then down the street, toward the Sorbonne. But none disturbs the leaves.

There is a rise in the wind, the sound of rustling, and the leaves lift and sail away, perhaps to the far corners of the city. Down a side street, already twisting into darkness and the foreign, spicy aroma of open-air cooking, an unseen musician plays a flute.

Across the square, the boulevard crosses Pont Saint-Michel, while along the *quai* traffic follows the river, blurring into a long stream of colors. A vendor on the upper embankment begins pulling in his wares. Others soon follow. The wind is blowing the edges of their old maps and sidewalk watercolors, teasing the pages of books left open for display. Suddenly the air quivers as the heavy bells of Notre Dame—too soon it seems—ring in the late afternoon. The September sun tries to linger on the ascending stone towers, the spires, the gargoyles. But mainly it is unsuccessful. It is a year filled with the unexpected, 1962, and the wind hints at a cruel winter.

Yet the island in the middle of the river and its great cathedral appear unmoved. Île de la Cité, shaped like a boat, rides in place, parting the dark waters of the Seine. The water flows calmly past, unperturbed, carrying with it the forgotten currents of history. The little flotsam of human lives. Yellowing leaves.

I can see Ivan just before our first Paris encounter, how he would have pushed his wire-frame glasses resolutely up, hitching them on the bridge of his long, sharp nose, trying to get a better fix on what he was seeing—the small foyer of a run-down hotel on Rue de l'École-de-Médecine, right off Boul'Mich, dirty marble floor, threadbare carpet covering crooked stairs, no elevator. I can see him thinking: But what was the *intent* of this? What were Jocelyn and J.J., rich and alluring, his most improbable friends, doing here? Solidarity with the poor? Unlikely. Perhaps it was merely theater, a stab at playing Left Bank student.

"Hein?" the fat-faced Monsieur Lepic would have growled, miffed at having to look up from his *Paris-Soir*. "Two American girls? What do you want? The room number, *hein*? They expecting you?" His eyes narrowing, Ivan would have adjusted his beret before starting up the three flights of stairs.

"Not now. Later," Jocelyn called out in French to his persistent knocking. Then, hearing at last the deep-throated "Ivan," she flung open the door. I peeked around the corner from the little closet holding a sink and my "throne," the bidet stuffed with pillows. "Is it really you? The existential Ivan?" I called out.

But neither of them paid attention to me as they stared at each other, trying to take in the changes—his French look, her tangle-haired disarray. Then Jocelyn cried out, "Look at you! Well, come on in!" She embraced him with kisses on both cheeks, then gestured to one uncluttered spot on the bed. "Sit!"

He glanced around at our dismal room, the dirty window overlooking the narrow street, wallpaper the color of spoiled cream buckling on the walls, the radiator with chipped paint. Seeing no alternative, he took the bed corner. I could almost hear him thinking: *They've changed so quickly.* He'd heard about the wretched boat ride, where Jocelyn ruled aloofly over the crowds who seemed to adore her, while poor old J.J., trying at last for a romantic passage on Rimbaud's *bateau*, did nothing but barf her brains out. *Now look at them. Just when they could be in some airy flat, reestablishing themselves in Paris as the glamour girls of California, they're here in this shabby walk-up. Even Jocelyn's color is off, disheveled like her hair, like the dark mess of this room, while J.J....*

What was he thinking about me? That, despite my usual quiet, my light so small it hardly illuminated the corner of a shadow, I had an uncanny charge about me? That is what I felt in those early days, a kind of electric energy that startled me when I looked in the mirror, as though my eyes were flashing question marks sketched by an excited hand in dark blue ink.

But all I said was something inane, something like, "Can you believe this?" as I crouched on the edge of the bidet so I could better join the conversation. "I mean that we're actually living here?"

Ivan shook his head yes. Then with a heavy sigh, no. "What I can't believe is all the paperwork shit," he answered, hunching his shoulders forward and seeming to deflate as he described the common afflictions of the newly arrived: identity cards, police cards, visas, student IDs, meal tickets, all requiring photos, official stamps in triplicate. He'd come to Paris in search of the headwaters of revolution and found, as he put it, "the fifth estate of bureaucracy."

I laughed at this, agreeing. But Jocelyn leaned back on the oblong bed pillows, distracted, her gaze fixed on the window where yellowing leaves drifted past like promises. Her eyes shifted color as she watched, now gold-flecked, now green, now opaque as sable.

What did he see us as? The light and dark halves of a pair of long-stemmed, strangely glamorous, unfathomable twins? I was certain that Guy, as his erstwhile roommate, had told Ivan of his agonies with me—our failures—but did he know that emptiness now took up that space inside me where I imagined love should have been? Did he know that vacuum in the center of both Jocelyn and me that sucked in everything around us? But why do I ask? Of course Ivan knew. After all, a certain hollowness at core was what we all shared, what allowed us to be friends.

The difference was that for Ivan there was another consolation—the bloody roots of history and the solace of rebellion. But for Jocelyn and me, who came from such different worlds inside his own native city that he could hardly imagine them, there was no such solace. Jocelyn, of course, deflected light from that dark cavity within by emitting flash. Song, dance, art, a mind that darted from math to philosophy to theater with equal and brilliant ferocity, and the chameleon colors of the actress—who knew how she would appear next? Yet I, whom Ivan knew better but understood less, I probably remained as enigmatic to him as I did to myself. Impenetrable, even, like the deep center of an opaque poem.

With my mind ricocheting off such thoughts, I listened half-cocked to his conversation and heard myself saying, "Sure, I'll come to a café with you."

But Jocelyn was having a different conversation. "Can you believe she'd actually write this?" she moaned, folding her long legs, wrapped in leggings, up to her chest. Then, pulling down the large horn-rimmed glasses jammed on her head, which added a scholarly air to her tone of disgust, she read, sounding just like her mother.

> My dear girls,
>
> I'm enclosing a little something extra because I'm positive you need to replace things that are wearing thin. I mean like good, solid nightgowns. You know I've been frantic thinking of winter coming over there. There might be that terrible flu. Remember, girls, vitamin C. Lots of oranges. They do have oranges, don't they?
>
> Love, Madge
>
> P.S. Don't worry, we're fine. But do write soon. And tell me how your underwear is holding up.
>
> P.P.S. Burt says, "Salubrious salutations. And don't forget to take all precautions."

Ivan hardly knew what to say. Exhortations from his own parents, I imagined, if they wrote at all, would read like *War and Peace*. Peace from his mother, the Quaker. War from his father, the Bulgarian ex-Communist (he belonged to the party) general who nearly had a breakdown when his two heroes, Stalin and Hitler, went to war against each other.

"So why don't you come out with us?" he asked again. "Meet my friends Yves and Roland."

"Right," I reinforced his challenge while unfolding from the cramped position on my misappropriated seat. "It's gorgeous out. They're playing 'September Song.'"

"I don't think so," Jocelyn removed her glasses and resumed staring out the window. "Looks gusty out there. Mean."

I imagine this: Jocelyn closing the door furtively, as if stealth could give her refuge, and belting the camel's hair coat (Burt's gift) tightly about her waist, before running soundlessly down the three flights of stairs. Monsieur Lepic, a beefy hand holding up his chin as he leaned against the registry counter, calling out to her, "They've gone out already, *vous voyez*, that *type de français*, and your friend, the dark one."

Jocelyn answering, *"Oui. Je sais..."* and smiling at Lepic's description of Ivan as a "French guy." But with his slender build, angular features, eternal winter pallor—now topped with a beret on that unruly black hair—she had to agree. Not that Ivan ever looked very American, and certainly not very rich. Ivan could pass in Paris. She envied him that.

"Don't know where they went..." Lepic continued as she stepped past him, marveling at how every building in Paris seemed to have an official spy. Following the sidewalk of the ancient, narrow street into the almost dark, into the persistent wind, she reached the boulevard where the twelfth and twentieth centuries intersected.

She did, in fact know where Ivan and I were going, and she had declined. Too windy, she'd told us. But it was not that. It was rather that the hour turned, and with its low light of dusk, now offered what she most craved, anonymity. Her willowy silhouette could almost hide in the falling shadows, and she could almost evade the calls, the hoots, the pestering that inevitably fell in her wake. *"Tu couches, chérie?* Sleep with me, baby. *Petit baiser.* Leetle kiss. *Suédoise? Anglaise? Ah, américaine? Une movie-star, yes?"*

We had talked of this, how the hectoring just came with the territory to any young woman on the streets of Paris (well, except Gracie), and I'd asked, unwisely no doubt, why Jocelyn found it such a big deal. She who had chosen, or nearly chosen anyway, stardom as a way of life. What could she expect?

I'm sure the question itself had furthered her gloom. Perhaps because she saw how much she was attracted to the magic screen at the same time she wanted to hide her real self. *And who might that be?* I can imagine her posing that pesky question in my voice in her head, because that question frightened her the most. *Alluring sexual goddess posing as virgin? Virgin posing as siren? Scared child posing as intellectual giant? Brilliant woman posing as scared child? All of the above, hiding out in Mormon dress?* She would curse me in her mind for asking, then lope from the plains across Boul'Mich, as if a stranger to its traffic, its young crowds and bright lights. Instead she would follow little Rue de la Harpe—the twelfth instead of the twentieth century—north to the river. She intended to find out some things by walking the streets of Paris alone.

In the month since she and I had settled in, we'd walked a lot, by way of orientation. But I think this solitary plunge into the blustery, falling dark felt different. She wouldn't have been able to define it, this exploration without maps, but she could feel her way by blind faith, following an invisible geography. And what would she find that evening, her scarf wrapped tightly around her head? Above all, she would have witnessed nightfall. How the cobbler and butcher had pulled in their awnings and closed the metal shutters over their storefronts. How a nun in black, white cross dangling in front of her habit, scuttled around a corner toward an ancient school. How three students in dark jackets pushed out from their table at a small café, leaving behind empty cups of coffee and a metal ashtray overflowing with cigarette butts, the hours for café-sitting being officially over. And how, at several small restaurants where the spicy aroma of grilling—lamb kebabs, shrimp, fresh fish—filled the street, the Greek or Arab or Vietnamese proprietors enclosed their open-air terraces, inviting diners to come in. Nightfall, the hour to come inside.

It was also the hour the streets became dangerous, because darkness is intimate, and intimacy the greatest danger. Surely Jocelyn had noticed before that even in the light of noon, lovers claimed Paris, openly kissing in full sun. But at night, those who refused to go in owned the city. Shapes of intertwined embraces and shadowy couplings took over the bridges, doorways, timeworn arched passages, the streets themselves. As if they were statues from some passionate underworld that had stepped out of their stone.

But for Jocelyn—and she couldn't say why—there was alarm in the sight of lovers kissing against a crumbling wall. Inside her coat pockets, her hands curled for warmth, the left one clenching a letter which, I knew, had also come in the afternoon's mail. Worse in its way than the one from Madge.

> Oh my God, I'm going insane. When I think that I had you here, over and over again in my arms, and that I let you go…over and over again. Christ, Jocelyn, don't write me you are *happy, well, and fine*. Don't write me at all if you don't share this misery, this craziness. I deserve at least that…

Despite herself, I'm sure she memorized it. And like the cold and the vision of some couple embracing, she probably wanted to wash it away with something warm, something comforting. It was then she turned to enter Bistro Saint-Jacques. Through the window, behind half-curtains hung on brass rings, she saw us, Ivan and me, a bottle of wine on the table, and the two Frenchmen she didn't know. She would have seen Yves best, his square jaw and light hair only half-hidden in my shadow, as he slowly swirled a beer in a glass, smiling that wry, knowing French smile. But Roland had his back to the window, so she could only have seen his slender shoulders and that slightly curled mop of black hair. Perhaps it was my eyes that alarmed her, for I was looking back into his, reflecting that daring way the French have of asking with their eyes, and electrified, I admit, by the experiment.

Perhaps that is what stopped her cold. What was she thinking? *Oh no, not you too?* Or: *Don't fall for this. We just got here, remember? And Guy. What about him, anyway?*

Did she really imagine I didn't see her, couldn't read her lips as she muttered *"Et tu, mon amie?"* under her breath, before she turned away?

Chapter 9

Gracie remembered everything. This was another one of her curses, as if extravagant brain power weren't enough. So it's easy to see her there lying on her bed in the dark back room watching desultory leaves float one by one past the window, and, despite herself, remembering. Leaves that detached themselves from the gold-turning plane trees in front of the apartment facing Boulevard Raspail to sail with dispatch over the roof and fall in wrinkled defeat upon the courtyard below. As if they blew past the window to remind her of something. And that memory then triggered another, on and on, until another leaf, like a well-known face, presented itself, and she thought and thought again, flipping randomly through her life like pages in a book she did not want to read but could not put down.

In that odd, zigzag, way she had probably begun by seeing her mother's face, tired but cheerful, empty but serene, in a perpetual state of passionless love, as she had always seen it. It was an immortal face, enough to make even a girl like Grace hold out for the saints. Gracie remembered the voice perfectly, Mama calling out as she stood at the stove, the sink, the table, the ironing board, gliding without pause from one to another, "Anna-Maria-Grace." Of course now Mama was dead.

All those years she'd been enraged at Mama for being Mama, and now, more than two years after it happened, she was still enraged at her for dying. At the same time, too, she suffered from a maddening longing, wanting Mama's sturdy arms, the arms that asked no questions, around her waist, and wanting the soft kiss that asked for no reply on her forehead.

These were thoughts she could never admit, not to the others. And as a twosome of leaves passed, nearly entwined, I'm guessing she spotted us, the two Jo's. What would she be thinking? A question, perhaps, of which of us she liked better, concluding that neither one of us was real in the sense of ordinary girls, like girls in her world before Claremont, the world of the convent school and nuns. But in the end I'm guessing Gracie liked Jocelyn best. With her astonishing beauty, her aloofness, her blonde aura, Jocelyn probably seemed more authentic in her distance, with no shred of pretense that she could ever be other than as she was, other than untouchable. I, on the other hand, had what Gracie came to see as a treacherous touch of human warmth, a certain, fatal gift of friendship in my wanting to reach out, to embrace, to assume equality. I know now Gracie had judged my stance on equality a lie. She had at first welcomed my embrace, had accepted my belief we were equal, on-a-par friends. And then, when I had insisted: "Of course you should come to Paris, Gracie, my God, why wouldn't it work out?" she had believed that, too. Only later, when she told me everything, did I know she condemned me as a purveyor of propaganda.

"You lied," she accused me through tears, "telling me my brains wouldn't show so much in Paris." Of course, I had never mentioned her intelligence—why would I?—but no matter. "Look at you," she went on, "so confident, it's all so easy for you with that Mediterranean look, your sexy dark hair and your curvy body like some kind of Sophia Loren or something. What would you know about the burden of brains?" Of course, I could say nothing in reply to such a biting truth. But I also saw the deeper betrayal. The Mediterranean accusation, the Loren thing…it was so *Italian*. So I had made Gracie feel a kind of kinship beneath the skin, a false comfort. For if I, who might be just a taller, more filled-out physical version of her subterranean Italian self, if I said that she could fit into thrilling, dangerous Paris (probably no more foreign than Claremont had been at first), well then she could. If I said she could achieve art and fashion and sophistication in the French manner, she could.

But by trusting me, by believing there was a place of revelation—Paris—where possession of all womanly secrets was obtained, she had simply been delivered into another of Dante's circles. In only a few weeks, she already felt doomed, by the language, which was, she said, "like being behind a two-way mirror where I could understand everything but say nothing"; by bad luck, for living comfortably in an elite neighborhood in a *pension* run by a retired professor of cuisine, "an old witch set on torturing me"; and—of course, though she didn't say it—by being short, ill-dressed, and homely in the world capital of style.

The leaves continued to drift by the window, twisted and brown. Perhaps they mirrored Papa's face, indistinct like her brothers, or mottled like that horrid pimpled

Georgie of her voyage, or one huge, golden leaf, broad and beautiful as a sycamore in the low hills. That one would have brought her to the vision she wanted and feared most—of Tom.

Then, the interruption, an unexpected curse to break the unhappy spell of falling leaves. *"Zut, alors!"* followed by *"merde!"* floating like music over the sound of rushing water. It would come from behind the closed door of the bath, which adjoined Gracie's room. Rising from the bed, she put her ear to the door. Madame had said a new resident was moving in, a girl, she said, like you. Well, perhaps not exactly like you, but from the *provinces*. The word was pronounced with such contempt Gracie understood she'd learned a new term.

Angoulême? Angers? Gracie couldn't remember exactly which place the poor girl came from. As she listened to her cursing the too-hot water, she tried to imagine what she looked like and probably had the urge to call out, by way of friendship, by way of warning. Something like, *Don't worry, I'm an outsider, a way way outsider, too,* or *Lucky the water's so hot—didn't she tell you about how great this place is and how she allows up to two baths a week if we want to be that foolish.*

No doubt what she actually said was nothing. And as she stood there with her ear to the door listening to this unknown, unseen person take a bath, one image soothed her mind: the ultimate Parisian bath scene—the overaged and overbearing aunt of the hapless Leslie Caron who played Gigi in the movie of the same name. The aunt with her perfumes and bubbles and baubles and baths, who plotted Gigi's future as a mistress to a rich and handsome playboy, the eternally French, eternally perfect Louis Jourdan.

Mama had loved sappy movies, and especially that one. She'd gone to the movie theater about six times to watch it after it came out that summer two years before she died. Such unusual self-indulgence—she'd admitted praying for forgiveness; she had even dragged Gracie along once. Gracie told me how hard it had been to hold back her contempt for Mama's infatuation—"all those snooty rich people with outrageously expensive clothes, and then the oily charm of that dirty old man of an uncle—Maurice Chevalier—who else?" I suspect, though, it was even harder to hold back the contempt for her own fascination with the seductiveness of Paris, with the irresistible Parisian acted with aloof perfection by Jourdan, and with the intriguing grittiness of a girl from the wrong side of the tracks who said no, stuck up for her own beliefs, and won in the end, by way of marrying the handsome prince. Maybe it was the character of Gigi that attracted her most. Later came the knowledge that made Gigi irresistible, the fact that the original story had been written by one of the greatest French writers of the twentieth century, a woman named Colette. But even without knowing, Gracie confessed that, though she'd never told Mama, she'd also snuck back to see the movie a second time.

I'm picturing this. Gracie backing away from the door, waiting for what seemed a suitable length of silence. Then, as if she might learn something about the newcomer who had just vacated the bathroom by entering its traces of steam and scent, she gingerly pushed open the door from her room and stepped inside, ready to make her way to the enclosed *cabinet*, as they call it, that held the toilet. The *bidet*, that peculiarly abbreviated piece of equipment, remained a puzzle in full view.

"Dieu!" pronounced a slight apparition entirely swathed in a huge white towel.

"Dieu!" Gracie answering back, blushing. "So sorry," she would have babbled in halting French, "I didn't know you were still, that is I thought you were finished…I'm Gracie, Grace, if it's easier. American. I'm staying in that room."

The small young woman would look up with clear eyes alert in her pale face, pointed and flushed with steam and water, then hold a moment like a figure in a frieze or temple carving from an ancient bath, towel wrapped around her head like a regal headdress. Then she would have smiled and melted into the present, into the funny moment of encounter when two housemates meet for the first time in a steamy Parisian bathroom. "I'm Camille," sticking out her hand somehow from beneath the wraps to complete the requisite courtesy demanded of all meetings, greetings, or exits, the handshake.

It was still an awkward gesture to Gracie, and she would take a moment to find her own. The energy from Camille's smile would give her courage. "Camille, a nice name. From Auvers, right?"

"No. Anjou. Auvers is famous for van Gogh's suicide. Anjou is famous for dukes and war and royal fratricide. And wine of course. You know Loire Valley wine?"

"No. But it's probably next on Madame's nightly oral exam. You've met Madame yet?"

"Briefly. But soon. As soon as I dress and we go to dinner."

Even now I can easily picture Gracie sliding onto her chair at the dinner table as soon as Marie finished ringing the bell, and, for the first time since the ritual ordeal of dining had begun two weeks ago, eager. Not for the cuisine, which so far she'd been too nervous to enjoy, and certainly not for the grilling that came with it, but for the company of Camille and the prospect of sharing the abuse.

She glanced up at the table with its slightly yellowed linens and sparkling wineglasses and ancient polished silverware and felt that strange stab once again of the familiar and the forbidding, like two currents of hot and cold running alongside in her body. Familiar because in its Old-World way it was known, as the bright modern kitchens with vinyl countertops and legions of machines and glass tables with plastic mats never were. But this was forbidding, too, for here Old World was not a red-checkered cloth stained with olive oil over a rough oak table in a Napa farmhouse. No candle wax melted down from old chianti bottles here, no sizzle of cooking and smell of garlic blended with the high-volume noise of a boisterous Italian family, mostly male. Here Old World meant polish and refinement, not the trappings of Tuscan family life two generations removed. Here all contradictions could be captured, simmered together, and boiled down to one word: Paris.

Gracie removed her napkin from its silver ring and placed it on her lap, waiting. It made her nervous to be first at the table. I can just see her studying the implements laid neatly on the linen cloth to see what strange new culinary and linguistic worlds she would soon be called upon to enter. "*Wheat-ers*" she heard in a rough bark behind her and glanced behind to see the thin, wiry figure of Marie, Madame Gautier's maid, at the buffet, and knew that in her asthmatic whisper she was trying to help, like giving an answer before an exam. Gracie smiled shyly. *Huîtres*. Oysters, which would explain the first small forks.

Antoinette Gautier entered like a steam engine, puffing, and lumbered forward on thick legs jammed into the house slippers she always put on when she entered the foyer. Tonight, Gracie noticed, the retired professor of cuisine had removed her apron, put on a dark green sweater with gold buttons, and dashed a bit of lipstick, not strictly on target, across her pinched lips. No doubt in honor of Camille of the provinces. She remembered how for her own arrival two weeks before, there had been no such attempt at making a good appearance. Clearly the provinces, then, so long as they were French, were still better than the untamed savage ones across the sea.

"Delighted we're having oysters, Madame," Gracie said by way of preemptive strike.

But Madame did not hear. Her jowls began to quiver in a way that was already familiar. "Mademoiselle is late. I said seven o'clock exactly. Strictly seven. Where is she? Marie, oh Marie," she called to the kitchen. "Ring the bell loudly, and if she does not come immediately, *fetch* her. Oysters cannot wait. We cannot wait."

At ten after seven, Camille, small, neat in a wool skirt and sweater and low-heeled pumps, slid into her seat. Madame had turned the color of smoked country ham. Gracie recounted the conversation to me later: "*Bonsoir* Madame, Mademoiselle Grace," Camille said in that, you know, bright voice of hers, like a bird in morning.

"'You are late, *mademoiselle*,' Madame spat out. 'We dine strictly at seven.'

"'*Eh bien,*' Camille looked up at her and gave her most dazzling smile and just said, like it was all news to her, like it was nothing. 'Sorry. So, then, seven it is.'"

Then—it's easy to imagine this—before looking down at her place setting, she gave a quick and saucy wink to Gracie, who instantly relaxed. And the meal became a pleasure, as Gracie followed Camille. The deft movements from oyster fork to soup spoon to serving platters as Marie passed them, to the correct plate or dish or, in the case of bread, to the table cloth. And as Madame bore down on her subject matter—the identification-and-name-of-dishes-and-way-to-eat-them quiz show—Camille cleverly tipped off Gracie. "What a lovely *potages aux légumes,*" she would say, and then, when Madame turned the next level of inquisition back on her, "I don't suppose you know all the secret ingredients, beyond the usual leeks and potatoes, that comprise an excellent potage, do you?" Camille would reply with that disarming smile, "Certainly not, Madame," and change the subject.

When Marie brought a bottle of red wine, Madame sniffed it, poured, and tried again, saying something like: "So, *mademoiselle,* since you come from the country of excellent wine, I suppose you will be able to identify this little vintage I have here before I propose a toast to you."

But Camille's small, pointed face lifted up, her short light hair curled like a cap, and her eyes laughed out loud. Gracie remembered her words exactly: "Ah, no, Madame, since I'm just a poor country girl, a provincial, shall we say, I only claim to know the wine of my own country, the Anjou that runs sweet as the Loire. And since I'll certainly not be able to identify this vintage, I'm not worthy of the toast. So let us toast instead my new *camarade*, Mademoiselle Grace from America. To Franco-American friendship."

Madame, beyond all the hues of pork, flushed the deep red of burgundy, which she drank, trembling. If she was angry or simply flummoxed, Gracie couldn't say. But she hardly spoke the rest of the meal, and after the crème caramel, when Camille pushed her chair away, complimented the cooking, and announced, "Mademoiselle Grace has kindly agreed to go out with me to find cigarettes," she uttered not a word of protest.

It was dark when they stepped out on Boulevard Raspail, but it had not been so long, and the sky held light over the rooftops the way that early autumn still holds the warmth of summer. And early night added its own luminousness, headlights, streetlamps, the subdued lights inside elegant old apartment buildings, then bright and jazzy rounding the corner onto Boulevard Saint-Germain. Maybe, Gracie thought, just maybe she would find Paris after all.

Another thing gave her hope. As she walked alongside Camille, who was slight, chic in that unadorned way of French birthright, and short—even shorter than Gracie herself—she could not help but see that men were noticing. There were the looks, the slowed cars, the occasional *oh là là* from young men—which up to this moment in her life had completely evaded her. With Jocelyn and me or Eve, or even Melanie and her amazing blonde hair, Gracie had always felt lost, completely unseen, like a twig among beautiful trees. But from what she said, I'm guessing how now she saw it was not just size that counted, and certainly not voluptuousness. How, glancing over at Camille who was walking fast, paying no heed to whatever to the attention she drew, she must have wondered: was it presence, carriage, that elusive thing called style? Was it Camille's artfully tied scarf, her long leather gloves, her shoes, soft calf, low-heeled, and classy?

Camille was saying something like "*Ah quelle horreur,*" meaning Madame Gautier. "She's the type that make us in the provinces hate Paris. You mustn't let her get to you."

And by the time they reached a café with a bar along the boulevard and stepped inside, Gracie practically stopped breathing. It was all she wanted, hoped, feared, and had not yet dared.

Camille went to the bar itself to ask for cigarettes, and Gracie stood, apart and happy in a shadow, and when Camille returned to ask, "How about a nightcap before going back?" Gracie could only nod yes and follow to a table on the enclosed terrace. All around them were men and women in dark clothes, black turtleneck shirts beneath casually stylish leather or jackets. They looked, she remembered, earnest and intelligent and sexy, and there she was in their midst, not more than a block or two from Café de Flore, or Deux Magots, headquarters of existentialism worldwide. And when the waiter asked what she wanted and Camille said a cognac, Gracie said make that two, and when Camille pulled out a long cigarette and offered her one, she swallowed and said no thanks, and then garnered all her courage to ask, "So what are you doing here?"

"You mean this café, or *chez* Madame, or in Paris?"

Yes, Gracie nodded. And thus she learned about Camille's aunt, Camille being motherless, and how Camille, being willful, had insisted on coming to Paris to finish her teaching degree although it was customary, indeed expected, to finish one's education in one's home city or at least province, and how the aunt, being worried, insisted on something respectable and knew someone who knew of the famous *pension* of the famous chef. And while Camille was saying all these things, Gracie studied her, her small curl-capped head and long, straight nose and the laughing clear eyes of no particular color and then the smile that came like an explosion, out of nowhere.

"So what are you planning to teach?" Gracie asked this last, working up to it.

It's easy to see how the air must have left her when Camille replied "Physics," her own secret, abandoned passion.

They left then to return to Madame's apartment, and on the way Camille linked her arm in Gracie's, the way French women do by way of friendship. And Gracie felt that rushing sensation again. Perhaps it was like high tide after the rains pouring in, or the creeks spilling over the riverbanks and into vineyards, perhaps it was the sensation of filling in all the known hollows and crevices in the cracked earth, plus others she hadn't known existed.

It was still early in those days along the Seine, when the trees yellowed, turned crimson, and dropped their leaves to dance into the streets, that Gracie took steps unlike any she'd taken. It was after a few days' observation, which she told herself wasn't really like scientific method (but which sounded to me like it was), that she made a bold decision. She had absorbed enough information from watching Camille and the rest of us, and especially those young French girls heading to high school, that she knew she wanted to move in a new way. Height and glamour at once, she figured, and headed to Galeries Lafayette to buy high-heeled shoes. She had never had them before. Mama had only worn flat-heeled pumps for good occasions and would have considered high heels impractical. The nuns, of course, would have considered them immoral.

So—and I do believe she was proud of herself for reaching such a momentous decision without consulting anybody—she went alone to the big department store. I like to picture her choosing, though she had no idea of her size in French, a pair of leather shoes with long, thin heels. They were the color of red rust or the leaves of the vineyards, Napa Valley in fall, she said. Across the toe lay a small strip of lizard skin. "They were classy. For once in my life, I said yes before even asking the price."

Perhaps it was the view of Paris from the perch of those new shoes, which elongated her short legs and made her conscious of each step as she lurched slightly forward then stood straight, that made the world seem an unaccustomedly rocky place.

On the upside, the constant whirlpool of the French language, which so demoralized other foreigners new to Paris (I had complained to her of feeling underwater, while Melanie said she feared drowning) was heady stuff for Gracie. French in its intricacies and complications of grammar and leaps of faith was an elixir, like physics. But when it came to speaking, to making herself known, she couldn't break the sound barrier. Silence dropped over her like a shroud, like another kind of invisibility not even height could help.

With her new gait, a direct result of the new shoes, she assumed she'd acquired the added boost needed to fit in as a *jeune femme du monde* on the streets of Paris. She had been quite sure, since that night she'd walked arm in arm with Camille, that all was possible. So as she hurried down Saint-Germain alone, past the birthplaces of existentialism, she tried to affect that pose of nonchalant sophistication that went with the look, yet at the same time she turned her radar on to pick up all signals of admiration she was sure beamed her way. In truth, she didn't catch any. Worse, the only ones who seemed to notice any positive change in her were her friends.

Well, not Jocelyn, who always seemed distracted when they had lunch together. And not Ivan, who walked with her part way to class on that particular Monday when he wanted to come over later for tea. But perhaps Melanie, who would have said something like, "You're looking very good, very French, you know."

"You were the only one who really noticed," she said later of her transformation. I had voiced an innocuous "Wow," looking her over in admiration. "Very chic, *mademoiselle*. Turn around. Hair in chignon, let's see, and wow, *talons*."

"Right, heels." Gracie grinned despite her best efforts at being nonchalant. "I needed a lift."

But then, right when she needed to concentrate on her walk, on how to make her hips move in the right way and carry it off without killing her feet, her mind would drift, not to the matter at hand, not even to the subjects of her courses, but surreptitiously to science. "I had forbidden myself to do this for the whole year," she lamented. Yet there she was, at the first opportunity, dreaming first of Pierre and Marie Curie, then of Descartes, his neat formulas and his unassailable logic. It seemed a kind of sedition. "I vowed not to let anyone know—especially not you or Jocelyn," she said before telling me of the turning point, the brush with her own Louis Jourdan.

It must have happened like this, with the light falling quickly on Rue du Bac and a chill riding the shadows. Too early, really, for this time of year, but one might as well shake one's fist at Charles *le grand* over there in the Elysée Palace as the gods of weather. Or so the tall man in the dark suit thought, as he rounded the corner from Boulevard Raspail. It was then he noticed a short figure coming toward him from the other direction. A girl, and immediately his attention wandered from weather gods, stories from the old crones in his childhood (say summers in Brittany), from the sale he had just brokered with the Americans, or from the woman who played in the back of his mind like a prospective mistress. Nothing to rivet one's attention like a girl. Short, but too distant to make out much else. He would have slowed to take it all in—the approach, bouncy and uneven and curious; the figure, hidden mostly in a coat so remaining a question; the legs, all right enough from a distance, but closer up their shape losing form as they slid into overreaching shoes; at last close enough, he viewed the hair, shiny and young but improperly styled; and then, the face itself, too large and awkward on the stump of neck, though skin passable and eyes. Ah well, they darted up to look at him directly, a little muddy but hopeful, and for that, that little motion of boldness, he saluted her. He raised his dark hat faintly and stared back, only hinting at a smile.

Pity, he thought, a homely woman, yet one who tried so awkwardly. Which made him think again of the gods, those of fate and of mercy—not much learned about them in those childhood summers—and the woman who would be mistress, whose presence once again he noted behind others in his mind.

But Gracie quickened her step, nearly stumbling on the uneven pavement as she passed him, hurrying so he wouldn't hear her heart beating hard in her chest. But why not, she asked herself as she reached the safety of Boulevard Raspail—her street. Had she not just met the eyes of a Frenchman, as dark and mythically handsome as Louis Jourdan, had he not followed her with his stare all the way down the street, tipped his hat to her charms, smiled? Had she not just, for the first time in her life, stepped into perfect harmony with her looks to arrive in some new land right there on her own little corner of Paris?

For once, she would fly up the stairs to the apartment, not even waiting for the antique lift, not even minding going "home." Even Madame, who, greeting her at the door with a bare civility, her small eyes narrowed with their usual suspicions, would scarcely bother her. *"Bonsoir,* Madame," she would say cheerily, brushing past to enter the dark salon smelling of old books. And so plopped down on a soft chair, content to sit there with eyes closed and remembering, she would await Ivan who was coming for tea.

Gracie was content—this much she admitted—to do nothing, to simply prolong the moment, its delicious spell, as long as possible. But Madame stuck her head around the door, like a sniffing hound. To preempt what inquisition might be coming, Gracie pretended to have purpose. She walked to a bookshelf and began browsing.

Her fingers ran over the matching leather hide of a series and she looked down, surprised to see the name Colette. *Gigi!* she thought, savoring the wonderful coincidence after encountering her own Louis Jourdan. And one by one she pulled out the volumes to look at the titles, *La Vagabonde, Chéri, Le Blé en Herbe*...all unfamiliar. By the time Ivan rang, she was lost again.

It was Madame once more who broke the spell. Shuffling in her bedroom slippers, she paused again at the parlor door. *"Voilà, votre invite,"* she said. Gracie didn't catch it all, except for the end, *"un type de français."*

"Ivan," she leapt up to greet him, and he kissed her properly, three times on the cheeks.

"So how are you surviving, *petite camarade aux armes*?" he would have said, pausing to take it all in. Then: "Wow, this is some pad. I'm just as surprised as I was at the Jo's, hanging out in that seedy hotel by the Sorbonne. So, Gracie, how did you pull this off? I thought you were as poor and out of it as I was."

Gracie was feeling cavalier, ready to match wits, eager to respond with words like, "Power of the purse, I guess. That is if you're poor enough you get rich by the inverse proportion law of charity cases. Didn't you know that? But so, sit." The gesture, though, would have been awkward as she pointed to the stiff horsehair settee. "Where are you living?"

And Ivan would sit, as ever uncertain what to do with his legs, pulling off that cheap new beret to uncover hair sticking out at unregulated intervals. He would tell her, "South side of town, Cité Universitaire, you know for outsiders, the dangerous and unwashed."

And she would reply that it must suit him on all accounts.

Ivan would appear not to hear that underlying tone, that cheerful banter. Maybe he didn't even hear her actual question. He perched rather, legs crossed like a girl, taking in the heavy treasures of the musty parlor, saying things like: "It's terrifying, of course, all the threats, the bloodletting which will come soon—even to Paris, don't think otherwise no matter what they tell you—and it's hard to know where to begin."

"Bloodletting?" Gracie was bewildered.

But he kept going on, as if reading from his usual script. "Well, I'm living there among them, so perhaps my days are numbered. But all our days are numbered. And it can't be stopped now, like a tide, they're coming by the thousands, and the Army's in revolt."

"I didn't know what he was talking about," she admitted, recounting how he'd finally looked at her directly, as if for the first time he realized he was speaking to another person. "But he was talking about Algeria and the godzillions of French foreign-born, the *pieds noirs* who are rushing back through France like a river at flood. He went on about land stolen then lost, promises made then broken, betrayal, the Army in resurrection, but Algeria still free."

It was then I imagine Gracie wished to close her eyes and dream of Louis Jourdan again. Ivan was bringing reality, like an unwanted guest, into the twilight of her best afternoon. She could have only been grateful for Marie banging into the door just then, pushing the ancient tea cart.

White-haired, thin, and merry-eyed, Marie did not let the loss of one lung shut down her stream of observations about the world, delivered in the barking tones of Parisian patois. That voice, intoning: "Tea's comin' Missy, a bit of a cake I swiped you too, plus those biscuits. Right from under her nose I snatched 'em, too, bless her miserly heart. Madame's eyesight's gone to the devil, praise God, and me I still see like an eagle." She would have winked, setting the cart by the settee before turning to go, leaving behind the echo of a cough that might have been the cry of a wounded animal.

"They serve you tea?" Ivan, pushing his glasses back on his sharp nose in that habitual gesture, would look at Gracie in wonder. She knew, for he'd come to invite her there, that he was living in a semi-squalid dorm with Malagasy students who sometimes brewed tea in the middle of the floor on a little brazier.

"Not every day. I mean I guess so if somebody's coming to visit." She said something like this, moving closer to the edge of her seat to reach the teapot, a piece of old *faience,* uncertain if he was impressed or disgusted. At least the topic might shift from the Algerian crisis.

"Wow," he would have answered, clarifying nothing. Then, "So what's the story on the poor old maid? Does she ever get medical care? How long has lovely Madame had her? Does she even get to eat here? She's so thin."

"I said I didn't know. I mean I hadn't gotten to know her very well, had I?" Gracie quoted herself, then added, "You know, it was just Ivan, with his endless supply of compassion, who had this ability to make me feel like I just flunked an exam."

She remembered watching him then as he stirred his tea slowly, and realizing that he, too, was used to this in his own way, because he also had these Old World connections—Bulgarian, was it? And Gracie acknowledged that in some way she'd always felt comfortable with him, despite politics. "Like me," she said, "he was also poor and a congenital outsider."

"He kept going on, though, with the questions, like: 'Do you know how she lives? I'll bet she lives in some goddamn little hole, unheated, beneath the roof. You know that's how they house their servants, don't you?'

"But I just wanted him to shut up, you know? I didn't actually want to hear this, didn't need this, you know…"

Of course I knew, because his was not the reality she'd come for. I can picture her glancing over at the table where she'd dropped a couple of those books by Colette, and thinking of the man who had saluted her with his admiring glance. It had all happened a little earlier that very afternoon, but it probably seemed a very long time ago.

Chapter 10

Following the sinuous curves of the back streets leading from the Seine toward Saint-Germain-des-Prés, Evelyn felt a rush of energy. Fall was the season when important things happened. As a child, she'd always tried out for things in fall, and always excelled—whether it was drama, or ballet, or kickball, or the church choir. In fall, she'd always been the one chosen for the lead role, the team captain, the soloist. One fall, she'd skipped a grade. And a fortune teller at a Halloween fair once told her she'd marry a Virgo even though she was a Gemini. She had made a note of that when she learned of Tom's September birthday. They'd celebrated that last year just after she'd been named football queen. Of course, bad things happened the previous fall too, like the car wreck and fire and the disasters that followed.

But those, she decided, were all in the past, the falls before Paris. She smiled slightly at the unintended play on words, and kicked some leaves that whirled in front of her. Many were red, like the strands of her hair that blew in the breeze, and for a moment she felt less foreign, less a stranger. *Hey, Paris, we match. I can do this!* she thought, and picked up her pace. She was headed to the Sorbonne to verify the lists of all the classes she was signed up for. Then as a gesture of goodwill and best intentions, she had determined to write the first of her reports to the church scholarship committee to let them know all she meant to accomplish, to assure them that their hard-to-come-by dollars would be well spent. *I'm turning over a new leaf,* she thought, and laughed out loud.

The stone steps leading up to the forbidding wooden doors caused Evelyn to slow her pace. The medieval church and gardens and the ancient building containing the Roman baths at Cluny behind her served as a reminder that she was entering very foreign territory. Though she'd already been inside the buildings of the Sorbonne many times, and had her student ID at the ready to prove that she *belonged* there, sometimes it was hard to convince herself. The flashbacks to Claremont always came as she climbed those steps and suddenly saw the grassy quad in sunlight, the mountains against a blue sky and airy classrooms beneath red tile roofs. The weight of centuries hung over the stones of the Sorbonne, and old air filled her nostrils as she inhaled in the dark corridors.

In truth, everything about this ancient university was different. It was crowded, teeming with students from around the globe; the lecture halls were unheated and so vast it was often hard to see the professor; worse, the course descriptions did not necessarily have anything to do with what was actually taught. There were no required reading lists either, because everything was required.

Melanie had already filled her in on this: "If the course is about seventeenth century lit, then you have to know *everything*. When exams come, they can ask about anything at all. And I've heard they will."

Exams. The very word sent a shiver through Evelyn, as she knew it did for all her *copines*. From what they'd learned, the exam process was itself akin to medieval torture. There were written exams at the end of the first term, and, if you passed those, you got to go through the bone-chilling process of orals. If you failed any one of these, you failed the whole term. And at the end of the year, the process was repeated, when you could fail the whole year. The failure rate for the Cours de Civilisation Française was about eighty-five percent.

Evelyn pulled out a notebook and began to copy the courses and hours she was registered to take onto the pages filled with squares. No use worrying about the exam thing yet, she said to herself, deciding to put it out of her head until necessary. As Melanie had said, the best way to prepare was to just keep up with your work—with *everything*, as was required. And feeling the weight of seriousness in studying at the Sorbonne, feeling even a pinch of penitence for her past frivolity, Evelyn turned back down the stone steps determined to make good.

I'll get on it right away, she vowed, deciding to head back to the apartment and start reading before even writing to the scholarship committee. The light, however, was so soft over the spires of Cluny, she slowed her steps a little to watch it change the color of the clouds as they drifted overhead. A part of her acknowledged it would be a shame to waste such a rare, lovely fall day completely bent over books inside. I'll just cut through the Cluny gardens, she told herself, knowing full well there was a little café with good espresso for less than one franc just on the other side. It would be good to sit there, study her class list, and make a firm plan about how to organize her schedule so as not to fall behind.

As Evelyn stepped up to the sidewalk café and chose a table in a slant of sunlight, a Vespa roared past and its rider made loud kissing sounds and shouted something about her red hair and making fire together. Evelyn turned away in annoyance. The shouting, gestures, kissing noises, even touching, from strangers was an occupational hazard of being a young woman in Paris—all the girls complained about it—and Evelyn was determined to remain unfazed. *Tom, Jay, the whole mess is behind me now. I had my fun on the boat, but now it's time to get serious,* she told herself as she opened her notebook and summoned the waiter for a coffee.

"Holy shit, can they be serious? I've got classes and practicums and lectures about forty-eight hours out of every day. Is your schedule half this insane?" Evelyn leaned toward Melanie, who had been hunched over the table studying when her roommate burst in the door.

Melanie glanced briefly over the list Evelyn had shoved under her nose: Literature from the Middle Ages through the Seventeenth Century, Tuesday & Thursday at 10:00 a.m. French art from Iron Age to Early Renaissance, Mondays & Fridays, 2:00 p.m. Art practicum with curator, Louvre 8:00–10:00 a.m. Wednesdays. French language, Monday & Thursday, with grammar sessions in Montparnasse from 5:00–7:00 p.m. Wednesday & Friday. Contemporary Political Science lectures and small classes alternating Tuesdays. Writing classes either from 5:00–7:00 p.m. Thursday or on Saturday morning. Finally, Melanie looked up. "Yeah," she said, "it looks about right to me. We've got lots of the same classes, actually."

"How can we do this? How can anybody do this? A million hours of classes a week. When are you supposed to read everything ever written in French on top of that?" Evelyn posed the question more to herself than to Mel.

Mel just shrugged in response. "I really don't know. I guess all we can do is not miss any classes, take a lot of notes, and read as much as we can." She paused a moment before adding, "And my parents were worried about all the wild things I might be doing over here. When would there ever be time?"

Evelyn sighed. "No time at all," she answered and looked at the stack of letters piled up on a side table for her. She had briefly glanced at some of them, then pushed them aside. Hearing from Tom, her father, the church scholarship committee, would only be distractions. No point in opening them now. Now what she needed to do was to go forward with her plan, which started with the letter to the committee. If she wrote to them first, before seeing their letter, she could keep things more on her own terms. And if she copied out her schedule for them, they'd have to be impressed.

She pulled out her only paper suitable for proper correspondence, and turned a black pen around in her fingers while she thought. For a minute her mind drifted back to the long Métro ride she had just taken from the Sorbonne to the posh neighborhood where she lived. It was not lost on her that she and Melanie were the only two among their friends not living on the Left Bank, but the Right. Right meaning rectitude, no doubt. Well, she was going to give it her best shot.

Then just as she poised her pen to begin writing, another random thought struck her. I'll bet every one of the members of the church committee thinks my name, Evelyn, means "desirous of God" because my mother told them so, just like she told me. I could set them straight then. I could tell them it really means just "desirous" and Mother added the God part. I know, because I looked it up.

Chapter 11

Dawn. A discovery, really, for eyes unaccustomed, like Jocelyn's. Hard, glittering fall, already stiffening with cold, making the towers, spires, and sighing rooftops of the old part of the city stand erect. Or perhaps they just stand out because many trees are prematurely bare. At this season, she notices, there was also room for the sun, that unruly invader from the east, ripping the cover from night and spilling red across the unknown vastness of Europe. The bells in the towers of Notre Dame shudder then, but do not give in to sound as daylight engulfs the great stones in a fiery rose.

She climbs up from the river walk along the Seine just as the first pigeons awake and fly from their granite perches, just in time to see the cathedral walls erupt in light, and she asks herself: Who else could be up at this hour? A few silent captains, working rusty barges up the river, drivers of tin-sided trucks delivering bread. The insistent lovers of course, the beggars, the occasional prostitute also walking the river's Left Bank before dawn. Or perhaps, in livelier sections of the city, cabaret-goers and artists wandering Montmartre, intellectuals and first-class hustlers in the all-night cafés of Montparnasse. The clerics, doing whatever mysterious things they do while others sleep or sin. And now, of course, the pigeons.

She stands, stranded in silence on the upper embankment, a short silvery half-river from Notre Dame singed rose in first daylight. She knows, certainly, there is meaning in it, but cannot see it. Perhaps because the other fire burned, once again, across her eyes.

The one that, after the winds stopped, licked the silent dome of a distant and perfect sky to race up the California hillside—odd how it followed the stone path they always walked—hurrying, as they always did, toward the house. She assumes no sound nor smell nor any kind of sensation in this vision. It is, rather, as if her native landscape is a mere prop, a studio set constructed for her to play out the small drama of her life. And then, too, she feels a tinge of guilt and the sensation of overwhelming regret that she had not, as she so ardently wished when J.J.'s Gran spoke the words, smelled the lavender in the fire.

But soon the bells of Notre Dame break the silence, followed by Saint-Étienne-du-Mont, Saint-Sulpice, Saint-Germain-des-Prés, and others all over the city. And for a moment, at daybreak, she concludes it possible to think that a known God could still exist in Paris.

But perhaps that is an observation only an outsider can make. I can imagine, for example, the *boulanger* hurrying to his bakery along Rue Racine; for him, church bells are merely an intrusion on his only holy practice, the worship of beautiful women. And the ones around at this hour rarely bring him closer to the divine. But this day is an exception. For this day he sees her, a tall, alluring figure wrapped in a foreigner's beige coat. Her head is covered with a dark scarf, but he can see wisps of loose blonde hair and a chiseled, oval face that might belong to a Viking goddess or be camouflaged as a Blessed Virgin in the stone statuary of a cathedral.

Perhaps that thought above all others in the morning chill makes him smile, the thought of another sacrilege committed by the church. Then he turns his attention once again to the girl, wondering why such a creature would be heading into the shabby Hôtel des Écoles at such an hour. But the smile doesn't fade even while he unlocks the door to begin his day of work. Perhaps it is a lucky day because of this good omen. A beautiful woman.

That, of course, he has to admit, is where trouble begins, too. He sighs, knowing this. All men know this. But he is not just any man; he is a Parisian. Therefore, he knows it doubly. For, as Jocelyn has just reminded him, Paris is a woman.

It was dark, crowded, and cold in the student lunch hall, just as it was inside the hallowed Sorbonne itself, and I was telling my story. Evelyn had pushed me into it.

"So, let's get to the main course," she said. "About your love life, J.J.? I hear rumors about a licentious night in a house of ill repute in a red-light district and I'm prepared to file my report to Spinster Krauss this afternoon."

My love life. My comedy of errors. My bad B-movie scripts. Still, the impulses of the storyteller took over, and I began my own version of my sojourn to Montmartre with Ivan: "Well, it was a dark and stormy night…"

We had been exploring Montmartre, the great hill dominated by the white basilica of Sacre Coeur, and home to artist haunts and little cafés and tiny clubs that had been at the center of *la vie bohème* for over a hundred years and were unhappily showing signs of what Ivan called "tourist creep." It was in fact a dark and cold night, threatening a storm, and we were hastily making our way down the foot of Montmartre, when he said to me with a kind of gasp, "Geez, J.J., what time do you have?" And I said, "Exactly midnight," and he replied, "Shit," because the last train left at twelve a.m. sharp.

Of course we tore to the Métro, and of course the door was shut in our faces. Resourceful, and fearful of rain, he asked how much money I had left, figuring if we pooled resources, maybe we could catch a cab. So I dumped out my few sous and so did he. Together we could have made it maybe halfway home. As I grew more frantic, probably verging on hysterical, I remember him growing more and more cheerful. I hated that. Especially that he was cheerful while revealing his great idea—that we hoof it across Paris, from the heights of Montmartre to the sinkholes of Pigalle and beyond, down to the banks of the Seine.

What he said was, "It is written in the stars that we shall walk across Paris in moonlight, my dear."

"Moonlight?" I wailed. It was pitch black, starless, and very cold. But Ivan was right; what else could we do? Within two blocks it began to rain, really rain. In two more, it was pouring. Fifteen minutes into this stroll, and I pulled under an awning, bawling. I was freezing and my feet hurt. So I took off my shoes for a minute—then couldn't get them back on. Damn if my shoes—cheap leather, I'll admit—didn't shrink! By then I was practically shrieking, Ivan was completely soaked but couldn't see because his glasses were like river bottoms, and there we were in pleine Pigalle, with every possible thing for sale except what's legal.

We stumbled around the corner to this all-night establishment, and Ivan pushed me to a remote table, ordered two coffees, and we began watching the night trade. *Putains*, some with leather and feathers, advertising their specialty. And customers, of course. Tough guys, thugs, pimps, pushers. It was a good thing that I had a practice run as part of my education at la Maison, attending the *bal masqué* dressed as a Parisian streetwalker, because the next thing you know, Ivan went off only to come back with this Cheshire Cat grin.

He was full of himself with another great idea. Great, of course, because it was the only idea we had between us. "I got us a room, J.J.... It's a runner-up idea to a cab ride, except we can afford it."

We linked arms then, and he said "Shall we?" preparing to tackle the rickety stairs as if they were the steps leading up to the Paris Opera House. Then he glanced back and I saw him cover his mouth to keep from splitting a gut. What? I wanted to know.

"It's your feet, J.J. Everybody's staring at your bare feet. They must think this is some weird new trick invading their territory."

I got to this point in my tale, and Evelyn bent over in appreciative laughter, Gracie shook her disbelieving head, while Mel nodded as if to say *no way*. And Jocelyn? Maybe she felt like saying, as she had when I dragged in well after my first morning class had begun, *Good grief, what are you up to now? You look like hell.*

Her mood distilled that of the whole displaced Maison Française band. My story had been amusing enough, but it couldn't change the fact that the food at the Sorbonne stank. The infamous one-franc meal was disgusting in its surfeit of starch—bread, peas, beans, potatoes. Hardly balanced meals, let alone cuisine in the French manner. Even Gracie complained, now that she was boarding with Madame Gautier and becoming a food snob. Evelyn, who couldn't afford better, and Mel, who could, both came to the dining hall for the collective company, the stories, and the jokes. But they pushed the stuff away, too.

Jocelyn just moved back her chair, as if getting ready to leave, when a poetic-looking young man, swathed in a long wool scarf, carrying a lunch tray, bumped her. He swore miserably. *"Type de français,"* she said irritably, *"tant pis, alors."* There had already been a tenseness in her body before, but when the young man bumped her, she seemed ready to snap. Gracie glanced up and decided to make peace by inviting him to sit down. I looked up, too, surprised. It was Yves, Roland's roommate. "Yves? Hello. *Asseye-toi*, join us."

"But J.J., I didn't see at first it was you."

I smiled, delighted. "So how was the exam?" I asked. "Have you eaten? How's Roland?"

With those words, with the mention of Roland's name, Jocelyn sprang from her chair, stood abruptly, and left without saying good-bye.

She slid lightly onto the long bench of the lecture hall. Except for the high, round dome overhead, coming to class she once remarked seemed indistinguishable from crowding into a train station. Usually we came to this "core" course on French politics together, or sometimes with Gracie if we'd had the one-franc special together, but today the food had been impossible, then Yves had joined us—and I offended Jocelyn by asking about Roland—so she simply left.

Or perhaps she'd left because she could hear Madge's voice in her head saying *Eat, eat*, again. "I'm afraid, you know," she'd confessed to me just the week before, "that the next round of health advice will come with money and instructions to eat at the Ritz."

What she decided to do instead was to *study, study*. She could master all her subjects, because it was easy, and she could claim her own winning role of star foreign student. Because studying would keep her from wandering, she could forestall her gathering sense of gloom. And what could be more natural for her than a segue from Kant and Nietzsche to Marx and Sartre, from all the intellectual territory she'd already visited with Samuel—beloved country—to the fertile new fields on the banks of the Seine?

That day after lunch I slipped into the lecture hall after Jocelyn did, but in time to see Alain Saint-Georges, professor of political science and pundit for *Le Monde*, stride in to take the podium. Tall, graying at the temples, eyes hidden behind tinted spectacles, he wore, with intentional flair, a cravat. A moment later, the room fell quiet.

"Alors," Saint-Georges began, "today we will depart from the prepared lecture to take up the matter of gravest concern. Today we have just learned, thousands of miles across the ocean, the superpower giants are playing nuclear games. The Americans, powerful but adolescent imperialists, are likely to do something stupid. We may all blow up…"

Jocelyn covered her ears.

Before the lecture was finished, Jocelyn made her way up the long corridor of the cavernous lecture hall to the exit. Soon she was inhaling the crisp October air in the courtyard, beneath the seventeenth century cupola standing like a grim sentinel over the cobblestones, worn down by centuries of worried student feet.

"Blow up," the professor had said, meaning the world as we knew it, herself included. "Incinerated," he'd said. And so she stepped outside needing air, trying to imagine, but all that came to her was the hill and the fire, the clean California afternoon, the flames, how the pool had been swallowed like a drink of water, and how the balcony from which we'd gazed at the stars had buckled and fallen silently into a river of fire, and the roof had lifted, in pieces, like burning angels flying in the wind. "Americans may do something stupid," he'd said in tones that reminded her of Grandfather in Utah. Did he mean Kennedy, whom everyone worshipped as a young god?

This much I know for certain. Alain Saint-Georges saw her just as she was turning away. Swiftly, he gained on her before she stepped outside the thick wall and placed his firm hand on her elbow. *"Mademoiselle,"* he said.

She stopped, blinked in surprise at seeing him up close. The smoothed-back gray hair, the well-tailored jacket, the cravat, the eyes not quite visible, somehow came together in a way that was more human, less forbidding than the figure at the podium. *"Professeur Saint-Georges, alors?"*

"Yes. I noticed you...that you left the lecture early. Perhaps the subject was too upsetting, no? But then, it *is* upsetting. I think, however, we should discuss this distress. You can explain to me your point of view."

"My point of view? I don't have a point of view. I mean, this was the first I learned of the missile crisis. From you."

"*Voilà!* You see. It's important that I keep in touch with foreign thinking."

For the first time since her arrival in Paris, Jocelyn wished for Samuel to be there, physically with her, to help bail her out. "But Professor," she finally blurted, "I'm sorry I cut out early. I admit I was upset, but I don't know. What could I tell you to be helpful? I mean, I'm only a student…an American."

"Oh no, *mademoiselle*, you're not 'just a student.' An American to be sure, and I like Americans very much. But you are a woman, no? A lovely woman. Please, we have much to discuss."

I first came to know of Jocelyn's entanglement with Alain Saint-Georges because of my own little drama with Roland. What do I remember of that night? How the light from the flickering candles played off the shadows on the walls of a little *cave*, making them exaggerated, monstrous, comical. *"La condition humaine,"* Roland suggested, shrugging, giving that Gallic gesture accompanied by pursed lips that by then at least I knew was the essential and inexplicable core of the French character. His little half-smile, enigmatic and inviting as it turned his long face from a look of melancholy into one of amusement. How he drew in on the cigarette poised delicately between two slender fingers, and the smile disappeared again, hidden in smoke. But inside this *cave*—literally a hole in the ground on the twisting side street off Place de la Contrescarpe—there was more smoke than light.

I remember trying to focus on my impressions as I made mental notes for my journal: packed-in bodies, sweat, the taste of cognac, the smoke of course, and Roland who, in his black turtleneck sweater, just smiled, smoked, watched. What could I say of him while he ran over me with those provocative dark eyes that challenged, yet promised patience; probed, but revealed little? I made a checklist of adjectives: charming, attractive, ironic, mysterious. Possibly dangerous.

"What are you interested in doing?" I heard myself ask, even then a little alarmed at my brashness.

He cocked his head in that sideways look, that long thin nose seeming to bisect his face as he tried to fathom my meaning. "*Eh bien,* I am interested in studying my philosophers and having a nice Bordeaux to drink, yes, and to be in the company of a beautiful, intelligent woman. *Une américaine* if I'm lucky."

But I persisted. "No, what I mean is, what do you want to do afterwards, after you finish your study of philosophy?"

The shrug again, mouth downturned. "Well, as philosophy is life itself, the studies never finish, no? Perhaps one day I'll go to the south, where my mother's family lives, and take up my residence there. Life is not so hectic in the Midi, you see."

Relentless now, bent on destruction, I went on. "And work?"

"Ah yes, well, of course when it is necessary." He smiled and took my fingertips, curling them gently in his.

But it was no use. I probably flushed and swallowed hard, trying to keep the next rush of words from spilling out, trying to grasp just where the hell I was. I confess I'd never felt so foreign. *Look,* I almost said, *have you no ambition? And what about injustice, poverty, and racism, don't you want to do something?* Then I swallowed hard again, conscious of Guy's voice shouting in my ears, furious at him for overtaking me once more.

"Roland," I said instead, trying to change course by twisting a napkin around my fingers so clumsily retracted from his, "the fact that a few days ago we nearly blew up, does that worry you?"

"On the contrary, it makes me grateful. For we did not blow up, you see, therefore we must be careful to not waste this time in stupid worrying or futile actions. Now I have more days to study philosophy and, if I am lucky, to also study you."

"Me? But I am an American, and according to your experts—like Alain Saint-Georges, for example—it is because of America we may all be exterminated."

"Baf," he replied. "Saint-Georges is an idiot. It is your Kennedy who is a real hero—in the classical sense. And yes, I want to study you, your territory, your golden California. Tell me while we dance."

I said nothing on the crowded, smoky little dance floor, but gave into feeling, as Roland's slight body pulled me close. And when the chanteuse with the long hair bowed over her guitar in a gesture so like Jocelyn's, I thought of her, and how her recent behavior, so odd, so elusive, troubled me. We were close in a way I couldn't define just then, but my well-being was wound up in hers. If she was off-balance, I listed too, and I was trying so hard to find my feet.

It was time to leave. On the way home, Roland pulled me close beneath the awnings to keep out of the drizzle, and we made a dash for it down a street with exclusive restaurants. There, on a corner across the street, I saw Jocelyn getting into a cab. Alain Saint-Georges got in after her.

The whole night, it seemed, was to be a continuous revelation.

"*Alors,*" Roland shouted as the rain suddenly fell on us like ice needles, "this is an outrage. Winter coming in too soon, cheating us of the promised days of sun."

"Promised?" I shouted back at him, trying to follow as he threaded mysteriously along narrow streets, hugging the buildings for shelter. "Who promised? God?"

"No. Much more serious than that. It's a guarantee by the government."

I could just feel his amused smile, though I couldn't see it. "So what are you going to do, sue?"

"*Alors,*" he laughed, then switched to his brand of English which always amused me. "Always this American combat solution, no? But I am a good Frenchman. Therefore, I will do my duty and strike."

We were by now outside the doorway of Hôtel des Écoles, laughing and wet. It was well past midnight, Monsieur Lepic had long since vacated his post, and the entryway was dark. I fumbled for my key when, suddenly, lightly Roland gathered me—that is the correct word—in his arms.

"They say, you know, that Americans are always so optimistic, perhaps naïve. Maybe it is true. But then you, Miss J.J., are from California and you just carry so much sunlight." And he looked at me, my face, as if studying a painting or rare flower, in a way no one had seen it before, kissing every new discovery before finding my mouth. *"Bonne nuit, Beauté,"* he said, then disappeared into the dark.

It was hours later when Jocelyn slipped out of a taxi and crept up the stairs to our room. She switched on that forty-watt light and was somewhat startled to find me, a shivering, coat-wrapped bundle, slumped on the bed.

"The damn heat isn't on," I said, by way of explanation.

Jocelyn nodded, then quickly shed her coat, dress, slip, and panties to escape into the warm comfort of one of Madge's flannels. Although half-frozen and more than half-asleep, I couldn't help noticing how her ribs stuck out, and how her legs, slender as straws, angled down from her sharp hipbones. My first reaction was to make another mental note about the unfairness of things. My own thighs, for example, were on a spreading spree, and there hadn't been a sighting of hipbones for weeks. Still, Jocelyn seemed to have crossed some threshold. This wasn't fashionably svelte, this was frighteningly skinny.

"Jo," I started in, "I don't know. You're so…" I didn't say thin. But she held up a hand, waved me to stop. "It's okay," she said. "I know…" Then, burrowing down as much as possible under the covers, she changed course. "That story you told today, the business with you and Ivan and the whores and the rain—true?"

"Of course," I answered, "but there was more." I told her then the rest of the story. How in that dingy whore's room I had stripped off my wet clothes to dry and had lain on the narrow bed wrapped mummy-style in thin blankets, listening to the rain. How the room had been cold and shabby, so unclean you could smell the dust.

How as Ivan undressed, there was a small thud as something fell from his coat pocket to the floor. "Good Lord!" he said. "I've been carrying this all day and forgot to give it to you. It's from Guy. He asked me to send it to you." He shoved a tattered package at me, then, assessing my immobile state, ripped the brown paper off and held a book up in front of my eyes.

Chinese Love Poems: Spring and Autumn Farewell. Stunned, I'd sat up and loosened the wraps around my arms to take it, reading inside the cover: "Dear J.J., I never had a chance to say farewell. Chinatown. September 30, 1962." I turned then to the encircled page in the index to find the poem "To One So Far." *Time was long before I met her, but is longer since we parted…*

I could hear Jocelyn listening in the dark, and knew what she couldn't say. Like how happy she was to know this story, how glad for my misery. And how it comforted her to know that Guy, ever since the night of the *bal masqué* and all our disasters, had not become my lover, but my obsession. She couldn't admit to the feeling of abandonment as I veered toward falling in love, but I know she felt it. Thus in some way, she welcomed my misconnections, my failures, my wounds from love, believing that such tortured incompletion, such longing and obsession itself were what bound us closest as sisters.

"I saw you get out of a cab with Alain Saint-Georges," I said as if to answer her silence.

"Yes," she said with a trace of weariness. "But it's not what it seems. Alain, you see, well, we *talk*. I mean philosophy, art, history, politics—"

"But you hate politics."

"I did. But in French, it's different. I mean here it's different."

By now my eyes were open wide in the dark. "I get it," I answered, adding in a dreamlike tone. "Because the talk is slow, like an exploration, and he doesn't seem to be in a great hurry—"

"And," Jocelyn broke in, "he seems to really care what you think. Then, you know—"

"You have to figure out what you think."

"Right. And there's this kind of, I don't know, atmosphere..."

"Yes. It has to do with lingering and..."

"...candlelight and long coffees, like he has only time and there's only you in the world. Who could ever know us so well?"

"Each other," I answered, half wistful.

But she didn't blink. "That's right," was all she said. And if she closed her eyes then, it was to close out the rest of the night. What was she thinking? Perhaps, hearing of the present from Guy, she'd given up fearing my liaison with Roland. Or perhaps she took note that we were finishing each other's sentences again.

For my part, I was momentarily stunned. Samuel, it was clear, had a formidable rival—the proverbial charming, famous, handsome older man, a Frenchman to boot, who had also discovered Jocelyn's mind. Surely the rest would not go undiscovered long. Taking advantage of the now-rare moment of connection, I decided to ask outright: "So, are you sleeping with him?"

Jocelyn just sighed and pulled the covers tighter. "We go to restaurants and meet in cafés and he introduces me to his friends. We read and debate ideas. But, no. It isn't like that."

It flitted through my head that if Alain Saint-Georges was taking Jocelyn to fancy restaurants only to explore her mind, maybe Samuel had no worries. Maybe Jo was safely asleep in her skin. But what was she doing in those restaurants instead of eating? How come she was so thin?

I wanted to bring this up, too, but couldn't think how. Instead, I only said something innocuous like, "*Merde, chérie,* it's freezing in here." But soft, rhythmic breathing was Jocelyn's answer.

Morning came and went without rousing us from our sleep, and we did not disturb the books and notebooks stacked next to the bidet and on the radiator. It had been some time since Jocelyn had actually been to class, but for me, this was a maiden voyage into dissolution. It crossed my mind as I woke up that I should have long since gone to the Sorbonne. To classes in French Civilization, Art History, and Lit from Middle Ages to 1600, to be precise. And at that very moment I should have been making my way to the dreaded grammar class in that miserable annex at Montparnasse.

But what actually concerned me was how intolerably cold it was in the little room, and how frost had formed on the inside of the windows. I dressed quickly to go down and protest to Monsieur Lepic.

He heard me out without registering anything on his beefy face. Then when he was sure he understood my complaint, he shrugged, hunching his shoulders up to his pink ears. "Well, *mademoiselle,* what do you expect me to do? We cannot turn on the heat until winter, and officially winter does not come for three more weeks. It's the regulations, *vous voyez*?"

"So we should all go on strike," I muttered, thinking of Roland. Then I remembered the night and how he had looked at me and called me *Beauté.* I kept the memory inside, my own secret, and let Jocelyn sleep on in peace.

Chapter 12

It was still October when Camille had first given Gracie the idea, on the night that Madame had been particularly ferocious about celery root. After a few weeks of dinner-table conversation filled with pointed remarks about provincials and their amusing rustic ways, she unexpectedly, Gracie told me, turned her guns on Gracie again. "So, *mademoiselle,* I trust your palate has improved already and you know something about the basics of cuisine at least."

"Oh, yes," Gracie replied. I can picture her trying not to disgrace herself because her mouth was full. "Very delicious."

"Not at all like home, I know." Madame beaming, lost herself in the sweet gloom of imagined horrors. No, Gracie was nodding, thinking of Mama's minestrone, cannelloni, that rich Alfredo sauce, and her divine San Francisco seafood specialty, cioppino.

"Pass the *céleriac,* please," Madame asked, still distracted.

Céleriac, celery. As Gracie told me this, I could feel her freezing as she glanced around at the dishes on the table and knew she had sampled them all. Nothing vaguely resembled celery. Madame looked up, the small eyes boring into her surprisingly wide. "I, I don't know what you mean, Madame," Gracie finally blurted out. Camille, who was chewing slowly, gestured to a dish in cream sauce, but too late, Gracie said, "too darn late."

"You don't know what *céleriac* is?" Madame's voice itself was charge and conviction.

"Certainly, Madame. It's a vegetable with thick green sticks that grows on a stalk."

It came then, like a flood bursting from a weakened dam. "Yes, but only animals, or humans who are nearly animals, themselves eat that fodder. Civilized human beings, when they eat celery, eat celery root," she began. As she continued, the flush in her face rose, as did her tremor of outrage until the wine jiggled in the glasses and Gracie wondered if she might have a stroke, especially when she got to the meat course, where Americans were the lowest on the food chain. "The national dish for Americans is only these 'amburg-airs,'' Madame concluded her tirade, "with that disgusting mélange of sauces and to drink, an abomination, Coca-Cola, not even a decent *vin du pays*."

Gracie had long since stopped chewing and perhaps stopped breathing as well. She could not open her mouth to begin when she thought of the wine that mellowed in barrels in the cooled storage rooms behind her house and ran through her Napa land as deep and red as her Italian blood.

But Camille, clear eyed and amused, could both breathe and speak. "Ah Madame, there you are wrong. While it is true that Americans love their 'amburg-airs—quite a delicacy when cooked the right way, you know, and you should try one at Le Drugstore on the Champs-Elysée if you've not had one—the true national dish, as everyone knows who has studied American culture, is the turkey." She pronounced this with particular relish, knowing full well that the retired professor of French cooking would sooner eat dinosaur than that disreputable and barbarian big bird from the New World.

It came to Gracie then, in a flash: She would cook Thanksgiving dinner and invite all her friends *chez* Madame.

If she'd given herself long to think about it, she would have been properly terrified. Thanksgiving was the ultimate American holiday, the one that left her feeling more an outsider than ever. And what could the rowdy Battaglias know about somber Pilgrims and frost on pumpkins? Only to prove their American credentials, they went all out, in that ridiculous way (in Gracie's view) of the second generation. Paper pumpkins and cut-out gobblers and crepe-paper streamers and, as usual, too much red wine, and Marcello insulting Favio before the soup was even finished, and shouting by the time the pies came out, and, if it wasn't raining, a good brawl outside the house by nightfall, and then the sounds—babies crying and the souped-up hot rods—finally fading away, signaling to Gracie that the ordeal was nearly over.

But there was the food, too, with Mama, whose family had been in the country longer than Papa's, always insisting that this one day they should eat like good Americans. Committing patriotism through food was a concept every good Tuscan could understand. And so in her magical way, she'd cooked: Italian-style squash soup, savory potatoes with Italian parsley, onions in oregano, and turkey. Turkey stuffed with olives, walnuts, mushrooms, sundried tomatoes, and sourdough bread crumbs, basted in olive oil and fresh herbs.

I think Gracie had watched Mama do all this unaware that she was even watching. But as these memories and smells pulsed through her, she did not think long enough to remember that she, Gracie, had never actually cooked a turkey—or much of anything—herself. So, giving in to a rare moment of impulse, she just blurted out something like "Oh, Madame, I have a wonderful idea. I would like to cook a Thanksgiving feast for you, and my American friends, of course. For one day, I will cook and serve you American specialties."

Then, remembering Madame's miserly nature, she would have quickly added, "I would do all the shopping of course and pay for the food. You could invite some friends, too."

Gracie was pleased with herself, for once flushed more than Madame, amused by her outrageous idea. What jumble of things could have been going through her mind? Perhaps a snatch of that old grade-school song, "Harvest Home," or the not-quite-articulated thought that, as hostess expatriate par excellence, she could at last become a full-fledged American.

"Madame looked pale as a turnip," she recounted, "and I might have come to my senses, except Camille jumped in. 'Madame,' she said in that deceptive, sweet voice she does so well. 'What a wonderful idea! A great suggestion, *mademoiselle,* my friends will be so impressed. I accept your invitation.' Madame, of course, was pre-empted, stunned, and defeated! She grunted something like 'Baf, if you wish,' and quickly left the table.

"Then Camille and I went out for our after-supper stroll—and the usual cigarettes and a nightcap—and laughed ourselves sick about how it would kill Madame's soul to admit that an American meal could be deliciously prepared."

As an afterthought, Gracie added, "I guess what we didn't get just then was that to do this in her kitchen was a kind of violation of sacred belief, a heresy, worse than eating meat on Friday or breaking fast during Lent. We didn't understand what we had done, but Marie did..."

As soon as Marie heard the news, she crossed herself and looked to heaven, saying only *"Dieu."* But Gracie was still too jubilant about her little coup to pay much attention, so she stood there, she said, drinking tea, while Marie went about washing dishes and wheezing. Without thinking, Gracie picked up a towel and began drying, just as she would have at home with Mama.

"Then Marie," Gracie said, "put out a soapy hand to stop me, saying, *'Faut pas, mam'zelle, faut pas,'* going on about how Madame, if she found me—a paying guest—doing kitchen work, would pop out of her skin like a parboiled tomato."

Gracie, of course, kept on drying and Marie quit protesting. Thus they became accomplices in the kitchen, co-conspirators in advance of the Great Feast. For once, perhaps the only time, Gracie felt at home in Paris.

It was Ivan who came to break the news. The day before, he said, that great human being, one of his heroes, had died. He'd heard it on the radio before seeing *Le Monde*. And before Gracie even heard the words, she saw the mournful slant of his beret, the moisture gathering in his dark eyes, and she looked out the salon window to the emptying trees of Boulevard Raspail. "Eleanor

Roosevelt," he said, and she could not even hear the rest, for her own tears. They came freely and astonished her. Eleanor Roosevelt dead. She could not sort out what emotion she was even feeling. Embarrassment, to be sure, remembering Mama and her primitive ideas and how she had lit a candle beneath Eleanor Roosevelt's picture as if the toothy old first lady were a saint, remembering how she herself as a balky child had turned away in disgust. There was something vaguely embarrassing, too, about paying homage to a busybody old woman who meant well to be sure, but who could never live up to the image of queenly, gorgeous Jackie, the true First Lady of the world. But mostly, despite herself, she felt sorrow. She remembered the picture of Eleanor Mama had hung not too far from the Virgin right above the votary candles. Losing the old lady Mama had so revered was like losing a bit of Mama all over again.

The weeks between early and late November, Paris appeared to her under a pall of melancholy she could not explain. As the river moved from the dappled light of fall into winter, all color seemed to drain from it and Gracie saw in its flat reflection not elegance and divine aloofness, but edifices of stone presiding over, at best, indifference, at worst, a mocking cruelty. The classical façade of the Louvre, the hulking specter of Notre Dame, the phallic obelisk of la Place de la Concorde, the monstrous Arc de Triomphe, what were these but immovable pieces on some grand, imperial chessboard, monuments to enormous egos—all male of course—in enormous games of power? Gracie tried to shake this unwelcome gloom. She of all of them had most easily pushed the dangers of the Cuban missile crisis the month before from her mind, and had willfully closed her ears whenever Ivan went off about the Algerian situation. Yet the gloom continued, and taking the Métro across the Seine at the Trocadéro in the late afternoon, the terraces of the Palais de Chaillot, which housed the Museum of Man, one of her favorites, seemed no more to her than slabs of concrete spilling without meaning toward the water where, on the opposite bank, the Eiffel Tower rose on its monstrous, ghastly industrial legs, casting the huge shadow of an iron spider.

The day before Thanksgiving came in gray, the cold hovering like one of those medieval humors used to explain the metaphysics of the universe, and Gracie stepped out with Marie just past dawn onto Boulevard Raspail, determined above all, with the Great Thanksgiving before her, to get beyond gloom. Gracie, I know for a fact, was not in the habit of going out barely past dawn. But Marie, whose damaged lungs suffered in the damp, no doubt coughed defiantly and scuttled like a tough crab, impervious, to the nearest Métro. Gracie, I'm just as sure, was happy to let her take charge.

"For the turkey, there is only the market at Clignancourt," Marie announced to her and she, in turn, reported to me.

"It was like a novel," Gracie declared. "Something out of Balzac, or Zola, or even Dickens. Like a whole little country existing inside the boundaries of stands, with dirty running ice water along the ground, and these hoards of poor people, pulled tight inside worn coats like Marie, exhaling steam and alcohol through broken teeth."

This was a different class of poverty, yet another world removed from the well-off rough and tumble of her own kind. After all, these people wouldn't take two baths a week at Madame's—they wouldn't even think of it. She didn't have to tell me this was not the Paris she had come for. She did tell me how she followed Marie further and further through the warrens of slaughtered animals hanging on hooks, the carcasses, joints, heads, flesh with remainders of fur, the pimple-skinned poultry, chickens, geese, game birds, until they finally reached a row of turkeys, and how she felt nauseated, then surreal, as if she had slipped over to a slightly different planet. How Marie marched ahead with determination, elbowing her way forward, muttering slightly, an old felt hat perched rakishly on her wayward hair. Finally, she stopped in front of a particular vendor, a small man with crinkled cheeks and burly arms, until Gracie came to rest behind her, out of breath. "They began bargaining. They spoke so fast in that Parisian argot, I hardly followed any of it. But I did catch Marie calling the guy an old crocodile, and I think he said something about not needing to buy a tough, ugly old bird since she was one. I couldn't follow the bargaining either—figures just started flying around, sometimes it seemed in the millions because they still calculate in old francs—and finally Marie said *'Oui.'* Well not really *'Oui,'* but you know, that sound that's like a punch in the stomach the way they say it in lower-class Paris."

I can just picture the trip home. Marie on the Métro with that huge bird, head and feet dangling outside the butcher's wrap. Gracie sitting next to her gingerly on one of those little pull-down seats, trying not to see the turkey carcass, maybe closing her eyes and seeing, despite herself, Mama catching a chicken in their own backyard and wringing its neck. Thinking, probably, that that sight had not remotely prepared her for this one, wondering why this felt so different, or why she felt a ridiculous tenderness for the awkward, ill-fated bird with the wobbly, limp neck. Perhaps it was remorse.

And maybe there, in the dark of the Métro ride home, for the first time her great idea suddenly loomed like a threatening cloud, a monstrous project of uncertain outcome. Soon, she knew, she would be grinding baguettes into crumbs, adding onions and herbs and mushrooms—and of course celery. And soon Marie would begin hacking the limbs from the turkey, severing its head. But then soon—too soon—it would be tomorrow, and the guests would come. "Thank God I asked for help," she said.

Ice formed outside the window before daylight in the dark kitchen. When I arrived, Gracie was already sweating, sipping the bowl with rich coffee and milk that Marie, who had gotten up even earlier, had made for her. I was by far the first to arrive, stunned and fragile from a blow that had arrived in the mail the day before, and eager for the balm of the familiar—a Thanksgiving dinner. Gracie was, happily, too distracted to notice my silence, to comment on my red-rimmed eyes. She glanced at me, then motioned to the odd instrument for grinding that Madame, in wordless black humor, had pulled out the night before. "Get a load of that." Beside it lay knives, cleavers, old wire whips, and worn metal spoons. Gracie stared at this array of weaponry in a kind of stupor, as if she were in some imaginary country or a dream which would soon end to send her tumbling back home again.

Then, mechanically, she began chopping the onions Marie had carefully laid out on an old oak sideboard, while I cut the rest of the ingredients for stuffing, including sausage. By the time Marie came back from the dining room, tears were streaming down Gracie's pale face. "*Sainte Marie et Jésus,*" Marie was muttering, "poor old mule, she's worse than damned. Not once in ten years."

"What?" Gracie looked up, crying as if heartbroken, and Marie laughed.

"*Pauvre petite mam'zelle,* even the onions are too much for you, *non*? Ah, what a bunch in this household." She shot me a glance and removed the onions from Grace to begin chopping them herself, deftly, with a clothespin clamped on her nose.

"What were you talking about?" Gracie asked her.

I perked up, too, when Marie answered, almost incomprehensible with the clothespin on top of her Parisian argot. She said something about Madame having *again* made a place setting at the table for her son, but never once in the ten years she'd worked here had the bastard set foot in his mother's house.

"Madame has a son?"

Marie nodded.

"Where? Here in Paris?"

She nodded again.

For a moment I guess even Gracie stopped worrying about the task at hand, about the debacle that could unfold before the end of the day. I glanced at her trying to make sense of this news.

"But *how*?" she finally blurted.

Marie stopped chopping and ran water over the offending onion in hand. "*Sainte Marie et Joseph,*" she sputtered, gnarled hands at rest on her thin hips, "how do you think, *mam'zelle*?" She looked at me again and shrugged. "In the normal way. *Oh là là.* Surely not even you would propose a virgin birth, her not being our Holy Lady," and she proceeded to cross herself.

"But has Madame been married?"

That surreal feeling that had been receding a little since Marie rescued Gracie from the onions began to overcome me again.

"Mais oui!" Marie now wiped her hands on her stained apron and tugged on Gracie's sleeve. "You haven't seen the pictures?" She led Gracie into the book-lined parlor with the family treasures, and I followed. Then Marie pointed to two photos, both in that faded brown that looks like sepia-tone. They were half-hidden on a shelf behind a leather-bound Bible, in an old-fashioned double-frame with gold gilt edges. One picture showed a small boy of five or so, posed in a sailor suit on a bench. Inside the frame was a lock of fine light brown hair. Opposite him was an unsmiling man with dark hair and eyes and a large mustache staring expressionlessly at the unseen eye in the camera.

"Voilà," Marie said with a touch of triumph. *"M'sieur et petit m'sieur*—only a young sprout in the picture."

"So what happened? Did Monsieur die?" Gracie's voice climbed into the higher scale of inquisitiveness.

"Ah non," Marie declared.

"Divorce, then?"

"Non, non, non," she wagged her head for emphasis. "Divorce, of course is a sin, not that Madame pays much account to that. No *mam'zelle,* Monsieur is alive and living on the Riviera. I believe with his mistress. Madame has not seen him for twenty-five years. And the son abandons her too."

This was not a conversation I wanted to hear, and I felt that blow to the gut that accompanies extreme bad news and undesired premonition. Marie's face contorted, as if she also were on alert for a coming storm. But Gracie, lost in her own surprise, did not see our alarm, and, of course, could not guess what I felt. In fact, by mid-morning, when the sun had broken through the frosted window leaving a smudge of light, she bent in a deep mood over the grinder, pushing through bread, sausage, herbs, mushrooms and celery, I suspect still trying to get a grip on what Marie had revealed. She had made little progress in grinding and began sweating again when the buzzer rang to announce Eve.

In a moment she sailed through the kitchen door, red hair flying. Eve, whom Gracie adored most. Eve, who was loved by Tom. Eve, who had the courage to live, to fail, to not give a damn. "So, hey, *ma petite choux*, what a shindig! Hey, J.J., *quelle surprise*, you beat me here you old morning thing. Look, I come bearing goodies, spuds—the holy route to salvation, via the church guild's cookbook—really good mashed with garlic though, you know? And the green beans. I thought small onions *avec*, you agree? Mel is coming with potables—she can afford them!" She threw her jacket over a chair and went to the sink to rinse her hands.

Marie watched from the corner of the table as she finished rinsing the brine, then greasing and readying the cavity of the big bird. The redhead, she seemed to note, apparently knew what to do in a kitchen, as Eve went quickly to work peeling potatoes. Gracie, who with my help was just finishing up the stuffing, noticed the same thing. Eve did seem at ease, even with all this bizarre Old World equipment. Being the pastor's daughter meant learning to cook, too. Just one more thing Gracie could envy. She moved over to the table and alongside Marie, and began stuffing the turkey.

"So, Marie," Eve spoke over her shoulder, "how'd you learn about this American meal? I thought French people didn't eat turkey."

"The poor, *mam'zelle*, eat anything."

Eve stopped and turned around. "I didn't think turkey, especially here, where it's sort of exotic, was especially cheap."

"Holy Mother and all the Saints, of course not. The only thing cheap is the lives of the poor. No, *mam'zelle*. But hunting is cheap."

"Hunting? In Paris? I didn't think turkeys lived here, at least in the wild. Did you, J.J.?"

Marie stopped her work to cough in deep wrenching waves that made her thin body contract. Then she looked up at Eve, at Grace, and finally at me, taking us in with her rheumy blue eyes. *"Hah, les jeunes filles que sachent-elles, ma foi?* I am an old woman and I have lived a long time, not all of it in Paris. I have seen things, my child…there are many ways to hunt."

Eve kept on peeling and I kept my head down, but Gracie stood motionless, as if seeing through a window she had never guessed existed, maybe the window on the life of the poor Ivan always was talking about. She stood as though seeing flashes of scenes that made no coherent picture, maybe a peasant shack somewhere, a paltry plot of vegetables, soldiers of course, and fire, and nimble-footed theft. Maybe Marie had stolen food. Maybe…

"Whoa, you know," Eve said, "no matter how good a job we do here, it's not going to be authentic without cranberries."

"Yeah, right," I agreed.

But Gracie didn't say anything. She didn't say, for example, that Italians, even Italians who were Americans, never ate cranberries.

The doorbell rang again. "Must be Jocelyn," Gracie said, listening to Madame answer the door. "Do you think she can cook?"

"Good question," Eve answered. "You never know about her. Can she, J.J.?"

Before I could reply, Madame passed by the kitchen door like a dark shadow, paused to sniff, and dropped a sack. "A messenger came with this," she said, and retreated, closing the door with a thud.

"What's that? Where's Jocelyn?" Grace and Eve asked together, while my heart inched toward my stomach.

"I don't know, but she's been feeling rotten," I said, plunging my hands into the sack to confirm my worst fears. There it was, a note hastily scrawled on square-ruled paper.

> *Chères soeurs,*
>
> Sorry, but I'm just too nauseated to be able to join you. This bug I have seems to linger. Please forgive (and pity me a little, too, for missing *la grande fête*). But I send a little contribution to the party with instructions to J.J. to do something respectable *avec.*
>
> *Baisers,*
>
> Jocelyn

I extracted from our stuffed plastic shopping bag several large cans. Two of prepared pumpkin. Two of jellied cranberry.

Marie crowded in as Grace and Eve stared at the booty, stunned. "How on earth…?"

"It was Madge. She airmailed them." I carefully lined the tins up, thinking my moment had come, for I did know something about making pies, and set about looking for a can opener.

But Eve and Gracie stared at each other knowingly, thinking I wouldn't notice or guess what was going through their heads. Airmailed big cans. Poor mothers, mothers of girls on scholarship, would never think of such an extravagance, of postage that was the price of several meals. Eve glanced at Marie, obviously hoping she did not understand this little national embarrassment. And Gracie looked at me, wondering perhaps what country Jocelyn and I really lived in, and if you needed a special passport to go there. "Well, it is a bit out of the ordinary," I said by way of a half-apology, "but, you know, she meant well." Then switching to my best French, I turned to Marie. "If it isn't too much trouble, show me where the flour and rolling pin are, and I'll get started on the pies."

It was a relief to begin mixing the dough, letting it rest, whipping together pumpkin and cream and eggs in a large bowl. This came easily to me, a fact that in retrospect I see made Gracie even more uncertain.

"So, did you learn this at home, from your dad, or what?" she finally asked. For a moment I was stunned, first with the sudden image of my most unculinary mother in the kitchen trying to teach me the art of pie crust rolling. Then unsettlingly, of my father, who did seem to know something of cooking, but never owned up to it. Finally, I looked up and seemed to see the kitchen in front of me through a filter of violet, as if through Gran's eyes. Or perhaps my own.

"Non," I answered Gracie softly in French, "I learned from my *grand-mère*. She is French." Then I turned back to the pie crust, my hair falling annoyingly over my face, and the small room, now steamy with pots boiling and the hot oven roasting the dressed bird, respired with a kind of sadness.

Madame sat quiet through the meal—the potage with harvest vegetables, the moist, perfect turkey with savory stuffing, the jellied cranberry, green beans with onions, and garlic mashed potatoes and gravy—in a russet dress, a gold necklace with pearls tight around her throat. She had said little, as one might not in the simple pleasure of eating a sumptuous meal. Someone among us knew how to cook, she knew that much.

Gracie glanced at her, noting her unnatural calm, the pallor of her usually flushed cheeks, and perhaps wondered if that air of unnamed melancholy in the kitchen had leaked through to the dining room. But it seemed impossible. Madame had not even reacted to the small pique Gracie had intended by serving a relish plate with olives and celery sticks. The table shimmered with candlelight that cast a warmth on the old *faience* Madame had used in setting it. Wine shimmered in the goblets, but the conversation was the sustaining liqueur.

To my surprise, even Mel seemed animated with the talk that moved quickly from Algeria and the *pieds noirs*, the missile crisis, music, theater, and art. "Where is Jocelyn when we need her?" Eve lamented as the question turned to film and the latest project by Roger Vadim.

"Poor Jo," Mel commented, raising her glass. We all followed suit, then, and I noted that even without Jocelyn, whose presence could fill a room, there were no empty spaces. The chair next to Madame, set for her son, was filled by Camille's guest, Madeleine, a tall, slim young woman with silky black hair, black eyes, and skin white as a cameo. She said little, while Camille made effortless conversation and jokes, and Gracie watched each time she spoke, noticing the tension between the two that made them shiver a little, like electricity on the fur of two cats who rub together.

Ivan had brought two friends, too. Good old Yves, ever the voluble blond. And Roland. His searching eyes, sheltered beneath his wayward coils of black hair, seemed to seek me out from the opposite end of the table. Did he sense my distress? Gracie noticed this, I think, and the fact that I was uncommonly quiet. But what could I say? Only when the moment came for Mel to pour the champagne and me to fetch the pies did I relax a bit.

I returned from the kitchen with the pies delicately balanced on two china platters and laid them as tribute, two jewels beneath their froth of *chantilly,* designed with deliberate intent to match her dress, in front of Madame. "Pumpkin pies," I finally said a bit lamely. And Mel poured champagne in flutes to make ready for the last toast. As though blessing a ship already safely launched, she raised her glass to say it was a day to give thanks, and thanks for friendship.

"Amitié franco-américaine," Roland shouted with enthusiasm. I felt a kind of smile growing in me, a radiant burst I hadn't experienced all day, and suddenly knew I had something to say.

"À la famille franco-américaine," I answered him, and sat down again to lift my glass. "To my own family in California," I swallowed carefully not to choke on my

words. "My grandmother is French, and she's the one who taught me to make pie crust, and to my extended family, here, at this table. Except, of course, for Jocelyn." It was hard to get the words out, but Madame didn't give me long to falter.

Camille lifted her glass in a little salute to me, while Madame lifted the knife to cut the pies. I was startled to see the look of transparent melancholy pass across her face, and for once felt I could understand her. It passed quickly, and she disappeared again beneath her mask of powder and rouge that unsuccessfully hid the face of a lonely old woman who longed for things she no longer knew how to name.

Then she took her first bite, and her color came back. "I can see the French hand at the bottom of this," she said, waving her fork at the pie, "so I congratulate the pastry chef. In fact, though a bit strong, this exotic *pompcan*, the dessert is in general excellent. But as for the matter of mixing French and American in the same family, *non*, I say, for the simple reason that some tastes cannot be mixed successfully. This is a question that the Americans simply do not understand very well." Her color gained a little with each word, as if a pink sunset were determined to settle over her face. Gracie leaned forward, alarmed at the strange turn of her conversation.

"For example," Madame went on, "I have heard, but only tonight at my own table actually witnessed, that Americans serve sweet sauces with meat. A lapse of subtlety, if I may say so, perhaps inherited from their forebears, the English, who make such unspeakable dishes as lamb with mint jelly." Madame quivered a little, setting off her chin, her color deepening toward aubergine.

"In fact it is said, but you Americans among us can only know the truth of it, that in America it goes much farther. In America, they say, it is common to mix salt and sweet, at which point the word cuisine must cease to be used. But for myself, I once tasted it at an affair where, alas, one could not refuse an abomination, what they call Southern baked ham. A ham, can you imagine it, cooked with sugar, fruit, and raisins. *Non, non,* I tell you in a world that pretends to be civilized, this is not possible."

She grabbed her fork now, like a peasant or a butcher, with her fist and waved it slightly as if to orchestrate the crescendo of her thought. "Everybody, of course, knows other abominations happen in America—divorce, for instance. Everybody has a divorce, whereas in France…but what I am saying, *demoiselles,* is how can you be surprised, cooking like that? Ham with raisin sauce! It is a scandal. Of course, what can you expect after such recipes, what but divorce and disgrace?"

The harangue rose and fell like a sword whose sharp edge landed squarely on me. All that I had been trying to keep down swelled up in me, and the words in Gran's letter swam in front of my eyes,

> …and so, my dear, though this is so difficult for you to accept from so far away, especially near Thanksgiving time, you know the separation may not be permanent and may not lead to divorce. And as I'm sure both of your parents have already told you, they feel this is the best course for both of them at this time, and not so difficult for you now that you're grown up. But of course it is difficult, one always needs family, so for the moment, my dear child, you and I will once again have to stick together tight, no?…

There had of course, been no letters yet from either my father or my mother.

I rose suddenly, nearly upsetting a wine goblet in my haste to push away from that table, warped now and hideous in my distorted vision. I turned without a word and fled.

Before I left the room, Roland stood, too, and I saw fleetingly how his slight frame half bowed like an ancient *chevalier* about to gesture with a feathered hat. As I ran down the hall, I heard him say "...feast worthy of a king. But you, Madame, have given us an unfortunate lesson in civilization today. They say it is dying in France. I never believed it until now."

I was already in the small cage of the lift when he made his own dash down the dark hall, past the parlor with its leather-bound books and incriminating, half-hidden photographs. But when the lift reached the ground floor, he was there to open the door and give me his hand.

It must have been somewhere between the fiasco of Thanksgiving and the deep cold of Christmas that the first letter came. It's odd, in a way, that Gracie didn't quite remember. But with her photographic memory she did remember what it said and remembered, too, every ambiance, every frisson, of the day. Ivan had come brandishing headlines about the front in Algeria, and they had withdrawn to the parlor for tea. Once again, Marie had arrived on the strength of one lung, pushing the tea cart; once again, Ivan had begun a monologue on the evils of the class system while Gracie's attention had drifted to the window, the sky now bared for winter against the naked plane trees, and to thoughts of the street below. In the varied sounds of its traffic, the horns, the braying of police sirens, she imagined Camille's gentle, protracted sigh, let out on the fumes of cigarettes. She wondered where, exactly, in the maze below, Camille was just now. In what café with Madeleine and her silky black hair, blowing smoke and laughing her heart out. Ivan went on, not noticing how Gracie's eyes kept scanning the shelves of old books, stopping on each volume of Colette. The tea grew cold.

Then, suddenly, a thump on the door.

Madame swung it wide open, stomping with unusual vigor on the faded Persian carpet. She nodded in brief acquiescence to Ivan. She had always, Gracie said, liked Ivan, calling him *ce type de français*, the ultimate compliment. Even more, she no doubt liked that in the fading afternoon, neither of them had thought to turn the lights on, exhibiting admirable frugality. "*Poste*," she said, and nodding to Ivan, threw a fat letter on a table, then retreated as quickly as she'd come.

Gracie snapped out of her fog and began to survey the letter from her chair. It didn't look like a letter from home, yet nobody but Papa or her sisters or Aunt Florence wrote to her. Marie returned to fetch the cold tea and a plate of pastry crumbs. Ivan proposed a walk to the boulevard, and, uncharacteristically, a visit to the churchyard at Saint-Germain-des-Prés. But Gracie declined, and as soon as Ivan retrieved his beret and she saw him to the lift, she retreated to her room, hand trembling slightly as it held the letter.

The word she used to capture her mood was "delicious."

Stretched upon her bed beneath the little reading lamp, to amplify the small light accorded by the window facing the courtyard, she read:

Hi doll,

It's been too long, and I did promise to write. No excuses really, but the football season is finally over, which is both a blessing and a curse. The blessing, if you can call it that, is now I finally have time to prepare for exams—though I don't have to say how much more difficult it's going to be without your help! Still, it has to be done… And the bad news? Well, of course the bad news is missing certain persons who used to reside at la Maison Française. God, it's like a ghost town over here. Which brings me to the point.

Gracie, angel, I need your help and don't know where else to turn. I really want to get over there. Evelyn's letters, though brief, have been like little bombs going off in my head—your cards, too, and thank you very much. I guess I'll feel like I always missed out if I don't get to Europe, too, like an education is more than just the books. You girls have always understood that, I know. But somehow, it's not just Europe—and here I know you of all people will get what I mean—but some kind of family tie, the Old Country thing that I want to experience. And, this is also not news to you, I very much want to see Eve again. I was thinking to surprise her, and, you know, maybe share something new with her that would mean a lot to both of us. Like maybe Italy! I haven't got the details worked out yet, but figured in order to go forward, I'd need an accomplice. Are you with me, doll?

I thought (knew?) in advance I could count on you. If you say yes, then I'll get back to you soon with Preliminary Plans, and SHHHH. Meanwhile, don't mess up those pretty curls with too many hard facts. Other stuff is okay. And keep warm. It's been a cold, dry year. No fires of any kind.

Take care, *bambina*, and, how do you say it, *je t'embrace*?,

Tom

Part 4

FROZEN RIVER, COLDEST NIGHTS

Chapter 13

The Rue du Pont Neuf begins on the Right Bank just where the "new" bridge, the oldest in Paris, ends. Covered with ice, its effortless arches, its Left Bank Henri IV bearded with snow, the bridge in winter becomes an abstraction suitable to the modern age. Beneath, the Seine flows, its secrets locked fast.

I'm guessing Jocelyn with her Nordic ancestry felt a kinship with that cold. She took in how the lights along either side of the Rue du Pont Neuf reflected like crystals against the banks of snow. Behind them, and along the elegant Rue de Rivoli, shops and businesses, where one window announced a coat sale, all showed signs of struggle. Like faces, storefronts then disappeared in frost, barely visible beyond her own icy breath.

In my mind I picture it all: Jocelyn rubbing her hands together, trying to warm them inside her gloves around the corner from Place de M. Quentin, outside Les Halles. To her dismay, it was nearly as cold inside the vast halls as without. But, as Fabrice, who was always explaining things, explained, Les Halles, the great central market, was more important than that. "If there is a single corner of Paris that above all defines *la* France, this is it, for here the primal meaning of France—the fruits of its soil—are brought like tribute to the centralized seat of power. Easier to centralize corruption, *tu vois*? That's it: *la Belle France*, a stinking, inefficient market, left over from the Middle Ages." Fabrice sputtering, then curling up the corners of his thin mouth, evidently pleased with himself, before carrying on again.

But Jocelyn, already lost in the contours of an incredible artificial landscape, wasn't listening. Those mountains formed by cabbages and potatoes, turnips, celery root, tender carrots, baby onions; seas of tomatoes rippling with waves, pyramids of citrus or melons smelling of summer or North Africa; whirling pools of biting olives, streams of milk and cream, islands of sweet butter. It was impossible to comprehend, especially in this winter where the snow fell and stacked like a deadly harvest, and the ice grew like ground cover overtaking all living things, including herself. Or so she felt.

"*Voilà*," Fabrice again. "Even through sheets of ice, all roads lead to Paris. And then, of course, OUT of Paris—that's what the silly bastards never take into account. No, no, they never think of that. How even the food must recirculate to the provinces, the people, and their little *pots au feu*."

Alain Saint-Georges, silent so far in the onslaught of his friend's impassioned speech, at last putting his hand on Fabrice's elbow, guiding him to the door. "Yes, yes." His tone was distracted. "But *la demoiselle* is hungry. Let us continue at one of the little cafés of the workers here, so she can experience the true flavor of the centralized market in France."

"Baf," Fabrice was insistent. "The workers here don't own the place anymore. They work through the night, but now their little all-night cafés are invaded by tourists...and capitalists. Americans!"

Then Jocelyn stopping, inhaling deeply. Cafés with funny names rimmed the outer edges of Les Halles, which leaked with savory smells: fresh bread, roasting chickens, and onion soup with garlic and crusty cheese. "Well, I'm American," she said at last, "so this must be for me."

Fabrice, frowning remorsefully. "No, no. *Mademoiselle*, please. You are a student—Alain's student. And a beautiful young woman, so it is a different thing, yes?"

As they slipped behind a table at Au Ventre du Cochon, Jocelyn caught her reflection—eyes like huge dark embers, hair shimmering gold—in the window. A perfect balance between Alain, that silver hair swept back, those beautifully lidded eyes traced with small tracks, the cigarette posed casually in a long holder dangling from his thin lips, and Fabrice, perfection, too, in his own way. The long face sunk with canyons of ennui, the rumpled beard, the graying hair lounging artfully over the ears, the fingertips stained from smoking Gauloises, the proletariat's cigarette. The perfect disaffected intellectual publisher. So they all look exactly as they should. And even the background players—the swearing, greasy drivers and warehouse men exhaling garlic, the consumptive-looking waiter with a voice like nasal drip and a dirty apron—were all perfectly cast.

This helped Jocelyn to focus, for her attention was slipping, though she could not admit that to herself any more than she could admit fatigue. Insomnia seemed much less agreeable to grapple with than the nobler quest, one she often spoke about to me, of staying up all night in search of meaning. How could she be bored, drinking red wine and eating onion soup at dawn with one of the most famous intellectuals in Paris? Or two, if Fabrice were to be believed. And, she had to admit, she was holding her own, enthralling them with her running discourse on Kant and Kafka, throwing them off even with little asides about the dark side of American theater, about which they could say nothing. The conversation was a gift, almost scripted, from her days with Samuel.

As for the wine, at first, of course, she had refused. But after a few times out with Alain, the charm had worn off the Mormon routine—"you know, it's just too alien for Paris," she announced one night, casually—so she'd decided to set it aside for the moment. Part of the learning experience, though she would never confess this to Madge, and made me swear I'd never tell either.

"What are you thinking, *chérie*?" Alain was asking, gently massaging her thigh beneath the table. "You look a trifle distracted, no?"

"Well, I was just wondering how dialectical materialism is manifest in this ancient market idea," she answered, pulling up a line from Samuel's latest letter.

"You were?" Alain and Fabrice, both at once, were caught off guard. It had been a long night for all of them, though after the late cinema when she and Alain had run into Fabrice, who proposed showing the young lady the Paris of the people, she assumed it was normal for them to stay up until dawn. But with the snow, it all seemed difficult, and even the tireless Fabrice was stifling a yawn. And Alain, who surely would have to begin another incredibly busy day soon, was looking haggard. Even, "I hate to admit this," she said to me, "old."

Best to veer away from dialectical materialism, since she couldn't remember what, exactly, Samuel had said. "No, I'm not really thinking about dialectical materialism, at least vis-à-vis the market, but I was wondering why we are sitting in the Pig's Stomach? Where do they get these names?"

Alain rubbed his eyes and began coming to life. "Ah, it's all about cuisine, which is really all about France. Pig's feet, pig's intestine—any part of the animal at all—are traditional delicacies of the *ancien régime…*"

"Mais, non," Fabrice breaking in. "It is all politics. Pigs, you see, being the ruling class…"

Jocelyn later admitted she tuned out his actual words, trying to get a measure of the man, this closest friend of Alain. She heard phrases—communism, anarchy—that she could fit into no meaningful pattern as he turned wild-eyed, expectorating into the hardened cheese at the bottom of his cold soup. All she knew for certain was that he was an ardent extremist of grand theory, who, being French and taking ideas to their logical end, came up with mind-bending conclusions. "Americans," he pronounced, quivering with the evil of the thing, "pay no taxes. Pigs of selfish consumption, monsters of individualism, they subsidize only Hollywood—and of course, spaceships to make interplanetary war." But other evils, such as mindless centralization, as exemplified by Les Halles, "were a result of the rule of the church compounded by sin and failed revolution into an even more nefarious formula, modern bureaucracy."

Jocelyn nodding soporifically, Alain's hand creeping higher under her skirt, Fabrice succumbing to worries on a cosmic scale. If the politicians and fools didn't ruin everything, if the Americans didn't succeed in blowing up the world, then one could always brood about other impending dooms: oil scarcity, deadly microbes in the water supply, waning sunlight, or worst of all, a French culture so impotent it would embrace English cuisine. Besides, as everyone knew who read the papers, the whole of France and Paris in particular was being overrun by *pieds noirs*, French refuges from Algeria who were the inevitable flotsam of failed colonialism.

"It is difficult to live with conscience in this world," Fabrice was saying, at last winding down, "when just to eat or drink, one must compromise one's principles." It was here that he poured himself the last of the wine. At the same time Jocelyn noted, Alain's hand went slack; he had fallen asleep.

"Look," she said, nudging him. "The sun's up. Shouldn't we be going?" Alain rousing himself, squinting. Fabrice's unnerving silence. Then Alain agreeing, "Yes, yes, I have a very important meeting."

"You'll not go home first?" Jocelyn chimed in, thinking to herself that unshaven and wrinkled, he really looked like hell.

"Ah, no, *chérie*. No time. I can take care of things in my office."

Then I see the three of them stepping out into the day. The cold was still bitter, but the sun on the streets threw light on the gritty edges of winter, where it turned to muck and frozen piles of trash. In daylight, the night workers looked grizzled and hard, Gauloises stuck between their yellowed teeth, emitting fumes and frost from their battered lungs.

Only a few hours ago, Jocelyn thought, *it had all looked so romantic. Now it seems just another variation on misery.* Her state of mind did not improve when Fabrice left them on the corner, nor when Alain negotiated, ("for an exorbitant price," she confessed) to have a cab take them back through the ice-bound streets across the river. And it certainly didn't improve inside the cab where Alain—cravat now straightened, shades in place—began whispering endearments in her ear.

Inexplicably, all she could think of was Madge and the last letter from home with its outrageous news: Madge and Burt meant to rebuild the house, replicate it "down to the art deco doorknobs." Sunlight through the taxi windows softened the frozen city, but Jocelyn was still longing for warmth. Longing for home.

"Next time, please, come to the office. There is so much I wish to share with you, my heart," Alain was saying, massaging her neck. Even with the shades on, he still looked old, over forty at least. *"Oui, oui,"* she answered, "next time in your office. Soon."

But even as she spoke, a different voice was playing in her head. *God, I may fail everything if I don't start going to class, don't start hitting the books. J.J.'s right. I've got to straighten up. Got to stop seeing Alain. Got to start getting some sleep.*

The cold kept turning Jocelyn inside. And because she could stop playing an impoverished student when it suited her, she reached frequently into her long pockets and browsed indoors. For a while, her favorite streets were the small light-filtered ones off Boulevard Saint-Germain, lined with antique shops, art galleries, and antiquarian book dealers. There she often found something—a book, an old map, a small objet d'art—that seemed custom-made for the new/old house being reconstructed in Hollywood, so she bought it, brought it back to stuff in some overcrowded corner of our tiny room, oblivious that she'd casually spent what many Parisians would consider a living wage. For propriety's sake, however, and for her own image, she did hide these purchases from the others. Especially from Gracie and Eve.

After one such expedition, with a small jade horse just purchased from a Chinese gallery, she rounded the corner onto Boulevard Raspail and, by chance, found herself directly in front of Gracie's apartment building. "I recognized the address," she shrugged, adding that, having missed "the wonders of Thanksgiving," she'd still never been inside. So, sliding the packaged horse inside her camel's hair coat, she rang the buzzer. After a moment, the concierge, a heavyset old woman with a lame foot, swung open the iron door, and eyed her with the withering skepticism for which her profession is famous.

"Eh bien?" the old woman barked accusingly, and with great reluctance opened the door to allow her into the dim foyer. After a probing interrogation, Jocelyn found herself in that ancient, tiny lift, closed behind iron grillwork doors like an animal in a primitive zoo. The dark floors, each like the one below, the courtyard behind, and a whole world hidden from the street but open to the sky. She knocked tentatively on the heavy door of Madame Gautier's fourth floor apartment. After a moment, it swung open.

A thin, white-haired woman in a maid's uniform answered. Her old blue eyes danced while she rasped a barely understandable greeting from clearly damaged lungs.

"Mam'zelle's waitin' for you," was all Jocelyn understood.

"Really?" she answered, wondering how that could be so, since she hadn't planned on dropping in.

Marie led her to a parlor, which, she said, reminded her in some vague way of Gran's, with dark Oriental carpets, thickset leather chairs and a horsehair settee, walls of old bound books and framed photos, yellowing over the memories of youthful hopes already dead for at least a half-century. But the thing that struck her most, "like a note off key" she said, was the "gaudy, eighteenth century thing, you know, with the frolicking naked cherubs and the yucky couple enclosed by a gold-gilt frame." I did know. I myself had remarked on the picture, so seemingly out of place with its pre-Romantic idyll of phony woods and meadows and a dreamy-eyed young couple dressed in vaguely Roman garb.

"So I just stepped up to look at this thing closer, to see if I was seeing, you know, what I was seeing, and I hear this voice: 'Well, what do you think? A masterpiece is it not?'"

The voice, of course, was Madame's, who had planted herself in the doorway. "But you know her. She just stood there all sort of short and dumpy, wearing this nondescript wool suit and this ancient felt hat that was plopped on top of her head. Mousy hair, don't you think? Bad dye job. But her legs, they looked like large poles sticking up from a pair of bedroom slippers. And she just kind of stared at me with these small squinty eyes—and the weird thing, you know, she had these jowls that shook like a hound's.

"Then she says to me, 'Well, my—ah, but you're not that other one, the wild redhead we were expecting. So who are you? Oh never mind, what does it matter. An American no doubt, and as ill-bred as the rest. Not of course that I expect you to have taste in such matters, but what do you think?'

"So I answer, 'Well my mother was an artist. I think…'

"But she just cuts me off. 'Hah, your mother, is it? Of course, who could know what terms like artist mean over there. This was painted by the great Édouard Constant, great-grandfather to my mother's mother, a regular at the court. Not that you would know about any of that. Well, where is she? Not only lazy, but lacking in all manners as you see.'

"Then she starts yelling for Marie. 'Get *mademoiselle* instantly. Her guest is here. You may bring them tea and one biscuit each. Just make sure they don't overdo it, and keep the electricity down.'

"So she turns back to me and says, 'I'm going out, frightful as it is, I have my duties. Sit, sit. She'll be here any minute, and…oh, never mind. I trust you'll not be here when I return, and so we'll never meet again.' And she slams the door."

Gracie appeared in the doorway of the parlor only a minute later. I imagine her rushing in, greeting Jocelyn with "Jo! What are you doing here? What a surprise."

Jocelyn, taking in then the shapeless wool skirt and sweater that hid Gracie's own shapelessness, had to wonder again, fleetingly, what it would be like to be short, homely, and disproportioned. But she said, "No. The real question is, what are *you* doing here, with that, that…?"

It is easy to see how the rest unfolded, as Gracie explained.

"Ah, Madame. The famed Antoinette Gautier, renowned professor of cuisine, retired, descended from the famed Édouard Constant, renowned *artiste* of rococo drivel and *constant* companion of kings, probably starting with Louis the Loony."

"So that's her? The slinger of the four-star soups?"

"She's the one. Soups with side dishes of insults, more than the minimum daily requirement, even for Paris." Picture Jocelyn sitting there, taking in how gingerly Gracie sat on the settee before asking again. "But you didn't tell me. Why are you here?"

"Would you believe it if I told you I was just walking by and realized I was in front of your building?"

"Sure. If you say so." There would be a slight question in the tilt of Gracie's head. "I haven't seen you for ages in class or… Where've you been?"

"Around. That is, at home, my room. Then taking things in, you know, museums and things. When I'm up for it."

"Are you sick, Jo?"

But mercifully, before she had to answer, Marie noisily entered the room, a red-cheeked Evelyn in front of her. "*Voilà, mam'zelle.* Here she is, the carrot-top, the one we were expecting. Now they're both here, isn't it lovely," she rasped. "Now I'll bring your tea."

"Jocelyn!" Evelyn fairly shrieked. "God, when was the last time… Wow, you look like a *Vogue* model. Everyone else here is fighting winter baggage, made worse by the food, and poor me, I live across from a bakery, and…"

"Eve of course came loaded with stories," Jocelyn told me. "And news. Seems she has a stack of letters from old lover boys too, you know, Tom the Hunk of course, but others as well. Some old boyfriends from before la Maison and even that good-for-nothing Jay who is now up and about on crutches and up to who knows what. I told her by all means to *burn* the damn things.

"But then the conversation turned to you. Eve was asking, 'So she's really going out with a real Frenchman? Do tell.'"

I imagine at that, Jocelyn shifted in her chair, twisting a piece of hair slowly. What could she say about me and Roland anyway? First, it was easier not to talk about it, because talking about me meant having to talk about herself. About betrayal. About Alain. About the letters that kept binding her to an increasingly surreal California. In fact, it was easy to not talk *to* me, since we were rarely home at the same time these days. "Haven't got much to tell," she would have replied, "you know how secretive she is! And, well, she's out so many nights. So make what you want of that."

To which Gracie would have said: "Really? I'm amazed. I see her all the time in class, and she says she's really studying just to keep up."

Here Jocelyn would have felt caught off-guard, revealed in her shaded storytelling. But Evelyn might have saved her.

"Poor thing!" Evelyn would have laughed. "Well everyone needs about nine lives just to make some of the scenes in Paris. So far, for me, my nine have run me ragged without even one for studies. But God bless Grace, who's helping me out with some notes. So Jo, what about you? Surely you must have some delicious scandal by now?"

Jocelyn could have only shaken her head in the mesmerizing way she had while singing on the stage of the *Jeanne d'Arc*. "Not really. Been, you know, just hitting the books pretty hard and trying to keep warm. And to that end, cutting class some. Too darn cold in that barny old Hall Richelieu, you know."

"Look," Gracie would break in, changing direction, unknowingly saving Jocelyn from further tiptoeing around the truth. "Madame hates me to do this because she's so tight she thinks I'll burn out her tube, but if you want we can turn on her TV. There's a big foreign policy statement by the foreign minister, and watching could save hours of studying for history and poli sci."

So Gracie switched on the large television in the corner, where the foreign minister, wearing an impeccable suit and elegant haircut, unloosed his mellifluous French and filled the screen. Jocelyn, as ever bored by politics, tuned out, catching only the usual references to *la gloire* and the nasty superpower which didn't seem to bow before it. What she thought about was how she needed to get back on track, vowing once more to really concentrate on her studies, at least enough to do well. There was, she had to admit, a mystique about a degree from the Sorbonne, and most students failed. A great mystique no doubt, then, for a degree with honors. Even Samuel couldn't top that. That concept, as it took shape in her restless brain, might have caused a smile just as the TV image of the minister faded and switched to a "distinguished commentator."

"Alain Saint-Georges," the announcer was saying.

Jocelyn described the scene.

"Wow!" Gracie broke in. "Our professor."

"So that's what he looks like," Eve sat up, alert. "I had no idea. Guess I'll have to go to class. Kind of cute for an old guy, don't you think?"

What Jocelyn didn't tell was the picture swimming in front of her own eyes. *Handsome, distinguished, in control.* His analysis was laced with references to Kafka and Sartre and American playwrights like O'Neill and

Tennessee Williams as "keys to inexplicable behavior on the other side of the Atlantic," she said. He mentioned dialectical materialism.

While he was still speaking, Madame blew into the room with an arctic blast.

But perhaps seeing the *demoiselles,* rich and giddy barbarians to be sure, improving their minds with a good dose of French perspective on the world momentarily softened her.

"'Ah, one of our finest intellectuals,' is what she actually said, and I could swear she sort of crossed herself," is how Jocelyn put it, adding that for a moment Madame blushed like a schoolgirl.

Perhaps that was the moment she thought to herself, *Well, he is good-looking. If Madame thought so, who could be immune? No doubt the whole country is watching him this very minute, thinking the same thing.*

It was then, without doubt, she made another vow to herself. *Like I promised, I'll make a visit to his office soon. Very soon.*

The letter from Samuel, fat and provocative as a dare, lay unopened on the bed. For once, I was there, upon my solitary perch, when Jocelyn unlocked the door.

"Guess what," I said, poking my head around the corner, "old Lepic turned the heat on. Sort of. Now its almost up to balmy arctic in here."

It was true. The chill had been taken off, giving Jocelyn the courage to undo her outer layers. As she did, she carefully removed the wrapped Chinese horse from her coat and set it on the only available space, the radiator. As she set it down, she moved aside my well-thumbed book, *Chinese Love Poems: Spring and Autumn Farewell.*

"How about that radiator, gurgling away like it's crooning a lullaby," I said.

"Yeah, it is making a lot of noise, giving a lot more noise that heat, actually," Jocelyn answered. "Like a lover." Then she settled down to read the latest treatise from Samuel.

Suddenly she could no longer accept her isolation, the loneliness of being alone with me in that small room. The wall she'd erected between us fell behind a flood of questions.

"What do you make of this?" she began.

Samuel, it turned out, had written about the newest brain-wave ideas he'd learned in neurology class. And about his latest passion, ceramic Chinese horses. And Jocelyn was desperate to understand whether these things were merely coincidences, or some kind of fatal entanglement that bound them at a cellular level and which it was hopeless to resist.

Long since fed up with arcane grammar and unpleasant poetry from the seventeenth century, I was ready to be drawn out, and, as if we were swimming side by side in her pool again, into the lapping, formless tide of conversation with Jocelyn. I made no pretense of answering her questions; answers would have been fatal. Before long, we lay stilled on the shores of our lumpy mattress, flannel-wrapped in Madge's gowns, once more sisters of the dark. An ice moon spilled cold light through the window.

I spoke, rather dreamily, of my increasing fascination with Roland, spoke of him without saying that he was everything Guy was not—dreamy, unhurried, given to all that was long, slow, and graceful, whether a book or a sentence or an afternoon in a café or a romance. The mystery of him. Where did he come from? Where he was going? And most mysterious, what did he see in me? The erotic, yet tender, regard between us had grown steadily. "It would be such a betrayal to not go on with this," I finally said.

"Betrayal?" Jocelyn asked, her voice rising with accusation. She did not utter Guy's name.

"Yes. Of experience," I answered, rolling over. "Of the great French lesson. How could I ever look Rimbaud in the eye again?"

But for Jocelyn, I knew, my fidelity to one mad poet was as puzzling as my infidelity in other matters. For her, there was no single sacred text, just a library of scripts. And as for the eye that could not be faced, it was not attached to any literary god, but to the modern Cyclops, the screen. As refuge from the cold, she had taken to stopping in the cinema and gorging on flickering images as others gorged on books. She was careless with ticket stubs, so I knew the particulars of her binges, though "feast" was most likely her preferred description. New American movies like *Fanny, The Hustler, Lawrence of Arabia*, even *West Side Story* with French subtitles, and the European greats: Bergman and Fellini and Godard and Truffaut. She had especially studied the stars, looking, I presume, for an image to follow. Sophia Loren, Jeanne Moreau, Brigitte Bardot. One by one she rejected those as, what? Too Latin, too complex, too cheap? Then she saw Catherine Deneuve in *Le Vice et la Vertu*, and mentioned she'd fallen under her spell. I believe Jocelyn knew right away she'd found her model. What could suit her better than Deneuve's cool, blonde, perfect beauty, her perfect morality, perfect desire, and perfect anguish?

Then, that very evening, she'd peered deeply into a different screen and seen the compelling image of Alain Saint-Georges. So when I said that experience was the great French lesson, I struck a chord. She knew I was right. Most of all, she decided if I was so determined to have it, well then, so was she. And if I could let the troubling questions of the past lie buried—that is how she saw me—then so could she. Better, she figured, to shrug them off, like conscience.

Experience. That would become her new mantra. Just to prove it, she said aloud to make sure I was still awake: "I've decided, you know, to sleep with him. I'm going soon to see him in his office. Alone."

I muttered sleepily, withholding the words "I know" as they formed on my lips.

Chapter 14

"Eh bien," Monsieur Lepic was growling, with Melanie standing before him, at last out of the snow, at last inside Hôtel des Écoles. "Who for?" Then hearing her reply, he'd say *"Qui? Oui.* I see it now, you're another one just like *la grande blonde*. But not so *grande, eh?"* Pleased with himself, he'd be chuckling, while Melanie began her climb up the worn stairs, belabored with so many clothes on, her boots already beginning to drip.

"Entrez," I called out, hearing her knock, unlocking the door. I admit surprise. Mel rarely came to our low-rent room, and never before without prior agreement. She had so many layers on, she looked like the little rubber tire man in the ads for *pneux* Michelins. I was very happy to see her.

"Mel, I don't have much to offer but the seat of honor." I gestured toward the pillow-padded bidet. "Oh, thanks, but…" She stood by our tiny closet and began shedding her outer clothes, then said, "Gosh, where's Jo? She said to meet her here—we have to make plans."

I looked at her with a cocked head, as if a slanting perspective could make me understand. "Plans," I repeated, trying quickly to figure what to say next to explain Jo's whereabouts. What could I say about Jo's pursuit of higher education with the eminent, graying, media idol, our very own specialist in American affairs, Alain Saint-Georges? I tried myself, clumsily I admit, to shut out the vision of Jocelyn's stated intent of conquest. Surely this was something no one, least of all Melanie, needed to hear.

"Well," I finally said, stating the obvious, "she's not here. She's out—at least out of sight, if not out of mind." I tried making a joke by gesturing to a mélange of wadded underwear, rumpled notes, and a pair of long red hose, draped over the radiator for drying. My own books, neat stacks of Voltaire, Rousseau, de Montesquieu, and Beaumarchais, encircled the bidet where Melanie now gingerly perched. "So what are the plans?"

"Well, we planned, that is she promised, you know, to go with me to visit Hans's parents over Christmas. I've already got the tickets. And we have to leave tomorrow. See…"

She thrust forward a well-worn note in formal French from the Boucher family inviting her to Strasbourg for a visit over the Christmas holidays. I read it, grateful my back was half-turned so Melanie couldn't see my face while I tried to figure out what in God's name to say.

It must have been one of those low, flat days when Melanie had approached and Jocelyn welcomed her in across the semi-wilderness of her conscience. Perhaps it was a moment of guilt *(be a real human being for a change, a friend,* that inner voice would have admonished). But it had passed so quickly Jocelyn had not even mentioned it to me.

"Mel, look," I spun around, trying to make contact with her dancing eyes. "I don't know what to say. She's been, well, *distracted* from time to time, and that makes her forgetful sometimes."

"You mean she didn't tell you that we're going?" Melanie's eyes were still for a moment, suspended above the bidet in disbelief.

"No. What I mean is, she's out tonight. It kind of goes in patterns. She may not come home."

"So, we have to go find her?"

"Melanie, what you don't understand is that I don't have the faintest idea where she is." I paused, not knowing what else I could possibly say.

I perceived a new order of paleness crossing Mel's face—the glaze of panic. Her gut must have become an icy knuckle, a knot of fear. I saw that she didn't have it in her to face Hans's parents alone. I moved up to balance myself against the water closet doorframe, trying to get closer. "Mel, look, I honestly don't know if she'll be back in time. But I promise, if not, I'll go with you...if you want. It was nice of them to invite you," I added, trying to soften the news.

Melanie seemed to focus on me then, on the reality of the situation, for the first time. "No it wasn't," she answered. "They had to, don't you see? Hans asked them to, since he's still stuck in the States, so they did."

"Ah, well, but they probably want you to come all the same. They're probably dying to meet you."

But Melanie just shook her head, wisps of yellow hair flying wild. "No. They're against us, too. It was only to be polite."

I could feel myself stiffen as I straightened up against the doorframe, offering a hand. "Look, Mel, you know you don't have to go if you really don't want to."

But she clutched my hand hard with her fingers—surprisingly, they still felt icy—and blurted out with a kind of bravado, "Oh, but I do! It means so much to Hans."

Jocelyn never came in at all that night, and I was bound to make good on my promise. But it didn't take long to have doubts about my sanity as we pushed and shoved through the Gare de l'Est. I felt miserable that Jocelyn had never showed up, that Melanie had so easily accepted the switch and had come so quickly to count on me, and that Jo and I could still be so seamlessly substituted one for the other. Then I let myself think about how cold it was, how crowded the station. And how above all I hated the strangeness of this Christmas, with my frozen errand of mercy, my love gone with no forwarding address, my home lost, my family in ruins. *"Merde,"* I said to nobody in particular, and tried to follow Mel, who darted and wove, worried about the time.

Being taller, I dragged the large pack and looked over the heads of the crowd to find the number of our train car, 58. At the rate we were moving, I calculated it could take a half-hour to reach the car, in which case we'd miss the train by fifteen minutes. The situation required desperate measures. *"Alors,* Melanie!" I called out. *"Halte!* I'm getting a redcap." And I waved to a porter, who parted the throngs with his baggage cart so we could follow in his wake. We ran through the crowds along the endless train. The massive engines began hissing. *"Numéro 58?"* the porter finally called out from the platform where the car should have been. *"Ça n'existe pas. Quand même, mesdemoiselles,"* he shouted, hurling the bags onto the nearest car, *"allez-y."*

I quickly jumped on the steps and turned to grab Melanie, who wavered on her high heels, and pulled her aboard just as the last blast of steam released the brakes. I remember how she stood there at the front end of the car, just blinking. "But what is this?" she finally said. I looked around. My eyes took in a sea of luggage—trunks, bags, skis, backpacks—but no seats. *"Alors,"* a voice called out to us from a far corner, *"venez ici."* Mel looked at me hesitatingly, as if for reassurance, then began making her way across the car on her treacherous spikes.

I made out four other young people who were sitting, more or less precariously, on pieces of luggage. They began speaking all at once. "The government, fraudulent bastards, sold us all tickets on a student car that doesn't exist. Pigheaded capitalists. Arrogant monsters. Dared to put us with the baggage. Wait until the student union hears about this." I felt heavy in my coat and boots and struggled just to keep standing while the car lurched. Or maybe I was just burdened by a strain of latent American practicality. *"Eh bien,"* I suggested all too breezily, "Couldn't we just get off at the next station and complain. Insist on our rights?"

"Impossible!" came the collective reply. "That would be seen as negotiating," one voice shouted. "It just plays into their hands to negotiate."

"Right," another said, in a voice that sounded familiar. "Besides, if we get off, they'll just think up ways to detain us. Better to plan a strike."

This certainly sounded familiar, and I bent to look more closely in the dim light to see if I could make out the speaker's face. I couldn't believe it. *"Yves?"*

By then Mel was pulling me back, tugging on my coat. "We *can't* get off and be late," she whispered, looking terrified. "We've *got* to be on time."

I saw then the extent of Mel's fear, of her determination, of her hope. "I understand the situation," I muttered, mostly to myself. "This is it then." And we sat momentarily on the edge of a large trunk, while Yves, also astonished, struggled to his feet to greet us.

"But this is unbelievable! And how far do you go? I myself go only to Bar-le-Duc to visit family for the holidays. But Ivan, have you seen him?" Ivan, he informed us, should have also been on the student car, heading for Germany. "But nobody has seen him." He shrugged.

I braced myself, then blurted "And Roland?" hoping of course to learn how my abrupt departure had affected him. "Did you by chance see him before leaving?"

"*Mais oui.* He came with me to the train. Did you not speak with him? I think he was going directly to find you, to invite you south for the holidays."

The train had by now long since left the station and my heart with it. Roland's news and the lost prospect of a warm Christmas by a friendly hearth only added to the fury of the cold as the wheels spun out screeching over the frozen tracks. Pelting snow assaulted the few dim windows and air whipped through cracks in the unsealed freight car, bringing in little jets of cutting ice. I sank to the floor with the others, on a created nest behind a barricade of trunks, as if a wall of luggage could protect us from the cold.

"Fraudulent bastards," I said, meaning everything, and accepted a swallow of wine from a bottle making the rounds. Melanie sank down too, and then we both just retreated into private thoughts over the clacking of the wheels and the high-pitched tearing of the wind, which was modulated, but not silenced, by the soft sounds of singing in French. I reached into my bag to pull out some extra clothes and passed them to Melanie. *They're against us too,* that was the refrain in Melanie's voice that kept playing in my head. Then I fell asleep.

The dreams seemed to roll with the turning of the wheels. A day at la Maison where the sky lapped down around the house in ever deeper waves of blue. The colors of Rimbaud's sail. Then these were shut down by the opaque eyes of Mel's mother, sweeping into la Maison on Parents' Day, that cucumber linen suit and those alligator shoes. She dazzled like a flare. That little arc she made, sweeping around to greet Hans, who looked as small and diminished as Melanie herself, saying once again, smiling, "Marvelous. And Belgium's such a sweet little country…"

The train slowed as the snow mounted on the tracks, changing rhythm enough to turn me in my cold sleep. Mrs. Hart faded, and I was confronted by Roland's dark eyes, inviting, desirous, gazing over Christmas candles. I sat up abruptly, heart thundering, to greet the face staring back at me in the dark and frozen window. Desire and illusion were enough to keep me from realizing, for a few moments, how cold I was. But then the train lurched, and I remembered.

"Nancy, Nancy," someone was bellowing into a garbled loudspeaker, followed by that screech and scrape of ice to announce the train's arrival in the station. I saw Yves jump off and breathed in a sharp pang of regret realizing that this was his stop, followed by a breath of relief that a parade of strikers didn't trail him. Then I noticed Melanie. Alarmingly, she had turned slightly purple and seemed to be praying.

"Mel," I tried shaking her, as if she had fallen into a trance. "Melanie," my own teeth were chattering so I know I was very clear. "You okay?"

Then her lashes, which had been closed tight, pushed open with effort, rather like sweepers trying to push back snow. *"Comment?"* she said. But before she got any farther, this bundled white figure climbed aboard, like a hoary snowman swathed in frost. "So you are here!" he called out in English.

Ivan! He squatted right down there with us, shaking off his outer layer of snow like a dog, calling out cheery greetings to everyone, who by this time were all pretty much sunk in misery or sleep.

"Jesus, Ivan," I said, "you have this way of turning up with the worst weather. So where—?" But he cut right across my ill-formed question and Melanie's half-thawed, questioning silence. "Been in the boxcar next door, couldn't believe what a student ticket was going to buy me."

"Fraudulent bastards," I said, trying out my phrase again, trying to find the right rhythm to express the outrage I knew Ivan felt. "Can you believe this? Yves says striking is the only answer."

"Wonderful, a transforming experience," Ivan was saying, seeming not to have heard. "Perfect. Ride into the heart of evil on a boxcar. Freeze. Feel the Nazi presence…"

Mel listened with her jaw half dropped. She knew, I suppose, he was speaking history, one of the things she was supposed to be learning. But studying facts was one thing, absorbing the marrow of collective experience was another. It seemed she could barely get a grip on her own. She began babbling some sort of catechism.

"What *are* you doing?" I asked irritably.

"Practicing subjunctives," Mel answered.

"Now? For exams?"

"No, not for exams. But it's terribly, terribly important not to make a mistake in subjunctives."

"You mean," I said slowly, trying to get the drift, "you mean so people won't think you're some dumb American or something?"

"I guess you could say that."

Perhaps Mel managed a faint smile, but if so, I didn't see it. What I finally did see was the outline of Melanie's plan. It was as though there, in her mind, a complex scene was unfolding and this was the final rehearsal. If the Bouchers were to catch her in some mistake, some fatal gaucherie, the curtain would ring down on her whole drama. Or maybe her whole life.

"So J.J., your *grand-mère* is French, right? What do you think? Do you think you should take your gloves off when you shake hands—Mother always said to—but in Paris, I've noticed, they don't."

"Keep them on by all means. Otherwise you'll die of frostbite."

She ignored the edge in my voice. "How about shaking hands in the morning, and kissing people even at home for greeting, what do you think?"

"Oh yes, kiss people. Handsome men especially, as much as possible. Others, three times on the cheek, like stations of the cross."

I reached into my bag to extract more clothing. We'd already put on sweaters beneath our coats, and Melanie's high heels, I noticed, had been replaced with fuzzy pink slippers. Now I dug for anything—mufflers, extra socks, a bathrobe—and Mel put on more layers without breaking her line of questioning. "I'm already pretty good about not eating American. You don't still, do you, crossing over the fork and knife? But I'm wondering about bread. Putting it right on the table seems so—"

"For God's sake, Mel!" I finally gave into my exasperation, exhaling so hard I made a telltale of frosted breath. Melanie retreated back to her subjunctives.

There was nothing more to do but lean against the frozen siding, wishing for sleep again, or if not that, at least fire. I squinted into the dark, trying to make out the others all huddled together, shivering and silent over the monotonous clicking of the wheels. Between rotations all I could hear were their breaths, heavy and lingering. Only Ivan, who had chipped some ice from the nearest window to look out at the frozen world, appeared serene.

"That I could; that you could, that he could…" Melanie was intoning.

"Now we know what it is like," Ivan was saying.

"That we could; that you could; that they could…"

"The difference of course, is that this is a pilgrimage, not a destiny, and at the end of the night, we can get off and walk away. We can't ride this to the end."

Yes, you are right, I agreed quietly to myself. At least I longed for history, even if I didn't own it. Yet Melanie, who codified the fears of one small life as she ran over the scales of grammar, was right too. *He/she/it might.*

They're against us too. That was the phrase which reverberated for a long time in that place between sleep and waking, when I tried to make sense of that impossible night and the days that followed. First, I tried to grasp who, exactly, *they* were, for surely some larger force than the suspicious and haughty Boucher family was required to orchestrate such a disaster.

What malicious gods were busily at work, I wondered, to turn the last stretch of that malevolent ride so cold that our outer clothes froze onto the boxcar siding, making it a struggle just to tear ourselves free? And what perverse little devil turned Ivan away from his metaphysical musings on evil back to his less original, if more vocal, neo-revolutionary self, who at the eleventh hour convinced the others to stage a protest after all? And why did I not see it coming, and at least threaten to kill him?

I got nowhere closer to answers than Jocelyn did during her phase of spiritual wanderlust, and accomplished nothing except to exhaust myself with speculation and recrimination. I fell back on my usual means of consolation—simply trying to order the facts as they happened in my mind, then rewriting my notes—but this failed too. Finally I took refuge in imagining a different ending. In a kinder world, I speculated, the Bouchers might not have met the train. Or at least they might have had the good grace to be late. Just a half-hour in that bitter dawn, in which Melanie could have thawed, found her tongue again, felt her feet, and fit them back into those slender heels, so little as that might have saved her.

But fiction couldn't save us; it was as it was. With the first slit of light, the Bouchers were there, already pacing the Strasbourg station, wrapped in lamb's wool and furs, their doubts firmly in place. I imagine they thought they had feared the worst—I mean, *une petite américaine*, what could be worse than that? But in reality, they hadn't begun to foresee what was coming. First Ivan, wrapped like an escapee from a winter scene in a Tolstoy novel, jumping down, shouting incomprehensibly. Next, the ragtag band of rowdy protestors, equally unshaven, disheveled and appalling, shouting slogans about *Capitalist Pigs*. Melanie followed. The image of her tumbling frosty and surreal out of that baggage car could never be erased, even with a lifetime of civilized behavior.

When she finally stood in front of Monsieur and Madame Boucher, she could only tremble. On her feet were vile pink slippers. And though, like a coach, I stood strong behind her, doing my best to get her to say her memorized opening lines, Melanie held her ground in silence. The perfect subjunctives remained inside, frozen shut.

It was as if those first few minutes with the Bouchers marked the beginning of a script that Mel was destined to adhere to. Her failure to deliver her prepared greeting was followed by an agonizing silence in the silver Mercedes that took us back to their large, excruciatingly neat house. Foolishly, I attempted to cover it up with meaningless chatter. Then, when Mel thawed out enough to try to speak, she began making mistakes that I had never heard her make before, and like an anxious mother hen, I would try to nudge her toward a correction.

"J'étais terriblement froide," she blurted out, as if they didn't know she had been very cold.

"Oh, c'est vrai," I replied, *"elle avait très grand froide, et moi aussi."*

Soon, it was not only her French that slipped, but things so inbred in Melanie that I imagined them to be part of her. When we sat down to dine at the large, formal table, she fumbled by picking up the wrong fork, making noises with her soup, and placing her bread on the dinner plate. I kicked her under the table and made a desperate pantomime, but too late. Later, she tripped on the edge of the carpet in the darkened drawing room, and nearly fell onto Madame Boucher who was already seated on the couch. By the time Monsieur Boucher, a music critic, began a discussion of great German composers—a subject Melanie had been thoroughly schooled in by Hans himself—and she chimed in by mixing up Schubert and Schumann, I realized there were no fixes for this disaster.

But I realized something else, too. For the first time I saw Melanie operate outside the programmed, nearly automatic behavior she had been so thoroughly schooled in. Maybe it was the first time she ever had stepped beyond the bounds of her upbringing. Although it was painful to watch her fall so badly, there was also an aspect to her large gestures, her freeform sentences, her clumsy stride that hinted at liberation. I believe I glimpsed a wholly different person who had been for too long trapped inside the confines of a propriety that had grown too small for her.

As soon as we left the Bouchers and made our snowy way back to Paris in a proper passenger car, the old Melanie reemerged. It was only later she concluded that in some subterranean way, the rebuff by Hans's parents fulfilled her expectations—and drew the two of them closer together. "We are bound tighter by this circle of resistance all around," she wrote in her journal. She noted, too, the perversity of the situation, "how much, in their mutual disdain for their 'wrongheaded' children, the Bouchers and Mother and Dad would probably admire each other."

I suspect the only consolation she found after the Black Christmas (my term) was to slip under the arc of cold things and keep her own stillness. Maybe she realized that was what Jocelyn had been doing, after all, when she pushed through great snowbanks to sit frozen in Saint-Étienne-du-Mont. In any event, I know that Melanie found her only moment of solace in Basel when she'd slipped alone into the cathedral and for the first time felt a shiver that wasn't from cold. "Beneath the red walls and soaring towers, I bathed in the pure winter light through ancient glass, and mostly the music that sounded in my ears, Hans's violin," that was where she found sanctuary. And there, the words from her only true scripture, Pascal's *Pensées*, shone with celestial beauty. *"Le silence éternel des espaces infinies m'effraie,"* she wrote on the top of each page of the Basel diaries.

Mel, the eternal silence of infinite space frightens me, too.

Chapter 15

It was, they said, the coldest winter in Europe for centuries. Ice made a solid landmass where water had made divisions. Snow became a new solid force to reckon with, and its weight broke confidence in human durability as it broke eternal monuments. I read in *Le Monde* that the Coliseum in Rome cracked for the first time in a thousand years. In fact, all the papers and airwaves were full of astonishing statistics—of temperature, of accumulations, of ravage. And in case I had missed the real story, Ivan cheerfully translated these for me from the abstract into particles per square inch of human misery. He emphasized that which was close at hand: "Think of those poor bastards, the *pieds noirs*, arriving from the heat of Africa into the arctic chill of France." Of course he meant more than the weather, but he did always seem to mention the world's "poor bastards" whenever I moaned about the cold.

But for Jocelyn, it was different. She seemed as inured to Ivan's dark view as she was to the misery of the cold itself. She took the statistics head on. She studied and memorized them, just as she memorized facts of history and dates, those scaffoldings that supported epochs of government, art, literature, and theater. She accumulated these with ease. What was more difficult to grasp was the context, seeing how one thing flowed from another. History itself.

Once while I was sitting on my throne surrounded by books, she cried out accusingly at some obscure observation I made. "The thing is, J.J., for some reason, you get this stuff. Nobody else will, except types like Ivan, get this stuff." But the fact was, I was slower and less agile than she at retaining large amounts of information (hence my overflowing and disorderly files) which she memorized like scripts. The main difference lay here: I cared how all the facts fit—I wanted a story line—however inept I was at putting it together; she didn't. It could have been another rift between us, as the campaign to ingest huge amounts of material intensified with the approach of term exams after the holidays and spilled over to the misery of winter, but our own thaw held. Still, the pain of thinking about California, lost warmth and home, seemed to soften for her by repeating a litany of facts about winter, while with each one I felt a new blast of ice wind.

Perhaps she was reciting some winter facts to herself as she stepped into the Rue Cujas going toward the Pantheon. I'm guessing now, for I have only Melanie's story, reconstructed from journals, to go by. But when Mel saw Jocelyn, she couldn't tell what was going on in Jo's mind as she headed into the wind. She did call out, "Jocelyn, Jo, *halte*!" hoping to get her attention, to get her to stop for a coffee, still hoping for an explanation of her strange disappearance before the promised, ill-fated, Christmas trip. But Jocelyn, who didn't hear, kept going. And Mel followed her.

When Jocelyn, after rounding the square where the classic dome of the Pantheon shone in the snow, just kept going, Mel stopped calling to her. Intrigued, she followed, placing her feet in the newly made tracks. They took her to the steps of Saint-Étienne-du-Mont, a church of late gothic flamboyance on Place Sainte-Geneviève. Inside the freezing nave, lit only by a few flickering candles, she saw Jocelyn sitting, as if entranced, before the roodscreen. Melanie did not know what to make of this sight of her friend, once so lustily glamorous, effortlessly popular, glitteringly brilliant. "She seemed so, I don't know, so thin, so elusive, so…" Mel didn't finish the thought. But she certainly saw Jocelyn sitting prayerfully in a Catholic shrine. "What was she doing there? What was she seeing in that place that I could not? I wanted to ask, but knew I couldn't. I mean I could have interrupted her, but she couldn't just then have told me anything I wanted to know." Melanie quietly slipped away.

In truth, Jocelyn could not have retraced, exactly, the circuitous route that had brought her to Saint-Étienne-du-Mont, most sacred shrine of Saint Geneviève. It had been her own private pilgrimage, begun at the moment when she'd decided, under the power of Alain Saint-George's persuasion, to cast off the Mormon façade. By then, early that brittle winter, she had walked Paris enough to understand its most fundamental lesson, which she pronounced to me herself: "Paris, you know, is untainted by any trace of Protestantism." I took that to mean unfettered by any heart-closed denial of the world, of any petty-minded work ethic.

It was soon after she grasped this idea that she appeared to stop her manic wanderings, her enforced starvation. She was determined, for a time, to study, to eat, to have her infamous affair. "I just want a normal life," she would say in those days, sighing, and trying visibly not to look at the growing stack of letters from Madge and Samuel.

But then the walks began again. They took on an air of purpose, destination, feverish quest. My guess was that since the normal, everyday life, *la vie quotidienne*, as it was put so poetically in French, had failed again, she went in search of the holy. And in her mind, the neoclassical or modern periods were too closely associated with the secular—or worse, were tainted by politics. That was how she worked her way back to the gothic and its edifices of glory. Notre Dame and its splendid gargoyles, Sainte-Chapelle and its miraculous light through glass. Saint-Séverin, Saint-Julien-le-Pauvre, the chapel at Cluny. One by one, she stalked the holy sites of medieval Paris through the late and endless winter. It was from this second wave of wanderings that she discovered another fundamental Parisian truth: that the spirit of Paris soared, like delicate gothic arches, with sensuality, wit, grace.

Revealing this discovery, she said: "It was of course Alain who told me, 'You know, my heart, that in French, mind and spirit, both found in the word *esprit*, cannot be separated.' And it was in Notre Dame, looking at the grotesque figures and the sublime ones next to them all carved into columns and figures, that I understood what he meant."

Of course, it was Alain, too, who had propelled her into the streets again.

How everything had shifted for the two of them with Jocelyn's soft knock on the huge oak door, its polished brass plate with the name *Prof. Alain Saint-Georges* inscribed in rich gothic script. I imagine she felt its intended weight and venerability when she placed her cool hand on the ornate door handle, and stood without breathing during the long pause before Alain's voice finally called out, "Yes, who's there?" How she had replied only, *"moi."*

In less than an instant, Alain yanked open the door, his eyes wide and for once without their protective glasses, his face flushed, like a pleased and lustful schoolboy. "He said, *'Mon dieu…* It is you after all. I thought… but Jocelyn, please come in.'" She recited this in monotone, as if replaying a sound recording in which all the highs and lows had been flattened out.

But I was able to fill in. The sound of her heart pounding as she slowly took it all in—the high ceiling and tall window, the shelves reaching the length of three walls crammed with books. The large desk covered with papers, books, folders, and its old-fashioned black telephone. His well-tailored jacket thrown over an antique desk chair fitted with rollers. "It was, well, charming, and impressive too, just like Alain was. I noticed, funny the things you notice, during that first minute he was trying to smooth down his hair, like a boy.

"He was also trying to make small talk while he was fumbling inside this bureau with a sliding door, pulling out a bottle of cognac and two small glasses. 'If I'd only known, *chérie…*' he kept saying."

She slid out of her coat, and leaned into a love seat where he sat next to her. An empire thing no doubt with scuffed lion claws, and she as exotic as an Egyptian creature herself in that green wool dress that fit her like a second skin and made her eyes look green, which is why she chose it.

"I felt strangely calm," she said, "as though having made the decision to, you know, do it, I could just surrender with a kind of detachment. 'I saw your press interview,' I told him. 'You were very persuasive. All those references to philosophers and dialectic materialism in the American context. You got it all so right.'"

I imagine Jocelyn said this to him, as she did to me, without any hint of irony. Perhaps that's why he chose to play the scene straight, handing her a cognac, touching her glass, and muttering something about the deep understanding that could only come after years of study, but then, the public could expect nothing less of "the number-one French expert on American affairs." And no doubt caught up in the fervor of his unique qualifications, he began at that moment to caress her.

"I think it was the setting," she said, leaving out the details of how Alain's mouth followed his hands down her long torso. It seemed clear she hadn't much thought beyond the moment of saying *yes, Alain, I will yes I will yes*. "But I don't know, it seemed a bit tawdry, a bit ordinary to just, you know, consummate everything right there in his office on that worn-out love seat." She didn't add that it was hard to see how this was different from any student throwing herself at any middle-aged professor, and that she needed this to be *special*. She didn't have to say how she pushed him off, saying, "*Ça suffit*, Alain. Enough. Of course, I agree with you, it is inevitable we should become lovers. But here…?"

It is amusing to picture what Jocelyn described next, Alain straightening himself, smoothing back his hair, taking charge again as a man of the world. "'Of course not here, *chérie*. I have this little place, a discreet hotel…more suitable for you'—he actually said this, if you can believe it—'more suitable for you to become the woman you are destined to be.' And oh, God, J.J., for a whole minute I actually believed it. Then, of course..."

Then, of course, it is easy to see how she played the part. Standing too, and rearranging herself, smoothing the sleek green dress. Glancing around the Great Man's office with a certain affection, taking it in to remember precisely because it was, was it not, the place where she'd sampled the hors d'oeuvres of her first great lovemaking. Then the casual stroll to the other side of the desk to glance out the window, and looking back, seeing, next to the ancient telephone, the picture. The pretty dark-haired young woman holding a small child.

"And who is that?" Jocelyn's voice asked dreamily, almost detached.

"Ah, my wife and daughter," Alain's voice equally detached. "Sometime ago."

The words raked her like a tongue of fire. I can imagine the collage of images—Alain on television, in the papers, standing in front of the Hall Richelieu of the Sorbonne, those nights in cafés, restaurants, and theaters with friends in deep conversation, and she had not once thought what other life he might have. She had not even thought where, exactly, he might live.

All that rushed through her before she sputtered out, "You're married?" hitting the notes of her high register, making it sound like the accusation it was.

"'But of course,' he answered. 'What did you imagine?'"

"What did I imagine?" For the first time in this recitation, Jocelyn looked at me, her blank eyes seeming to reflect only her inflamed cheeks. "I hadn't imagined anything, at least nothing like that..." and I could just see her turning from him, from the picture, gasping a little while he adjusted his tie and put on his coat. But I'm certain when the number-one French expert on American affairs faced Jocelyn next, he was shocked. For surely he had not expected the beautiful Jocelyn, a *vedette* truly, a star worthy of Hollywood, to stand before him red-faced and shaking with tears.

"He was so clueless. Can you believe he said something dumb like, '*Ah, chérie,* but what is the matter?' As if he didn't know what the matter was.

"Then I screamed at him: 'A wife and child? How could you?'

"So you know what he answered? This is a direct quote: 'Yes, my heart, but what has that to do with us? With anything?'

"I think I screamed again, and then my voice became calm, controlled. 'What kind of monster are you?' I said. 'Or what do you think I am? I'm a virgin'—I said it outright, J.J.—'I have morals. I mean I can't just *betray*…'

"But he just sort of stiffened into this huffy indignation, and he actually said, '*Oh là là, chérie,* I thought you had learned something from me, something about yourself, the true and sensual nature of a beautiful woman. This Puritanism, you know, doesn't become you…' By then, of course, I had slammed the door."

Yes, I nodded. Of course. I could hear the word *betray* hanging in the air after her departure, the word between them, hear it echoing in her footsteps as she ran down the corridor and into the courtyard of the Sorbonne. It would play over and over in her head as she told herself she didn't have it in her to betray that poor woman and the little girl. The one in the photo who was so like her small self with Madge, who had wept when the invisible professor at UCLA had gone back to his wife. But I'm sure she did not let the word so far into her consciousness that she saw its other meaning: that the deeper betrayal was to her own ego, which could not stand the idea of being the other woman.

And Alain? The door slammed so thoroughly that I don't remember ever hearing her mention him again for months, so I was on my own to speculate how the professor was in the wake of her departure. I can imagine him, slumped and stunned on that love seat where Jocelyn had so surprisingly put herself in his grasp, and more surprisingly retreated. It would be hard, of course, for him to admit that her behavior completely baffled him. To do so would mean admitting he hadn't understood her as a woman, something no Frenchman, no true Parisian, could readily concede. On the other hand, to admit he hadn't understood her as a young American, he could hardly concede either, being a world-class expert on Americans.

"Damned American bitch!" That is what I guess he would have said to himself in consolation. And then, from what I came to learn of the man, I believe he next would have turned himself to address the most puzzling thing she'd said to him in her outburst.

"A virgin? Surely a girl who tells such lies could never be trusted."

I believe that if, on that frigid afternoon in Saint-Étienne-du-Mont, Melanie had interrupted Jocelyn's solitude, if she had penetrated her icy aura of mystery, Mel would have learned as much about the affair with Alain Saint-Georges as I did, as much as Jocelyn knew herself. For the rest of Mel's questions, it is difficult to know how much would have been revealed about the fervent haunting of gothic spaces, the worshipful hours spent at the shrine of Saint Geneviève, the haunted walking she had resumed after her debacle with France's greatest expert on American affairs. There was no way Melanie could see the truth: Jocelyn had never been as miserable as she was at that moment, midwinter in Paris.

That much I know for fact. The rest—how Jo got there—I can only surmise. Casting off the Mormon trappings, had, for sure, been liberating. She even seemed to enjoy having a glass of wine with me, or taking a long, sensuous draw on a cigarette in a café, but—and here's the thing—if hedonistic discovery was the real lesson to be learned from Alain, she had failed miserably. Then she tried the gathering in of atmosphere, of the rose light in the great gothic houses of worship. The exercise intrigued, but eventually did not nourish her.

She spoke once of her frustration with the whole image of Notre Dame, the Virgin Mary, Mother of God. It was, she admitted, a better thing than those stern patriarchs of her recent past, but still cold comfort. "I don't actually get this Mary thing, do you? Here she is worshipped, holy, maternal, the whole bit, but I can't *grasp* her. It's like a role that's been overplayed so much it has no definition. And that's without even getting into the whole virgin birth thing, which is, when you think about it, pretty weird." Then taking a theological turn, she concluded, "They say this whole Mary-Jesus thing is about transformation and being *transsubstantial*. But it's only insubstantial, if you ask me."

It was by chance that she had entered Saint-Étienne-du-Mont, seeking shelter one cold afternoon, and there discovered the shrine of Saint Geneviève. The bond was instant. Had she not already picked her out by running her finger randomly down an index? She remembered the eerie night of the *bal masqué*—it seemed a lifetime ago—and realized she had chosen her patron saint.

With her teeth chattering, she was trying hard to concentrate on that connection in the freezing nave while Melanie slipped out unseen. And for once, perhaps history as I saw it made some sense to her.

When she talked about Saint Geneviève, it was with a kind of historical awe. Her saint had, of course (Jo knew the facts), a calling to the holy, but she had found it in this world. Her saint had done the hardest, the most admirable, thing: she had conquered fear. Fearless, Jocelyn's personal saint had led her little band to stand up to Attila the Hun (a character probably even more odious than Alain Saint-Georges), as later she would stand up to the marauding Franks. Mostly, her saint, who had once escaped invaders to bring back a barge from Champagne filled with food and drink, knew where she belonged. "Her place on earth was Paris," Jocelyn explained. "In a way, she was Paris." That idea, I knew, held for Jocelyn a kind of magic power.

Chapter 16

A pitiful willingness to go through the torture of actually preparing for the obvious insanity of examinations in the French university system was one thing Mel and I had in common. Roommates who flamboyantly refused to do this was another. For hours, we would sit on those Louis XV reproductions with red seats, drinking tea in the gray light filtered by falling snow. There was a comfort in the quiet back and forth of dates, facts, styles, points of grammar and literary criticism, which allowed us to avoid more painful, personal inquiry.

Paris in January. The anxiety of the coming exams only mounted as Melanie waited for me to arrive, half fearful that I wouldn't.

I imagine her pressing her forehead against the cold glass, waiting for me to press the bell, trying to stave off the panic with her frantically scanning eyes. Then I rang and entered the room and mumbled greetings, saying something lame, like "Thank God we can relax today and just share notes. There's plenty of time to be nervous later when exam week hits."

"Care for tea?" she asked, as we approached the dining room table to settle in.

For Melanie, it was discipline that, I believe, made her feel closer, for the moment, to Hans. European culture was, after all, his territory. But for me, whenever my attention waned, Guy appeared in my mind like a ghost. Guy, I knew, would devour this exercise, leaping at the opportunity to feed his rapacious appetite for facts about the underpinnings of human society and its discontents. Strange to realize, I didn't think of Roland, who embodied this history, lived, imbibed, and exhaled it, yet was completely indifferent to its unfolding. Perhaps that was the Old-World meaning of entitlement, and why we Americans, who could never thus be entitled, were instead restless.

As our heads bent toward our notebooks in the waning winter light, there was a turning of the key in the door, a loud slamming, and a second of silence that hovered over the faux Louis XV furniture with gilt trim, the heavy lamp shades, and the fake Persian rug. Then it shattered for good. Evelyn was home.

"Mail from lover boy," she shouted from the vestibule. "God, I made it to only one art practicum in the Louvre and I'm just pooped. Love those Renaissance nudes though. But should've gotten to bed—well hello." She spied me, then swooped into the living room, shaking her hair out from an angola knit cap. "*Tiens!* If it isn't. So what are you doing here?" She glanced at the table covered with books and notebooks, shook her head again, then pronounced: "Oh shit, you too, J.J.?"

I knew then that however futile studying might prove, Evelyn had decided to take a different path. By the time the first serious snows fell, she had abandoned all pretense of taking her classes seriously.

Later, on the Métro, tunneling through the dark earth on her way to exams at the Sorbonne, one of the thoughts buzzing through Melanie's mind must have been of Hans.

For once she was glad he was not physically with her, for she felt literally cursed—that funny term, she wrote, her mother always used. Often her period was late, or too light to notice. Once or twice, though, she'd been rocked by earthquakes, with rhythmic shudderings and showers of pain hitting her like falling rocks. Then more than ever, she had loved the dark, wanting only to curl herself into a fetal ball and crawl into another womb. Mrs. Hart had been efficient at such times, offering tea and a heating pad and firmly closing the door so she could rest. "'It happens to everyone, even to me once in a blue moon,'" is the way Mel remembered her mother's words.

She wondered, too, why she couldn't tell her father, who was a doctor after all and might have given her something for pain. But he was usually not there. Or if there, not to be bothered. Or, she quickly learned, if he were bothered, it had best be only about something worthwhile. That did not include a silly child moaning about a lost dog, a bad school report, a sprained ankle, nor a young woman bent double with cramps. Not the sort of thing one spoke to one's father about anyway, even if he *was* a doctor.

Better, she concluded, not to have Hans here to see her like this, white as death and holding herself. Better to be underground, hearing the rackety cars of the old train clack over the tracks reaching all the way inside the center of the city. Better to breath deeply like Eve had said, adding: "Christ girl, you've got it so bad it looks like labor." And better pray the "medicine" Edith poured down her, the two of them clucking over her like a pair of wet nurses, got to work soon. She leaned back against the glass door feeling light-headed.

Straight shots of brandy. Evelyn had told me about this herself, laughing, long before I had Melanie's own account in hand. "Maybe I was just getting drunk," she speculated. Maybe indeed. But whatever state of reverie she'd fallen into, no doubt the last ordeal of exams, the writtens, began to pass before her like flashes of life before the dying. We had suffered through that exquisite torture chamber together. The examination hall, a medieval fortress barred at the windows. The proctors, the prison guards keeping students chained to their desks. The flu epidemic, hand after hand waving frantically for permission to stand, to use the rest rooms. Permission denied, unless a proctor felt like accompanying the test-taker. The retching and vomiting in the aisles. It might have been the passage on the *Jeanne d'Arc* all over again but for the diabolical questions. Comparative French constitutions. The importance of iron grillwork as an art form in Paris. And the *coup de grâce*, the ultimate French form of torture by the Academy, dictation. Dictation with every known perversion of grammar they'd ever come up with. Dictation to die from. Could have died, too, Mel admitted after it was over, leaning back with her eyes closed, except for that roll of the dice, that passage by Pascal. *A roll of the dice for God.*

But there, feeling herself in the rock and rhythm of the train, she opened her eyes for good. The pain had almost subsided. Then she went light and numb and maybe a tad giddy. She looked in her satchel for a last glance at her notes and saw the little flask of brandy Eve had stuck in there, just in case, she said.

Inside the Sorbonne, the first thing Melanie remembered was her shoes. She pulled a pair of navy blue heels from her bag, traded them for her boots, and straightened her wool suit. I watched her do this near the front of the line that formed down the hall, and waved to get her attention. But her number was before mine and her vision was too blurred to focus that far. She didn't notice Gracie and Jocelyn either, further back in the line, nor the swarm of other students, each holding admission numbers and chatting nervously in a dozen languages. Mel appeared to hear only herself, that voice inside her head reciting its strange jumble of facts, perhaps to the strains of Hans's violin. Before entering the actual exam room, where she would face the two inquisitors—one male and one female, we'd been told—she slipped out of her coat. She was stopped briefly by a young woman on her way out, a German, who passed down the line saying conspiratorially, "Beware of the woman."

By the time Melanie got close to the door, I imagine she felt a twinge in her gut again. So she took another swig, followed by another, of brandy. She seemed beyond reach—of pain, of fear, of caring about the impression she made as a slender young blonde with legs, expensive clothes, and an uncharacteristic swagger.

But it's easy (because I was there, because I have Melanie's journals) to reconstruct what happened behind that door once she closed it behind her. For openers, Monsieur le Professeur Lapierre noticed everything and found her a neat little package, nicely shaped, appealing. Something earnest, shy, maybe even classy about her, though she was an American. Certainly not like that Teutonic piece of work who'd just passed through speaking French with the cadences of a storm trooper.

Madame le Professeur Grimbaud noticed too. How could she not? Another young foreign sexpot, having a fling in Paris on Daddy's money, without a fact or thought, or possibly even a brain in her head. Bad enough stupid foreigners of the male persuasion passed through the Sorbonne devaluing the diploma. They might amount to something somewhere, but these girls! They got by because her colleagues were such fools, they winked at the nubile charmers and passed them, ignoring the fact that they were complete idiots. Like that Brunhilda horror who had just gone through, and Lapierre giving her such high marks in physical geography that she was impossible to fail.

Applied female physical geography, that was his real specialty. Well, he wouldn't get away with it this time.

Monsieur le Professeur began fingering his soft brown mustache and coughing by way of preparation. A trim, mild-appearing man in early middle age, he looked up at one with sad brown eyes. At that moment they focused on the little blonde standing stiff as a soldier in front of them. *Pity*, he was thinking, not knowing quite what he pitied. *"Mademoiselle,"* he began gently, trying to make her less ill at ease. "Let us begin with physical geography. Can you please explain the importance of the Massif Central—" Melanie leapt in there, in the heart of France, and wound her way around it, hardly needing a prompt from her interlocutor. Moving down the Rhône to the south, she wandered the Atlantic Coast and the Loire, then approaching the harsher east on the way to Strasbourg, she loosened. First her stance, the high heels, and slim ankles moving apart, then back and forth, accommodating her sway. Her right hand began moving lightly, lyrically over the large brass buttons down the front of her suit, as though, with unconscious sensuality, she were calling the answers up from herself. Then her French, breaking the bounds of correctness, rushed forth with lightly accented fluid beauty.

Lapierre's territory expanded: history, art, philosophy. "The dates, *mademoiselle*, what do the dates 800 and 1800 have in common?"

Melanie rolled through the answers with intelligent assurance, as Grimbaud grew increasingly agitated. As unconsciously as Melanie was touching her buttons, she began stroking her mustache, her small black eyes boring into Melanie. Sex, she thought. Sex, that was all these young flim-flams had going for them. Look at this one, dressed for a shopping trip on Rue de Rivoli. True, her answers weren't as appalling as some of the others' had been, but still a woman like that existed merely to devalue a woman like herself, a true intellectual, an equal of men, a woman of substance.

"Mademoiselle," she said with an abrupt jerk, the way one would pull in a fish on the line. "Now it is time to turn to grammatical matters. Explain to me the *conditionnel, le passé antérieur, le plus-que-parfaits."*

Melanie, resuming her stiff posture, redirected her attention to Madame le Professeur Grimbaud, standing with her weight firmly on her heels. The earlier fumes of brandy fog were giving way to a kind of brazen clarity. For once, Melanie could see herself clearly—as well as Madame le Professeur—and knew that Madame le Professeur had just challenged her as one would challenge a man to a duel. Melanie was amused and at last most unafraid. Perhaps as a consequence, she would not be tripped up. Melanie began spitting out perfect subjunctives.

Grimbaud maneuvered skillfully before reaching for her *pièce de résistance,* the *explication du texte,* a diabolic piece of French torture devised by centuries of sadists, this anatomical deconstruction of a text's meaning. All students, even the French, quivered when forced to take a surgical knife to the sacred anatomy of French language structure.

But Melanie dug in, prepared to stand her ground as a passage from de Montesquieu's *Lettres Persanes* was thrust in front of her. Boosted by her brandy-enhanced confidence, and knowing that for some hapless students heads roll at that very moment because they couldn't begin to guess what they were reading, she began loudly: *"Ah bon, Les Lettres Persanes.* This passage demonstrates how these Persians, strangers in Paris, examine and satirize French society. In the eighteenth century."

"And why is it these Persians are writing in French, satirizing the manners of Paris?"

"Well, of course it is de Montesquieu's method," Melanie replied, "the guise of innocence that allows him to speak clearly."

"And who is de Montesquieu?" Grimbaud now, head slightly cocked like a fat bird, concealed her strike.

"But the author, *madame,*" Melanie answered blinking, flushing with agitation.

Grimbaud was upright now, spitting her words. "Ah. First you say these Persians are speaking. Then you say de Montesquieu. I suggest that *mademoiselle* should decide just whom she is talking about. And then we will discuss by what right and means one should critique French civilization."

"Alors," Lapierre broke in at last, flushed. "It's perfectly clear she knows…"

Grimbaud, brushing him aside, continued. "So why does he criticize French manners?"

"I suppose, *madame*, because he found them funny."

"Who?"

"De Montesquieu," Melanie now fairly shouted.

"A moment ago you said this Persian found them funny, being strange to France. Now you say de Montesquieu. Do you find him strange to France too? Or is it that all strangers to France cannot understand that which is French?" Grimbaud was now shouting too. "Is that the joke, *mademoiselle*, and foreigners just can't get it?"

Lapierre gasped, while Melanie stood silent, rigid again, clutching her sides. He began hesitantly, as broadsided as she at this assault and not knowing what to do to salvage the situation, only knowing that he must do something. "Ahem, *bien*, well then," he spoke softly, "one last question. Perhaps, *mademoiselle*, if it pleases, you might give a tiny exposition on the French author who has inspired you most."

Melanie, exhaling at last, was unaware that she had forgotten to breathe, unaware of the fume of brandy she released that recharged her courage. If meekness was required now, she was unaware of that, too. In her hour of need, *Les Pensées*, the thoughts of Pascal, clear, hard, brilliant as diamonds shining from the distant firmament of the seventeenth century sparked her now flashing eyes. She could recite them as a catechism, a holy text. They were the hard stones she tucked beneath her pillow at night—the truth as best she knew it—that guided her sleep even more than the letters from Hans neatly kept on her bedside table. When she exhaled again, and knew she was exhaling, she also knew it was time to stop. She had only one more thing to say: "Pascal, as a religious, as a Jansenist, of course also tried to understand, logically, the existence of God. He concluded belief was a roll of the dice, and he would roll for it. My fate here is nothing more than that, a roll of the dice. Except I do not hold them. Good afternoon."

Then she turned on her heels and left.

It was not long after that stunning ending, after the cramps had suddenly come back with force and the color had drained from her cheeks, leaving them paste, that Melanie wobbled out in defiant defeat, and I reported the good news.

"I was only a few back in line, so I got closer to the door to listen," I whispered loudly in her ear, feeling her breath still smelling of brandy. "You could hear them shouting. 'My God, you are so *dure,* you know, so hard-hearted, Hélène. She was very good, clear correct French, good grasp. You are just upset she did that tour de force on Pascal. You tried hard to trip her up with de Montesquieu, and even then she didn't fall. On what possible grounds do you want to fail her?'"

"'On the grounds that she is an idiot. But you probably didn't notice her head is completely empty. You didn't get that far up your famous physical geography, did you? Not much past those legs under that swish little skirt.'"

After more shouting, I told Melanie, Grimbaud had given her a complete zero, while Lapierre refused to come down one point. Averaged together, there were just enough points. "Mel, you passed, even if it was with the lowest possible mark."

Chapter 17

It was that season when winter still hung on the city like a coat, but Evelyn imagined it unbuttoned. For her the question was, what lay beneath? From the corner window upstairs of le Salon de Thé, the Rue de Rivoli below gave no hint. Yet for all her impatience, and Gracie said this too, Evelyn knew how to wait when she had to. She knew that the women in their fur-trimmed hats and leather boots and perfectly cut winter suits, the women who wore the clothes from the great fashion houses nearby, the women who belonged there, would slowly let her in on their secrets. So she would continue to come, to sit at a table with a linen cloth and a rose and order scented tea and a pastry, spend her church scholarship money as recklessly as she could, and watch.

Slowly the pervasive gray, the slush-iced streets, the wet that was neither snow nor rain, would pause, stop, and turn imperceptibly, and in that movement, a new dress, like a new season, would appear. Its emergence was best observed beneath the protected Italianate alcoves hovering over Rue de Rivoli. No doubt those arches, the curves and squares of finely cut stones that formed the elegant *maisons* along this street "spoke to her." She smiled to herself over that corny phrase used by the art instructor whose in situ raptures about two angles meeting a joint served only to make her know her bottom was freezing off, and helped her to drift into reverie about lying on the beach in the California sun. So she'd sworn off those extracurricular art sessions, as well as her regular classes. Instead, she'd discovered the architecture of elegance, architecture that could actually teach her something.

There, in the corner of le Salon de Thé, alien as a desert plant with her bright green sweater and shiny red hair, she knew she had much to learn. She knew from the way the ladies glanced at her, then turned away. She knew from their shoes, handmade high-heeled works of art in calfskin. She knew from the way they moved, the dainty, ritualized way they shook hands and dabbed their napkins at the corners of their mouths; from the way expensively cut wool, silk, and suede hung on them, draped as perfectly as stone robes covering carved saints on cathedral pillars; she knew from the way perfume wafted in the air when any of them passed. She knew, but could not yet explain, the difference between the dime-store fragrance her mother wore on holidays and real French perfume.

She did not know what exactly the French ladies thought of her, sitting too colorfully in the corner and all alone, but she knew (and how Gracie could understand this!) that they knew she was not one of them. The worst case, of course, would be to be taken instantly for an American. She thought of them, the gaggles pouring out of tour buses last September, with their plaid Bermuda shorts, stupid straw hats, Pepsodent smiles, camera bags, loud voices—and, most cringingly, their back-slapping, wave-and-wink, alarming friendliness. Encountering her countrymen in action was to live out her worst nightmare, being trapped at a church picnic.

Yet there was one exemplary American—Jacqueline Kennedy, who had stunned and won Paris last year. The American First Lady who dressed like a queen and spoke French like a *parisienne,* who glittered more than any movie star. The most famous woman in the world, and she too had, amazingly, once walked the halls of the Sorbonne during a cold Parisian winter. As Evelyn dipped one last sugar cube into her tea and stirred it around, these thoughts obsessed her. She swore to herself that, as soon as she absorbed all the lessons of le Salon de Thé and Rue de Rivoli, she'd be another Jackie with red hair.

It was Edith, her brassy and most unsvelte roommate, who had first brought her here, to introduce her to French manners and English high culture at once. Regardless, Eve told Grace, Edith was tasteless and a vulgar *nouveau riche,* "whereas I am well-brought-up genteel impoverishment. Besides," she added, "I have Jackie, and all Edith's got is the dowdy old queen."

Despite her mild contempt, Evelyn knew she had much to gain from associating with Edith. She'd understood that much way back, even on that the frozen day I'd come over to study for exams with Melanie. "A strange day," she told Gracie. "First coming in to find the two of them like little old ladies bent over their knitting, sweating over exams I hadn't even let myself think about. And then there were the letters." One from her mother, its ink all wobbly with virtue and hard work, sent to remind her what an honor (she stopped just short of saying duty) it was to have won the church scholarship, how people in their own parish had dug down to contribute to the fund, and how everyone looked forward to sharing her hard-earned knowledge when she returned. How they all prayed for her every day. And then there was another letter from Tom. His short, upbeat pages in neat handwriting, full of campus news, gossip, and football triumphs didn't actually say much. But it was his underlying tone of adoration and strong sense of physical presence that she felt. That day especially, she confessed to Gracie, she'd had the feeling of him, the gorgeous head with short-cropped hair and gray eyes, the strong neck and shoulders, the thick, hard chest he often pulled her against, the way his arms went around behind as he lifted her to kiss, the way he had held her the day she had been paraded across the football field in her white homecoming-queen dress and crown.

Just then, when Evelyn was trying to make sense of so many contradictory impulses, plump, rosy Edith burst in on our little scene. "Louis, Louis, Louis, *viens*," she was calling, trilling like a songbird. *"Viens, chéri, tu veux diner?"* The door blew open, and the poodle slid his elegant curls across the threshold like a bullied page. "Get in here, you bloody devil. I said dinner. *Dinner*." The door slammed shut, and Edith shouted "Crap," to nobody in particular, "they take so bloody long at Alexandre's." She shook her yellow newly permed hair, which looked not all that dissimilar to Louis's.

Only after all the commotion did she finally notice the two of us at the table, Eve standing to the side. Her manners changed instantly. "Evelyn, you didn't tell me we were having a guest, you must introduce us," she said in the voice she must have cultivated for presentation at Buckingham Palace.

Evelyn responded by mocking her, putting on a thick British accent. "Edith, my dear, may I present my old friend J.J.? She's come round for tea."

But Edith appeared not to notice and offered a gloved hand, a little nod, and said "*Enchantée.* Simply splendid of you to come, and do come again. Frightfully sorry I can't join you, but I'm afraid I'm late for a *soirée*—the Duke and Duchess you know—and one mustn't keep them." There were a few more door slammings and yaps from Louis, then she was gone again.

I looked at Evelyn, eyebrows raised.

"You explain it, Mel, she's your friend," said Eve.

"Hardly," Melanie looked up, rubbing her eyes. "Family connections. My mother and her 'mum' knew we would both be in Paris this year, so they decided we should room together."

"But tell her the dirt, Mel. The true story of Mary-Margaret Cooper, alias Edith, the new incarnation of Piaf—or the sparrow reincarnated as fat partridge. I mean, she has got this Voice. But then she's also got Daddy the rich industrialist trying to spread money like water to buy up what they don't already own, and Mummy—don't you just love that, as in Queen Mum—who's doing the social climbing thing to acquire a pedigree that overcomes those lower-middle-class origins. Ah, Edith—the sublime *and* the ridiculous. And that's not even mentioning the *masseur* she's hired to 'redo' those god-awful fat legs."

I mumbled something about how it must be quite a letdown for her to live with the two of them. Melanie broke in to say, "Well, we have insisted on sharing the chores. Remember that time she shrieked on the phone about what an experience it was to live with Americans and said, 'My God you won't believe what I've just done—I cleaned the *loo*.'"

"Yeah," Eve continued, "she's really very simple to understand. The girl has a single ambition in two-part harmony—to conquer *le tout Paris*, first as a great chanteuse, *à la* Piaf, then as part of high society. Edith, like Eliza, wants to go to the ball and be called a lady."

I could pretty much tell all this from my brief encounter with Edith. What I didn't know is what Gracie told me later: how just reciting Edith's story made Evelyn certain there were things in Paris, important things, to be learned.

Nonetheless, recognizing that "flunking out of the Sorbonne first term is probably not too smart," Evelyn temporarily put aside the real lessons of Paris in favor of the more familiar, if boring, activity of cramming. Melanie became her ready accomplice. It was as if all the hours of reading and memorizing had given her new power, and sharing them with Eve made her more powerful still.

Gracie, who, since getting that first letter from Tom, had started making pilgrimages to the apartment near the Bois, joined in too. "I already had good credentials in tutoring," she told me, almost savoring the irony of each word. It was easy for me to imagine how bittersweet those sessions must have been, Gracie brushing up against Evelyn's sleeve the way she used to against Tom's arm. The tag-team approach worked. Evelyn passed the first term, too.

Yet to my mind, the process had unhinged her a bit, as if she could not quite find her place in a cycle that left her somewhere between Edith's night-crawling and Melanie's rituals of study and sleep. So, with the orals behind her and a passing grade in her hip pocket, I asked her to join me after late class in Montparnasse. "Come with me to La Coupole," I said, "we can soak up some of that Montparnasse literary atmosphere, though God knows I shouldn't eat anything. I'm fat as a pig and starting to break out."

She looked me over critically. "You? I've been thinking you look sort of skinny lately. Wasted. Or maybe it's just craven. A Frenchman in the woodpile, J.J.?" She linked arms with me as we went inside, relieved, I think, to be out once again in the dark.

I didn't answer directly. "Well, I guess I could use some advice. You know, about French men?"

Eve pitched her head back and laughed from her belly. "*Moi*? The pastor's daughter? What would I know? I'm only a provincial *demi-vierge*."

By the time we left La Coupole, it was getting late enough for the real night people to start filling in the smoky tables by the glassed-in terrace. Maybe there was something in the air, a hint of melting softness that invited slowing down. I took my time getting to the Métro, and I know, because she told me everything the next night, that Evelyn didn't feel like hurrying, either. Despite her avowal to change her habits and begin studying in a rational way, I suspect that unnamed softening already sapped her will. Perhaps she told herself that reforming her habits was all well and good, but not a wise thing to do all at once. Perhaps she thought of home: not a patch of beach and a blue horizon, but Rue Boileau lined with all that was now familiar. Her *cordonnier*, her *tabac*, her *épicerie*, and her downfall, *la boulangerie*. Her *appartement*. And as the lift made its slow way up, maybe she cast herself in the best light, seeing her presence in this place as a vital force, a balance, in keeping Melanie from killing herself with work and pining, and Edith from completely overwhelming Melanie.

Maybe, stepping out of the lift and reaching her door, she felt vaguely proud of her pivotal role—and of her forbearance, which had so far kept her from doing in Louis, whose high-pitched yapping could be heard two floors down.

Chapter 18

February. The long tangle of underground tunnels from the Métro, one saying *Sortie Opéra*. A whoosh of heavy coats and neat, fur-trimmed boots with small heels, a southerly breeze—air pushed up from the closing of metal gates carrying expensive perfume. Gentlemen with cashmere scarves and slim, long-necked umbrellas. The crowd, climbing into the cold late sun, intent on reaching the wide plaza surrounded by elegant cafés and dominated by the gold-domed glitter of the opera house itself, did not notice the young guitar player with long hair, the old gypsy woman, the blind flute player, all wanting money.

But Melanie did as she dashed past and, despite herself, reached into her pocket for a few loose francs. As she did so, her fingers brushed against the thick pages of Hans's latest letter, the one she carried with her for ballast. The beggars snapped her out of her reverie, that longing for a garden in California, the music room, the filtered sun, the unearthly, soulful sound of Hans playing beneath the ground.

Anxiety rippled through her as she released the coins into the guitar player's case, the flutist's hat, the gypsy's creased, dirty hand. Hans would not approve. "'It is just a waste and teaches these people nothing, Melanie,'" she recorded, adding that his voice "sounded perilously close to Father's." Still, it was a small sin that she could not prevent herself from committing. It just seemed wrong to pass by and do nothing. "We have so much," she'd answered back to Hans, "maybe they need just a little hand now and then. For food or something." "They'll only drink it away." That was always the answer. She didn't say in whose voice.

But that small tremor of rebellion in her own voice had become clearer, then, too. She had passed her first rounds of exams, even if it was by a breath, and she felt a little emboldened—"unduly encouraged maybe, but still…" as if perhaps, somehow, she could get her diploma and actually make something of herself. Thinking that, she redoubled her efforts at studying—"I'm going to try really, really hard now and hope I can pull it off," she wrote, adding, "maybe even make a small mark." That was the thing. More than all else, though it was hard for her to admit it even to herself, Mel wanted to achieve some small recognition for serious work. Perhaps that's why she held back a little—just a little—from giving over to dreaming about Hans all the time. As she climbed up the last step into la Place de l'Opéra, that California garden sliding into the cool, late, almost bitter light of a winter afternoon, the little tinge of disloyalty she felt for thinking about herself instead of him was swallowed in the wind. "I am going to see *Don Giovanni*, after all, for him," she wrote to justify herself. I picture her as she slipped, anonymous, to the back of the line filled with fur and virgin wool coats.

All round, it was an unusual morning. Against my will, to say nothing of my general principles, I had ventured out early into the cold to slog all the way past the Bois. I needed to borrow some notes from Mel before my dreaded grammar section at Montparnasse. Instead of finding her alone, I walked into an early morning scene. Though Eve didn't usually budge before ten, and Edith usually dragged in about dawn (which in fact she had just done), there they were, the two of them, sitting quietly with a café au lait, happily discussing politics. Mel looked at them and just shrugged. I felt a little shortchanged, too, since she'd described their usual exchanges: yelling at each other about leaving a mess in the kitchen or cleaning up after the infernal Louis, or Edith (who, among other things, was envious of Evelyn's legs) calling Eve's behavior *déclassé*, to which Evelyn replied by calling Edith a *nouveau riche* slob who could use an accent adjustment.

But there in the dim breakfast light in their small kitchen, the two battling roommates suddenly found common political cause. "Oh *merde* the bloody French!" Edith was saying, enraged that her efforts at crashing the existing social order were being thwarted. "Piaf, baby, I toast you." Eve made an exaggerated motion with her bowl of coffee. "I who am also about to die, salute you." She smiled, hugging an old bathrobe about herself, then turned to me and said, "Come sit with us, J.J., a thousand and one tales of the night," before leaning conspiratorially close to Edith as they began sharing misadventures of the last few nights on the town.

Melanie shrugged again and made apologies for both of us. "J.J.'s got to dash, and I've got class," and we both were soon out the door.

Politics, I knew, bored her, and the fascination others found in the subject mystified her. "Along with religion, politics seems to be the major force behind human misery," she commented once. And I knew, for example, that by the French definition, her parents bordered on fascist. I also knew that to her, their politics seemed the least egregious thing about them. On the other hand, by American lights, most of the students, professors, intellectuals, playwrights—mostly everyone she heard voice an opinion in Paris—was a communist, or at least a fellow-traveler, whatever that meant. Those two labels alone were enough to begin World War III in either place.

Still, with her new determination to do well she was also determined to tackle the meaning of the political order because it was part of her curriculum. To that end she slipped out into the cold morning with me, each of us on our way to the Michel-Ange-Molitor Métro station, where we would go our separate ways. For Melanie, that morning brought the long ride to the Sorbonne and the early class on La Politique Moderne with Alain Saint-Georges.

I imagine her slipping into the Hall Richelieu, feeling confident enough to sit down in front when she could find a seat. She had been in the habit of sitting toward the back, often with Jocelyn who always seemed to understand everything, even the French, even without studying. But Jocelyn hadn't come for ages. And Melanie, who knew she drowned most easily in the swift-running tides of spoken French, now wanted to catch every syllable, every nuance of intonation, and felt emboldened enough to sit close to the podium where Saint-Georges lectured. She felt lucky to be so near him, seeing how students always pressed around him, how his columns in

Le Monde were always being quoted like gospel, how his face was always appearing, grave and intelligent, on the news.

"*Alors*, today we will address French foreign relations in the post-colonial era, in particular in Indochina, where America has moved in with typical misguided force, and the implications for world order," he would begin. Already, Melanie would feel lost.

After an hour, her head swimming, her notes a jumble, she'd notice she was hungry. Perhaps Ivan's perennial joke would ironically pop into her mind: "How do you feel after a meal at a north Vietnamese restaurant? Hungry for power," leading her to skip the usual horrid student lunch and seek out a little Vietnamese place instead.

This much I know from her journals: that day, she exited the Hall Richelieu, the dark corridors and the huge door opening on Rue des Écoles, passing the quiet desolation of Cluny in perpetual winter, graveyard of Roman baths and medieval political aspirations. Between the Romans and the gothic period, which gave the manor house its stony grace, there had been, she'd read, the Barbarians. They had invaded, overrun fledgling Paris, pillaged, looted, burned. The vast public baths of Cluny had been burned to the ground.

That image was in her mind as she wandered north, off Rue Saint-Jacques to a little side street lined with foreign restaurants. She found one that suited, Café Hanoi, and entered its dark portal. Inside, cooking smells—hot oil, seafood, ginger, garlic—warmed her. She ordered, and awaited her meal drinking fragrant tea. Her mind was clouded with a confusion of pictures. The horrifying ones Professor Saint-Georges had evoked of a country ripped apart with bombs and explosions—all somehow a result of being on the wrong side of colonialism, the wrong side of Marxism. Then, she focused on this odd observation, "the fresher and somehow more immediate image," as she put it, of ancient Paris being sacked by the Barbarians, "Cluny in flames." That, she knew, was only the beginning. The most recent calamity, World War II and the Nazi occupation, she was letting into her consciousness slowly, the only possible way to absorb it.

"How often have these streets been torched, with one era, one king, one idea being cremated to make way for the next? It's a horrifying, overwhelming concept, the endless ravages of human fire—I want to get it out of my head," she wrote. Back in the reality of the Vietnamese restaurant, "I paused on my way to the loo. The back door was open to a dingy courtyard and there in the middle was an old lady in a padded jacket next to a small girl. They huddled next to a round trash bin, rubbing their hands to keep warm. Flames leapt out of the top."

With the fire flashing in front of her eyes, she had a moment of rare clarity. Did the fire and the Santa Ana on the night of the *bal masqué* which had somehow not really touched her before flash into her consciousness? I don't know. All I know is what she wrote: "Fires. One made for human destruction, one from human need. Both burn. All fires are one... Does the personal devour the political, or is it the other way around?"

Next to this there is a one-word entry, "Daddy!" and a torn-out obituary, yellowed with the years, from *Le Figaro*. Sylvia Plath had just stuck her head in an oven and committed suicide in England at the age of thirty-two.

I imagine her sitting there, trying hard to keep so much in her head, eating her soup and rice with unusual haste. Wanting most of all to collect her thoughts, gather them in one place, make sense of the competing images of fire and ice. Alain Saint-Georges had said to read André Malraux? Remembering this, she reached inside her satchel then and touched the plastic-encased cover of *La Condition Humaine*, Pléiade edition, as yet unopened. I see her rubbing the edges of the pages as if caressing a talisman.

Chapter 19

Evelyn sat dazed and a little subdued on my bidet, and, as midday waned into afternoon, began talking about the night before, about her escapades on Île Saint-Louis.

"*Merde!* Bloody hell," were the sounds that had greeted her inside her flat. She stepped in the sitting room to see Edith, hair piled on top of her head in Marie Antoinette fashion, sidestepping Louis in a strange dance, blue satin gown and matching evening slippers swaying. She knew—Edith had spoken of little else for a week—that the gown, which had hung on the long front window to avoid wrinkling, was a Dior.

"I said something positive, like, 'Wow, kiddo, you look fit for a king… I see Alexandre's has been hard at work.'

"She answered with the usual 'Shit!' and kept up her little waltz, then started barking at me: 'Fasten this thing in back, will you? When I went for my fittings, I never dreamed of this problem. Hell!' She was in a froth—her word—that Charles would arrive in his limo, and she'd have to run out there half undone and have him fix her with his 'clammy little royal hands.'

"So I hooked her up, plus put on this fabulous strand of diamonds and sapphires, and told her she looked almost as great as I did as football queen last year. But she was so distracted, I couldn't get the smallest rise out of her. She just went to the window and stood there, watching and fidgeting."

Eve sat on the banquette to join the watch for Charles, whom she knew only by the highly incomplete description of "exquisitely titled." Edith had also added that he was a twit, but a twit she could live with because he was her ticket to the "in" crowd.

"'Thank God it's strictly platonic,' she told me, and then went on about how 'He, of course, tells *le tout Paris* that we're madly passionate and that he absolutely adores me—well, that part *is* true. But, my dear,' I swear she actually said this, J.J., 'he can't even get it up, and he's not half as naughty as my *masseur*.'

"Pretty soon old Edith started looking at the clock and pacing and shouting again 'Bloody hell! Where is he? We can't be late to this reception.' Then she went to the phone, but when she dialed out, it didn't work. So Louis, who's tuned into her every mood, started followed her, and the more she swore, the more he whimpered. '*Tais-toi*. Shut up, shut up!' she was yelling, then turned around and accidentally stepped on his paw. He shut up all right," Eve started laughing so hard, just as she had the night before into a pillow to muffle the sound, that she could hardly finish her story, "but our little poochie was so upset he *peed* right on her satin slipper."

In a moment, Edith stormed back into the sitting room. She finally had gotten through on the telephone. "Now she was yelling 'Swine! Monster!' and I was glad to understand that for once she didn't mean me, or even

Louis. Seems Charles wasn't coming in his limo after all. 'Talked to the valet,'" Eve recited in a perfect Edith voice, "'and his royal prick is having a royal pout. Fool! Idiot!' Then, without missing a beat, she started barking at me again: 'Come, quick. You've got to drive me, no other solution. It's simply too *déclassé* to arrive in a cab. And I'll show him up plenty. Did he imagine I wouldn't have the guts to show without him?'"

Edith gathered her wrap and evening bag, while Eve, as if with imaginary tape over her mouth, followed docilely to the street, not saying a word. Normally, Edith would have seized the wheel and driven her little Jaguar like a wild woman, leaning out the window cursing, shaking her fists, and steering in and out of traffic. But this was no normal evening.

"She couldn't fit behind the steering wheel without crushing her gown. So she tossed me the keys and did this command thing again: '*Alors,* you drive. There'll be a place to park—after I am ushered out by the doorman of course—you can take a cab home. Just put it on my bill.' Yeah, right! So then, she went around to the passenger side, pushed the seat back as far as she could, and slid herself in until she was more lying down than sitting up, terrified she'd mess up her hair or wrinkle the dress. So there I was, the official chauffeur, and I swear to God, J.J., I'd never have done this except it was so damn funny, and even then, lying there like one of those boutique dolls in fancy dress clothes, she still couldn't help herself. She was yelling directions at me even though she couldn't see out the window. We got to the Étoile, which was the usual circus with cars zooming around the Arc de Triomphe at terrifying speeds, and she'd bob up from time to time to make obscene gestures or shout '*Vielle peaux*, you bloody old bitch' at some poor fool who must have thought she was drinking too much. But, and here's the weirdest part, by the time we pulled into the circular drive at the little palace somewhere near Place de Voges, she sat up, smoothed her hair, and transformed herself into a princess.

"It was an amazing thing to see, how she allowed herself to be gingerly extracted from the car by two footmen and then escorted up the stairs as if this were the most normal thing in the world. After she disappeared, I started to leave and that's when I realized—can you believe this? Edith, *oh bloody hell!*, forgot to wait for the keys."

Taking a moment to recover, Eve went to park the car and came back to the palace steps. She meant only to go as far as the door, spot Edith, then hand the keys to one of the absurd footmen to deliver. She meant, since she was now reforming herself, to go home and study. But by the time she got to the foot of the stairs and peered into the vast marble entry hall, Edith was long gone.

"I kept looking to the footman for some kind of direction, feeling such a fool, feeling out of place, a silly schoolgirl in a green sweater and skirt. I tried explaining that I was looking for a friend, but they ignored me until one of them gestured with a sort of dismissive wave of a glove, and I realized I'd have to cross the entryway and into the salon itself to have a prayer of spotting Edith. It was amazing, J.J., packed with all these designer people and everything kind of twirling, like flashing diamonds reflecting in lights from these huge chandeliers. I guess I hesitated a minute, and the next thing you know, I felt this sort of slight pressure at the elbow and this person dressed like a maître d' began escorting me to the receiving line. So I panicked a little, saying "*Non, non, monsieur,* I don't belong here. I have no invitation. My friend, you see, the keys…" and I started waving them in front of him, but he ignored this completely, like it's part of footman school or something not to hear or talk, so there I am with my hand sticking out. Then this real waiter—one in a black tuxedo—came by and put a glass of champagne in it…'"

Soon, I gathered, another man in a tuxedo appeared, and Evelyn figured this one was a guest. Then another showed up. And another. "All I wanted to do was shrink and disappear. There I was towering over everybody like a giant American Christmas tree in bright green lit on top with neon-red hair. So I turned to one of these guys and said, 'Hey, *voyez,* I'm just looking for a friend, see. I'm not really here, not supposed to be here.'

"Then he did the look, up and down, slowly, you know the French way, and he sort of boomed out: *'Ah mademoiselle, mais si, vous y êtes. Et c'est magnifique.'* I felt so, I don't know, awkward, conspicuous, out of place, and then that gave way to a kind of dizziness. For a moment I felt like I was swimming, like I was on the boat with that music and the dancing and…and the way French sounds when men speak of love. I began hearing all these different voices, one man whispering to another: 'Ah yes indeed, she is here, like a Greek goddess in green.' So there was this whole crowd by then, looking me up and down, whispering, making comments, and all of it in admiration. And what could I do? Nothing, absolutely nothing. Absurdly, these lines of scripture—my father's voice—began running through my mind. 'My cup runneth over' was the one that stuck. I decided it was a message from God, so I accepted another glass of champagne."

Strange as it was, the moment must have been familiar, too. After all, Evelyn was used to being at the center of a circle of admiring men. I had seen her among the cheering huskies of the defending line as she paraded down the football field a queen, tiara in place. I had seen her at the mountainside cabin with Jay the night of the Santa Ana. But this was different, for in that Parisian palace she had been attached to no man, but rather stood on her own, bantering in surprisingly good French. She basked briefly in the little whirlwind of her own creation. "I forgot the keys in my hand. I even forgot Edith."

In no time, however, Edith, drawn to the small commotion at the other end of the vast salon, spotted her. And as she made her way toward the knot of men surrounding the tall figure in green, Eve looked up and watched her approach "like a steam engine about to blow its stack. For the second time in a couple hours it was all I could do to keep from cracking up. She was furious of course to see me there, crashing her party. But if she let loose, began cursing like a cockney fishwife, her house of social cards would collapse on the spot. She was almost puffing from anxiety, and her face got red—a terrible struggle that between her nature and her ambitions. So she just sort of came to a halt just at the edge of the circle, and broke out her loud, super-cultivated voice: 'Dahling'—can't you just hear it—'whatever happened? Did you take a wrong turn?'

"The *gentilhommes* all turned just in time to catch Edith, who was sort of spilling out of the blue Dior. I just held up the keys and waved them. Then I threw it right back at her.

"'Why, dahling, I just stopped in to give you these. You forgot them, you silly thing…'"

But at that point, Edith was no longer even looking at Evelyn. Her full attention fell on the short, balding man who had first attached himself to Eve and now looked her up and down. "Something was obviously going on here that I couldn't see, and then a minute later she said, 'Allow me to introduce my roommate, gentlemen, Mademoiselle Evelyn Richter from California.' Then she practically genuflected and bowed in my direction, presenting me to Monsieur le Marquis de Harfleur, *cousin du le* Count de Paris. Of course I knew right away, because of her tone and because of the litany of pedigrees she was always spouting, that this was a big one. Probably one of those direct descendants of the last Restoration and if possible, somebody even more important than her own Charles. So I did my best *enchantée*, and did my own princess-style hand thing just like I learned last year in my own royal court. Then I laid it on really thick, you know, 'Please excuse the intrusion, my deah Edith, but here are your keys, and I can make my own way out.'

"She threw me a glance like a skewer, and then there was a round of protest from several of the *gentilhommes*. 'Oh, *non*, please *mademoiselle*, you must stay. A pleasure, refreshing change, a young lady all the way from America, and so tall. Such a brilliant spot among women in such depressing gowns…'

"I could see Edith doing the mental calculations. Like she was adding up: *Okay, she crashed this with great success AND hooked the marquis. So maybe she is from California, she's poor, a minister's daughter, and a girl with no known social standing on any continent. But they seem to find her refreshing. Maybe I can turn her into some sort of minor social asset, turn this to my advantage.* What else could she have been thinking?

"Except maybe how much she hated me for having good legs while hers had to get worked on constantly—with no obvious improvement, I have to say. Anyway, she did see the handwriting on the wall, because she said: 'Of course, dahling, you *must* stay. You've already made yourself quite welcome. I'll have a tiny word with Madame la Contesse, you know, the hostess.'"

Eve grew tired of sitting on my version of a throne. Encouraged by a brave, rare showing of sun, we were drawn out into the world of daylight and walked toward the river. Spring is too strong a word, as no green even whispered along the exposed limb of any tree, but the strong dose of afternoon sun gave hope. And on the strength of it, booksellers returned briefly to their kiosks along the Seine. Across the river, whose surface rippled liquid silver in the stiff new breeze, Notre Dame seemed to throw off some shroud of gray sleep and find the new light intrinsic in ancient stone and glass.

In that little indentation along the Left Bank, where Shakespeare & Co. is set back from the river as if on a small square, I caught our reflection in a window. A street sweeper cleaning up around the outdoor book racks saw us, too. Two tall young women, one dark and pale, a classical look, Greek maybe; the other voluptuous, with hair like a crown of fire. Arm in arm, we strolled past, lost in conversation. But I saw him pull upright, pause, catch a little of our words on the wind. Maybe enough to confirm his suspicions, ah yes, that we were foreigners, *les étrangères*, drifting predictably along this path every year like newly feathered birds, chirping away in lightly accented French. Maybe he couldn't quite tell where we'd flown in from. Maybe he was thinking that some lucky *mec*—perhaps a guy with a broom just like him—had already got his hooks into me, for I was saying, "Roland, I think about him all the time even when he's not there."

Maybe the smile as he tipped his cap to us carried a response. *Eh, Roland mon vieux, you're a fool if she spends too much time thinking, old man, instead of being there in person to do the job properly. It's a question of French honor—la patrie—mon vieux. As for the redhead, oh là là, lucky devil who gets a piece of that business. A job for a real man, a street sweeper perhaps…* The cap went back on his graying head, he muttered, "*Eh bien*, the first long-stem roses mean the coming of spring," bent once again over his broom, and we went on along the river, following our own narrative.

"Oh, J.J., it was just perfect," Evelyn was saying. "I could just hear the wheels turning under that ridiculous lampshade of a hairdo—God, did I tell you how ridiculous she looked? So when le marquis, *my* marquis, suggested going to his 'hideaway' after the 'too boring trial we'd all been enduring,' Edith leapt like a cat. I mean, it's not like he invited her exactly, but she was purring. So the three of us, plus a couple of his really strange friends, you know, getups like those engravings in Balzac novels, linked up and marched out together, like a royal procession, people sort of bowing on the sidelines. She was beside herself, *especially when*, whom should we meet on the way out but Charles. He'd come late, maybe full of remorse and heartbreak. More likely full of shit…

"God, I wish you could have seen her. She literally pushed me aside so she could walk next to my marquis on the way out, barely giving a nod to poor old Charles *le pathétique*. And the next thing you know, we're back in the Jag, the Dior gown all squished to hell behind the wheel now and she doesn't give a damn, doesn't give a damn about anything except this incredible breakthrough. *Monsieur le Marquis*, she kept shouting as she tore around circles on two wheels and screeched across Pont Marie before we lurched to a stop on some small dark street on Île Saint-Louis. She even forgot to cuss at anyone or threaten to run over a single pedestrian.

"The 'hideaway' is actually an attic in one of those fantastic old buildings with a view of the Seine. It seems my marquis—Édouard, that is, and see how fast we got all chummy—fancies himself some kind of artist. Or he plays at it, sort of like Marie Antoinette playing at milk-maid, I guess. Or maybe he just likes to escape his dark old château or his apartment and just hang out there, like an ordinary person."

"So is he an ordinary person?" I had to ask, as we walked, still arm in arm, still tracing the emerging street with long-legged glides, still attracting the unblinking glances of every admiring passerby, still ignoring all of them, crossed the Pont Neuf, unconsciously making our way along the Right Bank there, to the Île Saint-Louis.

"Oh no, he's way, way below that. He's just a skinny old guy with a moustache and a toupee, ruined by money and bad blood and too many centuries of inbreeding, best I can tell."

"Sounds irresistible."

"Doesn't he just?" Eve laughed, throwing back her face to bathe in the sun.

"Oh, but the whole scene was a riot. There were about six of us in this little place, the perfect romantic artist's attic, and Edith figured it was her moment—the pinnacle, the crème de la crème, the top, and they're her captives. So Édouard opens not one but two bottles of this incredible Château Margaux that probably went back to the reign of Charlemagne, and after many toasts, including several to *'beauté'*—me, I'll have you know—he says he thinks it would be very avant-garde to eat in. So he rummages around and produces some bread and a bit of cheese he's stowed away, but before he gets too far, Edith starts in. She's coy, dropping her eyes.

"'Did you know,' she says in the cultivated voice, 'that my true avocation, or perhaps passion is the right word, is as a chanteuse? You see, Édouard, like you, at heart I'm an artist.' And she aims those beady little eyes right at him.

"'No?' he says. 'Really? Well then, amuse us. What is a party without entertainment? Sing for us. A ballad, an aria…'

"I can see what she's thinking. That she's got him, that she'll knock him over, the pinnacle of the pinnacle, Monsieur le Marquis, and that in no time she'll be playing the Olympia. She begins belting out "Non, Je Ne Regrette Rien," and, I have to admit, eyes closed, she *is* Piaf. Édouard and the other old boys are immobilized, thunderstruck, *boulversés,* as they said.

"But you know what, J.J., I'm also thinking, that she's here because of me. I got her in here, but as soon as we're out of here and she's had her little triumph, I'll be one of Louis's little dog turds again. But this is my party…so I do the damnedest thing. I start, ever so slyly, to flirt with him. She's too preoccupied to notice, of course, but while she's playing Piaf, I'm playing the marquis.

"I found my moment, too. As soon as she's finished, there is a minute of silence, then applause and bravo and *bis* and all that crap and talk of 'the star' and how they could say 'we knew her when.' Then Édouard wants to do his bohemian little supper thing to celebrate. The centerpiece of this operation, his main 'I'm an ordinary guy' routine, is a big can of baked beans, given to him, he says by an American tourist who toured his château and told him it was just the thing for an easy supper. They're all sitting around like something in a bar scene by Manet, sloshed on great wine, dressed in clothes from another century, and staring at this exotic wonder, a can of beans.

"So Albert, who's this youngish, squishy sort and does something in banking, starts whining '*Mais Édouard, mon vieux*, some kind of tin from America, are you trying to kill us? Anyway, how shall we open it? Wouldn't it be better to go out and eat properly?' '*Non, non,*' Édouard says, 'this is much more amusing. This is *comme il faut*. As for opening this little tin, *voilà*,' and he goes to the drawer where he keeps a hodgepodge of stuff and pulls out a tiny can opener. 'Just what the doctor ordered, *vous voyez*.'

"And so it begins. Édouard passes the can and opener to Albert, who fumbles with them clumsily, and he passes it to the next fellow, then the next. The can is getting pretty battered by now, the red Campbell's label torn and a few dents in it, but nobody gets the essential idea of how to make the opener open. Finally, Édouard passes it to Edith. It's an unspoken request to bail him out, to save his ass from humiliation. I mean, does it get worse? Edith, of course, thanks to Mel and me, knows more about cleaning the john than opening a can. Until we got this flat together, I doubt she'd ever even boiled water. She gives the can a few lame licks, then shrugs, defeated.

"So it's mine, all mine. *Permettez-moi*, I say, and take the can, the opener, and with them the marquis out of his misery. In a sec the stupid thing is opened, and I'm standing at the head of the little table in my green sweater and skirt pouring cold American baked beans into a bowl, and it's a triumph. Right there at that moment, I've opened up a whole world, and I'm pouring it into a bowl. They're putty in my hands, J.J., because I'm something completely different. Young, beautiful, foreign, the usual stuff, but also with know-how. I look from face to face and try to keep from laughing at my little conquest, because I know all I've conquered is the ruins of history. Then I think, but this is a new whole world opening to me. I need to grab whatever I can."

"Meaning?" I withdraw my arm and pause a moment to look at Evelyn straight on.

"Meaning I turn back to the marquis, ready to claim him as *my* marquis again. I know Edith wanted to pocket him, to use him, but I'm thinking, *no kiddo, this one's mine.* So I remain standing a minute, let him look me up and down again, and give him a big smile and a wink. 'Your beans, Monsieur le Marquis,' and he *is* mine."

She had pulled me across a small footbridge to the island. "See," Evelyn said, gesturing to the rooftop of an ancient *maison* on the corner of Rue Saint-Louis-en-l'Île, "the scene of the crime."

I peered up, trying to make out the window in question, but it was lost in reflection from the early setting sun. "From the way you describe them—him—they sound so well…maybe some things aren't worth spending time on, you think?"

"No," Eve answered, "I think everything is worth knowing. The trick is not to hang around too long after you've exhausted the subject."

"Yeah, well it sounds like you've already moved into the post-doc phase with this one. Aren't you tired of him already?"

"Oh no, not yet. See, there is this whole other world I already knew about from Edith. A ball at Versailles if you can imagine. I mean we came to Paris to learn what we didn't know, right?"

Thinking of Roland, I had to agree. I nodded, then said, "Versailles? You want to get there too?"

Eve peered into the darkening Seine. "Sure," she said. "If I can. But it won't be easy. I'll have to work on him."

"Like how? From what you said, he may not even be interested, at least not in girls."

"He isn't, at least not in that way. But in another, he's very interested. A would-be-artist, remember?"

"So…?"

"So, he wants to paint me."

Chapter 20

I am chagrined to learn, so long after the fact, that Melanie came to see us, to seek advice about Alain Saint-Georges. It is easy to see her winding her way down the narrow blocks of Rue de l'École-de-Médecine, making her usual zigzag in the snow, still trying to avoid the depths, but wearing fewer wraps. She would be wearing that smart navy wool coat with brass buttons and, despite herself, make a slim and graceful silhouette. Perhaps the clerk in the bookstore watched, fascinated, that this pretty young woman seemed to be doing the same snow dance as the other he had seen from time to time, the one who dressed in multiple layers like a blimp, not recognizing they were one and the same person. He would hurry outside with a small shovel as an excuse to speak to her. "*Allô*, cold enough for you?" She'd stop, then, surprised, and seem to look right at him. Yet, he'd noticed, her eyes moved quickly back and forth, as if she really didn't see him. There was, perhaps, a crescent of smile on her lips as she'd walked ahead. And then, as a way to call her back, he'd whistle. Something loud and off-tune. Something, she'd guess, from one of those cabaret singers. Maybe Edith Piaf. She'd feel light-hearted, chatty, her head full of Malraux.

But then, inside our hotel, Monsieur Lepic would inform her "The tall Americans are not there, *mademoiselle*. They have already gone out." And when she asked if we had gone to the Sorbonne, he would glower, blowing words like wind through his fat cheeks. "It's not my business, miss, to ask the residents' whereabouts. *Au revoir, mademoiselle.*"

Undiscouraged, she'd have made her way to the front of the Hall Richelieu, determined now that, despite lack of counsel, she was prepared to act on her own.

I see how it unfolded. How she sat firmly, a small gesture of proprietorship, on the bench, determined that after the lecture she would intercept Saint-Georges himself and pose her question. To that end, she'd have gathered her things quickly as soon as the great clock struck noon, stood, and buttoned her coat. Certainly the usual claque of hangers-on swarmed around the professor as soon as he left the podium, while he quickly responded to several questions without seeming to look directly at the questioner. Melanie hung at the back of the little crowd, but followed it, determined not to let this moment get by her. Finally, seeing her chance, she'd boldly move up to fill the space vacated by the others. At last, a pause filled only by the rapid strides of Saint-Georges's shoes on the marble floor.

"Alors, monsieur le professeur," she'd have begun in a firm voice. "I have one question from our readings on Malraux. It is about redemption. At the end of *La Condition Humaine*, there is a passage which moved me very much, but I'm not sure I fully understand. It's when Gisors says, 'Since Kyo died, I've discovered music…'"

Alain Saint-Georges would then have slowed his steps. Music. That was what he was hearing. The irresistible song of an American accent. Slowly, his head turning, he'd looked directly through those dark-tinted glasses, then stopped still. It was hard to admit to himself how much he had missed that sound, and there it was again. And again a striking blonde. Petite. Body of an angel, he was guessing, trying to size up what was beneath that well-cut coat. Classy. A delicious stroke of luck. Almost enough to make one a believer.

Well, but was he not a believer already? Perhaps it was hard to know which god moved him the most—the sweet god of sexual pleasure, or the martial god of revenge.

"You pose a profound and most intelligent question, *mademoiselle*," Melanie recorded him saying. "Please. Let us pursue this soon. Perhaps late in the day we could meet. I know this small bistro..."

Perhaps that's all she remembered hearing. But even if unconsciously, at least she had the presence of mind to keep in mind what he'd said. Yes, she knew the Opéra. And that little establishment behind Café de la Paix. She jotted, "Opéra, behind Café dl P. 18 heures."

She arrived fifteen minutes early, breathless, unbelieving, carrying her satchel of books. Inside the terrace section, closed to the outdoors for winter, she looked around, trying to decide where to sit.

"As I hesitated, a waiter approached and said, '*Monsieur* is waiting for you inside, *mademoiselle*, come,' and he escorted me to a table in a darkened comer. There Alain sat, drink in his hand, looking intent, reading a paper. I know my heart pounded. To think that a great man like that wanted to discuss my ideas on Malraux! I just stood there, holding my bag of books, uncertain what to do.

"He looked up, surprised. *'Eh bien, Mademoiselle Hart…'* And he pulled down his glasses for a moment like he was inspecting me. I felt dumb. Then he said, 'But I told the waiter to watch for a beautiful young woman with blonde hair and a—what do you say, na-vee *bleu* coat. Very nice. Very correct.' And he stood and kissed my hand, saying 'Please, sit down.' So I sat, or perched actually, on the little banquette next to him, trying to remember what I'd meant to say. But he just waited patiently, smiling, and then said, 'Why don't you take off your coat and tell me what you would like to drink.' So I ordered a coffee. But he ordered a bottle of Anjou, 'Something the young lady may enjoy.' And then I stammered something stupid like, *'Ah, monsieur, professeur…* I don't, well okay, thank you. Ever since this morning, I have been trying to organize my thoughts a bit better.'"

It was then she pulled out a notebook and a copy of *La Condition Humaine* from her bag and placed them on the table, just as the waiter brought the bottle of chilled rosé and began the elaborate ceremony with that Parisian flair of decanting, passing the cork, and pouring a bottle of wine. When he left, Alain Saint-Georges gently shoved aside the books and placed his hand, ("a gesture of friendly intent," she called it), near Melanie's wineglass. Imagine him looking at her steadily, head cocked to the side, a picture of sincere interest, *S'il vous plaît, Mademoiselle Hart—or perhaps I may call you Melanie?* And her heart, which had been pounding as embarrassingly as a telltale drumbeat out of Edgar Allen Poe, she feared, suddenly stilled, and she took her first swallow of wine. "He pronounced my name Mel-an-ee, exactly like Hans."

There was more, of course, in the sonorous, inevitable voice of Alain Saint-Georges. *First, tell me all about yourself. As an expert in American affairs, I am always so interested in the opinions and lives of my American students especially.* Perhaps this is when Melanie began reaching for the wine. This was a minefield she wasn't remotely prepared for. "How could I possibly explain my rich, practically Nazi, parents (who have recently gone to a fundraiser for their favorite Californian politician, Richard Nixon) to a leading leftish intellectual, who also happens to be the foremost expert on American affairs in France?" she lamented.

Then, as if to cross a chasm of ignorance, a divide of language, she threw out words. *"L'oppression,"* she heard herself say, followed by "struggle of the classes…patriarchal…domination…self-determination." Now emboldened by the wine, and the fact that her French flowed so well ("never mind that it made little sense"), she pushed on until he waved her silent with his hand. *Please, Mel-an-ee, why don't you call me Alain? It is so much less patriarchal that way.*

The rest I have to read between the lines. How Melanie blushed, trying out the name before plunging ahead, "Okay, Alain, well, but as for Malraux," then reaching across the table to seize her books. By now her discourse would have become a little dizzy, what with at least half a bottle of wine on an empty stomach. But Alain of course listened with undiminished attention, trying not to show that he thought she had clearly understood nothing of the great writer Malraux, greater than ever at that moment since he had become *le ministre de culture,* reigning king in a pyramid of official and political intelligentsia.

But unnoticing, undeterred, Melanie plowed on, making her case before reciting the killer paragraph, the one she'd even recited to me. "So, when I came to this passage, it just spoke to me," she would have said, adding perhaps, "I have experienced this. It's when Gisors says: 'I hear Kama, now, since he's been playing… And what, then, do I remember? My desires and my anguish, the very weight of my destiny, my life.'" She might have dared look at him directly now with her dancing eyes, blue as ice. "So, I was wondering if one could say that the key to understanding Malraux is in the universal sound of music…"

The great Saint-Georges would have pursed his lips, drawing his forehead into a thinking pose, before looking up at her with deliberate seriousness. Then: *Mademoiselle, Melanie, you have amazing insight, extraordinary originality. Truly, I have never heard quite this interpretation of the work. I believe you should write a paper bringing together your ideas. Of course, it goes without saying, such a paper would bring you an automatic pass with honors for my class, but we may find some further recognition for it too. Depending, of course, on how well you execute it.*

"We both rose then," Melanie recorded, "though I felt a little unsteady, but Alain is such a gentleman. He helped me put on my coat. And as we left the restaurant to cross the terrace, he sort of guided me outside with his hand on the small of my back. Everything looked so different in the dark.

"Then he said, 'But of course, we shall have to meet regularly to see how your work is coming along.'"

Part 5

SHIFTING LIGHT, DANCING LEAVES

Chapter 21

The first night Evelyn had climbed up the stairs to Édouard's atelier on Rue Saint-Louis-en-l'Île, she thought she felt spring. But she changed her mind quickly. Perhaps it was the cold inherent in stripping, sitting partially clothed on a chair, or lying completely naked on a thin blanket on the bare floor. Or perhaps it was because Édouard, with his frugal French nature, refused to turn on the heat. I can just hear her saying: "*Édouard, chéri, j'ai froide.* I'm freezing my ass off here, how about turning up the heat? *Un peu de chauffage alors!*" And his weak reply: "*Alors, chérie, là-là,* it won't be long now, *ma belle*, we'll quit for today soon." And then, just as she expected, he'd lit the match on the little gas heater, swearing as the flames leapt toward him. By that time, weary of posing, she'd strike a match, too, and reach for one of his cigarettes.

It seemed by Gracie's account to always be the same conversation; lying there, exposed and shivering, Evelyn asking herself why she was doing this. Suffering for one's art was all right, she supposed, but suffering for somebody else's art was not. Then she would ask again: "For

God's sake, Édouard, why me? You could just go over to École des Beaux-Arts, or any art studio, and find a real model, you know, for hire." To which she would get the ritual reply: "Precisely because you are not for hire, *chérie*. Because your beauty is so authentic, so pure...you are what I need."

In the stillness of her pose, with the goose bumps seizing her flesh, she watched his face. The twitchy little mustache, the balding head (covered, she said "like a cliché, with a beret against the cold"), the eyes dark and alert, I imagine, as they went back and forth from her form, her curves, to his easel and brush.

And there, shivering on the floor, she would always answer her own question. She did it in part because, there, naked and completely revealed, she was in that moment pure. "He saw me as no other man had and wanted to render what he saw immortal. What's wrong with that?" she'd put the question to Gracie.

That the whole thing was a charade, that he was only an amateur with no apparent talent, did not, just then, matter. But what she saw in his eyes as he looked at her—her perfect beauty—did.

There was another thing, too. In the six weeks since she had first gone there and "spilled the beans," as she drolly put it to me, the allure of Édouard's world, its extravagance, its decadence, its hints of power, had become increasingly seductive, a reverse image of her parents' world, with its righteous and pious self-denial. And as Edith shared more and more of the "royal" secrets, as if each were a shutter thrown open on a hidden window, Evelyn came to a profound and shocking realization, one that Gracie instantly embraced: "You know what, *paisana*, Edith doesn't belong there any more than I do." And

Gracie understood that Eve's unexpected conquest the night of the reception in the Place de Voges fed an equally unexpected sense of rivalry: She could beat Edith at her own game, which meant her own ticket to Versailles, the grand palace of all illusions, dreams, discontent, revolution. The palace *le grand* Charles had refurbished to royal splendor just last year to receive Jackie. The palace Jackie had conquered.

Once again, Evelyn stood, threw a blanket over her aching limbs, walked to the window and asked "Can I see yet?"

Once again he replied: "Oh no, I'm still just sketching. Nowhere near ready for viewing."

"So, when?"

"Whenever the Academy announces the awards." He ended the conversation with the ritual joke.

She would gaze down at the river then, which ran swift and clean, so transparent, so new, it held no trace of the past, no residue of fallen leaves. Maybe it was simply spring coming. "I just felt like shouting from that rooftop, Gracie, *'joie, joie, joie.'* God only knows why."

The weeks drifted, and Evelyn with them. She had no idea where they were taking her, no particular desire to know. Walking one day with Gracie, she pronounced the names of the new leaves—*maronnier, chêne, platane*—like incantations, and watched as they made dark patterns on the new and free-flowing Seine. "Say these are pictures," she said to Gracie, "they're abstract, but they still make sense, and so does the architecture of the branches that bind them together, if you see them that way. Which is more than I can say for all those thrilling angles and arches of basic baroque, or those Napoleonic pillars with hairy lions' feet we were supposed to have loved." Although she didn't say as much to Gracie until later, it was also more than she could hope for from the painting she had so mysteriously inspired.

Through the weeks of posing, of shivering on the floor, of pushing back the night at smoky little dives with Édouard and his fruity *copins*, she began to wonder if she would ever see it. Even more she wondered why she was throwing everything over for these pale blue-bloods and hangers-on. "Like that squishy Albert," she remarked to Gracie. "His most distinguishing characteristic is a ridiculous goatee whose only function as best I can tell is for harboring halitosis."

But then there was that night on Montmartre, in the tiny club not far from Au Lapin Agile, that cabaret of Degas and Picasso in the shadow of Sacre Coeur, and she remembered why she hung in there. "'*Une surprise, une surprise,*' Édouard kept whispering, like I didn't live with Edith and hear on an almost hourly basis where she had wrangled an engagement or a prized invitation. I mean 'Au Faim du Loup, Au Faim du Loup,' Edith had spouted off at least a hundred times, as if she'd been invited to perform at the opera, or on Broadway, or maybe the Hollywood Bowl."

But then, there they were, she and Édouard and a half-dozen others, crowding into the smoke-filled *boîte*, to be thrilled by Piaf belting out "*Allez venez Milord…*" Only this Piaf was incarnated in round blonde fluff, as Edith directed her vibrating notes, impressive white cleavage, and gaudy winks at him, Monsieur le Marquis. "*My* marquis," Evelyn declared emphatically. Perhaps there was just the taste of bitterness rising in the back of her mouth, like turned wine or stale smoke, or perhaps green shoots of jealousy were sprouting from the fertile delta of her imagination, or so Gracie speculated. Gracie, who knew of such things.

At least Eve remembered why she had posed: because she really wanted Versailles with its old candles and mirrors and marble, its murals with muted allegories, its gold. She wanted its style, its overstatement, its *luxe,* its class. Let others—Ivan, or the infamous Professeur Saint-Georges, or even Jay Greene—rail against the meaning of it. But let her waltz in the Hall of Mirrors just once, and she would own a piece of it.

So as she watched Edith gyrate, let loose her great voice, bow and inhale, Evelyn knew herself to be the lucky one. She was an American, better still, a Californian, and whatever pedigree, style, or power she could glean was hers for the taking. "Christ, I come from the land of Disney and Hollywood, after all," she told Gracie, "I ought to know something about imitation, something about reinvention."

For Edith, Eve foresaw only defeat. Edith was stuck in the detritus of a class system cemented by a thousand years of practice, one where the queen still ruled. For all Edith's aristocratic ambitions, Eve understood the French would never take her seriously. Nor would they take seriously her designs on Piaf, no matter how outrageously good her voice. If nothing else, Piaf herself, frail and degraded, would see to that.

Evelyn watched her roommate do her little bow and dance to Édouard, and saw in his eyes the final response. "It was like I was watching *La Bohème* or something," she recounted to Gracie. "I guess she might flatter him, or her talent might amuse him, but she was to him no more than a singer, a cabaret performer, a fat little foreigner who might come to Versailles to entertain—like courtesans entertain, you know?—but never as a true guest of that pompous-ass, stuck-up aristocracy."

That invitation, Evelyn grasped as Edith took a bow, was the crown jewel.

And it was to be hers alone. Édouard squeezed her hand, a reminder of the growing ardor she inspired in this man who worshipped her body but with artistic, not sexual, desire. She leaned over to whisper to him, to tease him, to flatter him, and finished by adding, "Do promise, *chéri,* I can go with you to Versailles." He said, *'Oui, oui, oui,'* a thousand times, and this is critical, 'When they are sent out, there will be an invitation for you, I promise.' But to tell the truth, my mind was already racing ahead, and by the time he said, *'I promise,'* I was already thinking: But where the hell will I come up with a gown?"

Chapter 22

For more than a month, Melanie's feet barely touched the ground. "Whoa, sweetheart, who *is* he? You have really got it bad." Evelyn recounted this wake-up call—and Mel's unusual behavior—on a rare day when she rushed off to attend lectures while Melanie, exhausted from staying up too late, was skipping class.

It was Evelyn slamming the door no doubt that caused Louis to yap, which woke Edith, who swore and threw something behind her closed door. At that point, Melanie wrote, she knew sleeping in was a lost cause. So she lay still on her narrow bed in the room she shared with Eve and thought about her roommate's words. It was true—staying out late to meet Alain and his friends, then staying up late to work on her Malraux paper, created the night-life style of a giddy romance. Moreover, she felt excited, humming, a little too prone to laugh, a lot too tired. Very alive. Very like falling in love.

"But it is not love." Melanie was certain of that. Of course she had not said this to Hans, because the denial would be almost as worrisome and confusing as a confirmation, given the strain of distance. But in her letters to him—more hasty and brief than usual, she conceded—she had tried to convey her extraordinary mood to him.

> …I still can't believe that my ideas could actually impress such a man, but it seems to be true. And his friends, too, this circle of respected intellectuals, writers, publishers, that wonderful filmmaker Fanton, and this real character, a publisher named Fabrice de l'Aunay. But what it makes me think, dear Hans, is what you already know and encouraged, even though I couldn't see it myself—that I do have a brain in my head, and that if I can just use it, maybe I can make something of myself despite the predictions of my family. If this paper turns out, maybe I'll have the courage to ask advice about pursuing a course in political science…

At the time she quoted sections of such letters in her journal, Hans had not written back. I believe by then she had given up feeling guilty for not thinking about him all the time.

Melanie and Alain met sometimes in the afternoon. They were quiet meetings in a café or bistro. Ever the good student, she always came prepared to discuss her work. But after a few sentences on the subject of music in Malraux, Alain seemed disinterested and changed the subject. "Today," Melanie noted on a Monday in March, "A. said, 'I think it best not to crush your ideas with the weight of too much talk. They are still fragile, in the chrysalis stage. We'll analyze them when they are ready to take flight, no?'"

Normally such talk, I think, would have sent Melanie into a furrow of despair, certain that she was foolish, her ideas weak. But when Alain made these comments, he showered her with such concern, such interest, she believed him. And as he hurried onto other subjects, sometimes even the embarrassingly personal ones she confessed to her journal—like how lovely she looked in this certain shade of blue—she knew he respected her opinion and cared about her well-being. At the end of these daylight encounters, she always came away invigorated and determined to redouble her efforts on the paper.

But the daylight meetings paled compared to the nights, when all the stars came out. As if on a Ferris wheel, she felt she was making a circuit, dipping high and low in a round of late-night cinema, theater, restaurants, and bars, where the brilliant lights were ideas and the energy that powered the magic was talk.

Conversation, a word that seeds these pages, was a concept she had never even known existed in stilted parties at country clubs where clichés were exchanged—and where, she now knew, people ate the culinary equivalent of expensively prepared plastic wrap. *Conversation*, an art form, an invisible network that bound a tribe together by secret flicks of the tongue, a rippling *tricolore* of intonation and sound waves. Yes, she was making a circuit, going round and round with dizzying frequency, bringing her into another foreign reality—night as the best time to be alive. "When do these Parisians sleep?" she once wrote peevishly. Clearly no one seemed to give even a nod to the precepts of her upbringing—work hard, all things in moderation, early to bed, early to rise. Oh yes, and be seen with the right company. Now it was not just the circuit she was making, but a circle in the French sense, and it had encircled her, too. "The most wrong people I could ever hope to meet," she wrote joyfully.

Because Alain had invited her, she had quickly been embraced by his friends. "Intellectuals, dissidents, the filmmaker, that young woman poet, journalists, haggard-looking professors from various faculties, well-tailored members of la Chambre des Députés, and that outrageous Fabrice. Apart from the poet and an occasional actress, I am the only woman," Melanie remarked.

The first time she had come out at night, after watching a performance of Ionesco's *Rhinocéros* at the Comédie-Française, she had walked with Alain to a little restaurant nearby. En route they had met Fabrice, who sat down with them, and soon three others had joined the party. "Alain introduced me as his student and an expert on Malraux. I shrank a bit at that because there I was in the company of Fanton, the filmmaker, Lemoine, a professor of physics, and la Rochelle, some kind of relic of a philosopher from the Faculté des Lettres, all just kind of looking at me, as if I'm supposed to say something. Then Fabrice de l'Aunay took off his glasses and sort of inspected me."

I can just see him looking her carefully up and down, taking in the neat black suit, the single strand of pearls, the little handbag from Hermès. I can also see Melanie freeze, almost as if reliving the moment in Strasbourg when she got off the train. But luckily, no one expected her to say much, or perhaps not anything. And as they launched into a dissection of the play, or the stupidity of American culture, or, once again, the Algerian question, I see her feet locking together in their black high heels beneath the table, as she sat rigid, listening and lost, cut off by the overpowering waves of French. It was one of those moments she wrote about, when she felt as isolated in incomprehension as she had been at first, when that art form, the French language, seemed a force of destruction, coming like a storm at sea to overwhelm and drown her.

But Alain sensed her distress and reached for her hand beneath the table, giving it an affectionate squeeze. Then he whispered in her ear, *Ça va, chérie. Don't worry. Nobody will ask you about Malraux tonight.* "I love that kindness, that fatherly concern of his. I actually started to relax. I also practiced sipping very slowly a glass of deep red Bordeaux—I'm actually coming to love it—and it helped too. Then surprise, almost without noticing, it was like I began to float on the current of French, or swim in it. It was like a religious experience, or some kind of revelation anyhow, to realize I could understand what they were saying."

She had lost the beginning of the conversation—of how they leapt from Ionesco's absurdist drama about conformity in a small town in France where everybody turned into a rhinoceros, to the more contemporary dispute of rightists versus leftists. Only there, at that moment in a small restaurant in Paris, it was accepted that these friends and colleagues of Alain's were all communists. The rightists believed in the Soviet model, while the leftists were partisans of Mao Zedong.

"'But the Russians were the architects, the great theorists, the founding fathers' Fanton shouted. La Rochelle then whispered in so loud a voice that everyone could hear that F. had recently made a film about the glory days of the Russian Revolution with incredibly expensive crowd scenes of the Russian Army 'liberating' Moscow. '*Alors,*' Fanton said, waving his fork, 'but you didn't show them mowing down the students, the protestors, the freedom lovers. *Non.* It was Mao who had to show the way for that true Communist spirit, the love of the peasants.' Frankly, la Rochelle looks like the sort who would be lost anywhere outside central Paris. It's hard to imagine him embracing a French peasant, let alone a Chinese. And he didn't seem to have much love for his own countrymen, either, if you count the *pieds noirs*.

"Maybe Alain guessed what I was thinking, because he leaned over and whispered to me that 'the old one has perhaps an overly romantic view of the Chinese, due to long family ties there with the banking interests in Shanghai.' Then he let out a long breath, a kind of wheeze of despair, and he said '*Ah, chérie*, this threatens to be the death of us. Algerians versus *pieds noirs*. *Pieds noirs* versus all of France. Left versus right. They can talk of nothing else in the *facultés*, and in the press, the whole enlightened intellectual class. The fight is so bitter. How can we make a united front against Capitalist Imperialism when we are acting like a quarreling mob?' He cheered himself up then by ordering two more bottles of the Bordeaux and a plate of the best cheeses."

By night's end, when Alain stood in a dirty snowbank for a cab, Melanie was reeling, and not just from drink: she still hadn't learned to maneuver in spike heels without near fatality. Just as she felt herself slide, a steady arm grabbed her firmly by the elbow. Saved by Fabrice. She turned to see his shaggy face hovering behind her like an apparition, his breath blasting her like the winds from hell. "So, he says to me, '*Eh bien*, young lady. Tell us—in only a few words for one doesn't have time nor wind left—what is the key to your gorgeous new theory of Malraux?' At that point, I was completely caught off guard and just said, 'I guess that would be music. The key to Malraux is music.'"

It is easy to see Fabrice's unctuous smile, as he closed his eyes in a sort of rhapsody and replied: *"La musique? La musique? Ah, c'est sublime, mademoiselle. Vous êtes sublime."* Then he opened his eyes just in time to see Melanie disappear into a cab with Alain, his best friend.

If I thought Melanie had grown unnaturally cocky, I guessed it was because of her close call on the orals, the fact that she'd survived what had been nothing short of a mighty thrashing. Her situation had been playing on my own conscience too, inspiring an announced resolve to do better in the new term. I, too, had passed my exams, but in such a lackluster manner as to give rise to the thought that despite my appearance of hitting the books, perhaps my real education, like Eve's, had little to do with the classroom. Of course, she had barely squeaked by her exams, while Jocelyn and Gracie had both excelled with little effort. I sighed and remembered a quote Eve had scribbled among others attributed to JFK beneath her picture of Jackie. "There is no justice," it said.

It was a nondescript afternoon of gray Parisian drizzle when Melanie invited me along on a jaunt recommended by the art professor to study iron as art in architectural expressions of the industrial age. *"Je m'en fous,"* I had replied using the great French epithet worthy of Edith.

"Well, you better give a damn," Melanie had answered back to me, clearly offended, "if you plan to pass the next exams." So she set out for the Gare Saint-Lazare alone, still stinging as she got off the Métro at Clichy not because she was mad at me for my language, or even really, for refusing to come. She was upset because of Roland, because his easy manner and lurking titles and the hint of old châteaux in the country impugned his character. She condemned him as an aristocratic, entitled snob—the kind of person she was trying desperately not to become. She wrote "I can see what he is, even if J.J. cannot. Even worse, I hate how she can so easily just 'not give a flying fuck' as she so elegantly puts it, and just kiss off work or even worrying about it when it gets boring or tedious or just because something better, like a fling with some titled no-account Frenchman comes along. After seeing all she has seen in Paris, after Black Christmas together at the Bouchers, how come she doesn't know better?"

The Métro pulled to a jerky halt. Melanie said *Je m'en fous* sourly to herself and stepped out into the embattled boulevards to seek the train station under a sky heavy with *grisaille*, a condition somewhere between grayness and gloom. Perhaps because of it, because the air itself seemed a blotter robbing the Place de Clichy of any particularness, she for once lost her bearings and began to wander in the direction of Pigalle.

"Women, some younger than me, with broken teeth and old eyes and skin advertising infectious delights, lurked even in the cold midday, peering through cracked-open doorways. An old woman in the blue drab of the working classes—like Gracie's Marie—was struggling up a littered street bent over with the cold and bundles of food or coal or wood. On balconies and in cracks between soot-covered buildings, no more black, really, than the Louvre or the Opéra, but without any kind of architectural grace *at all*, or seeming pleasure, there was laundry hanging in the dirty damp air. These weren't like the bright spots of a sort of dancing local color on the line, like on those vacations to Acapulco and the Bahamas. These seemed more like flags of despair.

"Then the worst—I can't tell Hans about this. When I went around the corner to Rue Moncey, I surprised a man buttoning his trousers. Gaunt, unshaven, unsteady, couldn't tell what age. Glass from a broken bottle lay at his feet. He looked like some kind of ghost in a white coat, and his eyes locked onto me with amazing boldness and determination. It was as if he were drilling a hole in me by looking. I imagine he saw me as stinking rich. He didn't move or threaten me with a gesture or anything. But his look was a weapon, and made me more afraid than fire, more than anything I can remember. As if I passed through an electric current, he jolted me with a look that said, *You are no better than some animal to be kicked.*

"A sense of darkness came over me, and I suddenly saw the black rim beyond the fire in the trashcan outside the restaurant, where the old woman and child had tried to warm themselves. Pascal again with his gloomy, trembling heart in the dark."

When she found the wide Rue d'Amsterdam, she also recovered her sense of direction as if she'd just escaped from the underworld. When she finally walked into Gare Saint-Lazare, she felt a sense of relief, stepping through the vast space of the terminal out onto the platforms where iron girders uphold a glass roof and beyond that the sky itself. Then she saw the maze of rails seeming to rise from beneath the ground, confusing as the unseemly wires overhead, and beyond, the blackened crisscrosses of the Pont de l'Europe making a marvel of ugliness supported by thick brick pilings.

"The elements of gothic—soaring space, intricate support structure, light through glass—were all there," she noted in her neat hand, "but as if inverted, as if to connect the traveler to the guts and engine of the earth by the muscle and will of mechanical power. A cavernous space where a person feels small, as one does in a cathedral, but here small like an ant, or a piece of machinery, not small before the awesome hint of God and the suggestion of a journey to a higher realm."

Of course there was nothing new in this, in Melanie's observations about an era's promise ending in the smoke and dirt of urban grime, in poverty's shabby despair. It was not even new, in a way, to Melanie. She had, despite her family's disdain, taken in with sadness the broken-down bungalows in low-rent sections of Pasadena, had brushed like a visitor from a different continent against the edges of Watts and East L.A. She had read Zola. But then again, what was new in the *grisaille* of the Saint-Lazare district was that Melanie saw it alone, for herself.

And inhaling the traces of stale smoke that lingered a century after the promising great white puffs of early steam engines had evaporated, she had stepped into the cold gray of a working-class afternoon far into the age of post-industrial existentialism. The Nuclear Age, Alain had called it. Thinking of him, she knew it was time to show him what she had written.

This is what she remembered: the smile on Alain's face as he saw her, that deep, concentrating, penetrating smile focusing all the power of his world on her. The thoughtful brow contracted in concentration at his desk as he read her words. And then the pause, him looking up and saying, *But, chérie, this is brilliant. Quite original.*

Her heart pounding as he sat next to her on the little settee, where she had slipped out of the blue wool coat and sat, expectantly, in a tidy sheath the color of new grass. Or perhaps celery. Her heart pounding because at last he was going to discuss her words, her ideas, her work. Only he had left the papers on the desk.

"'But you haven't finished reading,' I said. 'I make my strongest points in the conclusion.'" And then half-rising in the wool sheath, the hand reaching up, pushing her back down. That hand on her breast. A mistake of course, she knew it was a mistake, just reaching up like that, until it was there again, and he was saying, *No, no, not just yet, chérie, you see I am just boulversé…* Overwhelmed. Yes, that was the word, and the small cry and more pushing, and then she panicked. Melanie grabbed her coat, buttoning it as she ran, her mind not seeing anything but papers, floating gently, like leaves, from the desk. *Feuilles mortes*. And the voice of Alain, like a distant song on a scratchy phonograph, his *cri de coeur*.

Another fucking virgin? America, land of one-hundred fifty million vieilles filles. Old maids. The words rang like a siren in her ears.

She ran and kept running, out of the empty echoing corridors where old winter hung like a dirty rag across the windows, out into the street, across to the Cluny where the first vestiges of green peeked out, as if to mock her, beneath a sky of melted blue ice. There she flung herself on top of an ancient tomb, the wool of her blue coat a sponge to absorb the mud.

Among the tombs she suddenly remembered how the fire had come. On the top of the pages, she wrote *feu, feu, feu*, and scrolled the edges with licks of flame, imagining how hot it had been when the Barbarians arrived in Paris with their torches, how black and clean everything had burned. "Even the baths," she wrote. The baths where the Romans, and before them the Gauls, and before the

Gauls, the Parisii fishermen, had slipped naked into the water, into oblivion, into history.

She came to us to seek solace. She zigzagged down the narrow École-de-Médecine as if drunk, disheveled, her blue coat stained with mud. But we were not there, as Monsieur Lepic would inform her.

"Even the two Jo's let me down," she wrote.

Chapter 23

According to Gracie, it had been around the time that Evelyn made her first trip to the atelier that she also found out about Melanie and Alain Saint-Georges. In the weeks that followed, as spring determined to push through the strongholds of entrenched winter, Evelyn tried to make good on her vow to be attentive to Melanie, to prevent her from slipping into invisibility. She could expend an extra measure of compassion for one roommate as her duel with the other intensified. The rivalry with Edith grew fierce as the date for *le bal* got closer.

One evening she'd come home to find the apartment empty. A newborn, determined spring was playing against the window with soft light and the silhouettes of clouds like fat spring sheep, and she threw open the shutter to let in the smells of rising bread from the *boulangerie* below. Edith's things, she recounted to Gracie—"one alligator shoe, a playbill for *Le Bourgeois Gentilhomme,* some embossed envelopes addressed in a perfect hand, publicity photos"—were all strewn about. One by one, she picked them up and looked at them and saw with mounting dismay that they were only props: what they represented didn't exist. "There was only Mary-Margaret, rich little English girl of no-account stock, who wished to be Edith, *chanteuse extraordinaire,* and *habituée* of the inner sanctum of *le tout Paris.* But she would in fact remain Mary-Margaret, an ill-born English girl with a dumpy figure and a fabulous voice. 'Baise-Moi' was the song on the tape recorder, and I just sat and listened until dark. Hearing her voice, I had this realization that *combat-à-mort* with such as her—I mean, despite her gift, she's condemned to lose—probably isn't a worthy way of life."

But paying attention to Melanie, long neglected and grieving, by her lights, was. Besides, Eve told Gracie, "almost despite herself, Mel seems to have found some kind of strength, some sense of purpose—things I need to know."

I found the pages in Melanie's journals that describe how she asked Eve to a concert. "Not Piaf or Montand or anything like that, but classical. Bach. *The Brandenburg Concertos.* Some of Hans's favorites. And I told her she couldn't beat the setting. Sainte-Chapelle."

Melanie recorded that Evelyn was late and beyond excuses. Never mind that she'd been to a gallery opening with Édouard, that Edith had been there too *with Charles,* that the talk had been of nothing but the upcoming Bal de Versailles, that Louis had crawled in Edith's closet and peed on the other satin shoe. "'I've been living in the center of this storm,' she said, 'and I already know all the stories.'" There was nothing Evelyn could say to justify herself that would make the slightest case for her tardiness. And she must have known this, too, as she charged through the gold-embossed gate at the Conciergerie, across the stone-paved courtyard, and up the narrow round stairway to Sainte-Chapelle two steps at a time. When she passed through the lower chapel with its forests of painted gothic archways and little gems of blue glass windows, the music had already started. The sounds of the organ were the sounds that had reverberated through her childhood, and at last, there she was inside a church again. For Evelyn, coming to Paris had, after all, been about getting *outside* of church. But stepping into the soaring gothic embrace of Sainte-Chapelle was not church as she had previously experienced it. Melanie seemed to intuitively understand Eve's reaction, writing "This was not anything as she knew it. Certainly not light, which outside was dying into first spring night, but inside through glass, became life. Transubstantiation. Certainly not air, for air was nothingness that blew life through the body. But this air, this nothingness, through the prism of rose glass walls soaring toward heaven was something. It existed, fleshless with the color of flesh. Air, yet she could not breathe. Nor was this Bach as she knew him, for the notes rose into that colored emptiness and hung there, respiring but never falling. It also was not love, for there was no embodiment here, no sacrifice, no blood, not even carnal sin. I imagine the word God slipped into her mind, for this was about God, but she wasn't prepared to think about God. So she just sat down abruptly instead.

"Then she saw me. I guess so anyway, though my eyes were closed and my face tilted upward to the sound of violins and harpsichord, sounds I think that came as close to being the instruments of heaven as any I've ever heard. I remember that through the western rose-glass portal the sun poured all that was left of the day and spilled it down in a single shaft of light. She told me afterwards that it caught my hair like a torch and a rose flame shot up from my head to disappear high above. She said I burned like a candle. A holy candle. She said that word, holy, had not crossed her lips since confirmation class. Then another buried word rose up in her. 'It felt like worship, Mel,' she said. 'Only now I see. It comes from fire.'"

Eve's long confessional to Gracie filled in the rest of the details. Following weeks of hinting, spring had set its own starting line from which there was no turning back. By the Ides of April, she assured herself, all would be in hand. The promised invitation to the Bal de Versailles was to be mailed on the twelfth, and, to celebrate, Édouard had proposed a little party in the atelier—catered, no tinned beans this time, he said—to unveil his painting. He promised, despite three weeks of wheezing and red eyes, attributable to the miserable sprouting of the city's blooms and flowering trees. To alleviate his misery, he claimed a retreat to his château was in order. He also swore to entertain Evelyn there as soon as current distractions were over. That, she presumed, meant *le bal*.

His departure to the country coincided with the creeping onslaught of spring, and Gracie pointed out that Eve should have been suspicious right there. Retreating to the country to get away from pollen? But it's easy to see how the season itself could have lulled her into complacence. There had been those rare, mild days, where soft earth was shadowed by Monet skies, and the river rippled pink. Then there were the others, like remnant sales of winter, filled with vengeful, bitter rain and pitiless wind. The combination cleared away the last of winter's debris and left the city exposed in the new spring light, its wounds displayed for all to see: cracked bridges, collapsed walls, sunken roofs, ancient buildings cut adrift from their foundations, statues ready to topple.

Perhaps this seductive pull to the sensuous season contrasted with the bitter reminders of the relentless freeze made Eve restless. She began extended pacing—much the way Jocelyn had for months along the Seine. Walking was good for her, she said. She needed the exercise, to feel her body again. In fact, with the return of warm air, some small protective shell around her had melted too. The letters from Tom made her shiver a little, the way one shivers in heat. She read this one verbatim to Gracie.

> Dearest,
>
> It is rough over here without you. I keep seeing you on every street corner, or getting off the late bus, or safe and warm in my arms just outside la Maison. I'm studying, working on the damn physics (tell Gracie when you see her), trying to keep in shape for next fall's season. But I just want to hold you, feel you, touch that hair like fire and silk…

He added that Jay Greene was doing much better and was getting around on crutches. "He asked that I send his greetings, and gratitude."

That news, Eve confessed, made her shiver too. She began dreaming of Tom every night. Then, within a week, she received an envelope with the ragged handwriting of a child. Inside, on a scrap of notebook paper, was a cartoonish drawing of a stick figure with a mop of unkempt hair floating in the sky over a scene of fire and ruin. *"Lazarus rises and dreams of you,"* was the caption. It was signed with a childlike heart and the initials J. G.

With Édouard gone, she needed distraction. She missed the parties and little galleries and receptions where everyone had a title, old lands, or a new bank account—or at least, as she put it to Gracie, an aristocratic nose. Initially, it thrilled her that she could continue her conquest at these affairs with nothing more than her natural gifts, her sumptuous body, gorgeous hair, and beguiling French, dressed in cheap department-store sheaths and fake pearls. She especially liked it because she could, by playing herself, outdo Edith.

But then, having lost the taste for competing with Edith, the idea of owning something authentic grew on her. Real clothes, not hand-me-downs, church bazaar specials, homemade patterns, off-the-rack bargains. Especially with the Bal de Versailles close at hand. She still had not resolved the dilemma of what to wear.

She walked tall those days, Gracie said, so she could feel the sun with her face tilted upward to draw down its strength. Only two weeks left, and then the Ides of April.

Picture this. Early April, Evelyn walking along the Seine close to Pont Neuf, close enough to trail her hand in the water. Life as it blossomed here was beyond thinking. It was more like breathing, walking in sway with the river's tide and the breeze, feeling the bones of the city move in her bones, seeing herself in its eyes. It was knowing what she could not name, and laughing when her ears opened to take in the low whistles and calls, the hard purring Vespas gunning their motors in tribute, the long humming glances of black-eyed men passing in sleek sedans, the look in the pale eyes of the elderly gentleman tipping his hat. *Yes I will yes I will yes.*

Evelyn crossed the river to pass through the stylish Italianate archways of the Rue de Rivoli—architecture, which she said, she *got*, just as Melanie got the brittle gothic beauty of Sainte-Chapelle. She crossed the river this time to enter the one temple where she could in honesty worship—le Salon de Thé. She had not been there for a few weeks and, climbing the stairs, she prayed that the table in the corner—her table—would be available. Praise God, it was.

She ordered scented tea and some petits fours, then remembered her posture and straightened up, strengthened by the hot, sweet fumes and chocolate glaze. She looked around. Instead of feeling invisible, as she usually did, and needing to take mental notes on the manners, airs, and dress of the beautiful, she felt almost visible, almost comfortable, almost as if she belonged. If Jackie Kennedy had been sitting in her place, she told Gracie, all the French women of style would look to her, the American, to copy. But you know what she'd realized, she told Gracie: "I'm just as beautiful in my own way, and just as smart. Only not rich, not born with the silver spoon into class."

Yet she was on her way toward overcoming that disadvantage too. Going to Versailles was the breakthrough. She had to do right for herself, for her country—and, of course, for Jackie. All that stood in the way, really, was the right dress. As she was stirring her tea, looking at the elegant women around her dotting the tea room in delicate spring suits in shades of pink, blue, and yellow like new blooms, the solution came to her. The church scholarship fund!

This is how she put it to Grace: If she didn't pay her enrollment fees for the rest of the year (and what was the point, since she'd majored in socializing, had barely cracked a book for weeks, and had dim prospects for passing her year at the Sorbonne anyway?) then there was enough for a proper gown! Of course there'd be hell to pay, but she could deal with that later. Besides, maybe even the church ladies would be impressed at her success in the rarified world of international high society. They all, she knew, secretly admired Jackie even if they were Republicans.

So right there on the spot, proud of herself for having found so neat a solution, she got up, stood tall, straightened her plain cotton skirt, and walked with practiced grace from the room. All eyes, she knew, were on her and she felt their admiration all the way to Rue Saint-Honoré and the high fashion windows of the *grandes maisons*.

The ivory dress with beadwork along the bodice had slid halfway to the floor next to the plastic dress cover with *Givenchy* emblazoned across the top. Jacqueline Kennedy's favorite designer, she told Gracie. Evelyn's heart rate had quickened even as her feet slowed when she saw it in the window, and she had longed right then to feel its cool, elegant satin. We all heard how she walked into the *maison* with unaccustomed assurance, because for once she'd figured out how to get the money she needed, and because she knew in her heart that the dress was made for her. "I felt I had true courage," she said, "in the sense that the word comes from *coeur*, and boy had I lost my heart. It was love at first sight."

Buoyed by the feeling, Eve strode inside ready to meet the snooty salesgirl on her own turf. "I know she was ready to boot me out given my clothes, but my French was never better, and I don't know where it came from, but I figured I had to act like I owned the place, so I did." By the time Eve was alone with the dress in a fitting room, the model-perfect young salesgirl in black had exchanged her haughtiness for bewilderment, and Eve said, "I knew there was a heaven after all."

Though some alteration would be needed—the dress was too snug at the bust—Evelyn luxuriated in slowly turning around and around in the softly lit room of mirrors to see herself from every angle. No longer a make-believe princess on a cold football field swathed in cheap fabric from a Sears catalogue stitched up by her mother, she reveled in her transformation. As she fingered the beading, ran her hands across the satin on her hips, words came into her mind to describe the dress and how she felt in it: elegant, chic, glamorous, svelte, queenly. *Authentic.* "This is the real deal," she said aloud. That realization was the most amazing of all.

Like the rest of us, Melanie knew the story of The Dress. But what she didn't know when she came in the apartment was why Eve was on the window seat next to it, crumpled and sobbing.

Mel rushed to her, then hesitated, uncertain what to do. "I asked her what was the matter, then tried to comfort her, put my hand on her back (kind of awkward), and waited for her to straighten up. Finally she did, letting forth with a string of curses in French from behind a veil of fallen hair. 'Shit,' she finally said like an amen or something before telling me that today, at last, after two weeks of rushing to check after each delivery, she stuck her hand in the box and '*Voilà*, the thick envelope with the embossed seal on the back. Versailles at last! Only, can you believe this… it's addressed to Edith. There's nothing for me. Nothing! So I call Édouard's number in the attic, just on the off chance he's come back early, and I get this strange sound and then the operator's voice saying this number is no longer working.'

"'Meaning what?' I asked.

"'Meaning what?' she kind of wailed now. 'Meaning he ditched me. No invitation, no explanation, no painting. Can you *believe* this?'

"I tried to say maybe it wasn't so bad. Maybe the invitation was late. And maybe he just forgot to pay the phone bill…and he'd get in touch soon. But she cut me off saying, 'No, no. I wish you were right, but I know in my bones what the story is. He's just so weak, such a joke, a windbag in an old coat of arms, such a powerless relic he couldn't even raise so small a thing as a favor, so tiny a thing as an invitation. And on top of that, he's such a coward he couldn't even tell me. Meanwhile, I'm ruined.'

"'Ruined?' I say. 'I know you wanted to go to Versailles, but it's not like your life depended on it.'

"Then she says, 'In a way it does. I bet everything on it—risked everything—and spent everything. Now all I've got is that damned dress and nowhere to wear it.'"

Chapter 24

Spring was unequivocal. The sky lowered itself over the rooftops of Paris close enough to touch. Everything—the garden paths through the Tuileries, the storefront glass washed clean for new displays, the heavy shutters on tall windows thrown open with military alignment—appeared scrubbed, fresh, trim, and in place. Then came the breezes, and with them a wondrous tossing. Flowers bent fervently in their beds. Leaves blew whimsical and wide from their branches. Tulips separated petal by petal on their stalks.

What had been merely comprehensive misery all winter at the hotel on Rue de l'École-de-Médecine became, with spring, intolerable. Jocelyn, her spirits lighter, commenced walking again, but now rather like a cat who's slept away the dark months and wants once more to prowl. I, too, could hardly bear to remain in our cramped room. The piles of books (which had hardly led to my academic stardom) began to dwindle. The bidet gathered dust.

The only constant in our shift through the seasons remained the letters, which still poured forth, miraculously, through the vagaries of the French post. Letters from Gran urging me outside, urging me south to the land of almonds and olives, of sun and sunflowers, red poppies and lavender, to the land of ancestry. And the usual letters of contrary opinions from my parents.

The letters from Madge came, too, in a steady stream, often crammed with dollars and always with advice, which Jocelyn once again shared with me. Perhaps, Madge suggested, we might at last find fresh fruit (apricots or plums, she advised, might be particularly healthful at this time in France). Or perhaps we might at last be ready to come home. Jocelyn's rebuilt room with a new round red bed was nearly ready.

Samuel's letters, of course, arrived with unrelenting force. For whatever reasons, Jocelyn had been less inclined to leave them, opened or unopened, in full view of my inquisitive eyes, and I had been less inclined to ask.

The Prince of Dakar, as she called him, appeared often too, coming for Jocelyn. She never really explained how she had met the tall, handsome African. Seeing him from a distance, I wondered, who was he really? Truly a prince? Watching his posture, his regal bearing, I decided yes, and for once I didn't seek a convincing narrative as proof. Besides, it was spring in Paris, and anything was possible. When he came after dark to fetch her, and Jocelyn descended down the stairs, a perfect Desdemona to his Othello, they disappeared together into the night. As for who she might be in his eyes, "I dance wonderfully and that's enough for him," she once declared, and we did not discuss the subject again.

Our own *pas de deux* carried me away from her again. Not that there were any hostilities declared or undeclared between us now. But I felt overburdened with my own pitiful life, with the preoccupations of my friends that seemed to leak into me as insidiously as dreams. I also felt the charge from Jocelyn's electricity, and feared it like a live wire, never knowing where I might trip it, afraid it might make me wish to leave my own skin. With spring, Roland appeared and disappeared in zany, bewildering, passionate playfulness, like the sun in shadow. And Guy ran through the budding season, a deep, invisible current, its source and destination unknown, yet capable of pulling me down.

One day, my head full of these calculations, I turned the corner to Rue de Saint-Simon approaching Boulevard Saint-Germain, and stopped dead. In the plate glass of an antique store, surrounded by gilt-framed reproductions of eighteenth century nymphs, two landscapes in the manner of Corot, and a still life of undetermined provenance, was a large pink nude. A nude reclining on a white carpet, her inviting curves in hasty brushstrokes of muted color, underlying tones of blue, I guessed, her pose a faint reference to the ancients yet at the same time boldly modern. This nude leaned her head inquisitively on one hand, red hair cascading forward like a suggestion as she looked unblinkingly at her admirers. *"God!"* I said more as supplication than irreverence. There across the top was an attached paper announcing, in case I still didn't get what I was looking at, a price and title: *Eve réflechit au jardin après la chute.*

Right. It was Evelyn thinking everything over after the Fall.

It was then I thought of Gracie and went to find her. She lived closest by, but calling on her was more than convenience. It seemed important to have somebody else verify a sighting of the picture, perhaps to have a collaborator to help make a plan, before revealing to Evelyn what I had discovered. Walking briskly down Boulevard Saint-Germain, I turned onto Boulevard Raspail, threading my way through the old trees and the long reach of their new shade. The branches swayed and danced with a playful light I hadn't seen since fall. An almost unbearable sweetness in the spring breeze made me feel, in that old-fashioned word of Gran's, faint.

Marie let me in, Madame garrumphed, having never regained the bare civility of her pre-Thanksgiving days, and in a minute I was alone in the musty parlor. Gracie came in; freckles seemed to have bloomed on her pale cheeks, and her eyes, almost cloudy, focused on me in the most distracted way. Normally, news of the order I had come to bring, especially news of Evelyn, would bring her out of even the deepest hole of self-reproach. But my wild and rushed account evinced only a faint, distracted smile.

"Gracie," I said at last, "promise me you'll go to the shop and see for yourself. Go inside. Ask around. I mean, it's the least we can do for Evelyn, right?"

"Right," Gracie answered, seeming to rally for a minute. "I'll go later this afternoon. Promise."

"Meet me at Hall Richelieu then, before class? I'm dying over this. Have to tell Eve something. Maybe we should meet her together?"

"Uh. No. Don't think I'll make it to class tomorrow. If the phones work, I'll call your place and leave a message with Monsieur Lepic…"

I ran the rest of the blocks to the nearest Métro and the few blocks home from the stop at l'Odéon. Monsieur Lepic looked up in a kind of reptilian rapture from behind heavy lids as I passed him in the lobby and bolted the stairs three at a time to reach our room. *"Jocelyn, mon enfant, ma soeur, écoute…"* I called out, throwing open the door. But of course, Jocelyn was not there.

The next day when I returned late to Hôtel des Ecoles, Monsieur Lepic, perhaps suffering his own version of spring fever, was not behind the desk. But I noticed a note in the small cubbyhole where he placed our key. I pulled it out and stood in the shaft of daylight flooding the stairs to read it, not even waiting for the privacy of our room. The note, on a folded piece of notebook paper with small boxes instead of plain lines, was written in the straight and well-formed hand of a French schoolboy, but a boy obviously confused by what he was hearing. "*Mademoiselle*, your friend Mademoiselle Bagatelle regrets that she searched all her antiques, and even asked her proprietor, but cannot find your photograph. The picture in question, being no longer framed, is also missing."

Gracie's name did not make it onto this document, but Monsieur Lepic's did, in a large signature with a gothic flourish.

It was three days before I saw Jocelyn again. She came, I knew, during the day, no doubt to sleep; evenings, I'd come back to find my belongings once again rearranged or hidden beneath her latest clutter. I kept placing my note in dark ink upon her pillow: Urgent, Calling All Hands, You Must See This…, followed by the address, the startling object to be seen, and a hint to buy. Finally, on the third day, she burst in, humming La Marseillaise.

"Well?" I asked impatiently, "did you see her?"

"See who?"

"The picture of Evelyn. The nude. The one I told you about in the note."

She wheeled around to look at me, covering her own naked chest with a fresh shirt, her eyes once again their startled green. "Well, I did go to the antique shop 152 *bis* Rue de Saint-Simon, just like you said. Know what I saw? Some antique-y stuff, you know, tables, a chair, lamps, and a bunch of pictures. Frolicking cherubs and nineteenth century landscape knock-offs. Some drapes. Sort of like your mom's place if not her taste. However, there was not a hint of a nude."

"What?" I said, suddenly making sense of Gracie's garbled message.

"That's right, *ma belle.* I even went inside to ask, said I was an interested buyer. But *monsieur*—a pompous old windbag—told me I must be mistaken, said they had had no such picture in the window."

Chapter 25

Gracie knew, of course—we all eventually knew—of Jocelyn's final, humiliating encounter with the Alain Saint-Georges. She learned, too, through Eve, of Melanie's similar experience. So what could she have been thinking when, one spring day after class, she broached the gaggle of admirers around the Great One after his morning lecture and dared to speak up? Others would approach tentatively, or shyly, or seductively, and cast a question in his direction. But Gracie came in her unobtrusive way to make a slight correction. "I felt compelled," was how she explained it. "When he spoke about physical science in the colonial period, he made a mistake. I thought he'd like to know."

What did she say, exactly? The words themselves were not as important as the clarity of thought, the force of intellect behind them. Saint-Georges would have recognized those in the clear, if accented, American voice that reached him above the ring of "idolaters," as Gracie called them. He stopped speaking to a student in the front rung and came through the others to seek her out.

I do not know what went through his mind when he encountered the large head with the runaway curls, the short, squat body, the feet planted squarely in stumpy flat heels, for she had packed away her high heels before Christmas. I don't know what he saw in her earnest, intelligent gray eyes, or the tilt of her oversized, cleft chin. But I do know she engaged him, and before he left to vanish up the marble stairs to his office, they had conversed about Locke and Voltaire, Franklin and Diderot, and the correct reading of de Tocqueville. He had also told her he would like to discuss these matters with her again.

Gracie's heart beat like a rabbit's. She knew the pattern. She knew that she had crossed some great divide; that she, Gracie, could be counted as one of the attractive young Americans Alain Saint-Georges wanted to take to bed.

There were other signs, too. They began meeting in cafés, she told me, and sometimes restaurants in the evening. Fabrice came, and an ancient judge, and two young women writers, but she couldn't tell if they were fair game, too, or a couple by themselves. The conversation, especially when it came around to the philosophy of science and the relationship between atomic theory and existentialism, was amazing.

"And when he asked me to write my thoughts on the history of scientific theory in contemporary America, I knew I had arrived. *Mama mia!* Remember Melanie?" she said.

She had not felt so light-headed, so brilliant, since the hours in la Maison when Tom had learned basic physics at her knee. Their secret correspondence, their plotting and contriving to arrange a surprise lovers' tryst, even if one of the lovers was not Grace, gave off enough vicarious friction to carry her through winter. Then spring arrived and the unexpected thrill of a charged mental exchange with Saint-Georges (and Madame purring like a cat upon hearing his voice on the telephone), followed by the promise of consummation. The making of Tom's "doll," the permanent vanquishing of the dreadful memory of Georgie, and the final surrender to one of the intellectual giants in all France—it would happen, Gracie fantasized, in one sweeping seductive encounter.

If I'd known or been attentive, if I'd not been so oblivious to all except the dance I was doing so clumsily with Roland, if I'd not been distracted by Ivan and his oddly enthusiastic outings to charnel houses like Verdun, I might have noticed the change in Gracie. The way she "tarted up," as Edith would say, with rollers and hair spray to make her curls look more French, more chic, and less like the nether end of a mop. I might have noticed the too-large silk scarf draped around her short neck. And I certainly would have taken in the reemergence of the lizard-toed high heels. Of course, at the time, I saw none of this. But when Gracie told me of the events as they unfolded, it was as if she opened a window in my memory, and in a flash of light, I saw everything.

The paper, she said, had kept her occupied, "the way one is with a secret vice," for weeks. I can imagine her in the back bedroom of Madame's flat, slightly feverish as she worked at the small desk, Tom's letters for the moment stacked neatly to the side, while outside, through that window to the courtyard, spring brought birds to the ledge and a new sky and the sounds of children playing below. But she ignored them all. She had a more urgent mission.

For the first time since living at Madame's, she said, she'd lost weight. Camille even resorted to entreating her to come to the table, to come out for a cigarette or a nightcap, to stop working so hard—though she assumed Gracie was slaving over her studies (a foolish enterprise, in Camille's opinion). Even Madame, Gracie recounted, seemed more plainly melancholy, less vitriolic. "Maybe she missed having me to beat on every night over dinner, though I'd gotten so good at learning the names of things, I think the fun had gone out of it anyway."

No one, it seems, knew of Gracie's secret.

By May 1, the deadline she'd set for herself, the day the medieval poets had celebrated as a festival of love, she was ready. It is not hard even now to see her tricked out in that too-short beige linen sleeveless suit, the one she'd gotten because it seemed chic and expensive, but which she didn't understand made her limbs all wrong, made her fair skin look washed out. But she made up for it, I'm certain, by "amending nature with the paint pots," as Eve put it: fixing her lips with dark red lipstick when pale was all the fashion, rouging her cheeks to camouflage insurgent freckles, and carefully etching her eyes in black liner, rosy shadow, and dark mascara. I'm sure that the day Gracie tripped up the marble stairs on her burnt red heels with the lizard-skin stripe and followed the hall to Alain Saint-Georges's well-used office, her eyelashes were combat-ready. I believe she was prepared to surrender to his inevitable pass and to claim her place in that trinity of pale, beautiful sisters, who had, with their varying charms, trapped the great French intellectual and number-one expert on American affairs.

"Entrez," he had called out as she rapped softly on his door. Then she stood in its threshold, blinking a minute while she swept the room with her intelligent eyes. The settee, the walls of books, the old, cluttered desk, with

its framed picture turned away from her. And there, as if himself framed by the window over the courtyard, Alain Saint-Georges himself, sitting erect, wearing a dark suit.

"Ah, mademoiselle, enfin. Asseyez-vous." The greeting, the invitation to sit, these were, Gracie could see in retrospect, correct, formal. The proper sort of exchange between professor and student. And she took the chair he indicated for her, one with a straight back opposite him at the desk, not the settee where Jocelyn and Melanie had sat so inauspiciously before her.

He cleared his throat, lifted his glasses to look at her more directly, revealing the deepening creases around the corners of his eyes. The sunlight behind, she noted, flooded through the window, making it unclear where the distinguished gray beginning at his temples disappeared into the tone of his complexion.

"Mademoiselle," he began, and she remembered how he cleared his throat, as if to give himself pause to find just the right words. His eyes focused on her now, intently, as if to probe something beneath the surface. She feared the sound of her heart, feared he might hear it.

"Mademoiselle…ah, Battaglia, non?…" he continued, "I, I don't know quite how to tell you this. I have rarely in my long career been so moved by, that is to say, imagine finding one such as you among my students. I feel astonished, *mademoiselle,* and frankly, how should I say it? so lucky to have someone like you at last. You, if I may put it like this, make me realize my own worth, too, the validity of my efforts. To know that someone out there in that great sea of student faces, actually hears me, actually understands at a profound level—and frankly, the surprise of knowing that she could be an *American…"*

Gracie recited this much from memory, then couldn't seem to finish the soliloquy. What Alain Saint-Georges had said up to that point was rapture enough…the words, of love, she knew, of a great intellectual, a great Frenchman. It was almost too much to bear. She shut out the sound of his voice to wait, at the edge of her chair, for the next overture, while crossing and recrossing, like a nervous twitch, her rust-colored high heels at the ankles.

But, she had to notice, he didn't seem to be budging from his desk chair, didn't seem to be moving in her direction, and when he finally leaned toward her across the expanse of his desk, it was only to hand her a paper. "Permit me, *mademoiselle*," he was saying, "to show you what I have remarked on the paper—the most brilliant analysis of the scientific basis of the Enlightenment that I have read in the halls of the Sorbonne."

Gracie sat back, alarmed, realizing her hands and forehead had gone from wet to dry, from hot to cold, as if there had been a shift in the weather. The paper fell to her lap like a dead leaf, and still he went on.

"…what I mean, *mademoiselle*, and you must realize this has happened but rarely in my long career as a professor, as a specialist in American affairs, and, as you may imagine, never, but never before with a young woman, for in general they are so much suited to other things, but in you I see it plainly. A brilliant future as a scholar. A historian perhaps, or if you see my way of thinking, maybe you will follow me keeping one foot on each side of the Atlantic, and become a political scientist, a specialist in French affairs…"

He had stood by now, and was looking directly into her gray eyes, boring into her with a gaze of sincerity, and on wobbly feet, she stood too. What did she say to him then, at the most humiliating moment in her life? Probably little, probably nothing more than a perfunctory *"oui"* as he led her to the door, making the extraordinary promise to write a personal letter recommending her uncommon mind and scholarly potential "a guarantee for the success of the rest of your life," he said. "Thanks," she remembered saying back in English, as she tried to walk away without a collapse. And then, at last, he reached out his hand. Even years later, she could feel the burn of his touch, that collegial, avuncular, professional touch as he patted her on the shoulder before she fled, like her friends had done before her, in tears down the corridor away from him.

By the time I bumped into her again, Gracie's spirits had been buoyed by a new flurry of letters from Tom and plans for the secret tryst *à trois* were in full bloom. A stream of excited words brought her back from the brink of extinction where she'd tottered since Alain Saint-Georges had not tried to seduce her.

> ...think I can make it by mid-June earliest, doll, what do you think? I'm dying to hear back from you and can't wait to pin the very spot on the map. If you aren't staying on in Paris 'til then, where?

It was a mid-May day so fine it was hard to imagine any season had ever existed but spring. I was on my way to the Jardin du Luxembourg. "Come with me, sit a moment on a bench, and drink it in," I invited. But Gracie demurred. She said something vague about meeting Camille. Of course I was certain she was not, like the rest of us, gearing up for the awful finale of our academic endeavors—finals at the Sorbonne, which, in fact, she would not study for. Much to her dismay, she would end up once again with *highest honors*, mocking all her attempts to become a *femme du monde* instead of a brain. "Like the final nail in my coffin," she told me later. But that day, when she rushed off, I could not have guessed it was to run home to check the mail and pray for another letter from Tom.

She left me and I then went alone through the iron grill entrance, skipping puddles left from showers the night before and found a spot of sun on a bench between beds of tulips overlooking a pool. Small boys with knee stockings sailed their toy boats while grandfatherly old men in berets gave counsel. I wanted to believe in this snapshot, and in all the others—young mothers pushing prams, lovers embracing like those whose silhouettes had, in fall, forced Jocelyn to turn away, students like myself reading under chestnut trees.

There was plenty to worry about, the looming threat of exams for instance, and my rather impressive falling off from studying over the last several months. Or Roland, who now asked me directly to come south with him, to come home to Provence, showering me with images as sweet as Gran's letters. Then there were the letters from my parents, who now wrote from their separate addresses at nether ends of the city.

All I could see clearly was what was not there. Jocelyn, who in a way as vexing as in fall was largely absent again, dancing into the dark now, instead of hiding in it. Still, her absence felt like a room locked against me. Guy was missing even in my dreams, a lost obsession I was loathe to concede in daylight.

One day, Ivan knocked unexpectedly at our door. Jocelyn, who was out, had left a recent letter from Samuel on the chaotic mess of a bed, which included a homemade concoction to prevent wheezing, courtesy of Madge's anxiety and Burt's rebuilt "laboratory." The high window, opened to the whim of spring breezes, showcased blowing leaves and a sprinkling of fallen petals, carried aloft from some rare, last-blooming nearby fruit tree.

"Mais ouvre la porte," I called out. And he came in, flinging aside the threadbare beret, grinning. "Ivan the Terrible, at your service." He bowed low.

"Do not regale me with tales of human suffering," I said, not budging. "I came to Paris for *experience,* and I've succeeded. Human suffering is what I do best. Final exams at the Sorbonne. How can you possibly be smiling?"

"Have you read Camus's *Sisyphe*? But no, you're still stuck in the second empire, or maybe the first? Haven't gotten too far with existentialism, have you, J.J.? Well, when you do, you'll find it most enlightening—sheds all sorts of light on the French *experience,* as you put it. As for exams, think of old Sisyphus pushing that rock uphill for all eternity, and getting to the top and having it roll all the way down, and going to the bottom and starting again. That, *chérie,* is the perfect description of studying for exams at the Sorbonne. So why don't you do something reasonable, like come to Bistro Saint-Jacques with me? Haven't been there in ages. Going to meet Yves."

I had not been back to the little café since the night in long-ago fall when I'd met Roland. But it all seemed different in late spring, the narrow streets leading with bent light that seemed to follow us inside. Once again we sat near the window with the half-curtains hung by rings cutting the view of Rue Saint-Jacques in two. Yves came just after we did, his light hair also catching some of the day's late gold, his eyes the color of a laughing sea, his shirt collar unbuttoned. We sat, ordered a bottle of wine, and no one mentioned how the empty fourth chair—Roland's chair—loomed.

Then I looked up and saw Jocelyn, glancing in at us as she hurried past the window. In a moment, she entered, looking radiant. *"Eh bien, mon vieux,"* she said to Ivan, "got your note and hustled right on over. Yves, *bonsoir*. It's been a long time." The smile encompassed, took us all in, like it had in Jocelyn's old Hollywood pin-up shots. She acknowledged me with a wink, as if once again we were co-conspirators, as if I had been in on everything.

A long, slow meal and a bottle of wine consumed a piece of early evening; conversation consumed the rest. When we stepped out into Rue Saint-Jacques again, the street was dark. Jocelyn pinched my arm then and pulled me to her. "I saw her," she whispered excitedly.

"Who?"

"Catherine Deneuve. Going right down Saint-Germaine. She looks just like Sainte Geneviève. Twentieth century version."

She slipped away then, making her apologies to Ivan and Yves (she was, I knew, going to meet Yaousim, the Prince of Dakar) and I turned to thank them too. It had been a wonderful, unexpected treat and left me happy to wander home alone thinking of symmetry, coincidence, and the things we cannot see—pleasant distractions from worry. Anyway, there was no time for fretting, as I had promised to meet Roland late.

As ever, his presence had an immediate calming effect on me, his love of the absurd, his humor, his profound sense of *sans souci*. These were the very qualities that also frustrated and confounded me at times, but on that night, I once again fell under their spell. We walked the serpentine streets of the medieval city behind the Pantheon and ducked into a little club off Rue Mouffetard. Narrow stairs led to the cellar. Unlike the jazz or blues or guitar notes wafting from the other *boîtes*, Le Chat Bleu pulsed with percussion. My heart adjusted as I went down the stairs, resetting itself to the drums. African? Latin? Caribbean? I could not say what sounds these were, only what they felt like. Roland's fingers drummed on my back, pushing me gently but irresistibly down, down into the sound. It was the instant I knew that he was part of my future.

I felt ready to dance, but the space was small and already crowded. We made our way to a table in a back corner, and I leaned against the rough cellar stone that made up the wall. I felt Roland's eyes looking at me through the melted candlelight and I smiled. Then I saw her. Jocelyn. Hair pulled back into a blonde chignon, exaggerated eye makeup, rouge, and lightly painted lips, high heels, a sophisticated suit, a strand of pearls. Like Catherine Deneuve, the expensive, cultivated upper-class prostitute of *Belle du Jour.* Not a hair was out of place, nor a bead of dew upon her lip as she danced the wildest, most pulsating, devastating throb of a dance I had ever witnessed. As her long arms began to swing in opposition to her long legs, the other dancers moved back, and she seemed to fly around and behind and through the lightening-fast arms of a tall, impeccably beautiful black man in a perfect black suit. The Prince of Dakar.

I understood then her recent remark as she was about to tear out the door, leaving the usual detritus of clothes and letters about the bed. "He's been perfect, J.J. My dark angel, don't you see? He's cured me." She didn't say from obsession, from Samuel. But I could see how limp the letters seemed now, as if they had lost their power. *Feuilles mortes.* Dead leaves, ready to be swept away.

I hadn't actually met Yaousim, but I did, at that moment watching them, understand. She had claimed dancing as her only vice, but at that moment it looked like her salvation. Dancing with him she seemed close to holiness, the most evasive of all the things she so keenly sought.

I thought about that dance again on the train to the Cité Universitaire to fetch her. Holding that thought kept me a hair's breath from giving into the anger boiling inside. Her prince from Dakar lived there and I hadn't seen her for three days. It was the first day of finals and Monsieur Lepic beat upon the door before I was prepared to face the morning and all it would bring. *"Vite, mademoiselle,"* he called out, insensitive in the extreme to my sleep-deprived state, *"Téléphone. C'est l'autre, la grande blonde."* In three minutes I was in the dim lobby hearing the weak voice of Jocelyn entreating me on the other end of the line. "J.J. You've got to come get me. I'm sick. I know I can't get to the exam alone."

She'd made it to the café near the Métro, so I didn't have to bother going into the complex of buildings trying to find her, nor risk being waylaid by someone I knew. Like Ivan, for example, who lived there to mingle with the Arabs and Africans. It was not hard to spot Jocelyn, her hair disheveled and her face ghostly pale. She wore a light summer dress, sheer yet almost demure, knee-length, near-yellow. A recent gift from Madge and everything about it wrong, especially the color against the chalky skin and hair. I looked at her and opened my mouth to say something, then shut it again. She looked horrible, exhausted, hollow-eyed. If I hadn't known better, I would have thought she was drunk.

Jocelyn spoke before I could vent my annoyance. "Sorry. I know you have exams today, too. It's the flu. I missed it in winter, but guess I didn't get to miss my turn." I refrained from saying, "Yeah, right."

"Anyway, I was afraid I couldn't get back without, you know..."

"Barfing," I filled in unsympathetically.

"No, actually, fainting."

"Well, don't worry. I'll make sure you can sit on the Métro, and you can lean on me all the way back to the hotel."

"Oh, no," she looked up, suddenly alert. "I'm not going home. No time. I need you to help me get to the exam."

My astonishment and protests about this foolish plan could not penetrate a mind that had thoroughly made itself up. Evelyn might choose to fail by boycotting the tests, but Jocelyn, despite her best efforts, didn't know how to do anything but succeed. When I heard myself sounding like Madge, going on about health and responsibility, I knew it was time to give up.

Soon we were on the Métro, lucky to find seats side by side, and I sat back for the long ride into the city. Jocelyn had fallen into a kind of reverie, or perhaps a stupor. Her eyes had gone green, but green heavily tinged with yellow.

"So," she said, in an even monotone, "what can you tell me about political history, 1789 to 1960? I didn't exactly cover that after, well, I quit going to his class after, you know..."

I did know, and I softened. Reaching for my bag, I pulled out class and reading notes, not admitting to myself just then how much I, too, was invested in Jocelyn's success. Despite myself, my promises to the contrary, in my journals and in my mind, I was recording Jo's life as she lived it. I had a vested interest in it coming out right. Besides, as her soulmate, her other half, any failure on her part I took to be a failure on mine.

The notes were a jumble of names, facts, governments, and periods. Revolution and *Directoire*, reigns of terror and bourgeois amplitude, empires, republics and back again, all laced through with Napoleons, or modern dictators imitating them in the name of something else.

Jocelyn looked as if this dreary monologue could kill her if "the flu" didn't. She sat quietly, patient and enduring, the way one does when in great pain. Occasionally she'd ask something, as if she were paying close attention. "Say again about Clemenceau..." but I knew it was only to be polite. I didn't know why she bothered.

After a half hour, we were back at Boul'Mich and my head now throbbed, too. Still, I guided Jocelyn by the elbow as if I were the steady one, and we proceeded to the examination chamber of horrors, to repeat almost exactly the experience of winter. The only difference was that now the stakes were higher: If you passed each subject, you got a diploma; if you failed one subject, you failed everything.

After the ordeal, I vowed to put the whole bruising experience out of my mind, but it persisted, nagging like an incipient headache. It nipped at me through the more acute pain of leave-taking from Paris and the pleasurable anticipation of travel. Jocelyn and I were going south together. And when, weeks later, we approached the American Express office in Marseilles where we had directed the results to be sent, my anxiety rushed in like the tide. A background of ancient neighborhoods nesting in serpentine streets tumbled toward the blue port dotted with fishing boats, looking like a poster advertising Mediterranean life, which somehow only bolstered my apprehension. My hands were damp, my legs shaky, as Jocelyn and I approached the mail reception desk, quavering passports opened for identification. But the tanned young woman behind the counter only examined the names on these official documents and said a crisp *oui* without seeming to notice my distress. Then she produced them, two long mailing tubes. Diplomas from the Sorbonne.

I collapsed into the nearest chair, tearing open the tube to extract the elegantly printed document that would verify my passing, verify my existence in Paris, justify and proclaim all that seemed unreal and ready to recede into the uncertain terrain of memory. I could barely read past the words *Diplôme Supérieur*. Jocelyn, however, finding no chair, stood next to me and opened her tube discreetly, not like some child ripping open a birthday package. She pulled the parchment out gently and unrolled it with care and softly read each line. She hesitated a moment before pronouncing the course names for the history of art, modern French history, and contemporary politics, the subjects I had crammed into her on the Métro. Beside each of these was the word *Mention*, like applause in manuscript form.

I looked back at my own record, where the blanks next to the course titles remained simply blank, and then I looked up at her again with as much wonder as envy. What sort of person was it who could suck up another's notes on the Métro while sick and win honors on exams for which she had done no work whatever? But then, what sort of person was it who could do the reading, take extensive notes, cram them down a friend's throat on a train, and barely pass while the friend excelled? That was another thing about Jocelyn and me, one that I'd rather I didn't know.

She looked down at me at last, the yellows about her long since restored to promiscuous tones of gold, and she smiled a brief, crooked smile. *"Tiens,"* she shrugged, not even acknowledging that it was I, after all, who had saved her life. "So we did it. I knew we would. So, shall we go?"

Part 6

FULL SUN

Chapter 26

Taking leave. Funny, until that moment when it was upon me, I had never thought about the meaning of the phrase, and then I looked up, to see the sky had filled with leaves. Leaves so green and profligate, they altered the view—even the silver currents of the Seine beneath their lacy shadow-play—as if to promote forgetting. Vanishing love, unfulfilled promise, lost vows, nuclear shadows, embittered *pieds noirs*, missing pictures, misplaced virginity, lingering notes from an unfinished song, curlicues rising from a half-smoked cigarette, all seemed vague and shadowy under the canopy of trees. *Platanes, maronniers, chênes.* Taking French leave. A French pun, crafted centuries before, no doubt in a committee headed by an Alain Saint-Georges look-alike somewhere deep in the bowels of the Sorbonne.

I do not know exactly how we all left, except that unlike our arrival in Europe on the *Jeanne d'Arc*, our leaving was scattered, separate, a quiet disappearing.

For Gracie, I can imagine the packing up in the back bedroom overlooking the courtyard, the photos, brochures, postcards for Papa and the kids at home all carefully laid on top of the most precious cargo, Tom's letters, as she slid them in, then removed them from her trunk, unable to decide. Should she be prudent and pack them out of harm's way and the possibility of falling under Eve's curious eyes, or should she follow her impulse to hold them tight and tuck them somewhere close, to carry them near her heart? The dilemma would remain unresolved until Ivan came to say farewell, and then her sadness would break.

It was hard in its way to say good-bye even to Madame, who had for several weeks stopped her "assaults and pepper" as Eve called them, and had slumped into what seemed a sincere melancholy. Gracie was forced to trade her outrage for pity, losing a large measure of pleasurable anger in the bargain. Ivan, ever kindly, doffed his beret to Madame one final time, and she seemed overcome by a kind of moisture, nothing so visible as a tear, but rather as if she had found a new zone of humidity and had stepped into it to catch the dew, making herself damp and close to human in the process. *"Au revoir, mon fils,"* she said, and in that one moment of naming him son, made the poignancy of her affection embarrassingly clear.

Gracie mounted the narrow stairs to her little attic space, now insufferably hot and it only mid-June, and felt the oppressive weight of a desert on her chest. She knew what it was to say good-bye, as she had last year to Papa and her family, with the expectation that she would see them again. And she knew death. Saying farewell to Marie was to embrace both, and as Marie held her in her bony arms, rasping as if a lullaby, *"Ça va ma p'tite, ça va..."* Gracie cried as she had not since she left the safety of the nuns, since Mama had turned her head away for the last time, since Tom…

Worst of all, I think, was the sharp electric jolt, the frisson between pain and pleasure without words or sound, that she felt on the last long night in Paris, when the sun led the dancing through the Latin Quarter, and, after a last smoke and nightcap outside Deux Magots, she and Camille walked arm in arm back to Boulevard Raspail. There Camille, who smelled of rosewater and raspberry liqueur, kissed her gently three times in the French manner and said, *"Je t'embrasse toujours ma chère Gracie."* Somehow, more than all else that had not happened in Paris, Camille's embrace called up the most shameful secret of her longing—her failure to lose her virginity.

Perhaps Camille's touch also called up for Grace the memory of a conversation we had that spring, soon after I'd visited the Rodin Museum. I mentioned the visit to her and my own gushing reaction to *The Kiss*. She looked at me suspiciously, then countered, "Oh *that*. Well, did you go inside? You did see Camille Claudel, didn't you? In all the courses they just refer to her as the *mistress*, as if that were a profession. You know, moon in the shadow of the sun, the muse, a poor thing who went mad, *the little woman*. They never said she was the genius."

I had to admit that I hadn't made it to the floor with Claudel's work and had no impression of her at all. So within the week, I was on my way back to the museum, rushing through the streets to keep up with Gracie's uncharacteristically fast tempo. Once within the garden gates, we hurried inside, even brushing past Claudel's versions of Rodin while dying, Rodin in death, crafted by her fingers. We passed all the marble and clay, until Gracie pronounced "There," and came to a full stop before *La Vague*. "It's her response to him," Gracie said authoritatively, standing as if in possession before a large, fearsome green onyx wave about to engulf three little women. They were naked women, dancing, caught by passion, caught by love, caught by surprise.

I wondered which part of that wave she felt most when Camille kissed her farewell. Perhaps surprise. Then when the last night merged into dawn and Gracie left Paris, she packed that revelation away too, and headed south with Evelyn.

Eve spent her last night in Paris wandering alone. She was making, she told Grace, a tour of ruins. There had been so many in all the centuries and wars and fires of destruction, and in the late, long light of June, the unexpected warmth, she saw them all. Time and again, they had risen, rebuilt, out of the bones of themselves. They, at least, stood again both ancient and new. And so beautiful, reminding her, she said, "that Paris is a woman above all." But her own ruination seemed at that moment to have no such regenerative power. Her father would, she knew, instruct her to pray for forgiveness. But she had long since turned away from the God of her father. "If I have to believe in something, it might as well be a fairy tale. As for resurrection, I'd put my money on Cinderella, if I had any. And if I hadn't packed up the damn dress," she told Gracie, "I would have put it on. That was the night to pull out all the stops, turn any trick."

When Eve did return to the sleek apartment on Rue Boileau, it seemed particularly lifeless. Melanie, who had gone four days earlier, left behind only an emptiness where her spirit of neat order had been. Eve, of course, knew little about the particulars of her going, only that the Paris visit from the Bouchers the week before had been a quiet triumph. Melanie had suggested a restaurant near the Opéra, a place she knew well, she told them in competent French over the telephone, then met them there for lunch. She wore heels high enough to erase any vestigial memory of fuzzy slippers, and a light silk dress in the colors of summer. She had known what to order and what wine to recommend and had quietly insisted, invoking the ironclad rules of social scorekeeping instilled by her mother, on picking up the check. She had politely skirted any of their clumsy probes about her future, Hans's future, their future. After espresso in demitasse cups, she had stood, kissed and shaken hands correctly, smiled, then turned on her heels firmly to leave. When they in turn had called to invite her to dine, she had graciously refused, giving a reasonable excuse, employing impeccable French verbs, yielding no ground. "By then," Eve remarked, "she was grinning the biggest damn grin."

California, family, home, yes, we all had our homecomings, reconstructions to be made with our past. But in a way Melanie made the cleanest break; she put herself out of her family's reach as neatly as she had with Hans's parents. And yet she returned to Hans himself, not just as one might return to a boyfriend after a year of voyaging abroad, but as a way of life. But why? After her encounter with Alain Saint-Georges, I know she felt maimed, yet so many steps she took PFC, or Post-French-Creep as Eve called it, seemed circular. She appeared to take home only what she carried abroad: a nearly sacred devotion to

Hans and to Pascal. Flying across the Atlantic she made an entry in her journal that remains her only explanation:

> June 14. It's still uncertain if I passed, but I can always hope. The Sorbonne will mail the results home. But home, diploma, all of it means so little now. Somehow I survived all the nightmares and am soon to be with all that matters in this life, Hans. *Le coeur a ses raisons que la raison ne connaît point.*

For Jocelyn and me, leaving was a matter of stepping out on two pairs of long legs in such harmony they might have been one. We had not moved in this way since our earliest days in Paris. For Jocelyn, once she had struggled to the post with her mound of boxes, even enticing the nocturnal Yaousim into the full impact of daylight to help her, the weight of the year seemed to lift. He arrived, dressed casually for him, slacks and a white shirt open at the collar, and at last I was formally introduced. With charming correctness, he kissed my hand. I watched, a bit dazed, as he balanced several boxes at a time to disappear nimbly down the stairs, only to return with a beguiled and compliant Monsieur Lepic to help him with the trunk. Then Jocelyn and her prince disappeared in a taxi, and I was left to contemplate what remained.

The chaos that had buried our tiny room had vanished with no apparent plan, bit by bit into those boxes. I did not know if the letters from Samuel and Madge, which seemed to bring Jocelyn only misery, had made it into that packing, or if they had been relegated to the trash. Nor was it clear what souvenirs, artifacts, or clothes, what relics of shopping, what books, playbills, posters, what articles from *Le Monde*, notes from Saint-Georges himself, what matchbooks from what nightclubs, had made the cut. But when it had all disappeared into neat packages and the packages themselves were carried away, I felt the clean sadness of taking leave, and began my own preparations.

I ran my fingers over a dirty white wall, its cracks and smudges more apparent in the unrelenting light that poured in summer through the high transom, remembering the heartbreak in that same gesture when, as a tiny child, I had moved from Gran's, where the walls were papered with Babar, to our new house in the canyon in West L.A.

When it was at last time to leave, my chest was too full and too confused to begin to say *au revoir* to the streets, but I could manage a single farewell to Monsieur Lepic. He looked up from behind the barricade of counter, and I thought I detected a flush in his complexion beyond its first defense of ruddiness. His eyes hung a moment, suspended without movement over the expansive cheeks, and they held, fleetingly, the affection of a sad hound. We went through the formalities of parting, the exchange of bills and receipts and keys, all to his running commentary of non sequitur *"Eh bien, les grandes américaines alors, eh bien, après tout..."* And then, just as I was to go out the doorway where Roland had kissed me so deliciously the first time in the rain, Monsieur Lepic cleared his throat as if to call me back. *"Mademoiselle,"* he said, the hounds-eyes looking dark and bereft, *"soyez contente."* He did not wish happiness for me, that being far too American a sentiment, but rather that more subtle, more perplexing French prescription, satisfaction, contentment. *Find contentment.*

I was, at that moment, as far from achieving *contentment*, in the French manner, as I was from being well-behaved, as the French were always admonishing their children, in that oddly philosophical term, *soyez sage*, meaning "be good" by using the word *sage*, or wise. Hilarity, as in a kind of light-headedness, came closer than any other word to describing my state—and Jocelyn's state—of taking leave. Because we had not, really, said good-bye. Taking leave was, just as arriving had been, a measure of postponement. The doors to our houses, strange and rebuilt, were all still half ajar, waiting for us to decide whether to open or close them. Madge, and occasionally my father, still wrote with news and advice that was more and more distant from what we perceived as reality. Gran was still the only one in the universe I could count on to make sense.

And yet. As we headed out for the Métro, destination Porte d'Italie, to find the open road, Jocelyn, having lightened her whole load to her guitar case with a few belongings, every vestige of misery discarded, shouted into the giddy light of June, *"Au revoir Paris, putain, capital mondiale des misérables, je m'en foue."* Then, touching up this uncharacteristic outburst with a flourish for good measure, she added, "Fuck Paris," threw her head back, and laughed hysterically. It was a sound I could not remember, and we, *demoiselles* still, were on our way to the highway, to *faire l'autostop*—hitchhike—to rendezvous in the south with all we had left unfinished in Paris.

Chapter 27

It did not take long to stop a car as we hitchhiked our way south. Two *demoiselles*, long hair flying in the breeze, faces hidden behind large sunglasses, thumbs out, one carrying a guitar case. It quickly became a question of what sort of ride did we want, really, after the requisite questions of mutual destination, and, by the way, were we German? *"Eh bien, américaines alors, allez venez. Américaines? Okay you come."* We were offered meals, wine, tours of the countryside, and occasionally a ride to the youth hostel or fleabag of our choice. We were offered more too, much more, which is why we quickly adopted the strict "no more than one man" rule, and preferably one accompanied by a woman, and attempted to lower our skirts. We tried out all the luxury sedans, Mercedes, Peugeots, Renaults, and even, on a lark, hopped into a tin can Deux Chevaux, the little two horsepower Citroen that was the French answer to the VW bug. But no matter the car, nor the bumpy condition of any country road, the phrase *"desmoiselles américaines, alors, allez venez, okay you come,"* grew only more musical as the patchwork farmlands of brown and green south of Paris gave way to the rocky hillocks, terraced vineyards, and the perfume of lavender in the lands bordering the widening Rhône in its rush to the sea. "Ameri-can *jeunes filles*, we love you," was the refrain of the serenade to us echoing from the hilltops, the valleys, the city walls of Provence.

"I wish that jerk could see this now," Jocelyn said with that slight curl of a smile as we neared Marseilles in the plush back of a wide Citroen.

"*Which* jerk?" I asked.

"Alain," she answered, still lost somewhere down in that smile, "so he could update his *incredibly profound* theories on the state of Franco-American relations."

We were staying in a cheap hotel, a habit by now more than a conviction, near the labyrinthine old heart of Marseilles on that day we ventured down to the American Express to find what mail, grades, and fate awaited us. I was furious in a way with Jocelyn for turning everything upside-down and grabbing honors from my hard labor while I garnered only passing scores without comment. I was especially furious, I think, that she was so nonchalant, so ready to toss that triumph onto the heap with the others (all equally thrilling to which she was equally indifferent) and move on without a backward glance. But in truth, I can only now admit, there was more to it. The fury was within myself, at me, for being unable to make something of my own ability, for allowing Jocelyn to become my better half.

Even as I say this, I know the larger truth. I was also her better half. It was the distress of this knowledge that drove me sometimes to anger, and her to silence and distance. But it was the acceptance of this knowledge, the doubling power of our two best halves, that brought us back always to finishing each other's sentences. And never more so than those last days of June in Provence.

The darkness that clung to the cleft and tiny streets of old Marseilles as they wound, blind as worms, around their hidden core was the darkness of decay more than of mystery. Vanquished Greeks and enfeebled Romans, waves of Goths and Vikings and Carthaginians lay buried in the strata of time beneath stone streets, pungent still with the smell of bloody history. It stank of pirates and armadas and stale gunpowder; the tang of sea salt, the smell of fish guts, and spilled oil lived on its breeze.

By walking a few blocks to the center of the old port, we could burst into sunlight, as if suddenly breaking the surface after a long dive into the ocean. We would fill our lungs with air and light. It was an easy walk to the esplanade, and we took it more than once each of our few days in the city. Jocelyn had recovered her sense of balance in matters monetary, and once again chose impoverished circumstances when they suited and extravagance when it suited better. Happily for me, since my funds were running quite low and no one in my family had sought to replenish them, Jocelyn was feeling expansive now. In particular, she developed a taste for seafood fresh out of the water at a picturesque waterside restaurant, Le Soleil du Sud, with its fading earth-colored paint and shutters askew framing window boxes of red geraniums and tiny lobelias, blue as summer nights. The fact that tourists had discovered the place and tripled the prices didn't seem to concern her. It was as if she had found her own châlet on Sunset Boulevard and, as a regular, paid the bill (for both of us), hardly bothering to look at it.

On the first day we discovered what real bouillabaisse is, and Jocelyn also discovered, at least to my knowledge, the meaning of pleasure in food. We ordered a *vin blanc du pays*, and as the dish of seasoned broth with white fish, shrimp, scallops, langoustine, and oysters in the shell was set in front of her, her eyes turned a speckled golden color I hadn't seen for a long time. We sat, sipping slowly, savoring the mingled flavors of garlic, olive oil, seafood, and wine, saying little. Then Jocelyn looked up and out the window, watching the yachts slipping past in the breeze, the fishing boats tie up, the boatmen and stevedores, brown armed and muscular, some wearing berets, working in the unblinking sun. "It's not far, you know," she said, "now that we're all the way here. Just across a bit of water."

It, of course, was Africa. I had seldom seen her prince. Once the night we stumbled into them dancing their wildness together in the underground "cave," she Catherine Deneuve, he a dark figure in a black suit. Then, I had of course met him when he ventured into daylight to assist Jocelyn with shipping her appalling number of boxes. "Yaousim," she had introduced him casually, as though I had known him all along, known he had a name. Then he smiled, and I saw behind that alignment of grand and perfect teeth, the boldness and self-assurance of its greeting, a charm that explained its own attraction. The blackness of night, music, a smile bold as the sun, unknown magic, a prince of Africa, a caricature. Just as she, the slim model from Hollywood, the mysterious blonde with capricious eyes, was to him. *I see, I see,* I said to myself in that spellbinding moment of greeting. He turned soon, cheerful enough for a prince burdened by boxes making his way down a dimly lit staircase, and I never saw him again.

They had not said good-bye. In the days since our "liberation" from Paris, our days of stepping into the wind and freedom of the road and then the pushing through the tightly coiled secrets of Marseilles, she had alluded to her plans. "It's an easy hop to Senegal from Marseilles," she would say. Or, "Maybe shipping out across the Mediterranean would be best—a dash to Gibraltar and Tangiers, then on to Senegal."

I was not sure which category of fantasy to file this under, what sort of movie script was playing in her head. But I, too, had been less than forthcoming about my intentions. It was so much easier not to think about the future.

Then, inevitably, after unnumbered days of climbing hills to ancient churches and markets, days of browsing in galleries and sitting at water's edge in the sun, the future arrived. The end of June was at hand, and, despite myself, I had a ticket and a plan. As if by unspoken pact, on our last day in Marseilles, piece by piece we shed our defenses as if to let each other inside. It was hot and clear, the water with its film of oil at port uninviting, and what we wanted was the seduction of clear deep water, a clean sweep of beach. A homing instinct perhaps. "I have it," Jocelyn declared, poring over her guidebook. "There's a great public beach east of downtown."

We packed then with care, as if for once to give some determined structure to our day: bathing suits beneath cotton sundresses, sun oil and towels of a sort, pinched from the hotel, bread, cheese, wine, and fruit all tidily laid in my newly purchased straw basket. "No sardines, please," I'd said at the tiny market where we bought provisions. Jocelyn turned to me and raised her large, round sunglasses to stare. "Are you kidding?" she said. "They're disgusting."

We walked then the few blocks to the tram that wound along the edge of the city, with its brightly colored houses spilling like flowers over the edge of the hills, along the track overlooking the cornice, listening to the chatter of the other passengers with their patois of French and Provençal, thick as Italian soup. Then we went down, stopping before the blanket of bleached, pebbled beach, and the sea, whitecaps waving like flags over the deep calm of the Mediterranean. Salt blew into our hair while our feet burned at the edges as our sandals sank into the baking stones. We found a spot, a California kind of spot I should say, close enough to the gently breaking waves to hear them, far enough back to not find ourselves awash.

Jocelyn spread our gray little towels, barely a napkin beneath her long torso, and she quickly shed her dress to offer a winter-white, bikini-ed body to the sun. I hesitated, looked around at our fellow beachgoers, some older ladies in black shifts and straw hats with hampers of food for small children; some families, their children with buckets gathered under striped umbrellas; and some young like us, wearing briefs or bikinis or practically nothing. Awkwardly, I slipped my shift off too, and lay quickly beside Jocelyn.

As she turned her head toward me, blonde hair falling across her forehead onto the beach, her eyes were as startlingly blue as the sea.

"So, J.J., tell me your whole plan. Ticket out of here early tomorrow morning, right?" I nodded. "To the far corners of Provence, right?" I nodded again. "Tell all," she said. "Roland's family has what, a *palais*, a château?" The monologue was interspersed with the "so tell me" refrain, but at first, I said nothing because there was little space; for once, she was the interlocutor. I lay on the hot beach as if floating, watching her eyes turn from blue to green to blue, and listening as if she had stolen my thoughts.

"Okay," I finally said, "I'll tell you. Yes, I guess I do want to find some connection to, as you say, Gran's past, maybe through the backward mirror of Roland's world... well I *am* part French, part Provençal even, aren't I, so naturally I'm curious. Yes, I am going to Roland's house—maybe a château, as you suggest. But if so, I imagine it one of those ancient ones with drafty rooms and plumbing last modernized under Louis-Napoléon in 1848. There is so much I still need to learn. For one thing, to understand why in some ways Gran's world seems so much closer to me, even though I'm still a stranger here, than my mother's and her passion for junk and her West L.A. ways."

Jocelyn nodded slightly under her shades. "I get that," she murmured.

"And you, Jo?" I asked, "What about you?"

It was baking then, the sun boring down and we sat up in unison to face the inviting motion of the waves. We rose at the same time, not really speaking of it and walked slowly, soles against stone, to come to the welcome line of foam from broken waves. The water felt cold against my hot skin, and I realized I had burned, even as Jocelyn was slowly turning bronze. We plunged then into the water, a tame and soothing bath compared to the rough play of our California breakers, and swam out far enough to watch the shoreline diminish a little. We turned then on our backs to float. "So tell me," I asked again. "You?"

But Jocelyn's monologue had already started and it was not premised on my questions, nor halted by my breaking in. "Yes, it's firmly decided. I'm crossing over tomorrow, late morning, to Tangiers."

"By plane?"

"…like the Vikings did, you know, in ships. Then from there, a flight to Dakar. I read about one such in Saint-Exupéry…"

"Saint-Ex., of course, liked the desert better no doubt than the hot and steamy coast. Are you sure—"

"Probably you wonder if I'm sure, but of course I want, I must, see Yaousim again, I mean, well we've really only danced, you know, but the dance he does, I mean, I need to find—"

"Salvation? You have read *The Little Prince*, haven't you, it tells you plainly—"

"I mean he is a prince, after all, the prince of, well something, and I mean I couldn't just let that go, could I? Think of my career…"

"…let it go…" I repeated, not asking which career.

"I have a booking on Air France. From Tangiers."

We turned then and began the long, slow crawl to shore. I noticed, as Jocelyn turned toward me to draw in breath, her eyes had turned from sea blue to speckled gold, fool's gold, the old prospectors called it, as if she had captured rays rejected by the sun. Her arms, lifting gracefully from the water, were turning the same golden shade I had first seen in the hillside pool in California. Then, like now, her skin seemed the truest thing about her.

As we pulled ourselves out of the water, shook our wet hair, and flopped again on the ungenerous beach beneath, I started to ask more. Like, *What are you going to do, you know about Miss Calbrew, about the movies, about…* even in my mind I couldn't bring up the painful topic of Samuel. Gran's face, serene, suddenly appeared behind my closed eyes, and I felt her gentle patience. *All in good time, child.* Instead of speaking, I reached for Jocelyn's hand and squeezed it. *"Ah mon enfant, ma soeur, songe à la douceur d'aller là-bas ensemble..."* She was indeed my child, and Baudelaire's.

It was settled then. In the morning I would depart for the Maritime Alps near the Italian border, to find my little prince, while she would go into the heart of darkness to find her Prince of Dakar. I was surprised by her choice, but felt I understood it. In fact, when we rose at dawn to pack, I felt we had come together as one mind again, and had never been closer.

Chapter 28

It was not until much later that I understood that she had actually never intended to cross to Tangiers and fly to Yaousim in Dakar. Like a far ripple on a tranquil sea, she watched her link to him fade gently, then disappear. That was all right with her. What was not all right was that I had not done the proper thing; I was hanging on, insisting on meeting Roland again on some other ground. I was leaving her for the company of a man. So instead she had left me with her elaborate story, her dry-eyed cheerfulness—her lie.

When I think now of the trip from Menton to Sospel, I see the bright blue patch of sea disappearing in the rearview mirror as the road gets lost in the twists of climbing into the Maritime Alps. There is sunlight filtered through forest and shadows playing down the steep sides of cliffs. The air hints at pine and sea blown in on the breeze. Soon, in the garden of the villa, perfume will define all of Provence for me, then all of France, distilled in its uncaptured fragrance of roses, lemon blossoms, French thyme, and, always in the distant wind, lavender.

What I thought then was that it was a journey I could make easily, like the climb, say, from Laguna into the seaside hills, up and over through the honeycomb of canyons. But I was a girl yet, and California was easiest for me still, just as, I suppose, Gran had been a girl when she left Provence, and it remained forever the easiest corner of her mind.

I imagined Roland before I saw him, imagined his cryptic smile, his laughing, mischievous eyes, and his arms ready to enfold me as I stepped off the train. I imagined how falling into them would be easy. And I was right. *"Beauté,"* he sighed, pulling me to him, finding my mouth with his.

Soon we flew around the edges of the small mountains, hair flowing out the windows of his little sports car into sunlight, heading for Sospel. I stole shy glances at him, at his wild, curling hair, his lean arms now bronzed from the southern sun, his mouth with its amused half-smile. And beyond what I could see, I conjured: his vocabulary of gestures that could embrace the present and shrug off the unwanted; his philosophy, with its open-ended devotion to thinking; his delicious irreverence coupled with tenderness. He was everything I imagined and longed for. Being next to him felt right. Easy.

Even before we went down the long, graveled road lined with cypress to the tall iron gate leading to the Montrefor villa, his gentle concern circled me silently like an invisible net as protection against undue shock. I was, after all, about to enter the gates, the villa, and the unimagined tribal life of latter-day French aristocracy, Provence-style. "Don't worry, *chérie,*" he tried to reassure me, almost whispering as if an endearment, "it is, well, best to think of Ionesco, you know, *théâtre de l'absurd.*"

It was one of the most endearing of the many things Roland had ever said to me. Also, it was true. When he spoke of his mother's people, that is just what he meant. He had returned to the land of his maternal heritage and into a web of connections, inheritances, properties lost and found, titles won, discontinued, or sullied, in a cascade of time too dizzying to calculate for one of my paltry short-term California wiring. I longed to get it, to understand the banter, the in-jokes, the family patois, even to get the names with their ancient spellings resplendent with "y's" and "q's," but I did not. It was, just as Roland had forewarned, a drama, an ongoing piece of theater of the absurd, and I did not have a playbill.

It was easiest to be clear about what was not. Foremost, it was not, apparently, a chance to do what I had long wanted, to meet Roland's parents. They lived for the most part in Blois, south of Paris in the Loire Valley, the paternal, semi-urban and unlanded side of his provenance, and though they summered in Sospel every year, it was unclear when they would arrive. It was also certain that I would not meet Roland's only sibling, his sister Madelaine, who had just taken vows in a religious order. When seated at a long dining room table with a baffling number of cousins, aunts, uncles, and hangers-on whose names I could not begin to keep straight, I made what I thought was a rather tepid statement of surprise, that Madelaine would take such a drastic step. "Baf," came the nearly universal reply. *"Mais non,"* came the refrain from every direction, not at all unusual. Lots of it going around in the family they said, and I was treated to a litany of vow-takings. Perhaps this had been the family's population control, a way to keep the sprawling lands more or less concentrated over the centuries instead of letting them dwindle away in parcel allotments of patrimony, or maybe there had been some other explanation, a rampant sexual hysteria, or, it occurred to me, a simple desire for peace away from the incessant crush of relations.

As the talk buzzed, ever more loudly, around the table with its heavy burden of old plates and serving dishes, clutter of wineglasses, and scatterings of broken baguettes, I looked to Roland for comfort as well as explanation. But he gave his best shrug, his downturned mouth expressive of supreme insouciance, and the conversation between the relations, the Suzettes and Marie-Louises and Michelles, or the Michels, Michauds, Marcels, the Bertrands or Babettes, roared over me. All I got for sure was that in their own *grand-mère*'s generation, there had been a family of four siblings, two brothers and two sisters, and it was something of a record, even for this family, that all four had taken religious vows. The *grand-mère*'s legacy was instead this brawling crowd, a passel of old family holdings, most in disrepair, a yearly burden of taxes large enough to "run a few small colonies in the Caribbean," and rampant dementia. As to why so many members of the family had succumbed, over the centuries, to the rigors of poverty and chastity, the one reason never cited was faith. As I glanced around the room with its peach-colored walls and hand-painted floral design along the top, its high-arched glass door opening onto a terrace and fountain below, its long oak table surrounded by the babble of the present generation of Montrefors while their ancestors in oil glared down at them, I knew this was another thing I was not even close to understanding.

But I did understand the garden and Roland's place in it, hunched on a stone bench with a book, solitary and central in this little paradise. The garden was formal, in the French way, meaning plotted out logically, with trimmed hedges, carefully aligned cedars making sentinels along the paths, and regular marble roundabouts settled with benches; it was informal in the Mediterranean way, too, meaning fragrant, alive with unclipped rose branches left to waft as they will, olive trees, birdsong, water singing in tiny fountains, and replicas of classical gods stuck here and there, eyes bashful or distracted or looking backwards in time, the bases of their marble feet tickled by overgrowth. The large earth-colored arms of the villa, pinkish in slanted light and capped by red tile, not only enclosed some twenty-eight rooms inside, but reached out to embrace the garden as well. With its neoclassical flavor, its frescoes and balustrades, its oak-plank floors and windows arching to the sky, the house made a valiant and sturdy stand against the chaos of family that it contained and protected. But the garden was intimate. Its twisting paths led from one hidden corner to another without seeming design. Its heart was anywhere you found it. It allowed for solitude, silence, an existence apart from the tribe.

It was there, in the sun of his eternal present, that I knew Roland best. *"Eh bien, mon petit prince,"* I teased him, finding him with his nose in a volume of Voltaire. *"Non, non,"* he countered, smiling in that way that had always arrested the passage of time. "I believe I'm going to give up that crown, delightful as it is, to take up a new title: Candide II."

"Really?" I was laughing now and ready to banter, but he pulled me down to him on that bench in sunlight, and

I was happy the statues had already turned their eyes. The noise of the thousand cousins splashing in the pool down the terraced hill beyond the garden receded into nothing, as did all the world except that reckless moment in the light on the stone bench with a breeze through stalwart cedars, the roses waving their limbs to our rocking, and everywhere tender lips on my naked body. As he promised, no one disturbed us. "It is written, *chérie, ça va*, okay," and we made love for the first time. When I found myself again, and my clothes, the air settled around me with the scent of lemon blossoms.

And it was there, again and again in some corner of the garden, or standing naked in the scented breeze by the half-opened shutters of his bedroom, or on the white sands by the sea at Menton, eating fruits de mers freshly hauled in by the fishermen, or rounding mountain roads littered by altars to the recent victims of what I called driving by terror as we crossed the border into Italy and its flavorful open-air markets, it was there in that unspoiled sun, unlike the light of my soiled California, that I grasped the meaning of eternal summer. But it was also there that I knew I was suspended between things, waiting. My anxiety accumulated with time, and I began to complain. "So any word? When do you think they are coming?" I asked Roland, as I focused on the still hazy arrival of his parents. My increasing unease was answered by his eternal shrug. "Baf," he would say, like any true French *philosophe*, "any time. Who knows? They'll get here when they get here."

The future, it seemed, apart from the relations who had taken their vows and had some sort of celestial guarantee, was a place nobody in the Montrefor family was inclined to visit, even by speculation. I would say it was not so much forbidden territory as unpleasant and inevitable, like the taxes that had whittled away so much of their *patrimoine* (such an alien word to fall on my California ears, even in French). So we remained in the present, in the sunshine and laughter of Roland's adoration, his shrug, and his penchant to growl at writers already several centuries dead, just as, I remarked, my father would talk back to the TV news.

But the present seemed a circumscribed perch, one that for me was uncomfortable. It was the difference between us; Roland could stay in the present, happily thinking forever, because he had the security of a past. The past, I reminded myself, was what I had come for. So, as a way to allay my anxiety, I began to probe him for it, as if it were a commodity I could import. "So tell me," I would begin, playfully removing his book, and he would pull me to him, giving me that twisted, laughing smile that I began to realize contained what I was seeking. It was a genetic artifact forged by generations; with irony, wit, and sensual world weariness, Roland was never so French, and never so much what I was not, as when he smiled.

And he did instruct me. I confess now to have forgotten most of what he told me of a past buried in the deep layers of Provence, of Sospel itself. But of its most recent catastrophic era, World War II, I forgot nothing. The villa itself had been the hub of the town's changing fortunes and tragedies. "You see," he said taking my hand gently and leading me as one might lead a child through the garden, "they all, stupid sots, wanted it, took it, used it, and did their damage." First, when the Maritime Alps had been under Mussolini's command, the Italians took over the villa for their headquarters, scattering the family and servants, except for one beautiful young cousin whom they had tried to coerce into staying behind as a "local liaison." "Baf," he exclaimed, "such a weak excuse, even for Italians." What had happened to the young cousin had never been explained, but the worst injury that the family bore from Italian occupation was that, in addition to messing up the place, they drained the best wines from the family *caves*. This was a severe blow to the family's already diminishing patrimony.

The Italians didn't last long, for they were quickly taken over by the Germans, who also established headquarters in the villa. The Germans, Roland said, were the ideal tenants. "Cleaned up after the Italians, put everything back, revered our art and even our antiquity, very—what should I say—disciplined. Look here," and he pulled me down a shady garden lane where models of classical statues he named as we went—Diana, Apollo, Neptune, Proserpine, on and on—were lined up majestically under the trees. "They, the Germans did that. Before, the statues had been placed here and there, you know, by caprice, like the olive trees, and then the Germans come, and boom, they measure just the distance, find just the location, and bring in the young strong soldiers to rearrange the garden. It is charming, *non*?"

I had to agree.

"But then," he went on, "as the war progressed, *enfin*, the Germans were kicked out. The Americans came, and they of course took over the villa. More destruction, only worse this time. They pushed the statues around and trampled the garden, who knows for what reason," he shrugged, "and sometimes the statues fell and broke—like the little Venus over there." He pointed. "But *mon Dieu*, inside it was a catastrophe, *non*? These Americans, they know nothing about antiquity, the past. They write, how do you say, graffiti, their campaign plans on the walls, and the large salon in back, they used for a map room. Over the eighteenth century frescoes they put their big maps, using the big nails, pfft, pfft," he added, making a hammering motion. "Horrible!"

"So, you must have hated the Americans…"

"*Non, chérie*, we love the Americans. They came to give us back our liberty. The Italians, after all, they were only Italians, like cousins, we know them. But hate? Still, one cannot speak of Germans here without a whisper, as if saying a bad word. And Germans still do not dare to come to this corner of France. There are still no Germans among the tourists who visit Sospel."

That afternoon, in the village crossing the odd bridge spanning the Brevera River with its toll gate in the center, reconstructed after being bombed during the war, Roland pointed this out again. "See, English, Danish, Swedes, Spaniards, we even let in an American from time to time," he smiled again that smile that seemed more than ever a crevasse I could fall into, "but no German. Never." I scanned the tourist crowd milling about the center of the little village with its small plastered houses in the southern colors of red, yellow, ochre, with their small balconies and green shutters; they scuttled to sleepy cafés and a couple of kiosks selling souvenirs along the river banks where the river widens then splits around an agreeable arrangement of islets. I had to agree that, from what I could see, there were no Germans. I was about to ask why, but Roland was already telling the rest of the story.

"You see here, the town square, that's where they brought them. They went into the mountains as far as they could, and they brought the men down. Even from the villages where there were no known guerillas trying to sabotage the Germans. If only there was an old man or a boy of fourteen or so, that was enough. They came through all the towns, the filthy swine, and brought them here. But to the villa first, of course, lining them up in the garden. My mother's youngest brother, the only male left at home, he was about fifteen I think, they got him too. They all marched from the villa, down our road, to this square, and the Germans with their clean uniforms and clean hands lifted their rifles and shot them all. Just there. The blood ran into the river..."

I'm not sure that I said anything, but felt myself go pale. Roland drew me to him, then said in English, "The Germans...what kind of creature is it who plays Beethoven going to a massacre? *Tu vois, chérie,* we love Americans. How could we not? Yes, they do not take care with history, but it is a small crime, *non*?"

Chapter 29

As the train moved south into true countryside, rolling gently in a patchwork of farms and villages, Gracie strained to find the highway out the window, fancying she might spy us alongside. She, in particular, had thought Jo's and my determination to hitchhike mad, though Evelyn's eyes had grown round with delight at the idea. Briefly, Gracie had panicked that Eve might just decide to do it too, throwing Gracie's carefully constructed rendezvous plans into jeopardy. It had been hard enough to get Eve to commit to a certain place far enough in advance to tell Tom. For the longest time, she had simply said, "Hey, let's go where the spirit moves us," until Gracie insisted on a destination.

"I have to tell Papa," she pleaded.

"Okay, pick some big-deal place where the train goes a few hours south, and we'll stop there first."

"Like Lyon?"

"No, I read about it. Bourgeois and dull. Pick something more exciting."

Thus Gracie had studied the map and chosen Avignon. "Romantic walled city, once home to the popes," she read.

Tom would like that. So it was Avignon. And as hour by hour the train rolled toward the climax of all her secret plotting, Gracie tried to keep the jitters in her stomach away by concentrating on the road and on us, the two Jo's. Even then, she said, the irony was not lost on her that we were out there somewhere taking a flier, while she and Evelyn, the two poorest of the *demoiselles*, were riding in the relative luxury of a second-class coach. In the end, much to her relief, Eve had decided she needed her "loot," and wasn't willing to travel light enough to hit the road.

How do I know this, since the summer, so gently it seemed, blew us along separate paths until we had truly scattered? The fact is, I wouldn't have known if Gracie had not, just before the wedding, told me in such minute and painful detail, I felt I had been along every strange and twisted road they followed. She told me so vividly and so well, the story of their summer comes to me as easily as my own.

The sun was already sinking when they arrived at the station in Avignon outside the crenellated ramparts of the city walls, and the long walk through the ancient streets struggling with too much baggage was mainly silent. When at last they reached the Porte de l'Oulie and approached the bridge crossing to Île de la Barthelasse, Gracie began to worry. Evelyn had not said a thing about the enchanted town, with its encircling stone walls and fairy-tale towers and spires rising above them, its medieval papal palace, and its famous Pont d'Avignon, a bridge half-fallen into the fast-flowing Rhône centuries ago, where, according to legend and song, the townspeople danced.

Gracie was tired and discouraged once they began to follow the road that descended steeply back toward the river and the youth hostel where they planned to stay. What if Avignon were a bomb, and Eve insisted on leaving quickly? Pulling their bags into the foyer of the hostel didn't improve Gracie's mood. It seemed flimsy and was probably full of bugs. "For the first time in a long time," she said, "I remembered I was poor and how much I hated it."

But before she could sink into despair, Evelyn appeared behind her, the color back in her cheeks and her eyes wide open again. "Gracie, get your ass out here this minute. This you've got to see!" and she tugged Gracie by the hand. Gracie's jaw fell open as she and Eve stood side by side on the dirt road not far from the river's embankment. The last rays of the sun were bursting in streams of pink behind them to fall on the magnificent gothic spires and towers in front of them. The Popes' Palace on a high hill rose delicately into the deep summer sky, while the lights played magically on the city walls, and the graceful arches of the Pont d'Avignon spanned through mid-river in quiet symmetry. As darkness engulfed the last daylight, the lights of Avignon seemed to dance like fireflies. "My God," Evelyn said, "this is magic." Gracie remembered that the Youth Hostel International book had mentioned that the best view of Avignon was on its doorstep. "A million-dollar view," Gracie said, "and very much worth the price of admission, which turned out to be, among other things, mosquitoes." Most of all, she knew Evelyn was hooked and would not insist on packing up with morning's light.

It was not until the second day that Tom came. Gracie had memorized the train schedules and set watch along the steep road leading down to the youth hostel. There was a battered old sign saying *Auberge de Jeunesse* with an arrow pointing the way. Surely he would find them, but she needed to make sure. And so, early on the second morning when she saw Tom's familiar imposing frame turning down the road, her heart leapt before her feet did, and she ran to greet him. "Doll," he cried, swooping her into his arms, "how wonderful to see you." Within minutes, he was safely planted in the little grove behind the hostel that Gracie had scoped out as suitably private and she was running inside, her heart now thumping wildly.

As she flung open the dormitory door, she saw Evelyn in a thin cotton shift, a towel wrapped around her wet head turban-style. She was glistening as a water nymph, and strands of wet hair fell about her face. "I hadn't planned this part," she confessed, "and I knew that no way would Eve want it like that, a barefoot tryst with stringy wet hair. But there was no way to change anything. It was time…"

Uncharacteristically, she took command. "Eve, there is something amazing you have to see. Come on, right this minute."

"Well, hey, I'm not exactly dressed."

"Never mind," Gracie said, "you're fine." And she pulled a confused Evelyn by the hand to the opening to the little grove. "What are you up to?" Eve lamented.

The opening of the grove with its sweet smell of pines was as close as Gracie wanted to get. She could not bear to actually watch Eve fall into Tom's arms, as she assumed Eve did, and to see Tom embrace her in a very different way than he ever had, or ever would embrace Gracie herself. Feeling dizzy, she returned to her bunk and lay down on the rough cotton sheets.

Though she closed her eyes and ears, she could not escape the scene playing inside her mind, the way Evelyn would stumble in surprise then almost faint, as she had the night of the *bal masqué,* into the strength of Tom's arms. She could hear Eve moan, saying, "How good to see you, how good this feels!" And in fact she knew, because Evelyn, ever mindless of Gracie's sensibilities, told her that after kissing Tom deeply and well it was as if he cleansed her of the acrid smells and parched kisses of the marquis and his silly friends. Paris was gone, and she was in the arms of a man again.

Then she blurted without knowing what she meant to say, "But Tom, I failed, you know. I'm the only one of la Maison who failed."

Eve had instinctively said the perfect thing, the thing Tom needed and wanted to hear most. He was moved to put all his strength at bay, to gently hold Eve, who seemed so fragile, to protect her in the circle of his arms. She was sweet, warm, full, vulnerable, all he had dreamed her to be.

"Shhh," he hushed her, patting her wet head. "It's okay, baby. What did it matter anyway? You matter and I matter and I'm here now, with you. I'll take care of you now."

The next days blurred together in Gracie's mind. Often she sat in the third chair, sharing a carafe of cool Provençal rosé and a plate of bread and olives in the large squares or little side streets of town, feeling as if she belonged, as if she were family. Then Tom and Evelyn, "the lovebirds" she called them, would go off on their own, and leave her to her own discoveries. There was much to discover. The streets were packed with visitors for the summer theater festival, and on the long, late, warm nights the Place du Palais in front of the Popes' Palace and the Place de l'Horloge filled with musicians, jugglers, clowns—she warmed to their harlequin suits—and everywhere Gypsies panhandling.

Beneath the medieval structures were Roman ruins and beneath them the ruins of the ancient Gaulish people they had conquered. And beyond the walled city in the countryside all about were some of the greatest monuments of Rome. Cities, arenas, amphitheaters, great bridges, and the famous aqueduct outside of Nîmes, the Pont du Gard. These were interests she shared with Tom, who smiled at her with a nod to their common heritage. "For sure, doll," he winked at her, "gotta check those out." But Gracie didn't have to go as far back as the Romans to find the Italian connection; it all seemed to converge here, where the rushing Rhône parted for the Île de la Barthelasse. The famous feuding popes of the Middle Ages, of course, were all about the tug of war between French and Italian power, and once the papacy was safely back in Rome, the influence of Italy came back in more enduring ways. Painting in Avignon was heavily influenced by the school in Siena, and signs of the Renaissance crept in everywhere, in architecture, statuary, gardens, cuisine—even in Avignon's most famous poet.

More and more on her own, Gracie wandered to the tiny Place Didier and followed Rue du Roi René to Chapelle Sainte-Marie, whose facade looked nothing like a chapel, but more that of a large house with an arched doorway often firmly shut. Once she had peeked inside to see a courtyard and lush garden, and knew that very little remained of the ancient church. But it was here that Petrarch, the wandering Italian expatriate, first spied Laura, the beauty who inspired his exquisite sonnets, and his love for her remained undying and unrequited. In fact, it was said she never knew he existed. This was the corner of Avignon that touched Gracie most. She wondered what she might have done if she had had the gift of poetry.

A rhythm settled over all of them. Occasionally, Gracie would slip out of the drowsiness of the moment, the heat so still it seemed hardly to breathe (and made it hard to believe in the famous mistral) and imagine life beyond the ancient walls and the island in the Rhône facing them; she remembered sometimes how little time left there was in France, and puckered her lips trying not to pronounce the unspeakable word, future.

But for Evelyn and Tom, it was a happy thing to be circumscribed by the walls. Gazing back at the view of Avignon one night from the porch of the hostel, she said to him, "It's amazing how those walls seem to contain magic that cannot escape." In her expansive definition, she also meant the fertile valley, the surrounding hills, the fabled vineyards in every direction, and the majestic mountains visible from the Popes' Palace. And she was careful, as was Tom, not to speak thoughtlessly of the future, or plans, or where they would go from here. They did not want to burst the bubble of delight, of surprise, of old love renewed. Even the past was treacherous territory they dipped into timidly. Tom did give some updates on the current residents of la Maison ("standards are definitely slippin'," he grinned), on Spinster Krauss, on Jay Greene. "He's made a full comeback. Walking around on two legs again—well, four if you count crutches—but hell, he's doing great. Scar on his cheek makes him look like a jock."

After even so tentative a foray into the past, they happily gave reality the slip and reentered the safety of the sunny, windless present, the cafés, crowds, and shaded little squares under the protective leafy arms of ancient trees. And meticulously, room by room, they examined the extravaganza of art and theology contained in chambers and chapels of the feuding popes. Evelyn confided to Gracie that Tom was into "the Catholic thing" more than she was, and suggested maybe a trip into the country. They could take a bus to Châteauneuf-du-Pape, "see, it's a papal thing, too, all that great wine," to do some sampling. Or maybe go to Arles to see the town where van Gogh hung around.

Tom said "sure" and then, somewhat vaguely, "all in good time." Meanwhile he prowled Avignon, seeming to find images of Eve in frescoes, statues, and paintings everywhere. He told her that, but she shrugged it off. "Maybe it's the heat," she commented. "Makes your eyes swim."

But Tom persisted and one day after a drowsy lunch announced he had found Eve's exact replica. "You've got to see this," he said promptly at two p.m., when the buildings opened again after lunch. Evelyn stretched her long legs and replied, "You know, I think I'll leave it to you two. I'm not sure about seeing myself in pictures, all things considered. Think I'll sit here and have an espresso." And Gracie, who had been with them that day, looked questioningly at Tom. "C'mon kiddo. Somebody has to see this." Dutifully, she got up to follow, staying in Tom's shadow.

"My treat," he offered, stepping up to the ticket booth at the fourteenth century Petit Palace right near the Palais des Papes. Then he steered her straight to a room of Italian

Renaissance masters and stopped in front of a tiny masterpiece by Sandro Botticelli, *Virgin and Child*. "See," said Tom, "even though this was painted hundreds of years ago, that's her. That's Eve. It's like she's eternal."

Gracie stared hard at the Madonna before her as she gazed down at her chubby son with his golden halo to match hers. It was true that the perfect, rounded face under lovely arched brows resembled her, and the wisps of red hair that escaped a delicate ruffled white headdress were pure Eve. Then there was the suggestion of a full, rounded body beneath the beautifully draped robes. But there was something wrong. The sensuality, the hand reaching for the breast to nurse the infant, were all wrong, all subverted to maternal purity. The eyes, not open in Eve's eager directness, were cast down, finding all earthly joy now only in maternity. In short, the prostitute who had most likely been the model for this painting had been transformed into a saint of motherhood. Gracie looked at it from all angles but could not find its true likeness to Eve. Finally she said, "Well, yes, she is very lovely." But Tom gazed worshipfully and said nothing.

In the fallow hours, when Evelyn had time to herself to think a bit, she wondered about this art thing Tom had. Since he had brought it up, she'd tried to see if it worked for her, if she could find *him* represented anywhere. But on the whole, the males depicted in carvings, paintings, reliquaries, and statues were pathetic. Fat old popes or bishops in their ridiculous hats, wimpy sexless angels, or worse, what she called the "Weepy Jesus" school that she had rejected long ago from overexposure in too many Sunday school classes. Those sad, waif-thin specimens with scraggly beards nailed horribly to the cross, or those pious dopey-eyed creeps with their crooked haloes. No wonder church attendance was falling off. Scouring her mind for more recent attractions, her heart rate picked up considerably remembering *The Kiss*, then wondered why, at least from what she'd seen, the Italian masters hadn't done better with males.

Later in the evening, she mentioned her art theories to Gracie. Though Gracie made no comment on the Botticelli Madonna, she did take umbrage at Eve's shortsightedness on the Italian masters. "No males? What about *David*? It doesn't get more male than that!" And though neither had been to Florence, suddenly Michelangelo's huge perfect male body in marble, first viewed in schoolbooks with embarrassed giggles, overpowered both of their minds. Of course. That would be Tom.

Once the image of *David* was planted in Evelyn's head, she couldn't let it go. She had begun to understand what was so troubling about Tom's habit of looking at the art all around them trying to see her. The images were so angelic, so *virginal*. It explained what had been troubling her, Tom's restraint.

In the red and scarlet sunsets that edged into warm black night, they walked the darkened streets of Avignon, seeking hidden alleyways or doorways with eaves, or gentle slopes of the river bank, and finally the little grove behind the hostel. When they were alone, he would pull her to him, covering her with kisses, endearments, promises, vows that were so sincere he almost cried through hoarse whispers. Yet he was too tender, stopped too soon. Night after night, he would return her to the hostel door and visibly tear himself away with brutal self-control.

Evelyn knew that desire was not the problem. It was not that he desired her too little, but respected her too much. Adoration was a heavy burden. Besides, whatever long-held vision he had of her—of her purity and devotion—were distortions. She couldn't remember ever being the angel he imagined, but she certainly wasn't one now. His head had gotten confused with all this Catholic stuff, she decided, and all the images he looked for were the wrong ones. If there was a connection to be made with art, let it be with *David*. Only let him come alive, out of his stone. Let him be the man he really was, the one she longed for. And Italian, too, for good measure.

She chose the spot for the seduction with great care. They had been to the Jardin du Rocher des Doms several times during the day, walking slowly and with delight to the highest hill in town, usually bypassing the cathedral for the lush garden and views of jagged mountain peaks above it. There were fountains in the middle of small ponds, a miniature train to transport the foot-weary, shade trees and banks of flowers and children skipping with balloons and ice cream. But by nightfall, the garden paths were closed, gates shut, and everyone required to leave. It was perfect.

"So let's stroll up to the garden," she suggested after a late picnic supper on a bank overlooking the Pont d'Avignon. "Unless you'd like to dance off the end of the bridge."

"The garden sounds like a safer bet," he grinned, grabbing her hand.

They arrived in late twilight and strolled to admire the light on distant Mount Ventoux. Already families were making their way back down the path, soon joined by noisy teenagers, tourists in tacky shorts with cameras stowed in bulky cases, a few renegade musicians from the festival carrying a flute, drum, or guitar. Tom pulled her into an arbor near a little pond, pushed her hair back from her face gently before kissing her. Then again, and again. She waited a little before kissing him back, hard.

As his hands reached down her back to her hips, he held both her arms behind her and whispered, "Oh, my sweet Eve, it's time to go."

She looked at him with eyes open so wide even in the near dark he could not fail to see their light. "Why?" was all she said.

"We're not allowed to stay, you know."

"Most of the best things in life aren't allowed," she whispered back, remembering her confession that night on the *Jeanne d'Arc* that she'd been *born* a half virgin, and had gladly thrown away the other half. Now, whole, she'd like to give herself to Tom. She'd like to see *David* in the flesh. Even better, there promised to be a moon. She took him by the hand and pulled him to the ground. "Shhh," she whispered. "We'll have to be very quiet in case papal justice reaches up this far and they send around the cops."

When Tom could stand the silence, the holding in of his breath—his desire—no more, he fell on Evelyn. This time there was no restraint as he tore at her clothes, then his. "Mary Mother of God," he called before crying out, "let, me, oh for Christ's sake let me." Eve smiled wide in the dark while moaning hoarsely, *"Yes yes I will yes,"* as if it had been his idea.

At dawn, they scrambled to find the clothes that had been flung the farthest and did their best to put themselves back together before sneaking over a locked chain and down the path toward the Rhône. On the way up, they met a guard, who gave them a puzzled look. *"Bonjour,"* Eve said heartily, looking him straight in the eye. "A little walk before breakfast is so good for the digestion, don't you think?" Later over croissants and café au lait, she said, "So, *paisano*, you ever think about going to Florence?"

He wiped the crumbs off his chin and grinned broadly. "As a matter of fact, I have."

The next few days and nights found them hand in hand, or naked in each other's arms, nesting in little dens or beds of leaves like other creatures of the night. Gracie said one night they crept along the banks of the river close to the fallen bridge and sat, wrapped close together, when Tom suddenly declared, "Holy moly. It's so quiet I almost forgot. Do you know what day it is? It's the Fourth of July."

"Well God bless George and his wooden teeth, and God bless Martha—love the hats—and God bless Betsy Ross. I played her in the fifth grade play, you know. She could have come right out of the church ladies' sewing circle, and God bless—"

But by then Tom silenced her, presumably with his own lips, and that was the night they returned to the grove behind the hostel, the night Eve called out "David" while making love, startling Tom. "Who?" he asked.

"Just you, love, just you. It's a special nickname. You'll see."

Gracie never inquired when Eve stayed out all night. "What was the point?" she shrugged. "I already knew as much as I wanted. And the rest, between the two of them, I found out whether I wanted or not."

Perhaps Gracie was as content as Eve and Tom were to remain in their comfortable limbo, just living each moment as it came. But such passions could not be contained in the present, and time would not stop for them. Inevitably, plans started springing into their conversations. At first they were short term, referring only to the following week, or later in the summer, and were vaguely alluded to. Then, one morning, Tom put his arm around Eve and said, "Eve, honey, I've been given some offers, you know. When I go home, well, I was planning to sign with a new team in San Diego. It's pretty good for coming out of a small school, and it's a good contract and a good place. I think I could make a go of it. At least I want to. I don't know how far I'll get—if I'll make the big time, but it's what I do best. Playing ball. It's my talent."

"I know it is. That's really great, Tom." Eve looked at him with admiration and a little envy, for having a talent and a place in the world.

He looked back, seeing how her hair shone like copper in weaves of sunlight. "But I don't know how you'll like it. I mean, it's not terribly regular—there's travel and training and separations, and well, even abstinence. Yes, ma'am, Mrs. Tomacello."

Evelyn's golden glow turned suddenly red. "What are you saying?" She sat up straight, as if assaulted again by the old demon F word—future—that seemed to trip her up every time she was beginning to enjoy herself.

"I'm saying, sweetheart, that when we are married, I'll give up football if you want. Whatever you want. I just want it to be perfect for you." He touched her hair, burning metal.

"Married?" She pulled away from him. "But we never talked about it, Tom. I mean, you never asked…"

She broke off as if choked, as if suddenly trapped by too much devotion, and turned away from him, from his merciless sincerity, from his awful love. It was, she knew, so deep that he would do as he said, give up his dearest hope for her, something in a thousand years she would never do for him.

"Eve," he pulled her gently toward him by the chin, "there are some things people can say without words. As far as I'm concerned, in all the ways that matter, we're married right now. Even if it is just in the first stages. I would never have taken you that way unless..."

"For God's sake, Tom." She wanted to shout at him, but unaccountably began to cry. It was unbearable to think she was suddenly considered married to a man who would walk the earth barefoot for her, who would hold her higher in his esteem than she would ever hold herself, but who had never said anything, had never asked.

The sight of tears unnerved Tom more than he thought possible. He cursed himself for being a blundering fool, for being insensitive, for forgetting how delicate Evelyn was. Beside himself, he begged her to stop.

"Oh baby, please forgive me. It's all my fault. I shouldn't have just blurted out everything. I should have thought of a better way, a gentler way..."

Eve stopped crying and looked at him through the distortion of tears, thinking that she had never seen him so clearly. He was as he always was and ever would be. He adored her in a way that would change little for the rest of their lives. She knew that if she told him that it was the idea of marriage that disturbed her, not the style of his proposal, he would never understand. She looked at him and saw permanence and beauty. Like *David,* she thought, he was forever. But she herself was the opposite, impermanent, flighty, impetuous, a wild thing wanting to dart from petal to petal, happy for the moment to settle nowhere. She could tell him none of this. Drying the last tears from her eyes, she said, "Tom, you must never give up the idea of playing football. Not for anything, not for anyone."

He lowered his eyes in thanksgiving. He felt he had been given a benediction as well as absolution. She had forgiven him his clumsiness and beyond that had given him the greatest possible gift. If she thought first and only of his dream, obviously she loved him as much as he loved her, and once they were actually married would even sacrifice everything for him to let him play ball. He was overwhelmed with her love and the fact that they understood each other so well.

"Thank you," was all he said, then choked and could say no more.

Suddenly Evelyn noticed the heat. It weighed down on her, forcing sweat to run in little trickles at her temples and about her neck. She noticed the crowds that seemed to swarm the streets, and how now in full light the magical walled town seemed smudged and in need of a cleansing rain. Ideas in her head swarmed as if they were a nest of bees. She needed to lie down. More than that, she needed to talk to someone sensible. She needed Gracie.

For once, Gracie could not be found. Evelyn lay on her dormitory bunk and closed her eyes, trying to be still, trying to think. Tossing, she was flooded with all that drew her to Tom, until she was tempted to run and throw herself at him. No one would ever love her as much again, that she knew. But his devotion, his certainty, his unshakable sincerity, frightened her. She felt a small rush of panic she'd experienced before. Once again, she had acted on impulse, on desire, and now there were consequences. She hadn't planned on consequences. She didn't like the feeling of being out of control, of jumping into a tidal wave that would sweep her away quite powerlessly into marriage. Marriage. She knew the problem in talking about this to Tom was that for him it was a question of how and when; for her, it was a matter of if.

Gracie, red-faced and damp from the gathering heat, entered the dorm room noisily. Her sandals had little heels that clacked. Evelyn propped herself up on one elbow. "Oh, thank God you're here," she said, as though that were Gracie's duty. "Where've you been?"

"Actually, most recently I've been outside with Tom—Tom, who's loitering again." Gracie's gray eyes widened. "He says he goofed it up, talking about the wedding too soon. He says he messed up on the proposal."

"Proposal!" Then Evelyn began and repeated her stream-of-conscious thoughts to Gracie, who alternately paled and blushed in listening, but Evelyn did not see her. When Evelyn finished, she sat upright, suddenly feeling the need to breathe. "You say he's outside? I guess I should go out there. Tell him."

"Tell him what?" Gracie turned to look at Eve now, who in her cotton dress and sandals, was damp and flushed, her hair falling limply about her face. She looked, Gracie thought, much as she had when she ran to the grove the first time.

But Evelyn didn't answer, probably because she didn't know. She stepped outside, and Tom's breath caught in his throat. She looked like she did when he first arrived in what seemed another lifetime but was less than two weeks ago. She looked fresh and sweet, even more irresistible than when she was made up and dazzling. He reached for her, put his arm around her, and without a word they both turned to the grove where they had first lain together.

Evelyn recited it all later verbatim for Gracie. How the grove had always seemed cool and moist, but now the heat followed even there, and the dry needles fallen from the pines were uncomfortable beneath her. How Tom had started out, saying, "You know Eve, we can't just stay here forever. I mean we've got a few more weeks max in Europe, and then… Sweetheart, we have to talk about the future. About us, our plans." How her heart had raced, realizing he was right. Even now, facing him, she had no plan for what to say, no plan for the future. Yet it loomed, going home, facing her parents, facing school and the fact she had failed her year at the Sorbonne, facing the church scholarship committee, for God's sake.

The dizziness came back. Tom wanted to talk about marrying her. In a way, it was the ideal solution. To everything. But even thinking about it seemed to come with destabilizing vertigo. Then she spoke, hearing her own thoughts for the first time.

"Look, this is so big. And so sudden. You being here and all that has happened between us. Of course I love you, and well, you know. All the rest. But at least you knew you were coming here, and had, you know, more time to think about everything. I guess I just need time."

"Sweetheart," Tom answered, massaging her neck gently, "you can have all the time you need. It's not like I was going to whisk you away to church tomorrow or something. I'm just talking about when, where, those things. And how. We'll play it however you want, that's a promise. It's your call. I don't want to rush you."

Eve pulled back a little, so she could see straight into his eyes. "But there's one thing you forgot, Tomacello. See, you're so sure. You know how you want things to play out as far as you can see. But the thing you forgot is the 'if'—if we get married. See, I love you, but it's so confusing, so big, and well, unlike you, I'm not sure. About what to do I mean. And you never asked."

He looked back at her unflinching, the muscles in his jaw seeming to ripple involuntarily. "No, I don't see. I don't see at all…"

Eve's eyes, green at that moment as the surrounding glen, contracted, as if to reduce the pain she knew she was inflicting. She reached up to soothe his jaw. "I'm sorry, Tom. I'm so sorry. I knew you didn't see it that way at all."

He squeezed his fingers together, in and out, as if to knead a dreadful affliction. His voice rose and fell in shifts between anger and pain. "No, Evelyn, you're right. I don't see it that way. I mean we've been together a year. I mean together in our hearts, loving. You wrote to me, Eve, you wrote me that you loved me. I believed you. I came here to find that love again, to hold you again, to tell you again. To have you tell me. And you did, and we…we came together here, right here in this place. It was a pledge. How could we not be together forever? It's where we belong." He took her by the shoulders and pulled her close. "Look, baby, we love each other. That's it. It's easy, it's pure, it's fantastic. No complications. *Unsure?* It's the surest thing I ever knew." He began kissing her, hard.

She pulled away from his embrace. "I do love you, Tom. I do. But I can't help how I am. That it's not easy for me like it is for you. That's why I have to get away, to think!" Unexpectedly, she exploded in tears again and fled back across the path of needles to seek solace beside the river.

When Gracie saw Evelyn again, the decision had been made. "Gracie, we need to get out of here for a while, to think," she announced.

"You and Tom?" Gracie blinked, but this time not from the unforgiving sun.

"No! You and me. I can't think around Tom, he's too…" and she caught herself grinning. "It's hard to think around *David* when he's making his moves, you know."

So it was decided, and though Gracie hadn't exactly been consulted, she agreed. They would get away, go to the coast, cool off. In two weeks they would return, meet Tom, and everything would be settled.

When Gracie saw Tom next, he had resigned himself to the separation. Only two weeks, he kept repeating. Alone with him, with his wounds, Gracie felt as she always did in his presence, protective yet wanting, lost yet found. Then she wanted most to throw herself in his arms for comfort. She wasn't sure whose. "So where will you go?" she finally asked.

"I don't know, *bella*, haven't much thought about it." The sunlight made him squint, made her feel he was winking at her. She relaxed. "Maybe I'll kick around the Roman ruins in these parts, you know. Or maybe I'll even make a quick end run across the border, stick my toe in Italy, kiss the motherland." He laughed, and she shivered a little in the heat, savoring their private joke. "Oh, doll," he finally said, grabbing her in an exuberant hug and twirling her around, "how can I ever thank you? I wouldn't be here if it weren't for you."

They parted the next morning, this time taking the bus to the train station. Eve decided it would be better to say good-bye on the little hill where the bus stopped than in the crowded, public station. Tom walked ahead, carrying all the bags. They stood silent, waiting, until the bus was visible heading onto the other side of the bridge.

"So, two weeks isn't really long," he grinned, "only an eternity." And Gracie saw the grin waver into barely masked grief. "But sweetheart, if you want it, I know it's a good thing. Just remember how I love you…" It was all he could manage to get out.

Gracie, wearing a sundress and sandals almost identical to Eve's—"like a caricature," she said cruelly of herself—turned away. Then Tom found her, rumpled her hair, and said, "You're terrific, doll. Take good care. She's everything to me."

Gracie said *"Ciao,"* and boarded the bus, trying not to look as Tom kissed Eve good-bye. Eve, who climbed into the seat next to her and fixed her eyes on Tom, waving, until his strong muscular frame shrank and disappeared from view.

Chapter 30

They had decided on Nice, Gracie said, because it was the first stop the train made on the coast. For someone of her prodigious memory, it seemed that long stretches of their time there were vacant, hazy, or simply vanished in sea foam. But she did remember the long walk dragging their bags from the station to the section called Vieux Nice, close to the water, filled with students, carousers, vagabonds like themselves, and cheap hotels, like Vieux Trianon, where they had to haul their luggage up three flights. The room was stale-smelling, hot, and overlooked a crowded street closed to traffic, but open to late-night street prowlers. The toilet down the hall stank, and the public showers on the beach were more inviting than the communal tub one flight down. She wrinkled her nose recounting this, astonishing herself with the realization that she'd become a snob. "I guess despite everything, living at Madame's spoiled me for the 'real world.'"

Then she added as an afterthought, "We went to the Côte d'Azur thinking it would be cooler—and glamorous. It wasn't."

While Evelyn was absent for hours at a time, lost in the tangle of her thoughts, fears, and desires, Gracie had long hours to think too. Perhaps she questioned what had happened to her own plans, the things she imagined she wanted to do with her limited time and resources. But she never mentioned it. She seemed to have accepted her role as a kind of shell to surround, protect, and be filled by Tom's love for Evelyn, hers for him, and for the messes that came in their wake. The residue that came to her through Tom's affection, through Evelyn's need, was her reward. Still I wondered at it, wondered where she had disappeared when she recited Eve's thoughts as though they were her own.

Daily they made their way to the crowded public beach down the sweeping Promenade des Anglais overlooking the Baie des Anges, because that was what they had come to do, or at least what they could afford. Curiously, there Gracie had her small triumph. As they settled uncomfortably beneath a rented umbrella on the gray stones that covered the beach, and Evelyn made her daily complaint about how she'd take Santa Monica any day, Gracie spread her towel and began the daily routine of oiling herself. By paying scientific attention to just the right combination of oil, exposure, and withdrawal, she discovered to her considerable delight that her pale skin could turn a light toast color. It was an even greater delight, though she admitted this was mean, when Eve turned only a brighter and brighter shade of pink and had to spend longer stretches covering herself and retreating to the shade.

Protesting that she looked like a roast pig, she cried out in disgust and poked at her scorched thigh. But Gracie, of course, refused to agree. Then Evelyn retreated farther under the umbrella, where the pebbles beneath her towel still made a pattern of bumps along her fresh sunburn, and where the sweat glistened on her like Gracie's oil smelling of coconuts. French sun worshippers in bronzed skin and tiny silken strips covering their bulging virility swarmed about, but she waved them away as if shooing flies. Gracie knew she was for once thinking only of Tom, who must have loomed in her mind like a giant, his physical perfection putting all those oily imitations of manhood to shame. She seemed only to stare into the shifting blues of the Mediterranean, thinking.

The men swarmed around Gracie too, since she was sharing the same shade and corner of rough beach as Evelyn, but she knew too well none of the whistles, whispers, or admiring stares were meant for her. She, too, had Tom to think about and a responsibility to get Eve to see the light. Occasionally, they would plunge into the calm, lapping waters, and Eve would swim out deep enough to feel a cooling current, finding herself momentarily alone. Gracie, who was afraid of water, clung close to shore, trying to find the line where stones turned to softer sand. Then they would return to their uncomfortable spot on the beach and take a deeper plunge, the one that took them into the tangles of Evelyn's confusion.

"We had this conversation about it, with Eve saying things like, 'So he wants to marry me. It's simple really, isn't it? It's what people do…'

"And me replying, 'So what's your problem with it?'

"And then her saying, 'Well the *problem* is that it's so—it's so permanent—like forever…'"

I can see Gracie, perched on her elbows, staring back at Evelyn through those borrowed, oversized dark glasses, answering: "Right. So what's wrong with that? I mean isn't that what *everybody* wants?"

I can also see Evelyn wiggling on her stomach to follow the whim of shade shifting beneath the umbrella, trying to draw her pink legs away from the rapacious sun, replying at last: "'Yeah. Maybe so. At least that's what we're supposed to want.'"

Gracie was more than incredulous by now. "But you *love* him. *What else could you want?*"

They were both pretty uncomfortable, shifting on the stones, both knowing Gracie was right in what she had said and what she had not—that Tom *loved Evelyn*, and that he, like that eternally beautiful statue of chiseled marble he resembled, would never change. No matter what she did, he would love her forever. Where could this possibly be going but marriage? As her thoughts spun out, Gracie collected them. Eve *did* love Tom and didn't want to lose him. They couldn't stay where they were, and certainly couldn't keep on this way once they were back home, within the grasp of parents and coaches and churches. It was at that moment almost unimaginable for Evelyn to think of submitting herself for even one more year to the game of subverting Spinster Krauss and all the idiotic college rules. Besides, when it came down to the question of her future, she had no clue, no better alternative theory. Marriage certainly would solve a lot of problems.

Paris had been so delicious, she said, such a lark. She had felt such freedom, but with bailing out of the Sorbonne, cashing in the scholarship money, the stinging defeat of the marquis's defection—kind of like being left at the altar—she had nothing to show for her year. "Nothing," she reminded Grace, "except the goddamn useless dress."

Then she looked at Gracie in this penetrating way, like she'd never really seen her before. "I blew it. Not like you, kiddo," she said, and went on about how smart Gracie was and sensible, and how Gracie would never obsess about something stupid, like playing the marquis and going to a ball, the way she had.

Gracie told Eve to just quit worrying so much. To try to relax and enjoy everything. To go with the flow…

By then she also realized they'd really had a lot of sun, and that maybe the next day they should do something else to keep off the beach.

Evelyn agreed. She said it would be it be fun to go to one of those classy hotels with their own cabanas on the beach where they serve champagne and caviar. Or maybe go to Monte Carlo, to check out the yachts and playboys and casinos. Have lunch at the palace with Grace and Rainier.

I can see Gracie roll her eyes.

It was Gracie's idea to take the bus to Cimiez, the high hill above the city, and visit the Roman ruins. The fact that the whole of southern France had been an extension of the Roman Empire, that the word "Provence" had come from the Latin meaning province, made her feel a connection to her roots. It was a way of being in Italy without going there. Tramping along the neat excavation lines and tidy holes where wild roses and weeds still had their way, she followed the maps and explanations of what each section represented with an unexpected exhilaration. Houses, streets, baths, and higher up the hill an almost intact arena still in constant use. Even telling about them months later, she spoke with excitement, as though she'd found an escape from the unimaginable reality of the present in the crumbling but visible reality of the past.

Evelyn was more interested in the colors atop that high hill than with holes in the ground and broken artifacts over two thousand years old. She was the one who knew that Matisse had lived up here for nearly forty years, and when she saw the view, she knew why. Even Gracie had to admit it was like a stage set, with those grand villas and their semitropical gardens, the white-hot walls of the smaller houses with red-hot roofs, and a jungle of pink, orange, and purple bougainvillea spilling over the walls. She especially loved the palm trees fanning the breeze—like in Claremont—but with a view of the sea. Eve said it was like being in a painting under a van Gogh sun. She liked being up there because she could get a different perspective and a vacation from the heavy duty of thinking.

By the time the bus started its slow winding trip down the hill back toward the center of town again, it was sunset, and the startling orange fading to purple in the sky cast a new glow over the sea. Eve watched, mesmerized, their descent toward the rippling of what was by then a blood-red sea. Blood. That was the thing.

It wasn't until the bus reached the bottom and made its way through the city streets, stopping every three blocks, that Evelyn turned to Gracie with her startling announcement, blurting out, "Here's the deal. I'm late. Like about five days late. It should have started just when we were leaving Avignon. I *thought* it was just travel, or the water, or maybe tension. Or maybe those salades niçoises with all those anchovy thingies in them. Anything. But the thing is, I'm never late…"

I can imagine how she just stared at Eve, trying to put this in some kind of context, thinking that people like Evelyn did not just get pregnant. That happened to dumb people, like her cousins, or the girls who came all bent with shame to the convent schools to be finally and properly humiliated by the nuns. But Evelyn! Gorgeous, worshipped, adored, special Evelyn. And then those unwanted images in her mind of Eve and Tom lying naked together in some private hideaway. Gracie was in no way ready to picture Evelyn carrying Tom's child.

Stunned, Gracie blurted "Didn't you use anything?"

Eve replied that the way things had gone was sort of a surprise. She didn't expect Tom would have anything, being Catholic. But she had this douche stuff, a parting gift from Edith, and of course even the hostel had a bidet. She thought she was safe.

At this point, Gracie reverted to speech she didn't know she still had. "Jesus, Joseph, Mary Mother of God!" Then added that at least it kind of solved her dilemma.

That's when Eve went a little crazy. "*Solves* my dilemma? I don't get your thinking. Isn't this about the worst predicament a girl can get herself into?" And tears started spilling from her eyes. She talked about shame, and the impossibility of ever finishing college, and the certainty her family would turn her away when she needed them most. Eve wailed about how she'd become everybody's favorite cliché—the minister's daughter gone wild.

Gracie was too shaken to admit to herself how much she too was vested in seeing Evelyn as special, blessed in beauty and spirit, touched by the gods. I can hear her heated reply: "That stuff's for ordinary people. Any old minister's daughter. But not you. You're different. And this will make Tom only love you more." That Botticelli Madonna he so loved flashed before her eyes. "Anyway, now you'll have to marry him."

Gracie nodded, and Eve mumbled in agreement, while they slowly climbed up the stairs at the Vieux Trianon. The one thing that never came up was whether to keep the baby. Gracie guessed that Eve was the minister's daughter still.

And Gracie, knowing all too well Tom's Catholic sensibilities, didn't bring it up either.

Resignation did not come easily to Evelyn. "It was settled in one way, but in another Eve couldn't accept it, not yet."

They returned to their routine of escaping the unsavory Vieux Trianon and walking the few blocks to the beach every day to resume "Evelyn's Think-a-thon." Sometimes they walked up and down the great promenades facing the beach and ogled the sumptuous hotels, quaint and wealthy dowagers from another era. Sometimes they escaped into palm-shaded grassy parks to sit and listen to guitar-strumming musicians, watch children on a carousel, or look for a vendor selling Italian gelato. But they were never far from the shore, and Evelyn's growing obsession for finding what she now called "the red tide."

"She kept insisting it still could happen, that anything could happen. But…" here Gracie shrugged. With each day of blue sea and blood sunsets but no tiny spot of red, Eve's hopes were extinguished further. Five days after the ride down from Cimiez, she knew. She was pregnant by Tom and therefore would have to marry him. It was no use prolonging the debate about whether under other circumstances she would have married him or not. That was history. She needed to look ahead now. To a quick wedding, being pregnant, motherhood. She might as well relax and enjoy it, she told herself and Gracie. She and Tom would have a lot of explaining to do, a lot of peace to make with the world. Even better, the world would have to make peace with them.

On the morning of the fifth day, she pronounced, "it's a done deal."

It was Eve's idea to go back even though the two weeks weren't up. At one point, she even said to Gracie: "You know, kiddo, you don't have to come back with me. I mean, I guess I can take it from here. Maybe you want to slip on over the border to the motherland or something?"

Gracie admitted that she even thought about it. But as ever, she was running short on money and time. And in truth, where would she have gone in Italy alone? After all that had transpired, she couldn't imagine it. Besides, to leave with Eve pregnant would feel as if she'd abandoned her best friend in her time of need. What she didn't say—and it was hard to admit this to herself—was how much she wanted to see Tom one last time before, as she put it, "everything changed."

This time, in deference to Evelyn's *condition*, they scraped together the fare and took a cab back to the station. It was on the train going back up alongside the Rhône that Evelyn presented her last major surprise of that leg of the journey. She said there was this one thing, and she made Gracie promise that she would not say a word about this to anybody, most of all to Tom.

Gracie couldn't believe it. So she asked outright: "What do you mean?"

"I mean," Eve answered, as if in a trance, "I don't want him to know about the baby yet. He mustn't know it happened this way. And he won't have to. I want him to think I decided first, and then I found out later. *Please*… It's nearly true anyway."

Gracie agreed, but with this sinking feeling. She looked at it as a kind of sacred oath, romantic and secret. Then she came to wonder if she'd danced with the devil.

Chapter 31

Back in Avignon, Evelyn took to her bed, meaning she spent listless hours lying on the bunk in the hostel dorm in her peculiar limbo, waiting for Tom to come and the future to officially begin. Gracie took it upon herself, once again, to keep vigil. She posted herself at the bottom of the little hill, waiting for the bus to stop above. The second morning of her watch, the bus pulled away and out of its shadow stepped a tall, lean figure. The first thing Gracie noticed was that he limped. It was Jay Greene.

At first she thought he didn't see her, and she just watched. He looked the same, but graver. Listing, a bit gray, and then this slash across the cheek. Somehow that was the distinguishing mark, like an insignia for all his suffering. He looked, well…mature.

He came toward her with surprise and recognition, but without remembering her name. I can imagine Gracie having to remind him of who she was, how she was Evelyn's companion and closest friend. She of course didn't say confidant, confessor, guardian of secrets.

Jay folded his arms across his chest, taking her in, taking it all in. "Of course," he said. "I'm sure it's a surprise to see me here, but I'm not surprised to see you, a *demoiselle de la Maison Française,* traveling here with Evelyn. She's why I'm here, too."

Gracie felt her stomach constrict. "She's inside the hostel, resting," she told him, and tried not to give away a thing.

But then he asked if she could tell her that he was there, saying: "I had an intuition that she'd be back by today. That's why I got the first bus here."

Gracie turned deliberately to bring the latest news to Evelyn, as if it were her job in life to be a messenger between the gods. By the time she got to the dorm, she felt like shouting, as if to ring an alarm, as if there were a fire, as if she should warn Eve to run for her life. But she only said, "Your presence is required. A gentleman to see you."

"Tom! You mean he's back so soon?"

"Not quite," Gracie answered. "Check it out for yourself." Then she went as far as the door to watch Evelyn, breathless, look a long moment before saying, "Jay?"

He answered only "Hello," looking as if he was drinking her in.

Gracie did not have to listen to the rest to hear how they breathlessly filled each other in on where they had been, because Eve told Gracie all about it later.

She said the shock of brown hair that fell in an angle across his forehead seemed almost in direct line with the scar that now crossed his cheek. His light brown eyes seemed cloudy, as if fogged with the memory of pain.

She said it was like he was self-aware in a new way. Like he knew who had gone into the accident and who had come out of it. He told her that he was different. For one thing, he was alive, and not just physically. "He gave her some line," Gracie said later, "about 'knowing what it means to be able to say *I live*.'" They'd told him he'd never walk again, but oh God, how he wanted to. How he had to. He even admitted what a foolish, arrogant bastard he'd been. Flashing around in fast cars with a wad of bills.

"Imagine. Jay Greene saying all this stuff. Sounds almost like you talking, Gracie," Eve said.

But Gracie didn't say anything. What she feared was that only the flashy part of his arrogance was gone, like a layer of baby fat, but the wily, attractive charm was still there, lurking, even more dangerous behind the still handsome face now decorated with the defining scar.

Alarmed, Gracie saw how thoroughly Eve was taken in. Especially when she said: "I think he's chastened. He limps now instead of runs. For all of that, he seems more of a man."

Inevitably, he had asked questions, too. Yes, Eve told him, she had gotten his notes, but made some excuse about not being much of a correspondent. As for what he was doing there, she was as stunned as Gracie had been. Eve poured his answers into Gracie's ears as if she had asked.

He said he was just making good on his promise—one that Eve said she barely remembered. He said once in the hospital that he was going to give Tom a "run for his money." So he had come to do just that.

At first, he was waiting for Eve to return. But then it occurred to him that Tom might come first. If that happened, he'd never get the chance to even try. So he pulled out all the stops, including corny lines like, "You've inspired me out of my crutches six weeks early, Evelyn Richter. Just thinking of you inspired me. So now here I am, a knight in shining armor, presenting my colors."

No wonder Gracie was alarmed. I picture her sitting bolt upright, watching Eve's nervous fingers drum a small iron tabletop as if somehow she could hold back the flow of events that was running outrageously out of control. Finally Gracie asked: "So what did you tell him? I mean, what about Tom?"

"Everything," Eve replied. She said that she was waiting for Tom, that they were engaged, even that she was thinking about plans for the wedding.

Of course that wasn't quite everything. But when Gracie pushed her on it, she said no, of course she hadn't told him that. She repeated that Gracie was the only one who knew about that.

"So how did he take it?" Gracie finally asked.

"Oh, he was completely gentlemanly and only had good things to say about Tom, and asked where he was so he could congratulate him. He even said Tom is one of the finest guys in the world because he'd saved my life that night on the mountain…and for that he would always be in Tom's debt."

But Gracie wasn't buying any of this, and asked if she meant he was backing off, just like that. For once Eve was kind of calm, explaining it all matter-of-factly: that is, no, at first Jay didn't get the situation at all. He didn't get that Tom would come to woo and win her, so to speak, that they'd get engaged and all and then he'd just leave her "unprotected in this den of wolves." So Eve told Jay that she was the one who had needed time out, to think, and that we'd come back early to wait for Tom. To tell him.

Gracie heard her own heart fall before she heard the words she knew were coming. About how if Tom didn't know his good fortune yet, maybe it wasn't too late, maybe there was some slim thread of hope for Jay Greene.

Eve had assured him there was not. He said he respected that, but since all those days in the hospital and beyond, all that time he'd spent just thinking, he had things he needed to talk through with her. Maybe they could spend a day or two exploring the region and getting to be better friends until Tom came back. Then he could congratulate Tom in person.

Eve ran her fingers through her streaming red hair, while the knot growing in Gracie's stomach tightened. "You didn't agree, did you?" Gracie asked.

"Sure, why not?" she answered, flippantly, in Gracie's view. It was like no harm done, and then she emphasized how it would help keep her from getting too nervous waiting. "Besides, I don't really know him, except for that one night and all those awful days sitting by his bed." Eve said.

"So what's the point in getting to know him? He might have killed you if not for Tom."

But Eve just shrugged and said, "Funny, he talked about all that." He admitted how he had been prideful and arrogant, wanting Eve because she was beautiful and popular, because it would be a great notch to have on his belt. Great locker-room stuff. But then he came out with this: that all that had to do with the "old Jay."

Gracie was spared a definition of the "new Jay," but heard more than enough about where he was coming from. He believed, Eve said, that he had gotten to know her well through hours of observation when she came to sit with him. She was embarrassed to learn that he knew how uncomfortable she was with him, how it unnerved her to be with someone broken as he was. He surmised she did it out of a sense of duty, of shame for her own behavior, of pity. When Eve reluctantly admitted he was right, he brushed aside her apologies.

"Then," Gracie sighed, "boy, did he have her number! He went on about needing to get beyond it, moving onto something more. Life after physical rehab, I guess you could say. He told her how he started thinking about all the things she'd brought to read to him, the stories, the poems—some territory inside that was mostly terra incognita, but the place he needed 'to cultivate and make beautiful,' if you can believe it. Beautiful enough to be able to find and connect with Eve again. He told her it was the beginning of his 'return to the living.'"

When Eve recounted all this, she spoke so slowly, Gracie thought she was measuring her breath. Finally she inhaled and continued. "Then he actually said something like: 'That's when I vowed I'd meet Tom again to challenge him for your affection. But now that I'm too late, please grant me a day or two of friendship. It's part of my rehabilitation.'"

While Eve talked, Gracie lay back watching her preen. She was running a brush through her hair, which was shiny, and holding up a small mirror to check her complexion, which was smooth and glowing. Yet she kept up her line of chatter. "Hey, Gracie, maybe the beach did me a world of good too. You weren't the only one to catch the benefit of a few rays. Unless…" Then she stopped, kind of smiling. "Unless, you know. I've heard this condition is great for the complexion." She paused then and ran her hands slowly down her body, like she needed to verify what she already knew. "Well, my boobs are a bit tender, but at least my stomach is still the same. I mean, I'm not showing yet, am I?"

Then she laughed kind of outrageously, as if something were about to break, and said, "Can you just picture me with a watermelon out front?"

Gracie said she couldn't. Maybe that was because Evelyn at that moment looked more beautiful than ever. By the time she was lumbering and swollen, Tom would be there to look after her. For the moment, though, to Gracie's disgust, she was preening for Jay, and her secret *condition* added something exciting, something forbidden, about her that would only make her more desirable.

Gracie was left alone with her dark thoughts. The imaginary wall she'd built up, sealing her in with Tom and Eve, had just opened a very large crack. Despite herself, she began to think. "Thinking is the worst curse," she noted harshly, "like waking up from a peaceful sleep into a bad dream." Once it began, nothing was off limits, not even, she admitted, the dreadful Georgie MacKay and his pathetic letters. She thought of leaving the shabby hostel and its population of mosquitoes, or even sweltering Avignon and its mob of tourists. She had invested everything—vacation time, dwindling money, romantic hope—in what was rapidly becoming an outsized misadventure. Why not just leave?

But all her doubts came down to one word, the same word that kept her in place. "Tom," she said simply, not saying that she wanted desperately to see him again, that in the darkest corners of her doubts the hope flickered, however slight, that now more than ever, he might need her.

Evelyn, too, was feeling the heat; the initial charm of Avignon had worn away. Perhaps, she told herself, that was because the original enchantment was all about falling in love with Tom, and now he wasn't here. Perhaps she rationalized that when Tom came back everything would feel the same again. Or perhaps—I'm theorizing beyond Gracie's account—she was simply irritated at feeling so confused. She was, after all, sitting in a café where only a couple weeks before she had come for *petit déjeuner* with Tom after a delirious night of lovemaking. Maybe she was surprised at how comfortable it was, sitting there conversing so easily with Jay, how admiring she was of his transformation. She told Gracie how he had "given up the political thing, the mania for things Kennedyesque, and the big flash" (though she guessed he had the bucks to do that if he wanted). Now all he wanted was something quiet and substantial, a way to simply do good. That's why, she concluded, he was thinking of law school.

Perhaps most of all, being in the bright light of Jay's good company, Eve was able to do what she most longed for, to relax and forget. But it took only the slightest thing to bring her back to reality. As she sat in the shade sipping a lemonade and drinking in Jay's remarkable story, she casually lit a cigarette. "That's when it hit me," she told Gracie. "Yuk, it tasted terrible, and then I realized, oh God, I'm pregnant. And I felt like I just had to get out of there, or maybe just out of my own skin."

So she told him that she knew she'd promised to show him around Avignon, but the heat and the crowds were getting to her. She said she'd have to excuse herself.

Gracie told me how he stepped easily into each opening, saying things like, "Hey I don't blame you. It is too much here now. There's plenty of time to see it later. How would you like to get out in the country, where it's less crowded, cooler?"

But Eve still wasn't quite on board. The only way she knew to get around was by bus, and she certainly wasn't up for that. So he said he'd show her what he meant.

As she explained to Gracie: "He had this VW bug parked outside the city walls. Can you imagine? He even drove carefully. He certainly has changed his style."

That first afternoon, they took a short ride up the Rhône to Châteauneuf-du-Pape, home of some of the most prized vineyards in all of France. The fields and slopes, laid out in wondrous geometric design, were lush with heavy vines and dotted with estates, châteaux, and grand villas open to the tasting public. Bare, rocky hilltops sported romantic piles of stone, "lovely ruins," Evelyn said, and best of all, she had found a true remedy for getting out of the heat. "Get thee to a cave, woman," she told Gracie, as if she, too, had the option of going wine-tasting on a whim.

By nightfall, Gracie had plastered herself with bug spray and taken herself outside. She decided to keep watch by the river near the hostel instead of the road near the bus stop. Perhaps she half-acknowledged that she was now keeping vigil on two fronts and did not honestly know at this point which would be worse: to see Evelyn arrive with Jay or to have Tom arrive while Eve was gone.

Gracie watched the blue VW pull down that dirt road scattering dust, saw Evelyn step out with Jay, in a most gentlemanly fashion, holding the door. She saw how he escorted her to the hostel door and heard with her own ears how Eve called back to him, saying, "Come around again tomorrow morning. He'll surely be here by then." And Gracie collapsed on her back into the grassy riverbank, reassured.

Chapter 32

It was easy to pretend she'd seen nothing, knew nothing, so when Grace entered the hostel filling with the chatter of girls in a dozen languages, she went straight to Evelyn to ask how her day had been.

"Great," she said. Gracie went on, asking if Tom was back yet. Eve said no, but that it had to be soon. After all, it was coming up on two weeks.

"Right. And what about Jay?" Gracie snapped.

Then she stood rigid through Evelyn's long exposé of that day, the car, the vineyards, and ended up fatigued but happy to realize Jay had in fact, at the end of the day, gone away. She tried no doubt to keep the anguish, the loneliness out of her voice, when she asked Evelyn if she had dinner plans.

"No," she answered Gracie, "no plans. I'm just hanging around, waiting for the last bus of the day. Tomacello's got to be on it, no?" Perhaps, she suggested, Gracie would like to go to dinner somewhere.

For a moment, Gracie had difficulty conveying her feelings. Maybe she felt a pang of remorse, a softening.

After all, Eve had kept her promises to Tom. There she was pregnant, trying to hold it together while her life ran wildly out of control, and what was the harm if she made Jay Greene feel better about everything? After all, she had hardly invited him to show up. Of course, she was happy to have Eve to herself again, and happy at the prospect of dinner in town.

"Sure," she said nonchalantly. "I'd like to go to town for dinner." Remembering she could barely afford anything, she asked Eve if she could afford it.

But Eve just laughed and answered, "Hell no. But it was nice to have a man around who picked up the checks, wasn't it?" Meaning Tom. She also wondered out loud where old Tomacello got so much bread all of a sudden. But she'd find out soon enough, as he would be back any minute.

Gracie's mind briefly raced over the church scholarship money that Eve had so spectacularly blown. In her own case, she knew Papa would come through for her if she had any shortfall in her scholarship money. After all, he had promised. The fact that she was too proud to want to accept his help seemed like a small moral crisis compared to the size and dimension of Eve's.

They set out, and crossed the bridge from the island by foot, where the lights were dancing on the dark water sweeping beneath them like the fireflies in the night above.

Eve commented that it looked like *Starry Night*, one of her favorite paintings. She even said it was too bad they didn't get out of town to visit some of those places with Tomacello, since they had talked about it so much.

Gracie said, "Well, it's never too late."

They went to the same cheap little café with atmosphere just inside the city wall where they'd been with

Tom. In an odd way, it cheered them both up. Gracie thought about ordering a half-carafe of rosé, but then wondered if Eve could do that, what with nausea and everything.

But Eve just smiled, saying that was fine, that it hadn't occurred to her to get nauseated. Then she said how it was weird, like a whole new set of tides pulling on her, but from the inside. "There's a whole life in there I never imagined, Gracie. I can't see it, and we have never met, but it has such power."

After those words, Gracie said she felt she could relax further, and stop worrying so much about Jay Greene. She believed Eve was really coming to grips with her situation, was coming to understand her newly reordered priorities. Maybe the simple act of being able to talk about the baby made Eve more relaxed. And knowing that Gracie was the only one in the world she could actually confide in pushed her, no doubt, into an uncommon gratitude for Gracie's presence. Who knows what thoughts of gratefulness and friendship were driving their way into her consciousness as she told of her day with the "remade Jay Greene" and their lovely drive through Châteauneuf-du-Pape country. But somewhere in her narration she must have stopped suddenly to stare hard at Grace.

Because, Gracie said, it came more or less out of the blue: "Hey, I've been looking at you. I think you really ought to get one of those cute Italian haircuts that are all the rage—the real short curly one. You've got the perfect hair for it."

Gracie admitted surprise at the unexpected twist in the conversation. She didn't have to explain that she never in a million years expected Eve, of all people, to take an interest in her appearance. But before she even replied, Eve was rushing ahead, promising that the day Tom was due, they'd celebrate by going together to a shop in town and getting Gracie a new hairdo.

I can picture how they laughed, walking arm in arm back across that bridge, with the lights still running in the dark river, but the fireflies gone, leaving the warm summer sky invisible.

Eve was the one who asked, "Do you think he made it tonight?" while Gracie was the one who replied probably not, as it was still a few days early. Then Eve just looked up to that black sky and said, "Damn!" and didn't say another word.

The next morning Gracie slept in. It was as if a great burden had lifted, and Eve, not she, could be on watch for Tom. With all the decisions made, and Eve clearly eager to do the right thing, perhaps Gracie felt her role as intermediary was over.

Eve slept in too, though, given her *condition*, Grace thought that was understandable. Neither of them was there to see the arrival of the early bus, which was just as well because no one got off that morning on top of the hill near the bridge. And the other girls in the dorm, who mostly awoke at sunrise and filled the room with a pleasing, incomprehensible babble, had cleared out by the time a weary-looking pensioner who worked as concierge—one of those blue-uniformed characters, as if from another century, knocked loudly on the door. He proclaimed a gentleman was there for the American, if the American was still around so late in the day. Eve jumped up immediately, grabbed her watch, and moaned. It was after nine a.m.! She said she was coming.

But Gracie lay still, probably holding her breath. All she could think of was, how did he get here now? There was no bus at that hour. Had he walked from the train?

It was only a minute later that Eve was back, flying through the door.

"It's Jay," she said breathlessly. "He brought his car down again, just in case. So I said, 'Well, so be it. Tom's not here, and I promised you a day or two.' So I'm off. Why the hell not?"

By nightfall, Eve was back, ready to meet Tom. Once again, all the buses had been empty, and Eve and Gracie spent another evening together, waiting for the late bus. It had been, Eve said, a perfect day. They had visited Saint-Rémy-de-Provence, lunched in the old town, visited Roman ruins, and then driven a couple of kilometers out of town to see the asylum where van Gogh had stayed the year before he died. It was like stepping into his paintings with all the sunflowers, the twisted cypress trees, the olive groves, the tortured sun. She was enchanted. And Jay had said if she liked Roman ruins and van Gogh, there were plenty more where these came from. Next time.

"Next time?" Gracie could feel the alarm rising again as she looked sharply at Eve. "How that could be?" But Eve said reassuringly she meant *if* there was a next time. That Jay knew how things stood with her and Tom, and that there would only be another day if Tomacello didn't come for another day to claim her. "'If my luck holds,' is what Jay said."

Jay's luck held. The next day and the next. There was a trip to Nîmes to see more ruins and the Roman aqueduct, the Pont du Gard, whose graceful arches had been spanning a gorge for more than two thousand years. There was a trip to Arles, the ancient Provençal city where van Gogh had lived in the little yellow house, hosted Gauguin, cut off his ear in madness, and found starry nights over the Rhône. All of these, Eve said again, she had wanted to visit with Tom. There had been more, too, Gracie assumed, but not much of it was revealed.

What was revealed was the conversation they'd had on the fourth day, driving back from Arles. How Jay had taken her hand—only in friendship, Eve emphasized—and spoken movingly about how much it meant to him to have her ride in a car with him. The "old Jay," he said, would have destroyed her in his stupidity without even knowing who she really was. Eve had asked what he meant.

That person, Jay answered, was someone he couldn't even have imagined beneath such a beautiful exterior.

What he told her was he had found a beautiful girl on the outside, with a real woman beneath the skin. He admitted she had faults, he was pretty sure, but even more sure she had wit, excitement, and a willingness to be alive. She was a person he couldn't ever, ever see being held back. She was an adventure waiting to happen. Just thinking of her set his imagination on fire.

I imagine Gracie was on fire, too, just hearing all this.

Eve seemed sort of calm, even if somewhat surprised. All she said was that it was strange how different a person becomes according to the eye of the beholder. Then she said she didn't believe Tom would even recognize her by that description.

It was two weeks to the day since Eve had promised to meet Tom there, at the rundown hostel where her whole life had been uprooted as if in a whirlwind, and she awoke early. Gracie watched her perform the gestures that had become a habit, smooth down the red hair that had become unruly with a night of dreams, then run her hands across her belly for reassurance. Her body, after all, had always been the truest definition of herself, her immutable asset. It had, she'd told Grace, led her places she wouldn't have thought to go: to football queen, to posing nude, to a secret tryst with Tom, to pregnancy. That had become the pivot of her life, but so far her body would not betray her secret. Her stomach remained flat.

She was glowing with nervous energy, Gracie noticed, and was anxious for the bus to arrive almost with first light. "I know he's going to be on it, kiddo. I know it," she said. "What a day this will be. Everything will be sorted out at last."

Everything. Gracie considered the scope of that word for Eve: the failures of Paris, committing herself at last to Tom, planning a wedding, getting pregnant, facing motherhood—and then having to face the wrath of her parents on every account. Everything. Maybe, for once, it was possible not to wish to be Evelyn.

For her part, Gracie was content to make coffee in the unsavory kitchen and carry it down to the riverbank to wait. If I had to guess what she thought she was waiting for, I'd say it was a kind of bittersweet fulfillment. Her scheming and planning was finally to be realized. And, for one final time, she would have her own private moment with Tom, the benediction of his gratitude, affection...and, dare she believe, love? Perhaps, too, she recoiled at what was the most difficult part to admit: that she had long nourished herself on the passion and intensity that came with this wild affair, that she had let its blood run through her veins. Now that she would no longer be needed as intermediary, confidante, keeper of all secrets, maybe she would wither from some rare anemia for which there was no diagnosis nor cure.

She sipped her coffee, brooding calmly, waiting. Then she made out the shadow on the road, walking slowly. Evelyn alone.

She could see a furrow in her brow as she got closer. She'd noticed it a lot these days, actually, and figured it was a sign of distress registering in Eve's body, even if her mind wasn't yet acknowledging it. Then she kind of spit out, "Well damn. He wasn't on it. What's keeping him, anyway?"

Gracie reminded her that he wasn't actually late. That this was the day they'd agreed on. And he couldn't possibly know we'd been here all this time, waiting.

She admitted Gracie was right. Then she gave her this look, a real once-over, and said, "Okay, kiddo, let's do it. Go to town to get you a new haircut. Maybe a new frock, too." Gracie was beyond mentioning that neither of them could afford to buy one, even if one could be found.

They went back into the dorm then to get ready for town, when the old concierge knocked on the door again, saying, "A gentleman to see the American," like the voice on a groove in a phonograph that had gotten warped, then stuck.

Alarm filled Gracie's ears as she heard Eve's joyous yelling. "Thank God, he's here after all!" She threw down the brush that had not finished making its way through her tangle of hair. She actually leapt, Gracie observed, out the door.

There, the tall, now-familiar form of Jay rested against the doorsill.

Eve told him that Tom wasn't back yet, but would be soon. He answered something like, "Then I'm lucky by one more day. One more day of your good company before I turn you back to the lucky arms of my friend."

Eve swore she protested, assuring him that she couldn't make plans that day because she already had plans. Then she thanked him for the fine time they'd had, and for the friendship.

But Jay just smiled that slow smile, the smile that bent persuasively with an angle of gravity where it touched his scar. Clearly, he had no intention of letting this go.

By the time she returned to the dorm, she had spun around completely. "Look, Gracie, he insists you can live without me for one more day. I told him that's crazy, that's not the point, but he's pretty determined. He was ready to see Tom, you know, pay his respects, but said he made contingency plans in case he lucked out. Seems he's brought food and wants to go on some fool picnic. I'm really sorry, but he insists. I figure if I don't go, he'll just hang around and drive us both crazy."

Gracie noted that she made the smoothing motions with her hands again, but nervously, as if she was not quite prepared to believe what they told her. Then she stopped, looked at Gracie for a long, anguished moment with her brow furrowed.

"*Ciao*, little one," she said—something she had never before said—and kissed Gracie on the forehead.

Gracie waited for a while, probably for her breathing to become regular again, and walked to town alone. She decided to get a haircut.

Chapter 33

It seemed ordinary enough. The peak of summer, the sky a searing blue, the heat shimmering like the sheaves of wheat in a van Gogh landscape, the brilliant greens and yellows of Provence set out in blocks as if brushed by Cézanne. The VW bug took off up the hill, leaving a puff of smoke on the dirt road behind, without giving a thought to Gracie left below, watching and worrying.

The car did not swerve back to cross the bridge toward the city, but this time went straight ahead.

Artful in his casualness, as he was in all things, Jay had planned the day carefully, though to Eve it seemed to just unfold magically, like a rabbit out of a hat.

"It's time for a view from the top, don't you think?" Jay suggested, steering the car up to climb the high hill overlooking the Rhône on the right bank of the river to the walled "new" Avignon—established, Jay noted, by Philip the Fair, King of France, as a challenge, a statement of intent, to the old boys of the Holy Roman Empire and the popes that France was a contender. New, Jay said, if you get in the mindset of the thirteenth century.

They parked the little car and went inside the impressive city walls with its keeps and towers, seeking to climb the one with the best view. Evelyn did not admit to Jay that she felt slightly dizzy and that the most likely reason was not one she wanted to discuss. Jay, whose sensitivity amazed her, noticed anyway. There was her shortness of breath, slight perspiration on her forehead. But gesturing to the magnificent panorama, "old" Avignon by the swift-running river, the bridges and spires, the valley dotted with dark greens and browns, patches of yellow, the distant villages and road, and on the far horizon the purple shadow of mountains topped by the stony dome of Mount Ventoux, Eve had a perfect explanation. "'Vertigo,'" she said, not adding even to Gracie that it also perfectly described the disequilibrium she felt in the "new" Jay's presence, in the uncanny way he seemed to know her.

As they climbed down the endless spiral staircase made for the obviously dainty-footed watchkeepers of an earlier time, Jay laughed, trying to keep his balance. Not a good place for the halt and lame, he observed. I can see how Evelyn must have smiled at that. But Jay was rarely off balance for long, soon announcing that he was hungry. "What is that French expression," he asked, "hungry as a wolf?"

Perhaps in the straightforward telling of Jay laying out the picnic, even Gracie could see the charm in it. As if he knew perfectly where he was going in advance, he drove to a little wooded spot not far from the city walls, one that was secluded but with a view to Avignon, the Rhône, the towns and valley upriver. There was a Provençal tablecloth of gold and blue spread upon a shady spot of ground, and then, miraculously, a perfect yellow rose in a tiny jar placed in the center. "'I stole it from a garden fair and square. No proper picnic without a centerpiece,'" he said. There followed the wine, a bottle of Châteauneuf-du-Pape, roasted chicken still warm in its juices, dense local cheeses sweating in their skin, crusty bread still hot in the center, peaches and cherries soft and ripe. Evelyn began loosening—literally and figuratively—first the scarf she'd wrapped on her head to keep dust from her unruly hair, then the dark glasses that so successfully kept out unwanted rays and shielded unbidden emotions, then her sandals. It is not hard to picture this—Gracie surely did—Eve draped on the Provençal cloth, her red hair flying in mischievous strands as the breeze picked up, playing in the sun, her eyes green and flirtatious, her feet bare and smooth and long.

The words were, if not scripted, inevitable: "You know you are the most beautiful girl I have ever seen." And so, too, was this moment inevitable, when he would fall before her with his hopes—and even perhaps then she already knew, though she was afraid—that she would bare herself before him with her feelings. But what exactly were they? The wind was kicking up, blowing uninvited dust in her face.

At first she said she tried to stop him, tried to resist. Perhaps unconsciously she contracted her languorous body, laid out so invitingly on the tablecloth. Perhaps she pulled into a sort of fetal position.

"'Eve, you know we have to talk. It has come to this.'" He did not ask her permission. He knew she loved Tom, yes, yes, he accepted that. It would be hard not to. But loving him did not add up to marrying him. Marrying him would be a mistake. Why? Because he loved her too much and liked her too little. Because her wonderful spirit, wild as her hair, would be tamed, smothered.

The rest of his speech Evelyn recited verbatim to Gracie's horrified ears. "But today I must speak because today is different, it's free, it's an accident. He might have come back and we might not have had it, it might so easily not have happened, like we might so easily not be alive. But it's a gift, and we're bound to take it."

By now no doubt, he was covering her long pink legs with his game one, and held her arms fast in his as he began kissing her. "Why are you doing this? Why can't you just let things be?" Those would be the only words that escaped, along with her poor efforts to breathe.

"For God's sake, I love you." Of course he said more. That it was insane to go forward, for Eve to lock herself up for life without ever knowing how much he, Jay, loved her—despite his gentlemanly behavior. She needed to hear the truth. That he loved her in delirium, in extremis, that he loved her constantly and incessantly, that he had dreamt of her for months, dreamt of holding her, loving her. His hands delivered his message along the length of her damp, slender body.

Vertigo. Her body seemed not to belong to her anymore. It felt as if she were someone else, a spirit maybe, hovering over the pocket of forest on the hillside, the flowing river, the hazy distance, as the landscape itself began to weave in the strengthening force of the wind that folded the tablecloth over them like a protective cover.

Then, "You have to hear this, Eve. 'You belong with me, not with Tom. He has invented you, but I know you. I love what you are.'"

Her response was no doubt as dazed as she was, perhaps only a weak "Why?" And his answers came, as eloquent, as overwhelming, as forceful as the rest of the picnic had been. It's not that they were made for each other, no rubbish like that, he was sure. Nobody is made for another, only for oneself. But profound love comes from profound liking. He knew her, liked what he knew—and knew she liked him. Christ, they were good together, were they not? They saw the world with the same slant, laughed at the same things, and were so comfortable with each other it was as if they'd been together all their lives. There was no denying it, was there?

In that place that felt liquid, as if she were swimming, she acknowledged it was so.

The wind blew harder, and his words came stronger. It was stupid, damn it, to go ahead with her plans. She could break Tom's heart now, or she could break it later, and what was the point of later? It would only be harder to heal. It was better to be truthful. And he, Jay, was being truthful when he said he could do all that Tom could do—protect, honor, cherish, and love. But also and especially delight.

It was hard now to ignore the wind, which not only whipped up swirls of heat, but had changed from sighing to whistling to howling. She closed her eyes against the memory of the Santa Ana, but she could not shut her ears. "It was the sound of insanity," was how she put it. And through it, Jay's words came still. "So come with me. I'll take you away somewhere. Wherever you want to go. It's your happiness, our happiness."

Then the question she had not let herself ask rose from her throat. "But what about me? Do I love you?"

She of course knew the answer, though she didn't tell Gracie. She was ready to answer with the part of her she knew and trusted most, her body, which despite its hidden changes she still owned. She was ready to give herself completely to the earth as she lay upon it, to the whirling sky as she lay below it and to forget that tortured organ, her mind. She could whisper *Yes I will yes I will yes*, and turn fierce as the wind to Jay, into Jay.

But the hot wind became too strong, too menacing. Instead she answered only shouted words—the ones she repeated to Grace—"I don't know, I don't know."

And he helped her as she stumbled to the car, gathering the Provençal tablecloth as best he could to cover her. She admitted a state of shock. As if she had come to after a deep dream, a trip somewhere to an unknown world. She found herself half-naked, hair wild, glassy-eyed in the swirling heat. "It's the mistral," she said, looking at the trees and grass and flowers outside bending in madness, as if they had awakened in a tortured van Gogh world. It comes more rarely in summer they say. Usually it brings icy cold, but now, in summer it brought this strange heat.

They sat—it seemed forever—in the little VW bug watching the world bend in fury, remembering how only an hour or two ago it had been perfectly calm. Certainly Jay would have touched her again, run his deft fingers around the outlines of her full breasts before she drew the tablecloth to her more tightly; certainly Gracie would have known this even if she preferred closing her mind to the view.

Then, finally, more inevitable words. "So what is the answer to that question? Do you love me?" To which the only possible reply at that moment was, "I don't know." But she did know, and I like to think that beneath her breath she gave another, better answer. *I do know, but I can't tell you properly here, in this VW bug, with the storm raging outside. There is not enough room just now for my body to say all I have to say.*

By Eve's account, no more words were exchanged between them on the way down the hill to the hostel. The wind, she said, was doing more than enough talking. She had resettled her clothes and made a stab at smoothing her hair, though in the mistral no one would question its disarray. Jay parked the VW by the river beyond the hostel entrance and they sat in what passed for silence. He took her hand, only that. At last she was ready to go, or at least could no longer tolerate staying, and I imagine looked right into him with her eyes wide open. Then she spoke. "Tom," she said. It was the only word that could, at that moment, be spoken between them.

Eve stumbled into the hostel foyer, certain that Tom would be back. The mistral slammed the door behind her. She had no plan. She would simply walk up to him and begin.

It took a moment to realize she was there in the semi-dark room alone. I imagine her cursing in two tongues as she headed wearily to the dorm and her bunk and the prospect of waiting, once again, for the late bus. There were small consolations, though. At least Gracie, who was by default slipping into the role of her conscience, wasn't there. And this was the last time she'd have to wait for Tom.

By the time Gracie arrived much later, Eve appeared to be sound asleep. Gracie, who had spent the day in town getting a haircut, finding a new summer dress, and avoiding the dreaded revelations of *that day*, knew this much: that Tom had not come. She knew this because, taking refuge from the wind and the worrying, she had stayed inside the town walls until late, late enough to take the last bus across the river herself. It was no secret that she wished Tom would be on it and they could make the last walk down the road to the dirt path along the river and to the hostel door together. But she made the trip alone.

It was unimaginable, she said, that Tom would have missed such a date. Two weeks before, he had said it seemed an eternity. Once inside the dorm, she lay gingerly on her bunk trying to preserve her new curls and listened to the threats of the wind outside the thin walls. She could not hear anything from the bunk below where Evelyn lay, and seemed to have fallen into a coma.

In fact, Gracie would learn, that was not true. Evelyn's *condition*, compounded by her other conditions, had just become, if possible, more complex. She lay awake all night listening to the wind, which only just muffled the confused thumping of her own heart. She admitted to a burning sensation, no doubt fueled by the fear of wind and fire, which worked on her through the rampaging night to sear away layers of half-truths and deceptions. It was painful, she admitted, and at the same time cleansing. An ancient image, the legacy of being the pastor's daughter, "purification by fire—like burning at the stake," she said, shot in front of her eyes, before she pushed it away.

By dawn, when the howling had begun to quiet and the sun was struggling to rise over the eastern Vaucluse, her heart stilled too. At least she knew what she believed to be the truth. All that she had said and experienced with Jay seemed right. She did love Tom, but not in a way to make them both happy forever. Jay had been correct: Tom loved her too well and liked her too little, perhaps because his love was so confused with adoration. And Jay? How could the excitement, laughter, connection she felt with him be anything but love? She was in love with two men and pregnant by one of them, the one most devoted and least suited to her. She sneaked out of the dorm quietly, not wanting to have to confront Gracie and share these thoughts and this impossible turn of events, not yet.

She went to the shower stall to wash and to think before going out to face whichever lover. She still had no idea what she meant to do.

It was startling, she eventually did tell Gracie, to step out into the new day, a day so remarkably still after the havoc of the day and night before. Remnants of debris littered the ground, but her eye could not have lingered long upon them. What they would have fixed on was the blue VW, half-hidden in dust.

It was parked as if asleep in the spot where she had left it the night before. She walked up to peek inside. There was Jay in his same blue knit shirt, his same khaki pants, leaning back in a reclining seat with his eyes closed. His hair had fallen across his forehead and his face showed a day's growth of beard. Before she could open her mouth, he opened his eyes.

He rolled down the window and simply said, "I couldn't lose sight of you. I needed to know."

So she climbed in next to him. She guessed it was just preordained.

Eve did not say much about the rest of the day except to characterize it as surreal. She could not even recall, exactly, where they went or what they did. Because at some point—maybe sitting down there by the river, the water reflected back in their eyes, blinding them—Jay had asked outright what she intended to do. And she answered, "I guess I intend to marry you."

It was probably unclear who was more startled by the announcement, Evelyn or Jay or then of course Gracie, who heard it later. At least by Gracie's lights, Jay was pretty flabbergasted.

"Marry me? Wow, girl, you do move fast when you move, don't you?"

But Eve said, for the first time in days, she suddenly felt completely awake. She came right back at him saying, "Love, honor, cherish, isn't that what we've been talking about all this time? Certainly this wasn't about just shacking up?"

That got his attention because, she said, he just put his arms completely around her and called her Mrs. Greene. Of course he said he hadn't meant only shacking up, but it had all been so sudden. He had thought they would take things in stages, go off together somewhere romantic, get to know each other better, let the future unfold in its own time. But Eve was already worlds ahead of him. She told him that as far as she was concerned, the future was now.

I guess he was grinning by then and nodding his head. Okay, he agreed, fine. They could begin to telephone family, tell all the great news, let the plans begin. They could spend the rest of the summer together in romantic places, the Riviera maybe, or Venice.

"Like a honeymoon?" she asked.

Gracie was pretty sure it was then Eve began to cry, but didn't speculate about the devastating effect on Jay of those green eyes drowning in hurt and sorrow. All she knew was that he repeated a couple of refrains over and over, no doubt trying to get a grip on the reality that was shifting beneath him faster than he could define. "Wow," he said repeatedly, and "marriage" and finally, the phrase that Eve described as music to her ears.

"I never imagined this, not now, not so soon. I'm the luckiest man alive, Mrs. Greene. The luckiest." Then he said, "Why only one honeymoon, Mrs. Greene? We'll just have the first one *before* the wedding."

She agreed and probably stopped crying. There was a catch, though, she told him. The thing was, they'd need to get married as soon after the first honeymoon as possible. As soon as they could arrange it. She reminded him that she was a minister's daughter. She couldn't just let everybody think she'd been over here living in sin. She'd never live it down.

Eve did not tell Gracie Jay's response—puzzled no doubt, with his uncanny knowledge of her—she only reported his acquiescence.

Bright as the sun was on a hot July day after the mistral, still a large shadow growing larger loomed over them all. Tom. Or more accurately, the absence of him.

Before coming to find Gracie to tell her ("this may flatten you, but don't go nuts until you listen," Evelyn began), Jay and Evelyn had already had the first of two crucial conversations about how and what to tell Tom.

Evelyn began by asking Jay if he thought she should see Tom alone, or should they do it together? Jay replied with the obvious: Of course she should see him alone. After all she was his fiancée. But she answered no, actually she wasn't. If he had come back yesterday, she would have been. But she had never told him yes. As far as he knew, it was still an open question. Besides, she said, it was simply too difficult to face. She didn't think she could stand upright without Jay's arm to lean on.

"I can't bear this, any of it," she wailed to Gracie. "I mean it's hard enough. If Tom sees me with Jay, that would be pretty self-explanatory, wouldn't it?"

Gracie, who couldn't bear any of it either and whose head was no doubt splitting, just nodded, first yes, then no.

Chapter 34

History. When Guy had spoken the word, it was with a futuristic fervor regarding a thing just around the next corner, a thing to be grasped and shaped. But for Roland—for the French—it was more a matter of genealogy. I had neither history nor genealogy. It came to me then, after the long walk up the road back to the villa, in the garden where the Germans had tidily arranged the statues that Americans would casually use for war games, that this made me, by birthright, an orphan. Roland sensed my melancholy; his accounts had reminded me that I had no ownership of a past, and with each passing day I felt the weight of also having no ownership of a future. He offered a diversion. Monte Carlo perhaps, with side trips of hair-raising speed along the great and lesser cornices, visiting no doubt endless cousins in their ancient castles in impressive states of crumbling disrepair. Or Nice, with its grand palm-lined boulevards and faded elegance, its old-money ennui against the backdrop of the startling blue sea. "It is like a painting in a frame," he promised, "and very amusing on *le quatorze juillet*, when the rockets go off like crazy, my God."

"What about Avignon?" I countered, unable to say just then why I wanted no more mere diversion, no more days of drifting amusement in the perfect sun. I was unable to articulate any reason but an unspoken one to myself, that there I had a little piece of history, genealogy, geography of the imagination. Gran had often spoken of it.

"Avignon?! My God, chérie, but it is far. Across Provence up the Rhône, and full of hoards in summer...but why?"

"Because I always sang the song as a little girl. It was my first picture of France, dancing on the 'broken bridge.'"

The only response I remember is his short dark curly hair bouncing in the sunlight as he threw back his head to laugh. It was agreed, if we left immediately so as to be there in time for the rockets going off over the Rhône. It was also agreed that we would wait there to intercept Maman and Papa who would be traveling south on the train. Now Roland embraced the trip as a lark. He dashed to the village to make phone calls at the post office, to arrange train tickets, and of course lodgings with the endless network of relations. We left in a flurry of chaotic farewells, as if with the gates to the villa closing behind us and a din of voices chasing us, we were closing the curtain on a great theatrical performance. It was hard to believe I had been there barely three weeks.

The red sports car with Roland at the wheel shot out with such terrifying speed around the hairpin turns that I willed myself to blot out the trip as much as possible. The coastal hills, the castles on precarious rocks, the fields of flowers for the perfume makers, the wild roads carved into cliffs, the sea lapping at the foundations beneath, all was a continuous fragrant blur until we slammed to a halt at Nice. That, too, fit into the picture Roland had so neatly described. There we left the car and boarded the train for Marseilles, where, at the station I felt oddly like a *habituée*, as we waited for the transfer for Avignon. Through the long light of summer night, Roland held my hand in the gently swaying car, and I knew a sweetness in that comfortable zone between past and future, where his energy halted and my uncertainty stilled, temporarily at rest.

It was the morning of Bastille Day. The train stopped in the station outside the impressive stone portal to the walled city and we hailed a cab to the cobbled streets of its medieval heart where we would lodge in the apartment, dating from the fourteenth century, of another Montrefor, a professorial cousin who was in England for the summer. It was down the street from where they say Petrarch had lodged after first laying eyes on Laura, which began the cycle of love and longing that bled from his sonnets.

I remember everything about that day, and the days that followed, as if they were made of a hundred bright pieces of glass that fit into a mosaic, like a rose window through which exquisite color shines to form one amazing single image when I hold it up to the light. Yet somehow I can never bear to. I cling to the periphery, like the walls of the old city itself. I can look back upon the steep towers of the papal palace, the fortifications behind which wars of theology and religious fights (the Great Schism, they called it) raged, and over and over again replay the fireworks dancing over the Pont d'Avignon, where throngs milled around, some of them in the costumes of gypsies, minstrels, *jongleurs*, dancing off the half of the bridge that is standing to the half that exists only in the minds of magicians and children, dancing until they fell into the dark night of the river.

But beyond the heat and crowds, the music and costumes and pranks of Avignon in the bloom of its summer festival, it is hard to focus too much on the rest, the inside, the cobblestones of the square, the little roads leading to the ancient heart—our borrowed nest—the places of *explanation*, such as bookstores and museums or historical guides that all vied to make understandable the concepts of schism, that split down the fault line of the spirit, or the mysteries of unrequited love.

Roland still held me with the magic of the sun. I could still laugh at his crazy commentary. "My God, my God, what do we think here, a descendant of the Pope's mistress, reborn as communist block leader and, oh but this is *tragique, chérie*, yes then ordered by Kruschev himself to give her two front teeth as dowry, yes?" as we walked the cobblestones hand in hand, vetting the passersby with his terrible wit and funny English; I would quiver when he bestowed his tenderness on me with gentle, magician's hands, hiding his passion like a benediction of rain before a dangerous, thrilling tunnel of wind. But the waiting began to affect me, perhaps because I did not know what I was waiting for. His mother and father, who might never come? The conversation, by mutual silent accord, we could never have? A letter that would never arrive to give me clear instruction?

Roland, always exquisite in his sensibilities, felt my anxiety even before I could name it. He proposed a detour in the vineyards of the Rhône while we waited for his parents' train to arrive. The domain of Châteauneuf-du-Pape, he exclaimed, was the finest in all of France. There were the grapevines themselves, ripening and growing heavy with their fruit under the summer sun; there was the expanse of countryside with its varietals of color, the stony hillocks with broken ruins of old castles—very romantic, he assured me; there were châteaux and tastings from the great cellars, and, of course, there were cousins.

Without the cousins, I might have been persuaded. But there was no way around them, really, for Roland could not go to their territory and *not* see them, and if we stayed elsewhere but in their châteaux, they would be insulted. It seemed to me the only solution was for him to go, and me to stay. The prospect of some hours alone, when I would be free to wander the walled city without the strain of being embraced by the Montrefor family, seemed like a relief. Of course, I did not share that with Roland, who shrugged, smoothed my hair with great tenderness, kissed all the hollows of my face, and prepared to leave. Without his car, he would take a bus, and his cousins would fetch him in their car. *"Deux jours, mon coeur,"* he promised. A couple of days. Oddly, relief gave way to a rush of sadness that pushed against the effort of my smile when I waved good-bye.

There was a silence in the emptiness Roland left behind. At first I turned to tidying the apartment, trying to fluff its deep leather chairs and dust the bric-a-brac of the missing professorial cousin who smoked pipes ("like an Englishman," Roland had declared) and left the trappings of pipe cleaners, pouch tobacco, ashtrays, and the sweet residue of old smoke everywhere. There were his bookshelves, crammed with ancient leather-bound volumes on geology, geography, mining, land use. Though the subjects were of no interest to me, the feel of the books themselves, their gold-embossed spines, their hand-cut pages of rich rag paper, engravings, and photos carefully cosseted behind tissue leaves worked their seductive power over me. They smelled old in a powerful way, and I was suddenly transported to Gran's, where there was a study crammed with such books, and shelves of them in the living room and front bedroom too. Many of them were not hers, but Grandfather's, the man I never knew, whose books I had also never read.

Thinking of her, of him, was like a powerful jolt. The light summer air felt suddenly sharp, as if preparing for fall. And the unusual silence gave way to an unexpected sound, a distant song. I pushed open the glass doors of the salon to step out onto the flat roof, where generations of residents had gone for relief from the heat, to hang their laundry in the breeze, or perhaps to sleep under the spell of a full moon. Music and laughter from the summer festival floated overhead. By chance, and by the good fortune of Roland's endless network of family connections, I had landed in Avignon just at its most famous season. And now the festival, which I had not even known of, called out seductively. I decided to go down, to stand at its edge even without tickets to any performance. I noticed a breeze, a stirring from the south that seemed to dissipate the gauzy sunlight, and I turned my face full upright to the sky. There I saw, rising from the east, the outline of the full, round moon, even though it was only afternoon. Tonight would be a night for spells.

Of course, Roland was gone, so this night would not be a night of love. Before leaving the rooftop, I looked down into the tiny chasm of streets winding below in the direction of Petrarch's place, and, in the distance, as if brought in on that breeze, I heard a train. I knew then, as I hurried into shoes and down the twisting, ancient stairs to the bottom of the flat and the street below, that, instead of the festival, I wanted go to the train station. Not to meet or take a train, but to see again the scene that had been playing so obscurely in the deep regions of my mind.

What would she have been wearing? I imagined a long gauzy white dress, cinched tight at the waist, a bodice demurely buttoned to the neck, long sleeves fitting tightly at slender wrists. In truth, I don't know what a flower shop girl would have worn in Avignon in 1917. But I do know what he would have worn, because I'd seen it in the great painting hanging in Gran's front room. It would have been those high black boots and, tucked into them, the neat khaki pants with the razor-sharp crease, the fitted jacket with ribbons neatly arrayed on the erect chest, and, as an accompaniment, he carried what looked like a riding crop, though God knows his cavalry rode jeeps or tanks but never horses. I remembered, too, the cap with the visor, like a salute itself, reaching across his narrow brow. I could see the upper lip, closed unless bidden open, and most of all I could see the eyes, the deep, transparent blue of glacial lakes, but yet with a light in them, a mysterious beckoning. As for the rest, I knew little but this: she was twenty (my age), he was thirty-eight. She had recently come down from her mountaintop village to sell flowers in the open shop. He was a colonel with the American forces, in Avignon briefly, a few days only, on what business I did not know, but on his way back to the front.

I walked to the train station outside the massive city walls at Porte de la République and tried to imagine the engine of puffing steam that had carried him. How he would have cut a dashing figure as he strode up Cours Jean Jaurès, where even now a mosaic of vendors lined the edges, their bright awnings and merchandise of fruit, sweets, watercolors, and of course flowers mostly unchanged I imagined from 1917. I could picture him in his brisk military stride crossing the street to the little kiosks, pausing, selecting a piece of fruit, then glancing up to see the flower vendor next to him, a slender, chestnut-haired young woman with black eyes that smiled at the edges, even if there was pain in their center, eyes so large and dark that he fancied them a mirror in which he could find his own reflection. She could hardly have failed to notice him; after all, a tall American officer walking up the boulevard in Avignon in 1917 was not a common sight. But it would have been his eyes that held her, and made her breathe in double time, the transparent mystery of them.

He, of course, bought flowers, far too many bouquets to present, for example, to a hostess for dinner. Certainly, she thought, a man such as that would not fill vases for his own rooms, wherever he was lodging. On that first day, he nodded courteously and spoke only the barest words, revealing little. But his eyes spoke, and so, I was certain, did hers. When he returned the second day, she knew. She swallowed hard, nodding a polite, *"Bonsoir, monsieur,"* and making an effort to be businesslike, she gestured to freshly cut roses, peonies, bunches of daisies, pots of lobelia and brilliant geraniums, stalks of sunflowers, and, of course, bundles of lavender. Again, he purchased mounds of flowers, far too many for any reasonable use, and she swallowed hard, perspiring a little along her upper lip before asking, "But you are attending a funeral, *monsieur*?" The blue eyes registered laughter before his mouth did, but he did not hide his amusement, delight, in her question. Was she mocking him gently, or genuinely curious? I imagined the questions were raised and answered by the blue eyes searching the black ones while he lingered unaccountably long over making the correct payment and awaiting change.

On the third day—this much I'd been told—he changed his gait, walking with quick light steps across the square, pausing to give a smile deeper and more inviting than any salute he had ever snapped. The third day she was prepared, or thought she was, and had added freshly picked wildflowers, new colors of roses and canna red as Christmas candles to her repertoire. He smiled and sniffed, admired and selected carefully, asking for advice about what greens should accompany which flower. When he had selected even more than on the previous days, he set them aside and asked for the most "Exotic, fragrant flower of all, suitable for the finest lady, a gardenia." I could picture the way her chin dropped, and her long lashes fluttered briefly over her lowered eyes before she looked directly at him to say she was *desolée*, but she did not have such a flower.

"What?" he asked, eyebrows arched in mock anger, "how can that be?"

"But surely the lady will be very happy with the flowers you have chosen, *non*?"

"The lady?" the colonel had replied. "Ah well, who knows what a lady will like in the end? But you, *made-*

moiselle, you have disappointed me. So now I ask that you do something to make up for it. I request that you have a coffee with me, there in the café at the corner." He added a gesture to what may well have sounded like a military command.

I imagined the high color of roses coming into her cheeks as her black eyes blinked, a little shocked. "But *monsieur*, I am not free to go. I must mind the flowers."

"Well then, I will come back when you are closed. If you would agree. If you would do me the honor..."

I could see them sitting there. The Café du Soleil must have remained unchanged for a century in a town that had remained significantly unchanged since the days of the quarreling popes. I could see her flowing summer dress, a linen of a light pastel shade, and a large hat with a sweeping veil had been added to her ensemble. He would be standing, his military posture unendurably straight, while he waited by the chair for her to be seated. Then, in the cane-backed chair opposite, he would sit himself, stretch his long booted legs out beneath the table, and at last remove his hat to reveal his fully uncensored eyes. I did not know all that was exchanged in that fateful late afternoon in full summer, but some of the important facts of it had been spilled. That in order to make amends, in lieu of a gardenia, the lovely young lady had brought a bouquet of lavender for the colonel's friend; that he had said he wanted very much to see the young lady the following week, when he could return briefly before departing for a long time; that she agreed; that he leaned across the table, and, with great delicacy, pinned the bouquet of lavender on her bodice, declaring it, too, with its marvelous scent was fit for the finest ladies of the world.

It was as if in a trance that I walked up and down Cours Jean Jaurès, only faintly hearing the noise of the festival down the street, the shrieks and rumble of the trains as they came and went beyond the ramparts, leaving behind only plaintive whistles. But when at last I settled in at the Café du Soleil to order an espresso, I unfolded the menu as if reading revelations in a tongue I had just remembered.

This much I knew: The colonel had not in fact returned to Avignon the following week, but he did send a letter to the young woman in the flower shop in which he declared his love and his desire to marry her. Week by week she waited, hiding the letter against her heart, against doubt, and pinned lavender on her bodice. In fact, he would not come back for more than a year when the war to end all wars was over. She was amazed to see him again; he was amazed she had waited. Within months, the flower shop girl would become a war bride, moved to the distant and exotic sunshine of California. The next year, at the age of twenty-two, she would give birth to a baby girl, who would, at the age of twenty-two, become my mother.

On the second day, Roland was to return. I imagined his jaunty walk, his breathless whistle, the wind tousling his untamed curls, the wry smile waiting to break into a tender, lingering kiss when he saw me, his arms tight around my waist, gently nudging me inside, upstairs, to the bedroom. It would be a delicious greeting. He would set down his pack, and the wooden crate bearing gifts from another unknown cousin, this time the gift of the gods, Châteauneuf-du-Pape. Imagining his return, my lips, too, curled in an involuntary smile. But there was another vision in my head crowding him out. Grandfather striding the square in uniform, and Gran, young, black eyed, her natural energy spilling like a spring out of the flower stall, then dancing into his consciousness, now dancing into mine. I felt its surge as an irrepressible desire to go to its source. I knew I must visit Gran's small village clinging to a hilltop, *villages perchés*, they called them, in the Vaucluse. Roland could wait, could certainly find something to amuse himself, as he was the prince of amusement, for one day. I would leave a note explaining my trek in the *salon* of the professorial cousin's fourteenth century lair, next to the tidied-up pipes.

The details of that strange and wondrous excursion are etched still in my memory, all in place. Had Roland actually been back when I returned just before midnight, I might have shared my tale with him while he laughed, smoothed my cheek with his dear hand, rubbed my shoulders. But he was not there, and instead I began writing feverishly in my journal, writing, writing as I tried to capture what the day had meant. And as I wrote, the full moon that had so dazzled two nights before seemed to waft at the edges, its light wavering and diving into and out of the depths of darkness.

I noticed the light first before I became conscious of the wind, and then I think I heard it before I felt its punch. But the wind alone did not trouble me. It was the heat. I had heard, forever it seemed, of the ferocious mistral, and had shivered learning of its steely power as it blew down the Rhône like the breath of the mythical dragons said to inhabit the river. But in my mind it had always blown cold. The edges of my imagination had never bent far enough to conceive of hot wind. Perhaps, I told myself, this was not the mistral, but the sirocco that blew in from Africa. I had thought little about the winds of summer. I'd never imagined myself half-bent on a midsummer rooftop in ancient Avignon quaking with the smell of heat overpowering me from its nostrils. Like a child, I covered my ears that I might not see, and closed my eyes that I might not remember. Then I went inside.

I lay not on the bed, but on the divan in the pipe-filled salon, trying to assuage my trembling with some feel of friendliness, trying to avoid aligning the rhythms of my body with the tremors of what beast I imagined breathing outside. I became feverish. If I slept, it was in a high-pitched way, as one would in a storm at sea. If I dreamt, it was a replay of the wave-tossed gymnastics I'd performed at night on the lower bunk of the *Jeanne d'Arc*, a prelude to combat more than to peace. Morning could not come too soon. I was certain the winds would leave, that Roland would come.

For reasons I only learned later, he did not. I waited, restless, pacing, hot and half-crazed inside the little rooms tormented by wind, waited smelling and fearing what I smelled. In my nostrils—my brain—there was no lavender, as Gran had promised, only fire. And though the windows were tightly sealed against the fury, and in truth had been standing up to it since the fourteenth century at least, still the wind seemed to seep inside, not just into the rooms, where it lifted the edges of an open book ever so slightly and layered the floor with a sheen of fine dust, but it seemed to penetrate me. I felt fissures growing where I had hardly known cracks existed. I felt tiny lines creep around my eyes and knew if I looked in the mirror I would see the face of a hundred-year-old, scoured by time. I felt I might blow apart.

With the next dawn, I came to, still feverish, and could not tell sleep from waking any more than I could tell, in the whirling dusty hot air, day from night. The first thing I knew was that the wind had not slowed down. I had no reason to believe that it intended to. The second thing I knew with a clarity that still astonishes me, was that the eternal sunlight of the present—Roland's world—had been lost in the screaming furies of this wind. Even if he had been there—and he was not—he could not conjure it back. Without the kindliness of that Provençal light, without Roland and his ironic, infectious smile as armor against whatever ancient monsters tried to show their scaly hide, I had no place there. Through the haze, I could suddenly see my way clearly, and the labyrinth that had confounded me in Sospel's garden suddenly straightened into a clear path. The sweet confusion of all my days with Roland would right itself by following that path. I knew it led to the train station. I breathed normally for the first time in two days. I smelled neither wind nor fire. I began my letter:

> *Très cher Petit Prince,*
>
> My heart is so full right now because I know how much you will always be in it…

Chapter 35

By late afternoon, Eve decided it was time to find Grace. Eve and Jay spotted the bus just as they finished crossing the bridge, and Jay drove slowly, waiting for it to pull away and reveal whatever passenger was ready to descend the hill. It was not Tom, but Gracie in her full cap of curls, who headed down the path.

She stood in surprise, watching the bug come to a halt behind her as Evelyn, in a loose-fitting summer dress green as her eyes, got out and came toward her. Eve put her firm, bare arm around Gracie's shoulders.

Jay drove ahead out of sight, while Eve said to Gracie, "Look, we've got to talk, in private," and led her straight to the secret little grove where Tom had first met her, as if it were the most normal thing in the world.

But of course, it was not at first a conversation. It was rather Evelyn once again spilling the contents of her inchoate life. The dizziness, the sensation of floating, the crazy wildness like the wind itself. "The mistral effect," Gracie said to me wryly, acknowledging she had as little control over events as Eve did.

By the time Eve got to the part about realizing she loved two men and was pregnant by one of them, Grace could stand it no more. She broke in. "Right. And that's why the path you've got to take out of here is clear, isn't it? That kind of makes up your mind. Think of it this way, an Italian honeymoon."

And that's when Eve announced that yes, she was going on an Italian honeymoon. To Venice. With Jay.

"I went nuts," Gracie said simply. She told Eve she couldn't. What, was she crazy? What about the baby? "Think about the baby!" she began shouting. Rarely in her life had she shouted at anyone. She could never have imagined yelling at Evelyn, of all people. But then, she couldn't have imagined any of this.

And that's when Eve shouted back, "Think about the baby! For Christ sakes, I *am* thinking about the baby. I have to marry somebody, don't I?"

And Gracie replied something like: "Right. You do. You have to marry Tom. The baby belongs to him, you belong together."

But Eve always had an answer. She said that was wrong because nobody *belongs* to anybody. And how could she marry Tom? He wasn't there. He didn't even *show up*.

Even though months had passed before Gracie told me all this, I could see she was still shaken. Then it was her turn to experience all that Eve had: the dizziness, the surreal sensation of floating, vertigo, that in itself was a *condition*, she said.

Gracie had no defense against Evelyn's reasoning, because there was, in fact, no reasoning. There were twisted justifications, rehashed for Gracie's sake, already spun out to suit them in the conversations between Evelyn and

Jay. How it was better now than later to break with Tom, because in the end it would never work. How Tom could not really feel betrayed, because after all she had never told him yes. How the "new" Jay was deeply reformed, deeply wonderful, and with his *worldliness* (Gracie pronounced this as though she were spitting), deeply perfect for Eve. "Somehow this all came out as if it were *more honest*," Gracie said, "as if it were *the right thing to do*."

Unimaginable as it was, Tom did not appear on the last bus of the afternoon either, which led directly to what Gracie called "the last, crazy act in Eve's whole drama. I always thought the most shocking thing had happened when it hadn't yet."

Tom hadn't come and the wind started to kick up a little—only a little, Gracie emphasized, but maybe that was enough. That and the heat, which seemed unlikely to give in at all, even during the night. Eve had gone to the hill to wait, but when the bus had come and gone without letting out a soul, she returned to the hostel, frenzied-looking, Gracie reported, as she watched her from the riverbank, trying to cool off a little. Not wanting to speak to Eve just yet, Gracie remained by the river, fanning herself with a straw hat.

It was then that the VW pulled down the road, kicking up dust, and jerked to an abrupt halt in the spot where Jay customarily parked, not far from Gracie, who was out of sight down the embankment. She said she was waiting for Jay to get out so she could make a kind of getaway. But he didn't. Instead, Eve came running up, as if by appointment, hair flying, clearly beside herself. Jay got out then, held her for a minute, and they began talking. Gracie was so beside herself now she really didn't want to hear what she was hearing—but she couldn't help it.

It was what she termed a "dialogue of lunacy."

Eve, flailing her arms around and wailing, "I can't stand this. I can't just sit here and wait forever for him to show up."

And Jay responding, "Well I don't see what choice you've, or rather we've, got."

Then Eve's chilling coup de grâce: "Well we could *not* wait."

"What, like write him a dear John letter?"

"No, no. Well not exactly. More like a letter just explaining how it would never work between us. I never was *engaged* to him, you know. I mean, I don't have to mention you. He'll find out at a later, better time."

Jay, to his everlasting credit in Gracie's opinion, didn't exactly buy this. He protested. "Christ, I don't know, that seems so cowardly. Like the easy way out."

But Eve had the last, twisted word. "So, what's wrong with the easy way? In what scripture is it written that hard and hurtful is better?" She had gone, Gracie noted, from icily calm to shouting again. So, Jay wanted to know, what did she intend? To just pin it to the door like Luther and his Diet of Worms? That was a nice touch for the good Lutheran girl, Gracie added wryly.

But Jay was actually way ahead of her, because she hadn't actually thought through anything. She was just saying the first expedient thing that came to mind. And so, Gracie said, she came upon the final solution.

"Oh no, I wouldn't just leave it," she said. "I'll just give it to Gracie."

It wasn't hard to see the effect of these words on Gracie as she sank ever more out of sight down the riverbank. The reward for her unwavering and unrequited love in the threesome that had been split apart by Jay's intrusion was to be given the role of official executioner. Neither Eve nor Jay even questioned whether she, Gracie, would be willing to do such a thing, whether she would be willing to stay and wait forever, while they, in the quaint French term, were all too ready to *ficher le camp*—get the hell out.

"I couldn't bear it, any of it," Gracie told me quietly. "I didn't want any part of this sleazy scheme. I didn't want to talk to them or see them or give them the satisfaction of handing this off to me so easily. But I certainly didn't feel like arguing with them about it either. Everything was too exhausting. So as soon as they went inside, presumably to throw together Eve's stuff and write a letter, I just slunk away."

She decided it was time for her to leave, too. Her heart, she said, had its own schism, and the walls of Avignon seemed sinister and forbidding now, as if all the magic and sunlight and hope had been sucked up by some malevolent mistral.

"It was time to go," she shrugged. "It was over for me." With a train ticket and only a little money, she had a few days to get to Le Havre to catch the boat home. "It felt so strange to leave Avignon, though, because I was leaving so much of me there, so much unfinished business… I even left Eve without having really said good-bye."

Evelyn, however, did say good-bye to her. The farewell came in the form of a note left on the pillow of Gracie's bunk. It was a sweet note, charitable, full of thanks and even a semi-apology. "I know you don't approve, but I think at this point this is really the best, the kindest, way to go," she had written, then going on to ask Gracie the "small favor" of delivering the letter she had left for Tom beneath the note to Gracie.

"Small favor," Gracie repeated, "when what she was asking me to deliver was a bomb." It was Gracie's turn to hardly sleep. There was Eve going off on a honeymoon, and there she was left with the mess. In that long night, she decided she wouldn't—couldn't—be the one to do that to Tom. Especially not, knowing everything as she did. She determined to leave, to take the first morning train. She would leave the letter with the old concierge.

Gracie paused here, running her hands through her hair, perhaps unconsciously remembering the Italian-style haircut. "Funny," she went on, "it wasn't until much later that I realized that was just another version of running out on him, running away, taking the easy way out. In that sense, maybe for once, I became just like Eve."

Though the train north did not leave until midmorning, Gracie got up early, the effect perhaps of nervous exhaustion, packed her bags, and left them in the foyer. The concierge was not there yet, so she carefully tucked the letter—the bomb—in her pocket and strolled for one last time along the river and watched the early morning light do its magic along the walls of the town, the palaces and spires, the graceful bridge to nowhere, that had only the day before all appeared so malevolent. It was then she heard the familiar rumbling of the early bus, the wheezing of its brakes as it jerked to a stop, and walked by habit toward the sound.

She reached the bottom of the hill in time to see the mechanical door pull open and expected to see what she always saw, nothing. But then there was this form getting out. At first she couldn't see clearly because of the light, but suddenly there was this huge shadow swallowing the road as it came toward her. It was the one thing she hadn't imagined… Of course, the first thing he did was notice her hair.

She spoke sparingly now, parsing her words, and through the intervening spaces I could so easily envision the scene. How he would have grabbed her, kissed her on the mouth in that playful way that meant nothing but everything, whirled her around, and whistled. "Wow, doll. Let me look at you. Nice hair! And something else, too. Tan and glamorous. Very nice. So you two have really been up to something. But what can I expect, it's only been a thousand years." I can see him grinning, putting her back down on the earth that would keep spinning beneath her for a very long time.

She had her back to him when he said, "So how is our fair friend? Still getting some beauty sleep?"

Gracie didn't know what to say or do. So she just turned and looked at him for a long minute. It was then she realized he wasn't her *David*, caught perfect in stone after all. He was going to step into the sunlight, but that shadow would always partly cover him. He would still be a great athlete, still have that heroic kind of faith in life, and still be full of the passions he had always had, but from that moment on he would never be the same. And there was no getting away from it. And she was the one who would deliver the blow. The bomb was ticking in her pocket.

Not knowing what else to do, she took him by the hand and led him to the only place she could think of, the little hidden grove. He didn't ask anything and she didn't say anything, only that he ought to sit down. She sat too, then handed him the letter. He remained motionless, head propped up on his thick hands. She said she held her breath, afraid even that would shatter him, and watched the letter settle on the ground. "I never even wanted to see it, let alone read it," she said, "but I couldn't just let it sit there. I mean, someone else could see it. So I picked it up."

I could just see the remaining breath go out of her as she read the fateful words, "Dear Tom..." and moved through another thicket of Eve's artful, soothing, wondrously contorted justifications. "The truth is, you love me too well, and I am too restless for you. I would not be good for you in the end." Gracie quoted from memory. "The part that really got me was the P.S., when she said "I waited for days to see you, but you just didn't come. I couldn't stand it any longer. But maybe these words explain better than I ever could have otherwise."

Not knowing what to say or do, Gracie said she hit on the "worst possible thing." She asked him why *hadn't* he come earlier anyway? Why hadn't he come the day before when he was supposed to? He looked back at her "as if he were bleeding to death" and said he'd meant to, but something had come up. Then he added, "I don't think in the end it would have changed anything, doll. Except I would have, you know, seen her..."

Gracie, angry enough to explode, was ready to blurt out the truth. But then, she said, she looked at him, and thought no, it would just hurt him more and what was the point? He couldn't take that. She couldn't take that. And worse, much as she didn't want to, she realized in some twisted way, Eve had been right.

"He looked so awful, I decided maybe I should just go," Gracie recounted. So she asked him, did he want to be alone. But he said no, if she didn't mind he'd like her to stick around. He'd already been alone a lot and there was "a lot of lonesome ahead." He said she was a great comfort to him. "The best." She sighed here and paused before finishing this painful soliloquy, then blushed a little before adding, "So I did. Try to comfort him. We just stayed there awhile. On the ground."

I saw all too clearly what she was telling me. The nuance of the word *comfort*, and what she took that to mean. The way she would have reached for him with some awkward gesture that he was too bereaved to even notice. The way he would have responded, by pulling her close to him and putting her head to rest on his chest. How there, atop his wildly pounding heart, all stillness, all reserve, all reticence was broken for her. In the hidden den where so much passion had already been spent, it was now her time. Eve was gone, and she was now the one lying next to Tom's great, beating heart.

I don't know how or even if, at that moment, Gracie tried to come to terms with the twists and turns of fate that had brought her to that place. But what happened next only convinced her that, unbelievably, it was true: Tom needed her, and she alone was with him. After what seemed an eternity, Tom rose, pulling her up alongside him, and putting his arm around her, said, "So, doll, we better go. Get the two of us out of this place."

She asked where he meant for them to go.

And he replied, back to his room in town for the moment. "At least until we figure it out. Can't leave you in this hellhole another minute."

What happened in that room at the old Hôtel de Nice on the tree-lined Cours Jean Jaurès near the gate to the train station is mostly my guess. But the guess of an educated heart, I like to think. Naturally enough, Gracie only relayed the barest of facts: They had spent a lot of time "processing" everything. He had wanted badly for her to go to Italy with him. In the end, she couldn't, really. He had been uncommonly sweet to her—"chivalrous" had been one of her words. He had been sad to lose her company, promised to see her as soon as they were back in the same place again. He had given her a parting gift.

What I see is this. They spent the gathering heat of the morning going over and over what had happened, as if repetition were a remedy against shock and grief. For the last time, they knew, they walked the shaded streets of Avignon and went back, by habit now, to the table that had been theirs as a threesome, to sit under an outside umbrella at Lou Mistrau on La Place de l'Horloge. They sipped iced lemonade. He would have asked only once, did she know where Evelyn had gone? Unable to actually speak the words, or perhaps afraid of the treachery of a truth-telling tongue, she would have nodded no, gravely, and the topic of Evelyn's current state would not come up again. When no more could be said and the next level of comfort could be found in simple silence, they wandered off, she swallowed in his big shadow, seeking whatever odd, unexplored corner of town offered refuge. The old city museum, for instance, that had artifacts from formal digs and spoke of the "evidence of dragons," the beasts that had terrorized inhabitants of the Rhône Valley for centuries.

There were many places to be avoided, too: the site of the church of Sainte-Marie, where Petrarch had first sighted Laura; the park of the Dom des Rochers, where Tom and Evelyn had spent their first night of love, hidden in that green garden above the Palace of the Popes; the Palace of the Popes itself, with all its chapels, chambers, and churches, its gold trappings, schisms, and betrayals. From time to time, he would pull her up like a great rag doll against him in an affectionate hug, forgetful of the publicity of daylight. Holding her would comfort him, who had long since forgiven her small sin of homeliness and forgotten the larger, perplexing affront, that her fluffy curls concealed such a brain. She would feel only the strength of the moving muscles in his stride, and wonder at his sighs, like mournful whistles in the distance of night.

And yet, as day faded into evening and the bells of the cathedral began to ring, the church, in all its splendor and failings, and that Catholicism that linked them, arose naturally as spires as a place where conversation could begin again. They would be outside, ready to order a bite of supper, perhaps in a sheltered corner of the tiny Place Didier against the thick, cool wall of the small ancient church. He would say, "So, doll, I guess there's no harm in telling you that I went back to the Old Country. Florence, actually. I was trying to scout out, well I thought it would be the perfect place to…"

"Go on a honeymoon?" she would have finished that sentence.

"Yeah. And it was amazing. You should see that church called the Duomo, Gracie. Unbelievable. Marble in every shade covers the entire outside, so that the light…despite everything, it kind of makes you think about what's holy."

Gracie would be watching him now, looking closely into his eyes, nodding, but not saying anything. This was not a topic she'd want to get into.

He'd go on. "Anyway, there's so much more to see. And not just Florence, you know. I mean, think of Rome! My God, this little popes' thing here must be nothing compared to the real deal. There's so much of it, if you consider the coliseum where those poor Christians met the lions, and the catacombs, and Saint Peter's. Oh hell, Gracie, it's just great to be there, you know? In Italy, I mean. You just really connect to it. It's just so familiar even if you've never been there."

Perhaps at this moment she was having a seditious thought, wishing that somehow she could graft her intelligence onto Tom, so that he could begin to see things the way she did, and then his moral and physical perfection would be equaled by his mind's perfection, and he would indeed be a complete giant. But even if that thought was quickly and surreptitiously passing through her, it was just as quickly erased at the moment Tom looked directly into her eyes for once and reached across the table to grab her hand.

"Listen, doll, I know what. We should go together, you know? To Italy, check out the old family haunts. See Rome and the Vatican and get back to our roots." There would have been urgency in his voice as he spun out his plan as rapidly as it came to him, and the rising volume of his voice would have allayed Gracie's fear that her uncontrollable heart could be heard. "Look, it's perfect. I've ended up with, well more time and money on me than I imagined, and this is the only thing I can think of that would be good to do right now. What do you say, doll? Come to Rome with me. Just you and me, kid, that's all we've got in this miserable world."

I don't know how she answered in her dizziness and confusion, but it wouldn't have mattered since in the excitement of his new plan, he wouldn't have heard her. It wasn't until they were back in the small room at the Hôtel de Nice that he actually looked at her again, smiled his gentle smile, and ruffled her hair. Then he, too, would have to take into account the bed, the single piece of furniture in the room save for a stuffed chair, and seen her stand hesitantly before it.

"Look, doll, it's okay. Don't worry. Trust me, it'll be fine. We're in this together." It's then that his reassuring arms would encircle her as he began speaking again. "Tell you what. I'll go down the hall to the loo, get myself all cleaned up, and give you plenty of time to…to yourself."

I can't imagine what Gracie extracted from her bag to put on that was vaguely appropriate to her situation. Perhaps she chose only her best bra and panties before slipping underneath the sheet. But if she could not go there naked, not yet, her head had never been more full and at the same time more free. In those eight minutes or so that she lay in bed, waiting for him, the visions would have all been running like a forbidden filmstrip behind her closed eyes. The images of Eve, of what she had done, where she was, her *condition*, would have been pushed back into the darkroom to make space for Gracie's images of herself, as she lay there in bed, breathing shallowly, waiting for Tom to join her on the eve of their—did she allow herself to use the word *honeymoon*?—to Italy.

Tom came then and reached the bed only long enough to turn out the lamp and touch a pillow. In a moment, she heard, then understood, as Tom settled in on the floor beside her making a little nest with the pillow and a bathrobe and old coat. As if to reassure her, he said, "Don't worry, it's perfectly okay. You know old Tom after all those years in training can sleep just fine about anywhere. So don't even start to protest. I mean, it's important we get right with each other right the beginning. Who knows? We might have to be roommates again sometime and you need to be comfortable with that. You mean so much to me, doll, I wouldn't want to do anything, clumsy as I am, that might make you think twice, or worse, hurt you."

It wasn't until the next morning in the small hotel dining room over coffee and a croissant that Tom would hear Gracie and all the reasons she couldn't come with him to Rome. It was the first time Gracie would hear them, too. The obvious ones—she had too little money; it was wonderful of him to offer to pay her way, but she couldn't let him; she had too little time, and a ticket on a boat she had to catch—were the easy ones. The hard ones played loudly only in the echo chamber of her brain as it emptied itself through the night of all feeling, all delusion, all hope. The single thing she knew with certainty was that she was not then nor ever would be Evelyn. Therefore, for both their sakes, she could not go on with Tom.

It was in the train station along the quay where the impatient engine churned and steam rose up along the track between anxious wheels that Tom for the first time looked at her for a long moment while tears filled, then refilled in his eyes. She knew the tears were, at that moment, mostly for her, and she knew he meant it when he said he'd miss her. But then what was she to think when he said, pulling a little box from his jacket, "Ah, little Gracie, I'd like you to have something…special. It's the reason I was late coming back. They took an extra day to engrave it. Keep it please, just keep everything."

It was then that he reached for her and pulled her to him hard and kissed her, not kindly nor affectionately nor gently, not like he ever had before, but long and hard and deep, kissed her as if he willed her to be the one she was not, to be what she was not. It was her eyes that then ran with tears as she sat on the rolling seat of the departing train, trying to make her shaky fingers unwrap the ribbon, the paper, and open the little box. At last they succeeded and fingered the slender gold bracelet before her blurred eyes could read the inscription, *Te amo, Firenze 1963.*

At last she knew it was a place she never could go. And, it was, I believe, on the long, long trip back home Gracie finally understood she had to give up trying to get there.

Chapter 36

The road to Venice was a long one, full of mountain passes and impossibly twisty roads. And the new, mature, *repentant* Jay would never have attempted it, Gracie said. He hadn't even made a big deal of the fact that Eve insisted on Venice. When he had mentioned the Italian Riviera and Florence, and she got agitated, he just backed off. How could he know that Florence, the place where *David* resided, was off limits? And he readily acceded that a mountain road car trip in a small car was not a good idea for them, given their history.

In the end, they had agreed on Venice and the train. Romantic, Eve had insisted, not saying that a long train ride with its soothing rhythms was probably the most conducive to her *condition*. But before leaving, there were matters—papers, blood tests, dates—to be arranged. The good news was that Jay had the contacts to pull all the strings so they could be married quickly and privately, as she insisted. The bad news was that in order to make this possible, it had to be done on American soil, the consulate in Marseilles. To Eve, there was no luster in this ancient port city, only dark alleys and bad smells, a sinister sense of decay.

"If Édouard had been a city instead of a pathetic old fart,'" she told Gracie, "'he would have been Marseilles."

And because they had to visit Marseilles first to make the arrangements, then return two weeks later for their hasty ceremony, the taste and smell of it became brackets around the idyll of golden, liquid days in Venice, the honeymoon before the wedding. All the colors faded into rose—the naked color of Eve herself, Jay said—before dying into the light cover of summer night. He had told her this was a "time out," away from all of their worries, of all she had to face in the near future. He had no clue how big a cliff they were on, which meant that Eve could put it all out of her mind. She reveled in the gondola rides over rocking dark waters, in the gifts of silk and glass and perfume Jay lavished on her, in the meals laced with garlic and olive oil and washed down with wine. And secretly, she was buoyed by a new dose of self-confidence founded in that most basic part of herself, her body. "It, you know, held together," she told Grace. Meaning that she never succumbed to bouts of nausea, that despite slight swelling and tenderness in her breasts, she didn't show. Also meaning that she was able to bewitch Jay absolutely and lose herself in him to a degree that mercifully erased all memory. When Gracie said Eve used the word "sumptuous" to describe the days in Venice, I understood the word also meant Eve herself, and the banquet of their lovemaking that came with the night.

Gracie thought it was an unconscious thing, the way Eve settled into a kind of comfort with Jay, unaware that much of his quiet reserve of money and family connections had given her what she had strived for so ardently in her pursuit of the titled Édouard. "She has this ability," Gracie said with a kind of resignation, "to get what she wants even when she doesn't know she wants it—or is getting it."

One thing she did want was to visit Verona. "Hey, Romeo, wherefore art thou, and all," she repeated to Gracie, who wondered how Eve could possibly say those words without thinking of Tom, the lover whose baby she carried. Since the train stopped in Verona, it was easy to make the pilgrimage. And Jay, beside himself with both desire and amazement at the wild thing he was about to make his bride, was eager for anything she wanted.

If Venice had been an erotic dream, then Verona was a sheaf of pages from the poet's portfolio. Eve found what was said to be Juliet's balcony, and the central square with the old fountain, the one where Mercutio and Romeo fought with the Capulet boys. It amazed Grace that at such a moment, with all that had come before and was about to transpire, Eve could still imagine herself a kind of Juliet.

"But that's also where she first felt a kind of panic, isn't it? I mean she did know the end of the story." What Evelyn actually confessed was that in the end, it spooked her. The church with the stone crypts, the vaults of death. The feeling of waking in a cold tomb. When she came to, of course, there was Jay, no relation at all to Romeo, just Jay breathing away in a happy sleep. Somehow, that spooked her even more. And then realization hit her about the deal dealt those long-ago young lovers despite the fact that they hadn't done anything wrong. No indecision, no cheating, no little accident—nothing to make the world so mad at them. They had just loved each other.

The constriction of the tomb. That image above all others seemed to have been large in Evelyn's mind as she entered the labyrinth of Marseilles for her marriage.

The ceremony, if you can call it that, was brief and antiseptic. Eve seemed not to remember too much of it, nor want to. They arrived at the consulate where the flags flew over a building Eve described as only bureaucratic blah. She did remember that Jay had somehow come up with a dark suit and, as she stood in the tea-length white lace dress he had bought her in Venice, he had handed her a flower, a fragrant gardenia. She clutched it in surprisingly cold hands. They had been ushered into a room, a chamber she called it, by a gray-haired diplomatic type, suitably grave. She recalled that he had almost whispered to Jay that, if they wished to wait a little, perhaps a chapel could be made available. But happily Jay was adamant about not waiting, and about the need for discretion. Old friends of the family could be counted on for that sort of thing. Two middle-aged ladies who also worked there were called in as witnesses. Eve said she thought they got teary-eyed and a bit gooey after the ceremony and were inclined to hug her. But she stared straight at the red carpet and dark serious furniture surrounding them, and was slightly cheered by the official portraits. Not only of JFK in front of a flag, but one of Jackie too, wearing those pearls.

How weird does it get? she'd commented to Gracie. It had seemed to her that the pictures were the real witnesses to the ceremony—like the only friends in sight—while the others in the room were all strangers. "Well, my first wedding at any rate." I can see Gracie cringe.

The vows were exchanged quickly, the formalities over, and Jay kissed her once long and hard, calling her

Mrs. Greene. They signed some papers, were handed a certificate, and left.

The second honeymoon, the one that began after the ceremony, was to be a leisurely drive down the Côte d'Azur, where the twisty mountain roads overlooking the sea were deemed sufficiently safe. Perhaps the fact of marriage conferred a mantle of protection. It was, Gracie noted with some irony, not a bad ending for a twisted fairy tale, beginning with the poor minister's daughter who blows the church scholarship money.

Gracie had the itinerary down, the territory of a real Princess Grace in a make-believe world far from her own. The first night was Cassis, one of those romantic places on the waterfront you always see in tourist books. That was where, Eve said, she'd nearly drowned herself in champagne, trying to get the flavor of Marseilles out of her mouth. Or maybe even the bad taste of other things.

Gracie now seemed to own the narrative and told it at her own pace, by her own lights. Le Lavandou, Saint-Tropez, Cannes, Cap d'Antibes—she ticked off the landing spots of the second honeymoon, whose very names invoked magic, beauty, excess, as if she were spinning a tale worthy of Homer. "It was all supposed to end in Monte Carlo, you see. Jay in a tux and Eve in something shimmery, and they would conquer the world by proxy, outsmarting the croupier, beating the odds at roulette. Appropriate, I guess, to end the whole crapshoot with a high-roller moment. She meant, or says she meant, to tell him then—about his baby."

Gracie raised her eyebrows for emphasis as she said this, and I could see the fervor of emotion in the high color of her cheeks. But just what she was feeling, I couldn't say. And no wonder. As the tale spun out to its end, what could, or should, one feel beyond astonishment? Anger? Pity? Sorrow? Or like Evelyn herself in that moment, all of them, mingled with relief?

Though Eve didn't seem to pay attention to the continuing escalation of her lifestyle as she progressed through her honeymoons, Gracie did. It was clear that the humble VW bug and the low-budget charms of cheap rooms and picnics had steadily eroded, to be replaced by more upscale lodgings, fine dining, and an endless stream of gifts. But when, as the trip, and the story, approached Monte Carlo, with all its "name-brand pretensions," Gracie clearly was aggrieved. Perhaps it was because at the last stop, Nice, Eve had thrown out the name Hôtel Negresco. In what seemed like a different historical epoch, when she and Gracie both were penniless and agitated while Eve was debating whether or not to marry Tom, they had wandered in there on one of their strolls along the boulevard facing the sea. Gracie could actually conjure it—the sign featuring a black man in blackface playing music; the grand interior with a rotunda of Tiffany glass, gold leaf, and cherubs; fake Greek columns along the walls; obscenely ornate, thick carpet; the centerpiece of the oval room a chandelier made by Baccarat. Ordered, Gracie remembered, for the tsar of Russia. It was as far as Eve could get from where she had come.

By the time Jay and Eve got there it was already night, and they planned to hit the beach—just yards from where she and Gracie had been only weeks before—in the morning. After that they would make their leisurely way to Monte Carlo. They had one of those grand rooms overlooking the beach, and, with the shutters drawn, didn't stir until ten. But even though she was groggy, Eve said she had slept fitfully, and instantly when she awoke, she knew something was not right. There was a tugging sensation across her back and pulling at her stomach. She grabbed a robe and tried to stand, but only made it about halfway upright. In that position, she struggled to the WC.

It was a kind of horror, she said, seeing the first traces of blood. All the blood she waited and waited for that never came, and because it never came, changed her life. By now, she was pretty sure she was losing the baby. The baby she hadn't so far thought about as a reality. Yet she felt the loss of it, the loss of so much, and for what? For the shock of her body letting her down like that? She felt like screaming. In fact, she did scream. And when she emerged from the WC, pale and sweaty, Jay was sitting upright in bed, alarmed.

He called her "Evelyn, baby" and asked what was going on. But what, in truth, could she say? I think I'm losing Tom's baby, which by the way is the reason I married you, but stick around and help me out, will you? All that went racing through her mind, but of course she couldn't get into it, any of it, just then. She knew she needed a doctor, and fast. She said the obvious, which was of course factually true: that she was having bad stomach cramps and needed a doctor.

Jay wanted to call the concierge instantly and get the house doctor, but she knew that would be messy and inadequate. Her words. She had to get to a clinic or hospital, fast, and she knew it. She insisted, and Jay was so besotted that he was hardly going to argue. He found the address of one nearby, and they sped off in the trusty bug.

Sitting in the car, tearing around the twisty roads, Eve herself twisted in pain, until she almost lost consciousness. She had stuffed herself as best she could with pads, hoping to hold back major bleeding until she arrived. She fell into a pain state of unreality. She just kept staring at the sea, and at last all the five colors of blue gave way to that red tide she had watched and prayed for. Everywhere the water rolled red, and it was as if some great god, the god of her father, no doubt, was sitting up in the hot sky laughing. What she said to Gracie was, "It was the worst moment of my life."

And Gracie believed her. "No matter how she may be judged for a lot of things," Gracie said, "she did suffer and pay. At least for a while."

I was tempted to ask how Jay reacted to all this, what he could possibly have thought when it all became clear, but Gracie went on before I could interrupt. What saved her, Gracie said, at least so that she could take charge of things even in her terrible state, was that Jay didn't speak French very well. She just clutched her throbbing stomach and explained to the clinic attendant that she was having a *terrible crise d'estomac*.

Then she waved him a faint good-bye as they whisked her into an examining room.

I could see it as Gracie told the story. How the walls were white and so was the air against the crisp white hospital suit of the young doctor who stepped in to see her. And how, by that time, her eyes burned red with the smell of her own blood. I could just imagine his brief, clinical questions, softened somehow by being pronounced in French. He confirmed what she already knew: "About six or seven weeks along, my dear young lady, and I'm afraid, *alors*, we cannot save the child." *"Alors,"* Eve repeated. He said the procedure would be small—not serious—and that they would keep her overnight just for observation. Then the clincher. He squeezed her hand and said he personally would go explain everything to her husband. But at this point she nearly broke. Bursting out in her best French, she pleaded, *"S'il vous plaît, monsieur le docteur, non. Vous voyez, a ce moment il n'en sait rien de ce qui se passe..."* At that moment, she told Gracie, swear-to-God, she could have aced the exams at the Sorbonne just with her grammar alone.

Anticipating my question, Gracie went on. She told him that her husband actually didn't know their good fortune just yet, and the loss would hurt him so. Could he possibly be spared the truth?

"Did he buy it?" I asked.

Gracie gave a good imitation of the French shrug. "He was French, wasn't he?" Eve said at that point he just winked at her, and she officially had la grippe. Being a doctor, and being French, he no doubt had heard everything, seen everything, knew everything.

When Jay came to visit her that evening, Eve began crying and could not stop. He tried to console her, and said he was so aware of all the hours she had spent by his bedside. He even tried to joke about a new beginning now that they were married, and he could visit her in the hospital. But she knew he felt quite undone by her weeping. He couldn't begin to understand her mourning: she couldn't begin to explain the lies, the loss. What was that Pascal thing Melanie was always saying? *Le coeur a ses raisons que la raison ne connaît point?*

When Gracie finished, I felt dizzy. The miscarriage and loss of the baby that, in the end, neither Tom nor Jay knew anything about. The fact that Evelyn and Jay had actually gotten married before leaving France.

"You knew about that all along?" I asked, incredulous.

"Well, not *all* along, but well before anybody else. I mean I knew so much, I guess she figured it was safer if I knew the whole story. Maybe it would be easier for me to keep quiet? But it was hard. I mean, here I was back in California and from time to time I'd get a call from her parents. They were concerned about her, and wondered how in the world her scholarship money was holding out for so long, but they kept getting these reassuring postcards from the Riviera. She said she had met some nice young people she was traveling with. She had been straight with them, technically anyway, about failing the Sorbonne. They admitted to me they were worried she was extending her stay over there just because she was ashamed to show her face to them and the church people, who had such faith in her, and they wished they had a way to let her know how proud they were of her for trying. They just wanted her home, back in the fold.

"Of course, they knew, too, that Tom had been over there. He actually gave them a call before he left. And I think the fact that he didn't seem to be anywhere in the picture at the end was the one thing that cheered them—not that they didn't like him, but 'the youngsters are both too young,' and although they didn't say this, he is, after all, Catholic. Yeah, that was their big consolation, that she hadn't done anything rash, like running off and getting married, out of shame and despair."

Chapter 37

My sudden decision to leave Avignon had been like coming out of a fevered sleep. I blinked into the bright light, then stepped into shade in the narrow streets of the old quarter, surprisingly still. As I turned into the broad sun of Cours Jean Jaurès dragging my large bag, it seemed years, not days, since I had last walked it and strange to think I would not walk that way again. I knew almost by heart, because Roland and I had pored over them anticipating his parents, the train schedules to and from Paris. But for the moment, I was not going to Paris. Only when I got to the station did I learn that it was indeed not the train, but a bus I would have catch to take me into the Vaucluse and the tiny town of Venasque—Gran's village—perched somewhere east on a rocky hillock.

Standing at last in line with other passengers on the bus bound for Carpentras, I understood for the first time that I was traveling alone. There was no Roland to make mysterious phone calls to unseen relations or to hoist my bags, provide maps, translations into hilarious English, or to light every landscape with his crooked smile. The loneliness felt acute. I turned to a robust middle-aged man whose gray hair blew about a round face beneath a faded tan beret. He held two baguettes and a few bottles in a string bag. His great gray mustache gave me courage. "Nice day," I said slowly, always uncertain in the sing-song land of Provençal French, "now that the wind's stopped." He mumbled an agreement that it was nice, but what did I mean wind?

I smiled in reply, believing my French had failed in some primitive way. I tried repeating the conversation with others: a shopkeeper, a couple of school-age children going to visit their uncle, a peasant woman returning to her fields. Despite the accents, we understood each other. But whenever I mentioned the wind, the mistral that had brought so much sound and fury, so much dust, they all looked confused.

"Wind, *mademoiselle*?" the peasant woman finally said, "No, no. In summer now, down here, the dragon comes out of the water and sleeps on the rocks like a drunk. Too much good wine, hah? What we have now is more like a breeze, it is nothing. For wind, *mademoiselle*, you must get out of the lowlands. Go to the country of the high hills and maybe a little tickle, even in summer. But, in truth, there is no wind but the real mistral. Avignon, in this season, *mademoiselle*, she sleeps too, in the heat with no breath, snoring at noon to make music for the tourists. Hah! For some people though, the winds come in their minds. It's like the grippe." She paused to tap a rough brown finger against her crinkled brow. "But it is not a touristic thing, not a thing to visit foreigners. No, you have to be born to it." And she turned away.

I quietly fell behind her to climb onto the bus, sat heavily in my seat, closed my eyes, and replayed her words in my mind. *The real mistral is like a grippe, not a touristic thing, not a thing to visit foreigners. You have to be born to it.* Then the low-slung visceral pain of missing Roland rose acutely throughout my body. But when I opened my eyes again the broad stretches of fields with their rows of vineyards and sunflowers beneath rocky hills, and villages of stone and red earth seeming to grow from the land, felt strangely familiar. Then I knew that neither tourist nor native, by the old woman's definitions, I had to come to this place on my own. And beyond Roland, what I was missing in some acute, if buried way, was the others. Jocelyn of course, my second self. But Evelyn, Gracie, Melanie—where were they all when I needed them? Where were they to help me see where I was going and why? I needed them like I needed my own eyes and ears. My own mind. Did a story have any meaning—did it even exist—without the ones who in its unfolding can best give it shape?

My eyes closed again, overwhelmed with beauty and with questions, and I did not open them again until the bus stopped at Carpentras.

His name was Alphonse and I was certain I had met him before, either in a picture book or a story related to me long ago by Gran. He was round and craggy all at once. His pronounced belly stuck out like a boast from beneath his overalls. His well-muscled arms hung short from thick shoulders and seemed to move effortlessly as he hoisted large pieces of machinery into the tin-can back of his little Renault truck. Unruly dark hair spilled out from beneath a black beret, and a coarse black mustache seemed to reach up to it, as if in a perpetual smile.

Yet his cheeks, brow, and nose looked like the hills of Provence, cut with ravines and jutting with weathered outcrops. When he overheard my queries outside the bus station about finding a cab to Venasque, he said "But *mademoiselle*, that is where I am going, you must come with me." I saw his round black eyes filled with kindness, and replied *"Merci beaucoup"* without a moment's hesitation.

And so it was with Alphonse, a Gauloises-smoking gallant who stopped every now and then to take a swig from a large leather-covered bottle, a cheerfully chivalrous raconteur who sang between swigs while passing the bottle to me, that I discovered the road from Carpentras, baking in the red earth between fields of sunflowers, pointing the way to the great Mont Ventoux. It was with Alphonse that I leaned out the window of the truck's cabin to inhale the summer air sweet with smoke and honey. And it was with Alphonse, in a rush he proclaimed, but not too great a rush I concluded, to deliver the parts for some automatic washing machines, I was to first arrive in Venasque. I came with the innards of the town's first laundromat. "Think of it," he said, waving both hands in a swishing, circular motion, *"lavande automatique, pouf, comme ça,* is not the world a marvel, *mademoiselle*?" Automatic laundry. *Pouf.* It was indeed. And so was Alphonse, who like Roland seemed as organic a part of the marvel I was trying to grasp as the stone villages rising from the hills.

As Venasque appeared, its round Saracen towers cutting into the burning sky as it clutched the hilltop rising from the flower-strewn plain, I had the strange sensation of coming home. And when, by chance, I saw a small sign pointing to a dirt road that announced Prieuré de

Saint-Pierre-les-Thermes, I let out a small cry. "The holy water," I said out loud in English, remembering as if I had been there myself. The ancient ruin, the spring, the promise of miracles. The place where Gran's mother, my great-grandmother, had retreated after her husband, the schoolteacher who loved books, had fallen asleep one night over his papers and never woken again.

Alphonse, who had discreetly asked nothing of my origins nor intentions, startled at my words. *"Mais qu'est-ce que tu as?"* he asked gently. "Thirsty, then?" and he handed me the wine bottle again. I could hardly explain to him that it was quite the opposite, that I was drinking everything in, and then drinking more. As the road started to wind and climb the edge of the hill, I felt a kind of lightness, as though I were lifting into the air, into the sky pure as water. I looked up as directly as I could, to see if I could meet the sun's eye, but saw only its light playing on the dark ridge behind the blinding white dome of Mont Ventoux. *The Windy Mountain*, Gran had said, giving her own version of where the icy, flattening roar of the mistral came from. I had never heard her mention the dragons in the river, but staring at the silent white-caped peak, I could imagine the silent furies hiding in the mountain's majestic beauty, ready to unleash their devils. *You have to be born to it to understand*, the old peasant woman had told me. I knew then that the wind I—and perhaps only I—had suffered in Avignon had been real enough. It was a question of feeling for the wind beneath the calm and knowing how to bend inside it, just as now it was a question of how to see the face of each sunflower rising to the sun itself.

As if a messenger, a hawk drifted down and rested its wings mid-air for several minutes almost close enough to touch before floating away, then beating its wings furiously toward the mountain.

We were inside the great Saracen Walls on the northern edge of the village when I heard Alphonse say, "But where do you live, *mademoiselle*?" Live? I was startled into the present and the knowledge that he assumed I belonged there.

"Ah, here," I said. "Leave me here." We were near the tower gate where an old man sold tickets for those who wished to climb the towers and walk the ramparts. Alphonse protested, saying, "But no, I know the village like my own hand," showing me his square, lined palm. "I can drive these crazy streets like nothing, pouf, so I take the young lady and the valise, and drop you like that, pouf."

"But I am here," I said. "This is my street. Just there," indicating colored houses covered by climbing roses, whose shutters of blue and yellow opened like wings to let in the day. And I gestured to the tiny stone street to the side of the towers, with the small sandstone. And it was true. It all unfolded in my memory like a dream, a story told long ago. Alphonse kissed my hand and waved me off, before turning with a puff of exhaust as the rear of the truck sagged low, burdened by its cargo of washing machine innards, and nearly scraped the cobblestone street. I took my bags to the old *gardien* of the towers for safekeeping and headed down the street where Gran had lived as a girl. It was next to those magical towers, she had said, built to keep out unholy invaders—the Saracens, "who never much cared about our little village anyway, for what would they want there? And to keep out the plague, too, you see, which was interested and came as it pleased anyway."

I walked lightly through the village, for I had come to claim an inheritance that had never been directly willed. I took it all, though, a proprietor in exile. The low, vaulted archways tall enough, I guessed, for short knights on short-legged horses in retreat, or perhaps a lowly Renault truck bearing the necessary, if unsightly, mechanisms for the proper hum of modern life. The small central roundabout of stone built to encircle an ancient fountain from an ancient underground spring, also of stone, set in a street surrounded by houses made of the same, all sculpted from the rock beneath. Two cafés and a small open market stall, heaped with vegetables, peaches, plums, and the famous local cherries. Then more twisting stone streets and archways, more houses flanked by climbing roses, entangling sweet-smelling vines and purple bougainvillea, more riotous pots of red geraniums, orange hibiscus, and blue lobelia, more curtains flapping in the breeze, real or imaginary, inside the open arms of summer-colored shutters on houses either proudly displaying new paint, or just as proudly showing the layers of heredity beneath patches of multicolored plaster. Until, at last, I found the southern end of the village and the Église de Notre-Dame-de-Vie where Gran was baptized, its dark baptistery overlooking the sunny plains below, its sixth century Merovingian roots built upon the foundations of a Roman temple.

"How old?" I asked the gate ticket taker in his vestibule. "Who were the earliest humans here?" He raised his shoulders and turned his palms to the sky in a gesture I had learned first from Monsieur Lepic. "*Depuis toujours, mademoiselle, vous voyez.* Since forever, since twenty thousand years, since who knows? The beginning."

From outside the church wall, which seemed to tip, after so many centuries, away from the wind, I imagined I could see the Abbey of Sénanque in the far distance, imagined I could see Gran there, a young girl bent over the fields of lavender, tending them to make a small amount of income to help her poor mother after the schoolteacher, my great-grandfather, had fallen asleep forever over his books. I walked back to the northern end of the village, for some reason with Gran and Jocelyn together in my head, and how they had spoken the night of the fire. Jocelyn then as now, of course, had Madge, just as Melanie had Mrs. Richter, and Eve had her mother, the pastor's wife, and Gracie had had Mama. We all had mothers of one sort or another. But only I had Gran, by luck or birthright or inheritance. Such a treasure seemed, in that moment of yellow light and calling breeze, meant to be discovered and shared. But that had been my blithe promise to them all, hadn't it, about "voyaging abroad," about coming to France. For the moment, with so much wind in my mind, so many whirling visions, I was happy to hold my discovery to myself, alone, and claim ownership of what I was only beginning to know.

As I again approached the Saracen towers with their crenellated walls, I realized I was home, back on the street with the small houses where Gran had lived. Apart from the old man in the church, I had spoken to no one, yet my ears were full of voices. Though I had not invited conversation, when I returned to the tower where I'd left my bag, the *gardien* embarked on one voluntarily. He was under no illusion that I lived there, and began a weary explanation of Venasque that I assume he gave to all tourists. *"Vous voyez, mademoiselle,"* he began, "we're very old and small and set here on this rock for all these centuries. Not much to look at, lots of repairs to be made, but still proud. The earliest sort of Christians, *mademoiselle,* the best type, and then keeping back the infidels, so we are proud. A real contribution to civilization, don't you see, to France, after all, which is the same thing. Of course the wars, even the Great War—"

I felt compelled to break in, to give my identity, to make him see I was no random tourist. *"Monsieur,"* I interrupted, "I have come here because I am from here. That is, my grandmother lived on this very street, and..." I gestured, looking again at the small stone houses, settled now into the deep grooves of time. Then I saw a house, the second one down the street facing west, the blue-painted door ajar, invitingly open. "Ah, look, perhaps that is her home. I want to take a little look inside."

The *gardien* made a dismissive gesture with his hand. *"Mais non, mademoiselle,* you can't go there. It is nothing." Impatient with his chatter, and uncertain what in his thick accent he might mean, I went on down the street and approached the door, which needed paint, as did the flaking plaster façade beneath a red tile roof. Gran's house? Timidly, I stood for a moment, calling *"Allô,"* but when no one answered, I stepped inside. I imagined a little vestibule, a salon to the right, narrow stairs on the left. But my feet touched a ruined patch of worn stone floor. Before me the jagged remnants of walls reached toward the edge of the hillside, above me the tiles of the roof quickly caved into the vault of blue sky, and the open end where rooms had once been commanded me to admire the sweeping view of the plain below, its tiny roads and tidy vines, its fields of flowers.

Shaken, I retreated, half backing up to the tower and its voluble *gardien* again, who seemed to have continued talking as if I had never left. *"Vous voyez, mademoiselle,"* he went on, "we are very old. Many of our ancient houses give into time, unless someone in the family has the means," he made the French gesture of rubbing his thumb and forefinger together, "to put everything back. Of course outsiders," he said this with particular disdain, "they come too. Buy things, fix them, so-called improvements."

Alphonse and his makings of a laundromat, I supposed, was serving one of those, another horror of modernization. But by now the old man had moved on, rubbing his crooked, weathered fingers over his rough cheek. "Like a beast it is, *mademoiselle,* and so cold it rattles your bones." He had moved on to the mistral, I guessed, and couldn't tell if he was speaking with resignation or pride. "You have to be tough, you know, a true Provençal, to live here. The northerners, the foreigners," he shook his head, "they just come in summer, and they know nothing. Couldn't make it when the winds come." Then he looked at me directly for the first time, focusing with his rheumy eye. "Do you know what summer brings, *mademoiselle*?"

"The sun." I answered forcefully.

"But everyone knows that." He glanced at the fierce ball of heat still blazing in the late afternoon sky.

"Well, summer wind, then."

But my interlocutor was not interested in my answers. "Fire," he was saying. "Wildfire. They can catch in the brush beneath the mountain, the dry plains, even the dead crops if we don't have water, and then—"

"—and then everything burns." It was my turn to interrupt. "The winds come and spread the flames across the fields, the vineyards, the flowers. Not up here, of course, because you are safe on the hilltop. But below. And for miles and miles you know it's burning because you can smell the lavender."

Chapter 38

It was, on the face of it, an odd choice, returning to Marseilles. I wasn't as brave as Gracie, who at the last minute could step away from Tom and actually face going back to Paris ("like going home again after the family's moved away," she said). Nor was I as assured in caprice as Jocelyn, whose travel plans for her return home were nearly as serendipitous, as indirect, as her wandering in Paris had been. I certainly had no notion of once again crisscrossing her trail, nor, of course, did I have the remotest idea that Marseilles was still fresh with the scent of Evelyn, who was, at the time of my return, on her first honeymoon. The last person on my mind, I suppose, was Melanie; yet she was the one whose presence emerged most startlingly.

So by going completely my own way for my own reasons at last, I had come full circle into the lives of the others again, the *demoiselles* who had been so much a part of me that I hardly knew where their lives ended and mine began. By the time I left Marseilles for the last time, we were inseparable again. What I didn't know about where they had gone, I had to guess. With that, my *copines*, my friends, became irrevocably planted in my imagination.

When I had looked down across the long plain of the Vaucluse in the pure, scattered light of late afternoon, and realized that it was time to leave Venasque, I knew that leaving meant, one way or another, retracing my steps. In the first place, I would have to return to Avignon. From there, I would either have to go north and return to Paris, or go south to Marseilles. Going north was by far the more practical choice, since this time I would fly and not repeat the agony of the sea voyage by tin tub. (Only Gracie, because of budgetary constraints, would have to endure that.) Going south to find a flight home made little sense. Naturally, that is what I chose.

At the time, I had a lot of half-formed justifications for my choice, even including a tip from some student travel book that "real cheapie flights"—presumably with multiple connections—could be found there. But as I traveled in reverse the route I had so recently taken with Roland, there were only two things clearly in my mind. For one, the compulsion to ride Rimbaud's "drunken boat" was over. I had ridden it. When it finally came to a battered rest, listing over its anchor in some dark port, like all passengers, I had to choose what to do next. Rimbaud declared his death wish, then quit writing at the age of nineteen. Years later he came to Marseilles to die. But I was twenty, and decided to find another means of transportation. In the immediate sense, a train and plane would do. Beyond that, I held to an ill-formed desire to pick up the pen just where Rimbaud had discarded it.

I had wondered, of course, what became of Eve and Gracie after they headed out on the Auto Route du Soleil following in our footsteps. I had half-imagined we'd run into them somewhere, or our paths would cross at some American Express office, looking for mail. But such thoughts were a world away as I boarded the train in Avignon, bound for Marseilles. I had no idea where they were—where any of my *copines* were—and I gazed out the window distracted by my own vague sense of purpose, my own melancholy. Every ray of sun held Roland's face, every shaded street whispered with his laugh, and I could as yet not begin to let myself accept the cruelty of what I had done. And then in a far corner of the platform, I glimpsed a familiar shape and focused my attention. Impossible as it seemed, it looked like Gracie, and as she came closer, I saw that it *was* Gracie, shoving a large valise, pain furrowing her face. She passed close to my window, and I struggled to open it, but it wouldn't budge. Then I pounded on the glass, calling her name, but she continued to move past me in the other direction, and the train began to move.

The vision jarred me, and the image of her floated in front of my eyes, blocking out Roland's face, the unreal quality of the landscape as we rolled through it, even the jittery sensation of my doubts. Because there, on the train and alone at last, I could no longer run from the reality of what I was doing. I was heading south, going through the now-familiar country of Provence because it felt like home. Because I had made some connection to a past I never knew by visiting Gran's territory. And because of that, I could discard the shreds of poetry I had stolen from Rimbaud, I could set aside what I would later come to see as all my foolish youthful mantras, to find some other words, some other meaning that belonged peculiarly to me. I longed for a letter from Gran now, and I believed one might be awaiting me in Marseilles. I had sent her the address at the American Express office.

I arrived at dusk, almost jolted back into the collective life with the others I thought I had also left behind, with Gracie's sad and mysterious appearance everywhere in front of me. Because of that, in the morning as I retraced the aged and twisted streets I had not long before walked with Jocelyn, the faces of the others, and what I even felt was a hint of Evelyn on the breeze, came to me too. The words, *What has become of us?* almost escaped my lips as I approached the American Express office.

My surprises began in the line for receiving mail. I recognized the same efficient young woman who had dispensed the tubes with our diplomas from the Sorbonne. What I did not expect was for her to recognize me.

"Tiens," she said, *"vous voilà enfin.* The other tall one was here, too. Maybe ten days ago. So you are late." With that small reprimand to top off her revelation, she handed me my mail.

Gran, of course, did not disappoint. She had learned little of substance from me because the life I was leading that summer was much too precarious to commit to words. But she had received enough postcards to know where I was and that I had at last ventured into her country in the company of friends. In her reply, she was careful, as ever, to tread lightly. "I hope, dear child, that in the beauty of that landscape you can find a mirror to yourself, for it belongs to you as you belong to it, even though you had not before been acquainted." She spoke delicately, too, of those things that were difficult to hear: of my parents, of reconstruction plans in our lives after the fire, of my return. She was doing her best to create a soft place for me in what she knew, as no other could, would be a hard landing. Then, at the end, she threw in this surprise:

> I have one more piece of news for you. The other day your little friend Melanie called, rather out of the blue. It had taken some time for her to find my number, but she was hoping to find you here, not knowing when you would return. She said she had some news to tell you, so I encouraged her to write a note, send it here, and I would include it in a letter. She seemed, how should I say, aggrieved, that you weren't here in person, but took some consolation in the idea of writing you instead. I hope, of course, all news and love finds you in good time...

I remember looking at the pale blue envelope and the clear, legible strokes of Mel's hand with astonishment, and, opening the letter cautiously, as if I were facing Mel herself. I did not know, of course, that this would be the first document in what would become my Melanie archive.

> 6 August, 1963
>
> Dear J.J.,
>
> I guess your Gran will have told you I called and wanted to talk to you about something very important. She suggested I write instead, so I hope you get this. I had no idea you were still over there. In fact, I had no news of you or anyone, but guess I just figured everyone would beat it home soon, like I did. But of course, why would you? My circumstances are so different.
>
> Oh, J.J., I guess I wanted to talk to you because we had shared so much—that train ride to hell—and I thought

you'd understand. I mean, you have this way of giving advice by not saying much, if you know what I mean. Maybe it's just that you have a way of listening like you're hearing more than I even know I'm saying. Anyway, I tried calling Jocelyn, too, and talked to her mom, who seems awfully nice. But Jocelyn isn't back either. But you know that. Anyway, I felt a little relieved, even if that sounds mean. I'm not sure why, because Jocelyn listens too, so much so that sometimes I think she can play back to me what I've said. Maybe she doesn't *hear* in quite the same way.

But all this is nonsense. You can see I'm not really saying what's on my mind because it seems exhausting to have to write it, and then you're not really there to talk to and can't respond. But whenever you get back, call soon, and I can explain. Actually, things have been pretty rough at home, so I'm not sure exactly where I'll be staying, but I'll leave word with your Gran. Hans would say hello, too, if he were here.

I hope you've had a good, exciting—no, make that *safe*—summer, and that we talk soon.

As always, love,

Melanie

It would have been enough, that letter from Melanie, but it was not the end of my surprises. When I saw the second envelope the young woman handed me, with its subtle, mottled, finish looking now white, now rose, now beige, I saw Jocelyn in the sun. I knew, without even looking at the familiar, slanted scrawl, that it was from her. It was too much, just then, to take in more, so I held it lightly in my hand, as if a petal that would discolor from my fingertips, and walked slowly through the dark streets back into the sun. I found a place—that little restaurant by the sparkling sea where she and I had eaten bouillabaisse and she had found pleasure in the wine—and sat. I, too, ordered wine and stared for a long while at the postmark. "Paris," it clearly said, and I noted there was no return address. What the young woman in the American Express office had told me, and what the letter reconfirmed, was what I already knew. Jocelyn had not in fact gone to Africa to dance with her princely lover. She had found her own device and her own way, and had headed north.

The letter was brief enough, actually giving little explanation.

Dear J.J.,

As you can see, I'm still in France and in fact spent quite a long and wonderful time with Ivan at Carcassone and other sun-drenched remnants from the Hallucinatory Age of long ago. Will explain the whys and wherefores when we meet again.

And well, here I am, once again in Paris. No grand design here, simply the practical issue of getting north. I'm taking a train through Germany then will cross over to Denmark by boat and go on from there. I had an extra day and a half here, so decided to visit a few of the old haunts—and they do seem haunted. Even stopped by the old place to say hello to Monsieur Lepic, if you can imagine, and there he was just as fat and blustery as when we first met him. He seemed really happy to see me, though, which was different. And he asked about you. In fact, he was relieved to the point of near civility that I had come because he said a "postal matter" had come up after we left. A letter, it seemed, without enough postage, and he'd had to pay it. If he hadn't been so worked up, I would have let it be, assuming it was another letter from Samuel.

But no, chérie, this one's for you, as you see. I'm taking the chance that with your long stay in Provence, you'll venture out of the château once in a while—lover boy will insist on touring you around I'm sure—and that you'll check for mail.

I must close now. All the rest will wait for the day when we are face to face again, home in California.

Love, Jocelyn

The enclosure was a small, rumpled envelope, smudged with multiple stamps, a miniature masterpiece of wrong addresses and missed connections. Even without seeing the small, cramped writing, I knew right away. It was from Guy. Now my hands were cold and quivery, and, to steady them, I poured another glass of wine. The battered envelope seemed to dissolve as I opened it. Inside was a postcard. Mount Baldy with snow.

Dearest,

I know your birthday is approaching and with it my desire to see you and celebrate. Celebrate you. I can't tell you how I have missed you, and how lost I have felt not knowing how to reach you. I've thought so much about what you've said. I want to come see you at Christmas. Would you like that? Please say yes and respond to:

He ended with a post office box number in Los Angeles and the words, "I'd even ride the Drunken Boat to get to you."

Epilogue

It is getting late. As I look up from the table to the window and the mountains beyond, I see the sweeping palms, the shower of golden light slanting from the west that foretells a long sunset, a lingering twilight. I am startled away from the brilliance of Provençal sunflowers, the stretches of lavender, and the shadowy lanes along the Seine that have been filling my eyes. I'm also startled to realize all the *demoiselles* are still there, fixed in place around long-emptied lunch plates and cold cups of coffee. And I am chagrined to think that some have certainly missed classes because of me—a fact that certainly will not sit well with Dean Lutowsky.

But as I look from one pair of unblinking eyes to the next, I realize that I don't care what Dean Lutowsky thinks. Not really. Her view of what these young women are and should be is a lie based on her present theology. But it is no more a lie than the "advice" given so freely, so lovingly, by my own *copines*. No more than what I started to tell them myself. I think for a minute about the letters I read them a couple of hours ago and suddenly feel as I had that moment over a decade ago in Marseilles when I first sensed that the whole damn Maison Française had been transplanted inside my brain.

Now here was Jocelyn touting her pursuit of freedom, when she nearly went down in some kind of madness. And Gracie promoting motherhood along with that "surge of caprice, joy, desire," which, she said without apparent irony, characterized her year of voyaging abroad. As for Melanie, who knew what she would really have to say, since I made it up? But I imagine I was close—Melanie clinging for life to that one "thought" by Pascal as if it were holy scripture, a way to explain and deny everything at the same time. Perhaps Evelyn, who was always willing to live closest to the bone, came closest to getting it right, yet even she neglected to say anything about the possibility of disaster. She who knew it best. But I do give her credit for this: Although she advised the *demoiselles* to pay attention to that blood-rushing "lust for adventure," she also warned them of bombs, both in the world that had in so many ways already blown apart, and in the heart.

So were they wrong, my *vielles copines*, in pushing the young to risk leaving home, assured that they could never come home again? Were they wrong in speaking only of the glories of that year, sweeping aside the rest? Or is partial truth just the privilege of memory? More to the point, what do I have to say to these young women? That is what they asked before inviting me to lunch, what their eyes are asking now. If I had written a letter, instead of merely being the collector and archivist, I honestly don't know what I would have said.

But of course they deserve more. Certainly more than the pinched historical narrative pushed on them by the likes of Lutowsky, urging them to stay some maniacal, driven course, and way more than "the romantic crap" (his words) that Bud Purvis would have me fabricate. I suppose what they deserve is what they want—the real story. It's what I've tried to give them, and what I am about to deliver, like a body blow, to Bud Purvis. The real story is also the reason, I suspect, the *demoiselles* are so silent, so mesmerized.

I clear my throat, sip a bit of water, and begin. "It's late," I say, "and I've kept you all far too long. There is just one thing I have left to say. You may remember when I spoke to you of Evelyn's Eleventh Commandment—*Thou shalt not turn into thy mother.* Well every woman has to come to terms with that one. But there is one thing I've learned: It's okay, really, to turn into one's grandmother." I didn't offer any explanation. Perhaps I didn't need to.

But the one who looks like Gracie won't let me leave it at that.

"So do you think it was worth it?" she insisted. "And what happened to everybody afterwards?"

Afterwards?

There was a wedding. It was fall, one of those perfect days of sun where the palms seem to brush the sky clean and the mountains behind Pasadena rise clear and violet-tinged to the west, as if cradling the valley, or offering a buffer to the endlessness of the sea. As if promising definition. After the wedding, a few minutes from the church, there was a party.

The immense old hotel seemed to swagger a little on that hillside not far from Gran's, its dark Victorian shingles fussy beneath flowering vines. I was one of the first to arrive and watched Ivan come in, adjusting his wire-rim glasses and trying to tame his unruly black hair before entering the vast reception hall beneath chandeliers mounted in gold. He blinked, hesitated a moment before stepping onto the huge roses in the carpet, and made his way slowly down, through the ballroom, where the band in white tie was already playing waltzes. The tables, filled with rose petals and arrangements of chrysanthemums and orange blossoms, lilies and birds-of-paradise—all the seasons together—were piled in dizzying display. He glanced at the heaps of caviar in passing, then turned away. Behind him, outside, the limousines kept coming into the curving drive, disgorging guests in gloves and capes, satin, silk, dark suits, and tuxedos. Nervously, he smoothed his sports coat with his hands, hoping the stains from eggs thrown at the last demonstration were no longer visible.

Soon the wedding party began to arrive, Pastor and Mrs. Richter a little pale perhaps, a little overwhelmed perhaps, coming straight from the First Lutheran Church. And Gracie, the only one of *les demoiselles de la Maison Française* to be in the wedding, stepped hesitantly in her burnt-orange gown of taffeta and nestled like a weed in the bouquet of Eve's tall, languorous sisters. Then came the bride herself, her red hair regal in a *bouffant à la* Jackie as if to hold a crown. Eve, the color of roses but scented of gardenia, glided in as if at court, wearing (as the society columns would note) an ivory Givenchy gown with exquisite beadwork across the bodice. It was a gown fit for Versailles.

It had only been the night before, after the rehearsal dinner, when I'd offered to give Gracie a ride and a place to stay, that she told me her long, unbelievable tale of the divine union of Evelyn and Jay. We had sat late on the steps of Gran's house, staring into a black California night struggling for starlight. After a long silence, I finally asked the most obvious question left: "Why this? Wasn't the marriage in France legal after all?"

"Sure it was," Gracie answered. "You know Jay would pull all the right strings. It was just that they began thinking, how were they going to break the news? In the scheme of things, neither family would have been exactly wild about not having the wedding that both clans wanted so they could give their own stamp of approval. So in keeping with Eve's now hallowed tradition of not spilling the beans—maybe the most important thing Eve learned in France—she and Jay decided not to tell their families about the hasty trip to the altar. 'Why cause unnecessary hurt?' is what Eve said, as if I hadn't heard that one before."

"So they just pretended they weren't already married?"

"Bingo. They came home gushing with the good news of their engagement. That left barely enough time to get this all together, you know, announcements in the society pages and everything. When Eve called and asked me to be a bridesmaid, I nearly fainted. 'The only one who isn't a family member,' she pointed out. I have tried not to dwell on the fact that the invitation was also the price of my silence. After all, I'm the only one who knows everything—even more than the groom. That is, until now." She paused for effect.

I nodded, my head spinning. "So the two families were okay with this? They didn't have any suspicions, any questions?"

Gracie looked straight at me, and her gray eyes glowed like a cat's in the dark night. "No, J.J., they really didn't. I mean it was seamless, believable, a starstruck summer romance ending in a respectable engagement to be followed by a perfect wedding. But they covered their bases there, too. The Richters are getting a church wedding, even if it's not their home church, with Eve's father officially marrying them. And the Greenes are getting their society reception, which is perfect for the political career they have in mind for Jay after law school. Plus, the icing on the cake—didn't it strike you as odd to throw this bash on a Thursday?"

"Yeah, actually, it did. I noticed the date and—"

Gracie cut me off. "Well that was the *coup de grâce*, really. They picked the Greenes thirtieth anniversary."

At that point, I didn't finish saying what had been on my mind, but decided to share something else with Gracie. I told her about the note I'd received in Marseilles from Melanie, and how I'd called the number she left as soon as I found out, but it was disconnected. I had no idea how to reach her. Then, just a month ago, in October, she had called Gran's number again. I was overjoyed to finally speak to her. "Oh, J.J.," she had said, "I felt so desperate when I first got back. As you know, things did not go well with my family, and I just needed your advice. Hans wanted to get married right then, to run away somewhere and leave behind all that baggage. Meaning his family and mine. I just didn't know what to do." I interrupted with some incoherent and sympathetic words, repeating that I was so sorry I hadn't been there.

"Ah, but you were," Mel had answered. "I tried to think what you would say, and, more than that, what you would do. Unlike me, you always seem so certain of your steps, so clear in what you want."

I turned red into the phone receiver, glad that Melanie couldn't see me. "So what was my advice?"

"You told me to always be true to my heart, and to go for what I desired. So we took a bus to Mexico and got married across the border."

Though she couldn't see my color, she could hear me gasp. "It was great advice. So thank you. But it's just for you to know, okay? Making it public right now would be, well, complicated. I mean we're living not far from Pasadena while Hans is earning a bit doing some scoring for an old professor at Claremont, and we don't want any family involved with us right now."

That conversation and what Gracie had revealed played through my head like a record as I watched the party unfold. I saw Ivan take a breath, survey the scene, and step outside the vast ballroom, airy and light-filled as Versailles's Hall of Mirrors. He stood for a minute in the gathering light of late afternoon to compose himself. Then, noticing the terrace steps cascading to a pool festooned with floating camellias, he came down looking in every direction.

I took a goblet of champagne from a passing waiter and finally called out, "Hey you!"

He rushed to embrace me. "There you are! Thank God. I love them all, but this is a bit hard to take, you know, without a friend in hand."

"Right." I grabbed his hand. "Anyway, you are supposed to be my date." I was feeling a little unsettled myself. All my *copines* were arriving, regrouped for the first time since Paris. So much had happened in so short a time that time itself seemed to elongate. "I feel like I'm in a looking glass myself," I said. "Want to walk around a little before we go in to face the music? This is my old neighborhood. Well, Gran's actually."

Ivan slipped his arm through mine in that awkward yet delicate way of his, and we strolled, just as we had on the grounds of Versailles, down the gentle hill with its Japanese gardens and dainty bridge, its cactuses and rock formations, its flowering lily ponds. It felt as exotic as the Chinese book of love poems he had unexpectedly delivered from Guy that rainy night in Paris. Then, just as we had in France, we spun our thoughts into each other's sentences, until he said, "Well, I guess it's time to face reality again."

Reality being the wedding dance. We crossed the threshold into the ballroom where the filtered sunlight behind us gave way to the glitter inside. In the center I watched Eve, the crown of her hair threaded with pearls and gardenias, her neck encircled with diamonds, as she twirled and smiled in all that reflected between mirror and chandelier and candelabra. Her graceful movements camouflaged the remnants of Jay's lameness, hard to notice anyway beneath the boyish, dazzling smile, the shock of hair like a salute to his president-hero. I saw Jocelyn, too, now made up by Hollywood. Her long blonde perfection shimmered in a slim gold gown. She, too, was waltzing with a tall, deeply handsome dark man, a man who appeared to be Samuel.

"Jo!" I called out, waving. But she did not hear me, and her face turned to the light, a plaster cast. I had seen her only once since my return. In fact, she had come back only two weeks before, having followed the long summer light of Scandinavia into fall. We had floated then in the pool, newly constructed, outside the house also newly constructed and miraculously the same. In the familiar corner kitchen, Madge was working over vegetables and oranges. Burt wandered the lower levels in his skivvies, trying to find his glasses. I wanted to speak of this to Jocelyn, but our communication was in proximity more than words. Instead I watched her skin change color as her eyes did, reflecting the passing mood of sun and light. All was just as it had been so long before, when I had first noticed this startling aspect of my soulmate, my roommate, *ma soeur*. The difference was that now it didn't surprise me. Nothing surprised me. She did not speak of what choices, among her infinite array of possibilities, she had finally made. And I did not ask.

But as I watched her at the wedding, waltzing, I remembered how she had once declared dancing of a different kind her only vice. When she turned again, I saw her "Samuel" was not Samuel at all, but a drop-dead look-alike. Then I was struck, as the light passed over her, with the shock of understanding. The sense of betrayal she suffered, the way she always recoiled from the very word, was because of me. This was at the heart of our deep yet wounded friendship. For I was the one who could tell her thoughts before she did, finish her sentences, know precisely what she felt. Yet I was also the one who would drop our sisterhood in a heartbeat to pursue what I imagined to be a higher, more passionate, more prized union—the love of a man, whose perfection had so far eluded me. But she, Jocelyn, would waltz with Samuel and all his kind without succumbing to him, holding herself apart, intact, in reserve.

At that very moment Madge, draped in a feather boa, rushed to embrace me.

I fear I cut short the exuberance of her greeting. "*Who* is that?" I demanded.

"Not who, but what, I'm afraid," Madge answered. "That is, to put it plainly, a model, one sent by the agency that they felt would be suitable for Jo to be seen with, for publicity photos and all."

"But," I protested, "he looks just like Samuel."

"Of course, dear. She picked him out." Madge no doubt took in my expression of distress, before adding, "Well, but of course he's nothing like Samuel. I mean he hardly speaks in sentences, and is the sort that's afraid to sit because he might bend his creases wrong. But on the mechanical level, he's fine, and he waltzes flawlessly..."

Before Madge finished her summing up of Jocelyn's escort, I was suddenly transported back to the pool, remembering the sensation that all was just as it had been before. Now I knew what I had just understood was true. Jocelyn would be the Beer Queen and make publicity shots for Hollywood agents, while the difficulties with Samuel could be converted to an image, a model with just enough of Samuel for all the world to see. She would wear him like a coat. Paris too she could put on like skin, and all the discomforting truths of voyaging abroad might as well never have happened.

It was then I saw Melanie and Hans, making slow circles in a dark corner of the dance floor, so tightly wound together that from a distance they looked like one person. I rushed to find them and hugged them so fiercely, they stopped still to laugh. "Congratulations," I said too loudly, before they both shushed me. "It's a secret, you know," Mel reminded me.

Hans held tight to her hand, and he seemed for once to have blood in him. "We're kind of crashing this party," he said in a conspiratorial whisper. "You know we didn't have any kind of ceremony, so we're kind of sharing this one—a first-class reception with all our friends and all the champagne you could drink, so why not? Only nobody knows this is, what do you say, a double reception? Except you."

Why not indeed, I thought. Another jewel in a crown of deception. It was perfect.

Melanie took my arm and continued in Hans's cautious whisper. "But J.J., I was really shocked, weren't you? I mean who would have thought Evelyn and Jay Greene? After her, I guess you could say, *adventures* in France, I had heard rumors of Tom coming around again. Well, he did come around, to France, after I left—did you know?—but even so I wouldn't have dreamed she'd end up marrying a boy from home, and so soon after returning…"

Melanie went on in this vein awhile, and I nodded now and again, feigning surprise when it was called for, and wondered if she had any idea how surprising her news would seem to the assembled wedding guests. Then she said, "He was there, you know."

"Who?"

"Tom. Today, at the wedding. We came late on purpose, so, you know, and he came in just after us. Obviously he didn't want to be seen, so I pretended not to notice. But I watched. He sat in the far back, on the groom's side, and left just before Evelyn's father pronounced them man and wife."

Despite the late afternoon glow, I felt a bit of chill. As if I were a voyeur, watching from the edges as my life danced in front of me and absence were again my best companion. I pulled my wrap—a twin to one of Gran's—around my shoulders. It was French lace, a gift from Roland.

Ivan found me just then, and they all exchanged greetings. He appeared to be faring all right, but, I noticed his arm had gone limp on mine. I looked over at him, but the lights so filled his glasses I could not see his eyes.

"Want to dance?" I suddenly asked.

"You know I don't know how," he whispered loudly.

"Piece of cake," I answered, glancing down at what might well have been three actual left feet. "I'll teach you—think of it as taking radical steps."

"What the fuck," he finally said, giving his goofy, half-twisted grin and offering his arm. "Shall we?"

So we turned, stumbling and spinning, giving into the gods of laughter. Then, coming down the long hall from the reception, as if down the corridor of my recurring dream—the one where I drop a finished jigsaw and can't find a missing piece—Guy walked in.

He didn't spot me, and I dropped back against the wall, finding a shadow where I could watch unseen. It wasn't until he turned that I saw her, and everything became clear. She was plain, short, and frizzy, wearing a muslin dress, oversized African necklaces, hoop earrings, and sandals. She was everything I was not. I understood perfectly. Guy had flirted once with desire as I knew it, with my impetuous belief in discovery for the sake of itself. But as I watched him move deliberately across the ballroom floor, I could see nothing in him but purpose. With *her* at his side, I knew he had stepped irrevocably back into the New Frontier with intent. He planned to fix the broken world.

Absurdly, as he came closer, I wondered if he was thinking of me, remembering that tomorrow would be my birthday. My twenty-first birthday. After all, the last time he had reached out for me was on my twentieth birthday last year, saying he wanted to come to Paris for Christmas.

Such thoughts, I knew, were useless now, and probably pitiful. I turned away, postponing our inevitable meeting, thinking that all I had done was chase an illusion whose grand finale was this wedding, where all my friends were waltzing through their imaginary lives. But not Guy, who had grasped what life's meaning really was, and would live in that other reality which could not be shattered.

A waiter passed me just then, and I turned gratefully for a final champagne, while Guy paused for a moment to hug Ivan. As I reached for the goblet, my fingers paused. I hadn't noticed before, but beneath the glass covering the tray was one of the engraved invitations. I determined to read the words slowly, as if each were a revelation, until Guy interrupted me. I looked up and found only his eyes, which reflected the regret in my own. Neither of us could foresee, in that instant, that the next day the world we had known would be blown apart, and we would never be young again.

Rev. and Mrs. Arnold Richter
Request the honor of your presence
at the marriage of their daughter
Evelyn Ruth
to
Jay Harold Greene III
on Thursday, the twenty-first of November
Nineteen hundred and sixty-three…

Acknowledgments

So many kindnesses and so much support have gone into the making of this book, it is impossible to draw up an inclusive list of thanks, but I feel special gratitude to the following: Douglas Hale, for his love and incomparable "writer in residence" program; Jimmy Patterson for his long friendship and generosity; Rose Solari for her undying encouragement and superb editing; Linda Watanabe McFerrin for her great literary friendship, advice, and support; Lowry McFerrin for his helpfulness and professionalism; *les demoiselles de la Maison Française*, especially Josephine Jenkins Mitchell, Christine Weideranders Berardo, and Patty Kenny Immel, for sharing the long-ago experiences that inspired this tale; Garry Lambrev, for being there too, and for his insightful reading and comments; Sunny and Hugh Wallace, for buying my first ticket to France; Ron Wallace for carrying the torch of the French connection; and my children Rob Biggar, Hugh Biggar, and Heather Tomlinson, for always cheering me on, and for growing up to love Paris.

Follow the further adventures of *les demoiselles de la Maison Française* in Joanna Biggar's next novel, *Melanie's Song*.

Alan Squire Publishing (ASP) is an independent literary press founded in 2010. We are committed to bringing fine literary fiction, nonfiction, and poetry to discerning readers around the world, and to collaborating with other independent presses both in the United States and abroad.

Alan Squire Publishing:
A Small Press With Big Ideas